EXPOSITIONS OF SCRIPTURE

AND

PRACTICE OF PRELATES.

The Parker Society.

Instituted A.D. M.DCCC.XL.

For the Publication of the Works of the Fathers and Early Writers of the Reformed English Church.

EXPOSITIONS AND NOTES

ON

SUNDRY PORTIONS

OF

THE HOLY SCRIPTURES,

TOGETHER WITH

THE PRACTICE OF PRELATES.

BY

WILLIAM TYNDALE,

MARTYR, 1536.

EDITED FOR

The Parker Society,

BY THE

REV. HENRY WALTER, B.D. F.R.S.

RECTOR OF HASILBURY BRYAN, DORSET;
FORMERLY FELLOW OF ST JOHN'S COLLEGE, CAMBRIDGE, AND PROFESSOR OF NATURAL PHILOSOPHY IN THE EAST INDIA COMPANY'S COLLEGE AT HAILEYBURY.

Wipf & Stock
PUBLISHERS
Eugene, Oregon

Wipf and Stock Publishers
199 West 8th Avenue, Suite 3
Eugene, Oregon 97401

Expositions of Scripture and Practice of Prelates
By Tyndale, William
ISBN: 1-59244-701-5
Publication date 5/19/2004
Previously published by Cambridge, 1849

CONTENTS.

EXPOSITION

UPON THE

FIFTH, SIXTH, AND SEVENTH CHAPTERS

OF

MATTHEW.

[INTRODUCTORY NOTICE.

In the advertisement prefixed to the first volume of this reprint of the writings of Tyndale, the editor announced the intention of arranging them in three classes, viz. doctrinal and hortatory treatises; helps to a right understanding of the scriptures, consisting of introductory prefaces, expositions, and notes upon the sacred text; and lastly his replies, and exposures of the adversaries of the Reformation.

The first volume has accordingly comprehended the whole of the first class, and of the introductory prefaces, or prologues, as Tyndale styled them. Proceeding, therefore, to the expositions, the present volume will commence with Tyndale's exposition of the Sermon on the mount, as coming first in the order of the scriptures, though not published till 1532, and consequently some months later than his exposition of the first epistle of St John[1]. For the following reprint, that of Day in 1573, the peculiar readings of which will be marked D., has been collated with a copy of the exposition in the archiepiscopal library at Lambeth, numbered 401 in Dr Maitland's account of rare books in that library, and of which he has said that it may be a specimen of the first edition. The readings of the Lambeth edition will be distinguished by the letter L.; and the marginal notes found in it will have the initials W. T. attached to them, to mark that Tyndale is to be held responsible for them alone, the other marginal notes being probably composed by Foxe, as editor for Day.]

[[1] See Anderson's Annals, Vol. I. § 8 and 9; and Biogr. Notice of Tyndale, pp. li. and lii.]

¶ AN EXPOSITION UPPON THE V. VI. VII. CHAPTERS OF MATHEW,

WHICH THREE CHAPTERS ARE THE KEYE AND THE DORE OF THE SCRIPTURE, AND THE RESTORING AGAYNE OF MOSES LAW CORRUPTE BY THE SCRIBES AND PHARISES. AND THE EXPOSITION IS THE RESTORING AGAYNE OF CHRISTES LAWE CORRUPTE BY THE PAPISTES.

¶ Item before the booke, thou hast a Prologe very necessarie, contayning the whole summe of the couenaunt made betwene God and us, uppon which we be baptised to keepe it.

Set forth by William Tyndall[2].

THE PROLOGUE.

HERE hast thou, dear reader, an exposition upon the fifth, sixth, and seventh chapters of Matthew, wherein Christ, our spiritual Isaac, diggeth again the wells of Abraham: which wells the scribes and Pharisees, those wicked and spiteful Philistines, had stopped and filled up with the earth of their false expositions. He openeth the kingdom of heaven, which they had shut up that other men should not enter, as they themselves had no lust to go in. He restoreth the key of knowledge, which they had taken away, and broken the wards, with wresting the text, contrary to his due and natural course, with their false glosses. He plucketh away from the face of Moses the veil which the scribes and Pharisees had spread thereon, that no man might perceive the brightness of his countenance. He weedeth out the thorns and bushes of their pharisaical glosses, wherewith they had stopped up the narrow way and strait gate, that few could find them. (To dig the wells of Abraham is to open and make plain the scripture, which is the kingdom of God.)

The wells of Abraham are the scripture. And the scripture may well be called the kingdom of heaven, which is eternal life, and nothing save the knowledge of God the Father, and of his Son Jesus Christ. Moses' face is the law, in her right understanding; and the law in her right understanding is the key, or at the least way the first and principal key, to open the door of the scripture. And the law is the very way that bringeth unto the door Christ, as it is written, Gal. iii. "The (Abraham's wells. W. T. The kingdom of heaven, what it is. W. T. John xvii. Moses' face. The key, what it is. W. T. The law is the way that leadeth to Christ. W. T.)

[2 Such is the title placed at the head of this Exposition in Day.]

Gal. iii. law was our schoolmaster to bring us to Christ, that we might be justified by faith." And "the end of the law," that is to say,
Rom. x. the thing, or cause why the law was given, "is Christ, to justify all that believe[1]:" that is to say, the law was given to prove us unrighteous, and to drive us to Christ, to be made righteous through forgiveness of sin by him. The law was given to make the sin known, saith St Paul, and that sin committed under the law might be the more sinful. The law is that thing which Paul in his inward man granted to be good, but was yet compelled ofttimes of his members to do those things which that good law condemned for evil.

Law, what her office is. W. T. Rom. iii. Rom. vii.

The law uttereth[2] sin, condemneth our deeds, and driveth us to Christ. W. T.

The law maketh no man to love the law, or less to do or commit sin; but gendereth more lust, and increaseth sin. For I cannot but hate the law, inasmuch as I find no power to do it; and it nevertheless condemneth me, because I do it not.
Rom. v. The law setteth not at one with God, but causeth wrath.

Rom. iv. John i.

Moses gave the law, but Christ only giveth grace to do it, and understand it aright.

"The law was given by Moses, but grace and verity by Jesus Christ." Behold, though Moses gave the law, yet he gave no man grace to do it, or to understand it aright; or wrote it in any man's heart, to consent that it was good, and to wish after power to fulfil it. But Christ giveth grace to do it, and to understand it aright; and writeth it with his holy Spirit in the tables of the hearts of men; and maketh it a true thing there, and no[3] hypocrisy.

The brasen serpent. W. T. Numb. xxi.

The law, truly understood, is those fiery serpents that stung the children of Israel with present death. But Christ is the brasen serpent; on whom whosoever, being stung with conscience of sin, looketh with a sure faith, is healed immediately of that stinging, and saved from the pains and sorrows of hell.

The law and faith be of contrary operations. W. T.

It is one thing to condemn, and pronounce the sentence of death, and to sting the conscience with fear of everlasting pain: and it is another thing to justify from sin; that is to say, to forgive and remit sin, and to heal the conscience, and certify a man, not only that he is delivered from eternal death, but also that he is made a son of God and heir of everlasting life. The first is the office of the law: the second pertaineth unto Christ only, through faith.

The scripture, how it is locked up. W. T.

Now if thou give the law a false gloss, and say that the

[1 So Tyndale's Translation.]

[2 That is, detects.]

[3 L. *no;* but D. *none.*]

law is a thing which a man may do of his own strength, even out of the power of his free-will; and that by the deeds of the law thou mayest deserve forgiveness of thy fore[4] sins; then died Christ in vain, and is made almost of no stead, seeing thou art become thine own saviour. Neither can Christ (where that gloss is admitted) be otherwise taken or esteemed of christian men, for all his passion and promises made to us in his blood, than he is of the Turks: how that he was a holy prophet, and that he prayeth for us as other saints do; save that we Christians think that he is somewhat more in favour than other saints be (though we imagine him so proud, that he will not hear us but through his mild mother and other holy saints, which all we count much more meek and merciful than he, but him most of might), and that he hath also an higher place in heaven, as the Grey friars and Observants set him, as it were from the chin upward, above St Francis. Gal. ii.

And so, when by this false interpretation of the law Christ, which is the door, the way, and the ground or foundation of all the scripture, is lost concerning the chiefest fruit of his passion, and no more seen in his own likeness; then is the scripture locked up, and henceforth extreme darkness, and a maze, wherein if thou walk, thou wottest neither where thou art, nor canst find any way out. It is a confused chaos, and a mingling of all things together without order, every thing contrary to another. It is an hedge or grove of briars, wherein if thou be caught, it is impossible to get out, but that if thou loose thyself in one place, thou art tangled and caught in another for it.

Christ is the door, the way, and foundation of all the scriptures.

This wise was the scripture locked up of the scribes and Pharisees, that the Jews could not see Christ when he came, nor yet can. And though Christ with these three chapters did open it again; yet by such glosses (for our unthankfulness' sake, that we had no lust to live according) have we Christians lost Christ again, and the understanding of the most clear text, wherewith Christ expoundeth and restoreth the law again. For the hypocrites, whatsoever seemeth impossible to their corrupt nature, unrenewed in Christ, that they cover over with the mist of their glosses, that the light thereof should not be seen. As they have interpreted here the words of Christ, wherewith he restoreth the law again, to be but good

When by glosses of our own imagination we darken the clear text of God's word, then is the scripture locked up from us.

[4 Fore, i. e. previous.]

Christ used no temporal regiment. W. T.

counsels only, but no precepts that bind the consciences. And thereto they have so ruffled and tangled the temporal and spiritual regiment together, and made thereof such confusion, that no man can know the one from the other: to the intent that they would seem to have both by the authority of Christ, which never usurped temporal regiment unto him.

Notwithstanding, most dear reader, if thou read this exposition with a good heart, only to know the truth, for the amending chiefly of thine own living, and then of other men's (as charity requireth where an occasion is given); then shalt thou perceive their falsehood[1], and see their mist expelled with the brightness of the inevitable truth.

Christ is a gift given only to them that love the law, and profess it. W. T.

Another conclusion is this: all the good promises which are made us throughout all the scripture, for Christ's sake, for his love, his passion or suffering, his blood-shedding or death, are all made us on this condition and covenant on our party, that we henceforth love the law of God, to walk therein, and to do it, and fashion our lives thereafter: insomuch that whosoever hath not the law of God written in his heart, that he love it, have his lust in it, and record therein night and day, understanding it as God hath given it, and as Christ and the apostles expound it, the same hath no part in the promises, nor can have any true faith in the blood of Christ; because there is no promise made him, but to them only that promise to keep the law.

He that professeth not the law, hath no part in the promises. W. T.

Thou wilt haply say to me again, If I cannot have my sins forgiven except I love the law, and of love endeavour myself to keep it; then the keeping of the law justifieth me. I answer that the argument is false, and but blind sophistry, and like unto this argument: I cannot have forgiveness of my sin except I have sinned; ergo, to have sinned is the forgiveness of sins. And it is like to this also: no man can be healed of the plague but he that hath it; ergo, to have the plague doth heal the plague.

Works do not justify. W. T.

And like sophistry are these arguments: If thou wilt
Matt. xix. enter into life, keep the commandments; ergo, the deeds
Rom. ii. of the law justify us. Item, "The hearers of the law are not righteous in the sight of God, but the doers of the law shall be justified;" ergo, the deeds of the law justify from sin.
2 Cor. v. And again: "We must all stand before the judgment-seat of

[1 So D., but L. falshepe.]

Christ, to receive every man according to the deeds which he did in the body;" ergo, the law, or the deeds of the law, justify.

These, and all such, are naughty[2] arguments. For ye see that the king pardoneth no murderer but on a condition, that he henceforth keep the law, and do no more so; and yet ye know well enough that he is saved by grace, favour, and pardon, ere the keeping of the law come: howbeit, if he break the law afterward, he falleth again into the same danger of death.

Even so, none of us can be received to grace but upon a condition to keep the law, neither yet continue any longer in grace than that purpose lasteth. And if we break the law, we must sue for a new pardon; and have a new fight against sin, hell, and desperation, ere we can come to a quiet faith again, and feel that the sin is forgiven. Neither can there be in thee a stable and an undoubted faith that thy sin is forgiven thee, except there be also a lusty courage in thine heart, and a trust that thou wilt sin no more; for on that condition, that thou endeavour thyself to sin no more, is the promise of mercy and forgiveness made unto thee.

By keeping the law we continue in grace. W. T.

And as thy love to the law increaseth, so doth thy faith in Christ; and so doth thine hope and longing for the life to come. And as thy love is cold, so is thy faith weak; and thine hope, and longing for the life to come, little. And where no love to the law is, there is neither faith in Christ for the forgiveness of sin, nor longing for the life to come; but instead of faith a wicked imagination, that God is so unrighteous that he is not offended with sin; and instead of hope a desire to live for ever here, and a greediness of worldly voluptuousness.

Faith, love, and hope are inseparable in this life. W. T.

And unto all such is the scripture locked up, and made impossible to understand. They may read it, and rehearse the stories thereof, and dispute of it, as the Turks may; and as we may of the Turks' law. And they may suck pride, hypocrisy, and all manner of poison there-out, to slay their own souls, and to put stumbling-blocks in other men's ways, to thrust them from the truth; and[3] get such learning therein as in Aristotle's Ethics and Moral philosophy, and in the precepts of old philosophers. But it is impossible for them

They that love not the law cannot understand the scripture to salvation. W. T.

[2 That is, worth nought.] [3 L. *to get.*]

to apply one sentence thereof to their soul's health, or[1] to fashion their lives thereby for to please God; or to make them love the law, or understand it; either to feel the power of Christ's death, and might of his resurrection, and the sweetness of the life to come: so that they ever remain carnal and fleshly; as thou hast an ensample of the scribes, Pharisees, and Jews, in the new Testament.

Care. Another conclusion is this: of them that believe in Christ for the remission of sin, and love the law, are a thousand degrees and not so few, one perfecter or weaker than another; of which a great sort are so feeble, that they can neither go forward in their profession and purpose, nor yet stand, except they be holpen and borne of their stronger brethren, and tended as young children are by the care of their fathers and mothers. And therefore doth God command the elder to care for the younger: as Paul teacheth, saying, "We that be stronger ought to bear the feebleness of the weaker;" and, "Brethren, if any man be caught in any fault, ye that be spiritual," and are grown in knowledge, and have gotten the victory of your flesh, "teach such with the spirit of softness," not calling them heretics at the first chop, and threatening them with fire and fagots: but, *alter alterius onera portate* (saith he), and *sic adimplebitis legem Christi;* that is to say, "Bear each other's burden, and so shall ye fulfil the law of Christ." Even so verily shall ye fulfil the law of Christ; and not with smiting your brethren, and putting stumbling-blocks before their weak feet, and killing their consciences, and making them more afraid of shadows and bugs than to break their Father's commandments, and to trust in words of wind and vanity more than in their Father's promise. And for their sakes also he hath ordained rulers, both spiritual and temporal, to teach them and exhort them; to warn them, and to keep occasions from them, that with custom of sin they fall not from their profession.

How God careth for the weak. W. T.

Rom. xv.

Gal. vi. By bearing each others' weakness we fulfil the law of Christ.

Rulers, why they were ordained. W. T.

Now when they that take upon them to be the elder brethren are become hypocrites, and turned to wily foxes and cruel wolves and fierce lions, and the officers be waxen evil and servants to mammon, ministering their offices for their own lucre only, and not for the profit of their brethren, but favouring all vices whereby they may have a vantage;

Why God scourgeth his. W. T.

[1 So L., but D. has *for*.]

then is God compelled, of his fatherly pity, to scourge his weak himself, with poverty, oppression, wrong, loss, danger, and with a thousand manner of diseases, to bring them again, if they be fallen, and to keep their hearts fast to their profession. So that *diligentibus Deum omnia cooperantur in bonum:* they that love God, that is to say, the law of God (for that is to love God), unto them God turneth all to the best; and scourgeth them with the lusts of their own weakness, to their own salvation. Rom. viii.

Another conclusion is this: God receiveth both perfect and weak in like grace, for Christ's sake, as a father receiveth all his children, both small and great, in like love. He receiveth them to be his sons, and maketh a covenant with them, to bear their weakness for Christ's sake, till they be waxen stronger; and how often soever they fall, yet to forgive them if they will turn again; and never to cast off any, till he yield himself to sin, and take sin's part, and for affection and lust to sin fight against his own profession to destroy it. And he correcteth and chastiseth his children ever at home, with the rod of mercy and love, to make them better; but he bringeth them not forth, to be judged after the condemnation of the law. The conditions of the covenant. W. T.

Another conclusion is this: every man is two men, flesh and spirit; which so fight perpetually one against another, that a man must go either back or forward, and cannot stand long in one state. If the spirit overcome the temptation, then is she stronger, and the flesh weaker. But and if the flesh get a custom, then is the spirit none otherwise oppressed of the flesh, than as though she had a mountain upon her back: and as we sometime in our dreams think we bear heavier than a millstone on our breasts; or when we dream, now and then, that we would run away for fear, our legs seem heavier than lead; even so is the spirit oppressed and overladen of the flesh through custom, that she struggleth and striveth to get up and break loose in vain; until the God of mercy, which heareth her groan through Jesus Christ, come and loose her with his power, and put his cross of tribulation on the back of the flesh, to keep her down, to minish her strength and to mortify her. Flesh and spirit. W. T.

Wherefore every man must have his cross to nail his flesh to, for the mortifying of her. Now, if thou be not strong Cross. W. T.

Evil lusts and affections are to be purged with the cross of Christ.

enough, and discreet thereto, to take up thy cross thyself, and to tame thy flesh with prayer and fasting, watching, deeds of mercy, holy meditations and reading the scripture, and with bodily labour, and in withdrawing all manner of pleasures from the flesh, and with exercises contrary to the vices which thou markest thy body most inclined to, and with abstaining from all that courage the flesh against the spirit; as reading of wanton books, wanton communication, foolish jesting and effeminate thoughts, and talking of covetousness (which Paul forbiddeth), and magnifying of worldly promotions; and takest, I say, up such a cross by thine ownself, or by the counsel of other that are better learned and exercised than thou; then must God put his cross of adversity upon thee. For we must have every man his cross in this world; or be damned with the world.

Eph. v

To sin under grace, and to sin under the law. W. T.

Of this ye see the difference between the sin of them that believe in the blood of Christ for the remission of sin, and consent and submit themselves unto the law, and the sin of them that yield themselves unto sin, to serve it, &c. The first sin under grace; and their sins are venial, that is to say, forgiveable. The other sin under the law, and under the damnation of the law, and fight (for a great part of them) against grace and against the Spirit of grace, and against the law of God and faith of Christ, and corrupt the text of the covenant with false glosses, and are disobedient to God, and therefore sin deadly.

Lambs. Swine. Dogs. W. T.

Of this also ye see the difference between the lambs of true believers; and between the unclean swine, that follow carnal lusts and fleshly liberty; and the churlish and hypocritish dogs, which, for the blind zeal of their own righteousness, persecute the righteousness of the faith in Christ's blood. The effeminate and careless swine, which continue in their fleshliness, and cease not to wallow themselves in their old puddle, think that they believe very well in Christ's blood; but they are deceived; as thou mayest clearly perceive, because they fear not the damnation of evil works, nor love the law of good works, and therefore have no part in the promise.

Swine have no faith. W. T.

Dogs love not the law. W. T.

The cruel and doggish hypocrites, which take upon them to work, think they love the law; which yet they never saw, save under a veil. But they be deceived; as thou mayest perceive, by that they believe not in Christ for the forgiveness of sin. Whereby also (I mean that they believe not) thou mayest perceive that they understand not the law: for if they understood the law, it would either drive them to Christ, or make them despair immediately.

True faith is coupled with love to the law. W. T.

But the true believers behold the law in her own likeness, and see the impossibility thereof to be fulfilled with natural power; and therefore flee to Christ for mercy, grace, and power; and then, of a very thankfulness for the mercy received, love the law in her own likeness, and submit themselves to learn it and to profit therein, and to do to-morrow that they cannot do to-day.

The difference of faiths, and how it is to be understood faith justifieth. W. T.

Ye see also the difference of all manner of faiths. The faith of the true believers is, that God justifieth or forgiveth; and Christ deserveth it; and the faith or trust in Christ's blood receiveth it, and certifieth the conscience thereof, and saveth and delivereth her from fear of death and damnation. And this is that we mean, when we say faith justifieth: that faith (I mean in Christ, and not in our own works) certifieth the conscience that our sins are forgiven us for Christ's blood's sake.

Faith of hypocrites. W. T.

But the faith of hypocrites is, that God forgiveth, and works deserve it: and that same false faith, in their own works, receiveth the mercy promised to the merits of their own works; and so Christ is utterly excluded.

And thus ye see that faith is the thing that is affirmed to justify, of all parties. For faith in Christ's blood (which is God's promise) quieteth the conscience of the true believers: and a false faith, or trust in works (which is their own feigning), beguileth the blind hypocrites for a season; till God for the greatness of their sin, when it is full, openeth their eyes, and then they despair. But the swine say, God is so good that he will save devils and all; and damn no man perpetually, whatsoever he do.

Faith of swine. W. T.

Another conclusion is this: to believe in Christ for the remission of sins, and, of a thankfulness for that mercy, to love the law truly: that is to say, to love God that is the Father of all and giveth all; and Jesus Christ, that is Lord of us all, and bought us all, with all our hearts, souls, power, and might; and our brethren for our Father's sake (because they be created after his image), and for our Lord and master Christ's sake, because they be the price of his blood; and to long for the life to come, because this life cannot be led without sin. These three points (I say) are the profession and religion of a christian man, and the inward baptism of the heart, signified by the outward washing of the body. And they be that spiritual character, badge, or sign, wherewith God, through his Spirit, marketh all his immediately and as soon as they be joined to Christ, and made members of his church by true faith.

The right baptism. W. T.

The church of Christ. W. T.

The church of Christ, then, is the multitude of all them that believe in Christ for the remission of sin; and, of a thankfulness for that mercy, love the law of God purely and without glosses; and, of hate they have to the sin of this world, long for the life to come. This is the church that cannot err damnably; nor any long time; nor all of them: but as soon as any question ariseth, the truth of God's promise stirreth up one or other to teach them the truth of every thing needful to salvation out of God's word; and lighteneth the hearts of the other true members, to see the same, and to consent thereto.

Whosoever derogate any thing from the faith of Christ are not of the church.

And as all they that have their hearts washed with this inward baptism of the Spirit are of the church, and have the keys of the scripture, yea, and of binding and loosing, and do not err; even so they that sin of purpose, and will not hear when their faults be told them, but seek liberties and privileges to sin unpunished, and gloss out the law of God, and maintain ceremonies, traditions and customs, to destroy the faith of Christ, the same be members of Satan, and all their doctrine is poison, error and darkness; yea, though they be popes, bishops, abbots, curates, and doctors of divinity, and though they can rehearse all the scripture without book, and though they be seen in Greek, Hebrew, and Latin: yea, and though they so preach Christ and the passion of Christ, that they make the poor women weep and howl again.

They that have not the law written in their hearts cannot understand the passion of Christ to salvation. W. T.

For when they come to the point, that they should minister Christ's passion unto the salvation of our souls, there they poison altogether and gloss out the law, that should make us feel our salvation in Christ, and drive us in that point from Christ, and teach us to put our trust in our own works for the remission and satisfaction of our sins, and in the apish play of hypocrites, which sell their merits instead of Christ's blood and passion.

A short repeating. W. T.

What the inward baptism of the soul is.

Lo, now, dear reader, to believe in Christ's blood for the remission of sin, and purchasing of all the good promises that help to the life to come; and to love the law; and to long for the life to come, is the inward baptism of the soul, the baptism that only availeth in the sight of God; the new generation and image of Christ; the only key also to bind and loose sinners; the touchstone to try all doctrines; the lantern and light that scattereth and expelleth the mist and darkness of all hypocrisy, and a preservative against all error and heresy; the mother of all good works; the earnest of everlasting life, and title whereby we challenge our inheritance.

Thau. W. T.

Faith, hope, and charity, are inseparable. W. T.

And though faith in Christ's blood make the marriage between our soul and Christ, and is properly the marriage garment; yea, and the sign Thau, that defendeth us from the smiting and power of the evil angels[1]; and is also the rock whereon Christ's church is built, and whereon all that is built standeth against all weather of wind and tempests; yet might the profession of the faith in Christ's blood, and of the love to the law, and longing for the life to come, be called all these things, were malice and froward understanding away; because that where one of them is, there will be all three; and where all are not, there is none of them. And because that the one is known by the other, it is impossible to know any of them truly, and not be deceived, but in respect and comparison of the other.

Faith, hope, and charity are known one by the other. W. T.

For if thou wilt be sure that thy faith be perfect, then examine thyself whether thou love the law. And in like manner, if thou wilt know whether thou love the law aright,

[1 Tyndale alludes to Ezekiel ix. 4—6, where the Latin, of the Vulgate translation, makes the Lord say, "Put the sign of Thau on the foreheads of the men." The Hebrew verb means *setting a sign*, or *marking;* and the substantive formed from it, תָו, signifies *a sign*, or *mark*, and is also used as the name of the letter ת, Thau, the last letter of the Hebrew alphabet. Hence Jerome, copying the Hebrew substantive in Roman letters, translates, *Signa Thau,* where the Septuagint renders, Δὸς σημεῖον, and our authorised version, '*Set a mark.*' Unhappily, too, though neither the Hebrew nor the Samaritan characters for Thau bear any resemblance to a cross, the Greek and Roman character for the corresponding letter, T, obviously has a resemblance to it; so that the text, as read by the Romanists in their Vulgate, conveys the idea of the outward sign of the cross having a defensive power in it.]

then examine thyself whether thou believe in Christ only for the remission of sin, and obtaining the promises made in the scripture. And even so, compare thy hope of the life to come unto faith and love, and to hating the sin of this life; which hate the love to the law engendereth in thee. And if they accompany not one another, all three together, then be sure that all is but hypocrisy.

If you say, Seeing faith, love, and hope, be three virtues inseparable; ergo, faith only justifieth not: I answer, though they be inseparable, yet they have separable and sundry offices; as it is above said of the law and faith. Faith only, which is a sure and an undoubted trust in Christ, and in the Father through him, certifieth the conscience that the sin is forgiven, and the damnation and impossibility of the law taken away, as it is above rehearsed in the conditions of the covenant; and with such persuasions mollifieth the heart, and maketh her love God again and his law. And as oft as we sin, faith only keepeth that we forsake not our profession, and that love utterly quench not, and hope fail; and only maketh the peace again. For a true believer trusteth in Christ only, and not in his own works, or aught else, for the remission of sin.

The office of faith. W. T.

And the office of love is to pour out again the same goodness that she hath received of God upon her neighbour, and to be to him as she feeleth Christ to herself. The office of love only is to have compassion, and to bear with her neighbour the burden of his infirmities; and, as it is written, *operit multitudinem peccatorum*, "covereth the multitude of sins;" that is to say, considereth the infirmities, and interpreteth all to the best, and taketh for no sin at all a thousand things, of which the least were enough (if a man loved not) to go to law for, and to trouble and unquiet an whole town, and sometime an whole realm or two.

The office of love. W. T.

James v.

And the office of hope is to comfort in adversity and make patient; that we faint not and fall down under the cross, or cast it off our backs.

The office of hope. W. T.

And thus ye see that these three, inseparable in this life, have yet separable and sundry offices and effects; as heat and dryth[1], being inseparable in the fire, have yet their separable operations. For the dryth only expelleth the moistness of all that is consumed by fire; and heat only destroyeth the

[1 Drought, or dryness.]

coldness. For dryth and cold may stand together; and so may heat and moistness. It is not all one to say, the dryth only, and the dryth that is alone; nor all one to say, faith only, and faith that is alone.

Go to then, and desire God to print this profession in thine heart, and to increase it daily more and more; that thou mayest be full shapen like unto the image of Christ, in knowledge and love, and meek thyself, and creep low by the ground, and cleave fast to the rock of this profession, and tie to thy ship this anchor of faith in Christ's blood with the cable of love, to cast it out against all tempests; and so set up thy sail, and get thee to the main sea of God's word. And read here the words of Christ with this exposition following, and thou shalt see the law, faith, and works, restored each to his right use and true meaning; and thereto, the clear difference between the spiritual regiment and the temporal; and shalt have an entrance and open way into the rest of all the scripture. Wherein, and in all other things, the Spirit of verity guide thee and thine understanding. So be it[2].

[[2] Thus L., but D. has *Amen.*]

AN EXPOSITION

UPON THE

FIFTH, SIXTH, AND SEVENTH CHAPTERS

OF

MATTHEW.

THE FIFTH CHAPTER OF MATTHEW.

WHEN he saw the people, he went up into a mountain and sat him down, and his disciples came to him; and he opened his mouth, and taught them, saying: Blessed be the poor in spirit, for theirs is the kingdom of heaven [1].

CHRIST here, in his first sermon, beginneth to restore the law of the ten commandments unto her right understanding, against the scribes and Pharisees, which were hypocrites, false prophets, and false preachers, and had corrupt the scripture with the leaven of their glosses. And it is not without a great mystery that Christ beginneth his preaching at poverty in spirit; which is neither beggary, nor against the possessing of riches, but a virtue contrary to the vice of covetousness, the inordinate desire and love of riches, and putting trust in riches.

Poverty in spirit.

Riches. W. T

Riches is the gift of God, given man to maintain the degrees of this world, and therefore not evil; yea, and some must be poor and some rich, if we shall have an order in this world. And God, our Father, divideth riches and poverty among his children, according to his godly pleasure and wisdom. And as riches doth not exclude thee from the blessing, so doth not poverty certify thee; but to put thy trust in the living God maketh thee heir thereof. For if thou trust in the living God, then if thou be poor, thou covetest not to be rich; for thou art certified that thy Father shall minister unto thee food and raiment, and be thy

Neither riches nor poverty exclude or assure us of God's blessing.

[1 In these expositions Tyndale appears to have translated the Greek text afresh, as each passage came before him, instead of copying his own previously published version.]

defender: and if thou have riches, thou knowest that they be but vanity, and that as thou broughtest them not into the world, so shalt thou not carry them out; and that as they be thine to day, so may they be another man's to-morrow; and that the favour of God only both gave and also keepeth thee and them, and not thy wisdom or power; and that they, neither aught else, can help at need, save the good will of thy heavenly Father only. Happy and blessed then are the poor in spirit, that is to say, the rich that have not their confidence nor consolation in the vanity of their riches; and the poor, that desire not inordinately to be rich, but have their trust in the living God for food and raiment, and for all that pertaineth either to the body or the soul; for theirs is the kingdom of heaven.

Who are poor in spirit, is here pithily declared.

And contrariwise, unhappy and accursed, and that with the first and deepest of all curses, are the rich in spirit; that is to say, the covetous that, being rich, trust in their riches, or, being poor, long for the consolation of riches; and comfort not their souls with the promises of their heavenly Father, confirmed with the blood of their Lord Christ. For unto them it is harder to enter into the kingdom of heaven, than for a camel to enter through the eye of a needle. No; they have no part in the kingdom of Christ and God. Therefore is it evident, why Christ so diligently warneth all his to beware of covetousness; and why he admitteth none to be his disciples, except they first forsake all together. For there was never covetous person true yet, either to God or man.

Rich in spirit. W. T.

Mark x.

Eph. v.

If a covetous man be chosen to preach God's word, he is a false prophet immediately. If he be of the lay sort, so joineth he himself unto the false prophets, to persecute the truth. Covetousness is not only, above all other lusts, those thorns that choke the word of God in them that possess it; but it is also a deadly enemy to all that interpret God's word truly. All other vices, though they laugh them to scorn that talk godly, yet they can suffer them to live, and to dwell in the country: but covetousness cannot rest, as long as there is one that cleaveth to God's word in all the land.

Covetousness is a thing contrary to the word of God, and to the ministers of the same. W. T.

Take heed to thy preacher therefore, and be sure, if he be covetous and gape for promotion, that he is a false prophet, and leaveneth the scripture, for all his crying, 'fathers,

By covetousness is a false prophet chiefly known. W. T.

fathers,' 'holy church,' and 'fifteen hundred years[1],' and for all his other holy pretences.

2. Blessed are they that mourn, for they shall be comforted.

Some cry, The world is naught, not for their own and others' iniquity; but for waywardness they cannot enjoy their own lusts.

This mourning is also in the spirit, and no kin to the sour looking of hypocrites, nor to the impatient waywardness of those fleshly, which ever whine and complain that the world is naught, because they cannot obtain and enjoy their lusts therein. Neither forbiddeth it always to be merry, and to laugh, and make good cheer now and then, to forget sorrow, that overmuch heaviness swallow not a man clean up. For the wise man saith, "Sorrow hath cost many their lives." And, "An heavy spirit drieth up the bones." And Paul commandeth to "rejoice ever." And he saith, "Rejoice with them that rejoice; and sorrow with them that sorrow, and weep with them that weep:" which seem two contraries.

Prov. xvii. Phil. iv. Rom. xii.

Godly mourning. W. T.

This mourning is that cross without which was never any disciple of Christ, or ever shall be. For of whatsoever state or degree thou be in this world, if thou profess the gospel, there followeth thee a cross (as warmness accompanieth the sun shining), under which thy spirit shall groan and mourn secretly, not only because the world and thine own flesh carry thee away, clean contrary to the purpose of thine heart; but also to see and behold the wretchedness and misfortunes of thy brethren, for which (because thou lovest them as well as thyself) thou shalt mourn and sorrow no less than for thyself. Though thou be king or emperor, yet if thou knowest Christ, and God through Christ, and intendest to walk in the sight of God, and to minister thine office truly, thou shalt (to keep justice with all) be compelled to do daily that, which thou art no less loath to do than if thou shouldest cut off arm, hand, or any other member of thine own body. Yea, and if thou wilt follow the right way, and neither turn on the right hand nor on the left, thou shalt have immediately thine own subjects, thine own servants, thine own lords, thine own counsellors, and thine own prophets thereto, against thee; unto whose froward malice and stubbornness, thou shalt be compelled to permit a thousand things against thy conscience,

As warmth accompanieth the sun, so followeth the cross a true christian man.

[1 Alluding to the priests' common assertion, that the customs then prevalent in the church were instituted by the apostles fifteen hundred years before Tyndale's time.]

not able to resist them, at which thine heart shall bleed inwardly; and shalt sauce thy sweet sops, which the world weeneth thou hast, with sorrows enough; and still mourning, studying either alone, or else with a few friends secretly night and day, and sighing to God for help to mitigate the furious frowardness of them whom thou art not able to withstand, that all go not after the will of the ungodly. What was David compelled to suffer all the days of his life of his own servants, the sons of Zeruiah[2], beside the mischances of his own children! And how was our king John forsaken of his own lords, when he would have put a good and godly reformation in his own land![3] How was Henry the second compassed in like manner of his own prelates, whom he had promoted of nought, with the secret conspiracy of some of his own temporal lords with them! I spare to speak of the mourning of the true preachers, and the poor common people which have none other help, but the secret hand of God, and the word of his promise.

King John. W. T.

Henry the second. W. T.

But they shall be comforted of all their tribulation, and their sorrow shall be turned into joy, and that infinite and everlasting, in the life to come. Neither are they without comfort here in this world; for Christ hath promised to send them a Comforter to be with them for ever, the Spirit of truth which the world knoweth not. And they "rejoice in hope" of the comfort to come. And they overcome through faith, as it is written, The saints "through faith overcame

The promise of God's word is the comfort of the afflicted in this world for Christ's sake.

John xiv. Rom. xii.

Heb. xi.

[2 Seruia, D.]

[3 In so saying, there can be no doubt that Tyndale alluded to what passed in 1207—9, as related by the monkish historian, Matthew Paris, who mentions how John forbade ecclesiastical appeals to Rome; telling Innocent III., that 'Cum archiepiscopi, episcopi et alii ecclesiarum prælati, tam de regno Angliæ quam aliarum terrarum suarum, in omnium scientiarum plenitudine sufficienter abundent, si necessitas coegerit, extra terras suas justitiam vel judicium ab alienigenis non emendicaret': also that by John's orders, 'Presbyterorum et clericorum focariæ per totam Angliam a ministris regis captæ sunt, et graviter ad se redimendum compulsæ:' and that John patronised a preacher who affirmed, 'ad papam non pertinere de regum sive de quorumlibet potentum laica possessione, vel subditorum regimine; cum præcipue principi apostolorum Petro nihil a Domino nisi ecclesiæ tantum ac rerum ecclesiasticarum sit collata potestas.'—Matt. Paris. Hist. Angl. f. 188—92. Lond. 1686.]

Faith is our victory. W. T. 1 John v. kingdoms, and obtained the promises." And "this is the victory that overcometh the world, even our faith." But the blind world neither seeth our comfort, nor our trust in God, nor how God, through faith in his word, helpeth us, and maketh us overcome.

How overcome they (wilt thou say) that be always persecuted, and ever slain? Verily in every battle some of them that win the field be slain: yet they leave the victory unto their dear friends, for whose sakes they took the fight upon them; and therefore are conquerors, seeing they obtain their purpose, and maintain that they fought for. The cursed rich of this world, which have their joy and comfort in their riches, have since the beginning fought against them, to weed them out of the world: but yet in vain. For though they have always slain some, yet those that were slain won the victory for their brethren with their death, and ever increased the number of them. And though they seemed to die in the sight of the foolish, yet they are in peace, and have obtained that everlasting kingdom for which they fought. And besides all this, when God plagueth the world for their sin, these that mourn and sorrow are marked with the sign of Thau in their foreheads, and saved from the plague, that they perish not with the wicked, as thou seest, and as Lot was delivered from among the Sodomites.

By persecution and death for the truth's sake we obtain life, and get the victory.

The mourners for righteousness are saved, when God taketh vengeance on the unrighteous. W. T. Ezek. ix.

And contrariwise, cursed are they that laugh now, that is to say, which have their joy, solace, and comfort in their riches; for they shall sorrow and weep. And as it was answered the rich man, "Son, remember how that thou receivedst thy good days in thy life-time, and Lazarus likewise evil; and therefore is he comforted and thou tormented."

Luke vi. Luke xvi.

3. Blessed are the meek, for they shall inherit the earth.

Meekness possesseth the earth. W. T.

By the earth understand all that we possess in this world; which all God will keep for us, if we be soft and meek. And whatsoever trouble arise, yet, if we will be patient and abide, the end will go on our side; as it is written in the thirty-sixth Psalm, "The wicked shall be weeded out, but they that abide the Lord's leisure shall inherit the earth." And again: "Within a while the wicked shall be gone, thou shalt behold the place where he was, and he shall be away; but the meek (or soft) shall inherit the earth." Even as we say, 'Be

[Psal. xxxvii. 9.]

still, and have thy will;' and, 'Of little meddling cometh much rest;' for a patient man shall wear out all his enemies.

It is impossible to dwell in any place where no displeasure should be done thee. If it be done unwillingly, as when thy neighbour's beasts break into thy corn by some chance against his will, then it is reason that thou be soft and forgive. If it be done of malice and self-will, then with revenging thou dost but, with pottering in the fire, make the flame greater, and givest an occasion of more evil to be done thee. If any man rail on thee and rebuke thee, answer not again, and the heat of his malice shall die in itself, and go out immediately; as fire doth, when no more wood is laid thereon. If the wrong that is done be greater than thou art able to bear, trust in God, and complain with all meekness unto the officer, that is set of God to forbid such violence. And if the gentlemen that dwell about thee be tyrants, be ready to help to fetch home their wood, to plough their land, to bring in their harvest, and so forth; and let thy wife visit my lady now and then with a couple of fat hens, or a fat capon, and such like, and then thou shalt possess all the remnant in rest: or else one quarrel or other may be picked to thee, to make thee quit of all together.

Refer the revenge of thy cause to the magistrate whom God appointeth to forbid such violence.

Choose whether thou wilt, with softness and suffering, have God on thy side, ever to save thee, and to give thee ever enough, and to have a good conscience and peace on the earth; or with furiousness and impatience, to have God against thee, and to be polled a little and a little of all together, and to have an evil conscience and never rest on earth, and to have thy days shortened thereto. God hath promised, if thou be meek and soft and suffer a little persecution, to give thee not only the life to come, but also an hundredfold here in this life: that is to say, to give thee his ownself, and to be thy protector, and minister to thee ever enough, which may of right be called an hundredfold, and is a treasure passing the treasure of all princes.

Hundred fold. W. T.

Finally, Christ teacheth here how every man must live for himself among them to whom he is a neighbour, and in private matters in which he is but as a neighbour (though he be a king), and in which thou canst not be too soft. But and if thou be an officer, then thou must be good, kind, and merciful; but not a milksop, and negligent. And to whom

The private person may not avenge, but the officer must. W. T.

thou art a father, them must thou rule, and make obedient, and that with sharpness, if softness will not be heard, and so in all other offices.

4. Blessed are they that hunger and thirst for righteousness, for they shall be fulfilled.

Righteousness. W. T.

Righteousness in this place is not taken for the principal righteousness of a christian man, through which the person is good and accepted before God. For these eight points are but doctrine of the fruits and works of a christian man, before which the faith must be there, to make righteous without all deserving of works, and as a tree out of which all such fruits and works must spring. Wherefore understand here the outward righteousness before the world, and true and faithful dealing each with other, and just executing of the offices of all manner degrees, and meek obedience of all that are under power. So that the meaning is: happy are they which not only do their duties to all men, but also study and help to the uttermost of their power, with word, deed, counsel, and exhorting, that all other deal truly also, according to the degree that every man beareth in the world; and be as desirous to further good order and righteous dealing, as the hungry and thirsty be desirous to eat and drink.

How this word righteousness ought here to be understood.

And note, that it is not for nought that he saith, Hunger and thirst. For except thy soul hunger and thirst for this righteousness of her new nature, as the body doth for meat and drink of his old nature, the devil and the children of this world (which cannot suffer that a man either deal truly himself, or help other) will so resist thee, plague thee, and so weary thee, that thou hadst lever, of very mistrust, and desperation that thy state[1] should be better, to forsake all, and make thyself a monk or a friar, yea, and to run into a strange country, and leave all thy friends, than to abide in the world, and to let it choose whether it will sink or swim.

Monks.

Monks, why they run into religion. W. T.

But to comfort us, that we faint not or be weary of well doing, Christ promiseth that all that have this thirst and hunger shall have their lust satisfied, and be translated into a kingdom where none unrighteousness is; besides that

[1 So D., but L. has *that aught.*]

thou shalt here at length[2] see many come to the right way, and help with thee, and many things that cannot be altogether mended, yet somewhat bettered and more tolerable; so that all righteousness shall not be quenched.

And contrariwise, "Cursed be all they that are full," as Luke in the sixth saith; that is to say, the hypocrites which, to avoid all labour, sorrow, care, cumbrance, and suffering with their brethren, get them to dens, to live at rest, and to fill their bellies; the wealth of other men not regarded. No, it were a grief to them that other were better, that they alone may be taken for holy; and that whosoever will to heaven, must buy it of them. Yea, they be so full, that they prefer themselves before[3] poor sinners, and look as narrowly on them as the Pharisee did on the publican, thanking God that he alone was good, and the other evil. Cursed are they yet for all their fulness; for they shall hunger with everlasting hunger, where none shall give them to eat, nor they have any refreshing of their pains.

Luke vi.

Monks cursed. W. T.

Blessed be the merciful, for they shall obtain mercy. 5.

To be merciful is to have compassion and to feel another man's disease; and to mourn with them that mourn, and suffer with them that suffer; and to help and succour them that are in tribulation and adversity; and to comfort them with good counsel, and wholesome instruction, and loving words. And to be merciful is lovingly to forgive them that offended thee, as soon as they knowledge their misdoing and ask thee mercy. To be merciful is patiently long to abide the conversion of sinners with a lusty courage, and hope that God will at the last convert them, and in the mean time to pray instantly for them; and ever when he seeth an occasion to exhort them, warn them, monish them, and rebuke them. And to be merciful is to interpret all to the best; and to look through the fingers at many things; and not to make a grievous sin of every small trifle; and to suffer and forbear, in his own cause, the malice of them that will not repent nor be aknown of their wickedness, as long as he can suffer it, and as long as it ought to be suffered; and when he can no longer,

To be merciful, what it is. W. T.

[[2] So D., but L. *hear and see.*]

[[3] So D., but L., *compare themselves to open.*]

then to complain to them that have authority to forbid wrong, and to punish such evil doers.

Monks. W. T.

But the hypocrites, clean contrary, condemn all men for grievous sinners, save them only that buy their holiness of them. And because they will suffer with no man, they get them to silence. And because they will help no man, all that they have (say they) pertaineth unto the covent[1], and is none of theirs. And if they be offended, they will be avenged immediately. And to cloak, that they should not seem to avenge themselves, the matter (say they) pertaineth to God and holy church, or to some saint, or to one or other holy thing: as if thou smite one of them on the one cheek, he will turn to thee the other, ere he will avenge himself; but the injury of the holy oil wherewith he was anointed, that must he avenge, and that with a spiritual punishment; that thou must be accursed as black as a collier, and delivered to Satan. And if thou come not in, and ask absolution, and offer thyself to penance and to paying thereto, they will not suffer till the devil fetch thee, but will deliver thee to the fire, in the mean time; and all for zeal of righteousness, say they.

Convent. W. T.

Oil.

Holy oil must be avenged. W. T.

Zeal of righteousness, what it is. W. T.

O hypocrites! the zeal of righteousness is to hunger and thirst for righteousness, as it is above described: that is, to care, and study, and to do the uttermost of thy power, that all things went in the right course and due order, both through all degrees of the temporalty and also of the spiritualty, and to jeopard life and goods thereon.

Care.

How the spiritualty care for the temporal commonwealth. W. T.

All the world can bear record what pain ye take, and how ye care, for the temporal commonwealth, that all degrees therein did and had their duty; and how ye put your lives in adventure to preach the truth, and to inform lords and princes, and to cry upon them to fear God and to be learned, and to minister their offices truly unto their subjects, and to be merciful, and an example of virtue unto them. And how help ye that youth were brought up in learning and virtue, and that the poor were provided for, of food and raiment, &c.? And how provide ye that your priests be all learned, and preach, and do their duties truly every man in his parish? How provide ye that sects arise not, to poll the people and lead them out of the way, under a colour of praying and hypocritish holiness, living themselves idle, and being utterly

[1 Covent: convent.]

unto the commonwealth unprofitable? Who smelleth not the sweet odour of chastity, that is among you? What righteousness is in your sanctuaries, and what indifferent equity is in all your exemptions, privileges, and liberties! By your works we judge you, and your zeal to righteousness; and not by your sophistical subtle reasons, with which ye would claw our ears, bleer our eyes, and beguile our wits, to take your tyrannous covetous crudelity[2] for the zeal of righteousness!

Finally, he that will not be merciful, to be blessed of God, and to obtain mercy of him, both here and in the life to come, let him be accursed with the unmerciful, and to him be "judgment without mercy," according to the words of St James in the second chapter of his epistle.

As thou art merciful, so shalt thou obtain mercy in the life to come.

James ii.

Blessed be the pure in heart, for they shall see God. 6.

"That which entereth into a man defileth not a man, but the things that defile a man proceed first out of his heart," as thou mayest see Matt. xv. "Thence come out evil thoughts (saith Christ), as murder, adultery, fornication, theft, false witnessings and blasphemies. These are the things that make a man foul." A man then is not foul in the sight of God, till his heart be foul. And the filthiness of the heart are thoughts that study to break God's commandments. Wherefore the pureness of the heart is the consenting and studious[3] purpose to keep the law of God, and to mean truly in all thy words and works, and to do them with a true intent.

The filthiness of the heart, what. W. T.

Matt. xv.

The pureness of the heart, what. W. T

It followeth then that thou mayest be pure-hearted, and therewith do all that God hath commanded, or not forbidden. Thou mayest be pure-hearted, and have a wife and get children; be a judge, and condemn to death them that have deserved it; hang or behead evil doers, after they be by a just process condemned. Thou mayest be pure-hearted, and do all the drudge in the world. Lot was pure-hearted among the Sodomites. Nicodemus, being in the council, among them that conspired the death of Christ, was pure-

[2 Crudelity, i. e. cruelty, from the Latin form of the word]

[3 Study and studious, are here used in that sense which they have in the Latin; that is, to desire, and desirous.]

hearted, and consented not with them to the death of that innocent.

The end of the law is to justify all that believe. Rom. x. [Matt. xi. 27.]

If the law be written in thine heart, it will drive thee to Christ; which is the end of the law, to justify all that believe. And Christ will shew thee his Father. "For no man seeth the Father but the Son, and he to whom the Son will shew him." If thou believe in Christ that he is thy Saviour, that faith will lead thee in immediately, and shew thee God with a lovely and amiable countenance; and make thee feel and see how that he is thy Father, altogether merciful to thee, and at one with thee, and thou his son, and highly in his favour and grace, and sure that thou pleasest him, when thou dost an hundred things which some holy people would suppose themselves defiled if they should but think on them. And to see God is the blessing of a pure heart.

Impure-hearted, who are. W. T.

Impure and unclean-hearted, then, are all they that study to break God's commandments. Impure-hearted are all that believe not in Christ, to be justified by him. Impure-hearted are all hypocrites, that do their work for a false purpose; either for praise, profit, or to be justified thereby; which painted sepulchres (as Christ calleth them) can never see God, or be sure that they be in the state of grace, and that their works be accepted; because they have not God's word with them, but clean against them.

7. Blessed are the peace-makers, for they shall be called the children of God.

Peace-making, what.

To inherit this blessing, it is not only required that thou have peace in thyself, and that thou take all to the best, and be not offended lightly and for every small trifle, and alway ready to forgive, nor sow no discord, nor avenge thine own wrong; but also that thou be fervent and diligent to make peace, and to go between, where thou knowest or hearest malice and envy to be, or seest hate or strife to arise between person and person, and that thou leave nothing unsought, to set them at one.

Princes, what they ought to do ere they make war. W. T.

And though Christ here speak not of the temporal sword, but teacheth how every man shall live for himself toward his neighbour; yet princes, if they will be God's children, must not only give no cause of war, nor begin any; but also (though he have a just cause) suffer himself to be entreated, if he that gave the cause repent; and must also seek all ways of peace, before he fight. Howbeit when all is sought, and nothing will help, then he ought, and is bound, to defend his land and subjects: and in so doing he is a peace-maker, as well as when he causeth thieves and murderers to be punished for their evil doing, and breaking of the common peace of his land and subjects.

If thou have peace in thyself, and lovest the peace of thy brethren after this manner, so is God, through Christ, at peace with thee; and thou his beloved son, and heir also.

When thou mayest assure thyself to be the son and heir of God.

Moreover, if the wrong done thee be greater than thou mayest bear: as when thou art a person not for thyself only, but in respect of other, in whatsoever worldly degree it be, and hast an office committed thee; then (when thou hast warned, with all good manner, him that did it, and none amendment will be had) keep peace in thine heart and love him still, and complain to them that are set to reform such things; and so art thou yet a peace-maker, and still the son of God. But if thou avenge thyself, or desirest more than that such wrong[1] be forbidden, thou sinnest against God in taking the authority of God upon thee, without his commandment. God is Father over all, and is (of right) judge over all his children, and to him only pertaineth all avenging. Who therefore without his commandment avengeth, either with heart or hand, the same doth cast himself into the hands of the sword, and loseth the right of his cause.

Vengeance pertaineth to God only. W. T.

And on the other side, cursed be the peace-breakers, pick-quarrels, whisperers, backbiters, sowers of discord, dispraisers of them that be good, to bring them out of favour, interpreters to evil that is done for a good purpose, finders of faults where none is, stirrers up of princes to battle and war; and above all, cursed be they that falsely belie the true preachers of God's word, to bring them into hate, and to shed their blood wrongfully, for hate of the truth: for all such are children of the devil.

Blessed are they that suffer persecution for righteousness' sake, for 8.
theirs is the kingdom of heaven.

If the faith of Christ and law of God (in which two all righteousness is contained,) be written in thine heart; that is,

In the faith of Christ and law of God all our righteousness is contained.

[[1] So L., but D. *wrongs.*]

if thou believe in Christ to be justified from sin, or for remission of sin, and consentest in thine heart to the law, that it is good, holy, and just, and thy duty to do it, and submittest thyself so to do; and thereupon goest forth, and testifiest that faith and law of righteousness openly unto the world, in word and deed; then will Satan stir up his members against thee, and thou shalt be persecuted on every side. But be of good comfort, and faint not. Call to mind the saying of Paul, how
2 Tim. iii. "all that will live godly in Christ Jesus shall suffer persecution." Remember how all the prophets that went before thee
Luke vi. were so dealt with. Remember the examples of the apostles, and of Christ himself; and that the disciple is no better than his master; and that Christ admitteth no disciple, which not only leaveth not all, but also taketh his cross too. We be not called to a soft living, and to peace in this world; but unto peace of conscience in God our Father, through Jesus Christ, and to war in this world.

The peace of Christ is a peace of conscience. W. T.

To suffer with Christ in this world is to be glorified with him in the world to come.

Moreover comfort thyself with the hope of the blessing of the inheritance of heaven, there to be glorified with Christ, if thou here suffer with him. For if we be like Christ here in his passions, and bear his image in soul and body, and fight manfully[1] that Satan blot it not out, and suffer with Christ for bearing record to righteousness; then shall we be like him in glory. St John saith in the third chapter of his epistle,
1 John iii. "Yet[2] appeareth not what we shall be, but we know that
Phil. iii. when he appeareth, we shall be like him." And Paul, "Our conversation is in heaven, whence we look for a Saviour, the Lord Jesus Christ, which shall change our vile bodies, and make them like his glorious body."

It is an happy thing to suffer for righteousness' sake, but not for unrighteousness. "For what praise is it" (saith Peter, in the second of his first epistle), "though ye suffer, when ye be buffeted for your offences?" Wherefore in the fourth of
1 Pet. ii. iv. the same he saith, "See that none of you suffer as a murderer, or a thief, or an evil doer, or a busy body in other men's matters." Such suffering glorifieth not God, nor art thou thereby heir of heaven. Beware therefore that thou deserve not that thou sufferest. But if thou do, then beware much more of them that would bear thee in hand, how that such suffering should be satisfaction of thy sins, and a deserving of

[1 L. has *yea that.*] [2 L. has *yet it.*]

heaven. No; suffering for righteousness, though heaven be promised thereto, yet doth it not deserve heaven, nor yet make satisfaction for the fore sins: Christ doth both twain. But and if thou repent and believe in Christ for the remission of sin, and then confess, not only before God, but also openly, before all that see thee suffer, how that thou hast deserved that thou sufferest, for breaking the good and righteous law of thy Father, and then takest thy punishment patiently, as an wholesome medicine to heal thy flesh that it sin no more, and to fear thy brethren that they fall not into like offence, as Moses teacheth every where; then, as thy patience in suffering is pleasant in the sight of thy brethren which behold thee, pity thee, and suffer with thee in their hearts, even so is it in the sight of God, and it is to thee a sure token that thou hast true faith and true repentance.

No bodily pain can be a satisfaction to God, save Christ's passion. W. T.

And as they be blessed which suffer for righteousness, even so are they accursed which run away, and let it be trodden under the feet, and will not suffer for the faith of their Lord and law of their Father, nor stand by their neighbours in their just causes.

Blessed are ye, when they revile you, and persecute you, and say all 9.
manner of evil sayings against you for my sake, and yet lie.
Rejoice and be glad, for your reward is great in heaven. Even so
verily they persecuted the prophets that were before you.

Here seest thou the uttermost, what a christian man must look for. It is not enough to suffer for righteousness; but that no bitterness or poison be left out of thy cup, thou shalt be reviled and railed upon; and even when thou art condemned to death, then be excommunicate and delivered to Satan, deprived of the fellowship of holy church, the company of the angels, and of thy part in Christ's blood; and shalt be cursed down to hell, defied, detested, and execrate with all the blasphemous railings that the poisonful[3] heart of hypocrites can think or imagine; and shalt see before thy face when thou goest to thy death, that all the world is persuaded and brought in belief that thou hast said and done that thou never thoughtest, and that thou diest for that thou art as guiltless of as the child that is unborn.

What the most cruel persecution is. W. T.

[[3] So D., but L. *poison hearts*. See Vol. I. p. 17, n. 4.]

Well, though iniquity so highly prevail, and the truth, for which thou diest, be so low kept under, and be not once known before the world, insomuch that it seemeth rather to be hindered by thy death than furthered, (which is of all griefs the greatest;) yet let not thine heart fail thee, neither despair, as though God had forsaken thee, or loved thee not: but comfort thyself with old ensamples, how God hath suffered all his old friends to be so entreated, and also his only and dear son Jesus; whose ensample, above all other, set before thine eyes, because thou art sure he was beloved above all other, that thou doubt not but thou art beloved also, and so much the more beloved, the more thou art like to the image of his ensample in suffering.

Set the example of Christ before thee. W. T.

Did not the hypocrites watch him in all his sermons, to trap him in his own words? Was he not subtilly apposed, whether it were lawful to pay tribute to Cæsar? Were not all his words wrong reported? Were not his miracles ascribed to Beelzebub? Said they not, he was a Samaritan, and had a devil in him? Was he not called a breaker of the sabbath, a wine-drinker, a friend of publicans and sinners? Did he aught wherewith no fault was found, and that was not interpreted to be done for an evil purpose? Was not the pretence of his death the destroying of the temple, to bring him into the hate of all men? Was he not thereto accused of treason, that he forbad to pay tribute to Cæsar, and that he moved the people to insurrection? Railed they not on him in the bitterest of all his passion, as he hanged on the cross, saying, "Save thyself, thou that savest other," "come down from the cross, and we will believe in thee;" fie, wretch, "that destroyest the temple" of God?

Yet he was beloved of God; and so art thou. His cause came to light also, and so shall thine at the last; yea, and thy reward is great in heaven with him for thy deep suffering.

And on the other side, as they be cursed which leave righteousness destitute, and will not suffer therewith; so are they most accursed, which know the truth, and yet not only flee therefrom because they will not suffer, but also, for lucre, become the most cruel enemies thereof and most subtle persecutors, and most falsely lie thereon also.

Most accursed, who. W. T.

Works justify not. W. T.

Finally, though God, when he promiseth to bless our

works, do bind us to work if we will obtain the blessing or promise; yet must we beware of this pharisaical pestilence, to think that our works did deserve the promises. For whatsoever God commandeth us to do, that is our duty to do, though there were no such promise made to us at all. The promise therefore cometh not of the deserving of the worker (as though God had need of aught that we could do), but of the pure mercy of God, to make us the more willing to do that is our duty, &c. For if, when we had done all that God commandeth us to do, he then gave us up into the hands of tyrants, and killed us, and sent us to purgatory (which men so greatly fear), or to hell, and all the angels of heaven with us; he did us no wrong, nor were unrighteous, for aught that we or they could challenge of deserving: howsoever that God useth his creatures, he ever abideth righteous; till thou canst prove that, after he hath bound himself with his own word of mercy, he then breaks promise with them that keep covenant with him. So now, if nought were promised, nought could we challenge, whatsoever we did. And therefore the promise cometh of the goodness of the promiser only; and not of the deserving of those works, of which God hath no need, and which were no less our duty to do, though there were no such promise.

Not the worker, but the pure mercy of God is cause of the promise made unto.

Ye be the salt of the earth: but if the salt be waxen unsavoury, what 10.
can be salted therewith? It is henceforth nothing worth, but to
be cast out, and to be trodden under foot of men.

The office of a true preacher.

The office of an apostle and true preacher is to salt, not only the corrupt manners and conversation of earthly people, but also the rotten heart within, and all that springeth out thereof; their natural reason, their will, their understanding and wisdom; yea, and their faith and belief, and all that they have imagined without God's word concerning righteousness, justifying, satisfaction and serving of God. And the nature of salt is to bite, fret, and make smart. And the sick patients of the world are marvellous impatient, so that, though with great pain they can suffer their gross sins to be rebuked under a fashion, as in a parable afar off; yet, to have their righteousness, their holiness, and serving of God and his saints, disallowed, improved, and condemned for damnable and devilish, that may they not abide: insomuch that thou

It is a jeopardous thing to salt hypocrisy. W. T.

must leave thy salting or else be prepared to suffer again; even to be called a railer, seditious, a maker of discord, and a troubler of the common peace; yea, a schismatic, and an heretic also; and to be lied upon, that thou hast done and said that thou never thoughtest, and then to be called *coram nobis*[1], and to sing a new song, and forswear salting, or else to be sent after thy fellows that are gone before, and the way thy Master went.

Salt.

Who is meet to salt. W. T.

True preaching is a salting that stirreth up persecution; and an office that no man is meet for, save he that is seasoned himself before with poverty in spirit, softness, meekness, patience, mercifulness, pureness of heart, and hunger of righteousness, and looking for persecution also[2]; and hath all his hope, comfort, and solace, in the blessing only, and in no worldly thing.

A true preacher of God's word must use no partiality for fear of persecution.

Nay, will some say, a man might preach long enough without persecution, yea, and get favour too, if he would not meddle with the pope, bishops, prelates, and holy ghostly people that live in contemplation and solitariness, nor with great men of the world. I answer, true preaching is salting; and all that is corrupt must be salted: and those persons are of all other most corrupt, and therefore may not be left untouched.

The pope's pardons must be rebuked; the abuse of the mass, of the sacraments, and of all the ceremonies must be rebuked and salted. And selling of merits, and of prayers, must be salted. The abuse of fasting and of pilgrimage must be salted. All idolatry and false faith must be rebuked. And those friars that teach men to believe in St Francis' coat, how that they shall never come in hell or purgatory, if they be buried therein[3], may not be passed over with silence.

Monks, why they run to cloisters. W. T.

The pain and grief of salting made monks flee to their cloister. Nay (say they), we went thither of pure devotion to pray for the people. Yea, but for all that, the more ye increase, and the more ye multiply your prayers, the worse the world is. That is not our fault (say they), but theirs; that

[1 *Before us:* the expression is taken from the old Latin form of a magistrate's warrant, summoning the accused.]

[2 So D., but L. has *longing for persecution too.*]

[3 See Vol. I. p. 122, n. 2.]

they dispose not themselves, but continue in sin, and so are unapt to receive the influence of our prayers. O hypocrites! if ye were true salt and had good hearts, and loved your neighbours (if dead men be neighbours to them that are alive), and would come out of your dens, and take pain to salt and season them, ye should make a great many of them so apt that your prayers might take effect. But now seeing, as ye say, they be so unsavoury that your prayers be to them unprofitable, though their goods be to you profitable, and yet ye have no compassion to come out and salt them, it is manifest that ye love not them, but theirs; and that ye pray not for them, but, under the colour of praying, mock them and rob them.

Finally, salt, which is the true understanding of the law, of faith, and of the intent of all works, hath in you lost her virtue; neither be there any so unsavoury in the world as ye are, nor any that so sore kick against true salting as ye: and therefore are ye to be cast out, and trodden under foot, and despised of all men, by the righteous judgment of God.

By salt is understood the true understanding of the law, as of faith, of works, &c.

"If salt have lost his saltness, it is good for nothing but to be trodden under foot of men." That is, if the preacher, which for his doctrine is called salt, have lost the nature of salt, that is to say, his sharpness in rebuking all unrighteousness, all natural reason, natural wit and understanding, and all trust and confidence in whatsoever it be, save in the blood of Christ; he is condemned of God, and disallowed of all them that cleave to the truth. In what case stand they then that have benefices and preach not? Verily, though they stand at the altar, yet are they excommunicate and cast out of the living church of almighty God.

Spiritualty: why they be despised. W. T.

And what if the doctrine be not true salt? Verily then is it to be trodden under foot: as must all wearish[4] and unsavoury ceremonies which have lost their significations, and not only teach not, and are become unprofitable and do no more service to man; but also have obtained authority as God in the heart of man, that man serveth them, and putteth in them the trust and confidence that he should put in God his maker through Jesus Christ his redeemer. Are the institutions of man better than God's? Yea, are God's ordinances better now than in the old time? The prophets trod

Ceremonies must be salted. W. T.

[4 Used by Ascham for *sour*. Johnson's Dict. weerish.]

under foot, and defied the temple of God, and the sacrifices of God, and all ceremonies that God had ordained, with fastings and prayings, and all that the people perverted and committed idolatry with. We have as strait a commandment, to salt and rebuke all ungodliness, as had the prophets. Will they then have their ceremonies honourably spoken of? Then let them restore them to the right use, and put the salt of the true meaning and significations of them to them again. But as they be now used, none that loveth Christ can speak honourably of them. What true christian man can give honour to that that taketh all honour from Christ? Who can give honour to that that slayeth the soul of his brother, and robbeth his heart of that trust and confidence, which he should give to his Lord that hath bought him with his blood?

Ye are the light of the world. A city that is set on an hill cannot be hid. Neither do men light a candle, and put it under a bushel, but on a candlestick, and so giveth it light to all that are in the house. Let your light so shine before men, that they may see your good works, and praise your Father that is in heaven.

Christ goeth forth and describeth the office of an apostle and true preacher by another likeness; as he called them before the salt of the earth, even so here the light of the world: signifying thereby that all the doctrine, all the wisdom, and high knowledge of the world,—whether it were philosophy of natural conclusions, of manners and virtue, or of laws of righteousness,—whether it were of the holy scripture and of God himself,—was yet but a darkness, until the doctrine of his apostles came; that is to say, until the knowledge of Christ came, how that he is the sacrifice for our sins, our satisfaction, our peace, atonement and redemption, our life thereto, and resurrection. Whatsoever holiness, wisdom, virtue, perfectness, or righteousness, is in the world among men, howsoever perfect and holy they appear; yet is all damnable darkness, except the right knowledge of Christ's blood be there first, to justify the heart, before all other holiness.

All knowledge is darkness, till the knowledge of Christ's blood-shedding be in the heart. W. T.

Another conclusion: As "a city built on a hill cannot be hid," no more can the light of Christ's gospel. Let the world rage as much as it will, yet it will shine on their sore eyes, whether they be content or no.

Another conclusion: As "men light not a candle to whelm it under a bushel, but to put it on a candlestick, to light all that are in the house;" even so the light of Christ's gospel may not be hid, nor made a several thing, as though it pertained to some certain holy persons only. Nay, it is the light of the whole world, and pertaineth to all men; and therefore may not be made several. It is a madness that divers men say, 'The lay people may not know it:' except they can prove that the lay people be not of the world. Moreover it will not be hid; but as the lightning, that breaketh out of the clouds, shineth over all, even so doth the gospel of Christ. For where it is truly received, there it purifieth the heart, and maketh the person to consent to the laws of God, and to begin a new and godly living, fashioned after God's laws, and without all dissimulation: and then it will kindle so great love in him toward his neighbour, that he shall not only have compassion on him in his bodily adversity, but much more pity him over the blindness of his soul, and minister to him Christ's gospel. Wherefore if they say, 'It is here or there, in St Francis's coat, or Dominick's, and such like, and if thou wilt put on that coat, thou shalt find it there,' it is false. For if it were there, thou shouldest see it shine abroad, though thou creepest not into a cell or a monk's cowl, as thou seest the lightning without creeping into the clouds: yea, their light would so shine that men should not only see the light of the gospel, but also their "good works," which would as fast come out as they now run in; insomuch that thou shouldest see them make themselves poor, to help other, as they now make other poor, to make themselves rich.

The lay ought to have the gospel. W. T.

The property of the gospel. W. T.

The true gospel is not hid in dens. W. T.

If the spiritualty were a light, as they ought to be, they would make themselves poor, to make other rich; but they make other poor, and themselves rich.

This light and salt pertained not then to the apostles, and now to our bishops and spiritualty, only. No; it pertaineth to the temporal men also. For all kings and all rulers are bound to be salt and light; not only in example of living, but also in teaching of doctrine unto their subjects, as well as they be bound to punish evil doers. Doth not the scripture testify that king David was chosen to be a shepherd, and to feed his people with God's word? It is an evil schoolmaster that cannot but beat only: but it is a good schoolmaster that so teacheth, that few need to be beaten. This salt and light therefore pertain to the temporalty also,

Kings ought to be learned. W. T.

and that to every member of Christ's church: so that every man ought to be salt and light to other.

The order how every man may be a preacher, and how not. W. T.

Every man then may be a common preacher, thou wilt say, and preach every where by his own authority. Nay, verily; no man may yet be a common preacher, save he that is called and chosen thereto by the common ordinance of the congregation, as long as the preacher teacheth the true word of God. But every private man ought to be, in virtuous living, both light and salt to his neighbour: insomuch that the poorest ought to strive to overrun[1] the bishop, and preach to him in ensample of living. Moreover every man ought to preach in word and deed unto his household, and to them that are under his governance, &c. And though no man may preach openly, save he that hath the office committed unto him, yet ought every man to endeavour himself to be as well learned as the preacher, as nigh as it is possible. And every man may privately inform his neighbour; yea, and the preacher and bishop too, if need be. For if the preacher preach wrong, then may any man, whatsoever he be, rebuke him; first privately, and then, if that help not, to complain farther. And when all is proved, according to the order of charity, and yet none amendment had, then ought every man that can to resist him, and to stand by Christ's doctrine, and to jeopard life and all for it. Look on the old ensamples and they shall teach thee.

None ought to preach openly, but such as are admitted by the ordinance of the congregation.

Spiritual and temporal regiment do differ.

The gospel hath another freedom with her than the temporal regiment. Though every man's body and goods be under the king, do he right or wrong, yet is the authority of God's word free, and above the king: so that the worst in the realm may tell the king, if he do him wrong, that he doth naught, and otherwise than God hath commanded him; and so warn him to avoid the wrath of God, which is the patient avenger of all unrighteousness. May I then, and ought also, to resist father and mother and all temporal power with God's word, when they wrongfully do or command that hurteth or killeth the body; and have I no power to resist the bishop or preacher, that with false doctrine slayeth the souls, for which my master and Lord Christ hath shed his blood? Be we otherwise under our bishops than

[1 So D., but L. *overcome.*]

Christ and his apostles and all the[2] prophets were under the bishops of the old law? Nay, verily: and therefore may we, and also ought to do as they did, and to answer as the apostles did, *Oportet magis obedire Deo quam hominibus;* "We must rather obey God than men." In the gospel every man is Christ's disciple, and a person for himself, to defend Christ's doctrine in his own person[3]. The faith of the bishop will not help me, nor the bishop's keeping the law is sufficient for me. But I must believe in Christ for the remission of all sin, for mine ownself, and in mine own person. No more is the bishop's or preacher's defending God's word enough for me; but I must defend it in mine own person, and jeopard life and all thereon when I see need and occasion.

Acts v.

Every man must defend Christ's doctrine in his own person.

I am bound to get worldly substance for myself and for mine household with my just labour; and somewhat more for them that cannot, to save my neighbour's body: and am I not more bound to labour for God's word, to have thereof in store, to save my neighbour's soul? And when is it so much time to resist with God's word and to help, as when they which are believed to minister the true word do slay the souls with false doctrine for covetousness' sake? He that is not ready to give his life for the maintenance of Christ's doctrine against hypocrites, with whatsoever name or title they be disguised, the same is not worthy of Christ, nor can be Christ's disciple, by the very words and testimony of Christ. Nevertheless we must use wisdom, patience, meekness, and a discreet process, after the due order of charity, in our defending the word of God; lest, while we go about to amend our prelates, we make them worse. But when we have proved[4] all that charity bindeth us, and yet in vain; then we must come forth openly, and rebuke their wickedness in the face of the world, and jeopard life and all thereon.

Whoso refuseth to die for Christ's sake, cannot be the disciple of Christ.

[[2] So L., but D. has *the other prophets.*]

[[3] The words *person* and *parson* were not yet made two, by the adoption of the letter *a* into the first syllable of the synonyme for a Christian minister, as a means of distinguishing between them. Tyndale has therefore employed the word person here in each sense. At one period, in our language, the name of person was given to a rector, when meant to be distinguished from a vicar. Of this examples are given in Johnson, Dict.]

[[4] That is, *tried;* as in 1 Sam. xvii. 39.]

Ye shall not think that I am come to destroy the law or the prophets: no, I am not come to destroy them, but to fulfil them. For truly I say unto you, till heaven and earth perish, there shall not one jot or one tittle of the law scape, till all be fulfilled.

A little before Christ calleth his disciples the light of the world, and the salt of the earth; and that because of their doctrine, wherewith they should lighten the blind understanding of man, and with true knowledge drive out the false opinions and sophistical persuasions of natural reason, and deliver the scripture out of the captivity of false glosses, which the hypocritish Pharisees had patched thereto: and so, out of the light of true knowledge, to stir up a new living, and to salt and season the corrupt manners of the old blind conversation. For where false doctrine, corrupt opinions, and sophistical glosses, reign in the wit and understanding, there is the living devilish in the sight of God, howsoever it appear in the sight of the blind world. And on the other side, where the doctrine is true and perfect, there followeth godly living of necessity. For out of the inward belief of the heart floweth the outward conversation of the members. He that believeth that he ought to love his enemy, shall never cease fighting against his own self, till he have weeded all rancour and malice out of his heart: but he that believeth it not, shall put a visor of hypocrisy on his face, till he get opportunity to avenge himself.

False doctrine causeth evil works. W. T.

True doctrine is cause of good works. W. T.

And here he beginneth to teach them to be that light and that salt of which he spake, and saith: Though the scribes and Pharisees bear the people in hand, that all I do is of the devil, and accuse me of breaking the law and the prophets, (as they afterward railed on the apostles, that they drave the people from good works through preaching the justifying and righteousness of faith;) yet see that ye, my disciples, be not of that belief. For heaven and earth shall sooner perish, than one jot or tittle of the law should be put out. I come not to destroy the law, but to repair it only, and to make it go upright where it halteth; and even to make crooked straight, and rough smooth, as John the Baptist doth in the wilderness; and to teach the true understanding of the law. Without me the law cannot be fulfilled, nor ever could. For though the law were given by Moses, yet grace and verity, that is to say, the true understanding

Grace and truth through Jesus Christ. W. T.

and power to love it, and of love to fulfil it, cometh and ever came through faith in me.

I do but only wipe away the filthy and rotten glosses wherewith the scribes and the Pharisees have smeared[1] the law, and the prophets; and rebuke their damnable living, which they have fashioned, not after the law of God, but after their own sophistical glosses, feigned to mock out the law of God, and to beguile the whole world, and to lead them in blindness. And that the scribes and Pharisees falsely bely me, how that I go about to destroy the law, and to set the people at a fleshly liberty, and to make them first disobedient, and to despise their spiritual prelates, and then to rise against the temporal rulers, and to make all common, and to give licence to sin unpunished; cometh only of pure malice, hate, envy, and furious impatiency, that their visors are plucked from their faces, and their hypocrisy discovered. Howbeit what I teach, and what my learning is concerning the law, ye shall shortly hear, and that in few words.

Whosoever breaketh one of these least commandments, and teacheth men so, shall be called the least in the kingdom of heaven. But he that doth them and teacheth them, the same shall be great in the kingdom of heaven.

Whosoever studieth to destroy one of the commandments following, which are yet the least and but childish things, in respect of the perfect doctrine that shall hereafter be shewed, and of the mysteries yet hid in Christ; and teacheth other men even so, in word or ensample, whether openly or under a colour, and through false glosses of hypocrisy; that same doctor shall all they of the kingdom of heaven abhor and despise, and cast him out of their company, as a seething-pot doth cast up her foam and scum, and purge herself. So fast shall they of the kingdom of heaven cleave unto the pure law of God, without all men's glosses.

Glosses.

They that destroy the law of God with glosses must be cast out.

But whosoever shall first fulfil them himself, and then teach other, and set all his study to the furtherance and maintaining of them, that doctor shall all they of the kingdom of heaven have in price, and follow him and seek him out, as doth an eagle her prey, and cleave to him as burrs. For these commandments are but the very law of Moses, (the

[[1] So D., but L. has *which the scribes, &c. have smeared to.*]

draff of the Pharisees' glosses cleansed out,) interpreted according to the pure word of God, and as the open text compelleth to understand them, if ye look diligently thereon.

The church. W. T.

The kingdom of heaven take for the congregation or church of Christ. And to be of the kingdom of heaven is to know God for our Father, and Christ for our Lord and Saviour from all sin. And to enter into this kingdom it is impossible, except the heart of men be to keep the commandments of God purely; as it is written, "If any man will obey his will," that is to say, the will of the Father that sent me, saith Christ, "he shall know of the doctrine, whether it be of God, or whether I speak of mine own head." For if thine heart be to do the will of God, which is his commandments, he will give thee a pure eye, both to discern the true doctrine from the false, and the true doctor from the howling hypocrite. And therefore he saith,

Law. John vii. Except a man love God's law, he cannot understand the doctrine of Christ. W. T.

The righteousness of Pharisees. W. T.

For I say unto you, Except your righteousness exceed the righteousness of the scribes and Pharisees, ye cannot enter into the kingdom of heaven.

The righteousness of the scribes and Pharisees cannot enter into the kingdom of heaven. The kingdom of heaven is the true knowledge of God and Christ: *ergo*, the righteousness of the scribes and Pharisees neither knoweth God nor Christ. He that is willing to obey the will of God, understandeth the doctrine of Christ, as it is proved above: the scribes and the Pharisees understand not the doctrine of Christ: *ergo*, they have no will nor lust to obey the will of God. To obey the will of God is to seek the glory of God: for the glory of a master is the meek obedience of his servants; the glory of a prince is the humble obedience of his subjects; the glory of an husband is the chaste obedience of his wife; the glory of a father is the loving obedience of his children. The scribes and the Pharisees have no lust to obey the will of God: *ergo*, they seek not the glory of God. Furthermore, the scribes and the Pharisees seek their own glory: they that seek their own glory, preach their own doctrine: *ergo*, the scribes and Pharisees preach their own doctrine. The major thou hast Matt. xxiii.: the scribes and Pharisees "do all their works to be seen of men: they love to sit uppermost at feasts, and to have the chief seats in the synagogues,

Glory. He that seeketh his own glory teacheth his own doctrine, and not his master's. W. T. Matt. xxiii.

and salutations in the open markets, and to be called rabbi." And the minor followeth the text above rehearsed, "He that speaketh of himself," or of his own head, "seeketh his own glory:" that is to say, he that preacheth his own doctrine is ever known by seeking his own glory: so that it is a general rule to know that a man preacheth his own doctrine, if he seek his own glory.

John vii.

Some men will haply say, The scribes and Pharisees had no other law than Moses and the prophets, nor any other scripture; and grounded their sayings thereon. That is truth: how then preached they their own doctrine? Verily it followeth in the said seventh of John: "He that seeketh the glory of him that sent him, the same is true, and there is no unrighteousness in him;" that is to say, he will do his master's message truly, and not alter it: where contrariwise, he that seeketh his own glory, will be false when he is sent, and will alter his master's message, to turn his master's glory unto his own self. Even so did the scribes and Pharisees alter the word of God for their own profit and glory. And when God's word is altered with false glosses, it is no more God's word. As when God saith, "Love thy neighbour," and thou puttest to thy leaven, and sayest, "If my neighbour do me no hurt, nor say me nay, I am bound to love him; but not to give him, at his need, my goods which I have gotten with my sore labour;" now this is thy law, and not God's. God's law is pure and single, "Love thy neighbour," whether he be good or bad: and by love God meaneth to help at need. Now when God biddeth thee to get thy living, and somewhat over to help him that cannot, or at a time hath not wherewith to help himself; if thou, and thirty or forty with thee, get you to wilderness, and not only help not your neighbours, but also rob a great number of two or three thousand pounds yearly, how love ye your neighbours? Such men help the world with prayer, thou wilt say to me. Thou wert better to say, 'they rob the world with their hypocrisy,' say I to thee; and it is truth indeed that they so do. For if I stick up to the middle in the mire, like to perish without present help, and thou stand by and wilt not succour me, but kneelest down and prayest, will God hear the prayers of such an hypocrite? God biddeth thee so to love me, that thou put thyself in jeopardy to help me; and that thine heart, while

He that seeketh his own glory, altereth his master's message. W. T.

Word.

God's word altered is not his word. W. T.

To love is to help at need W. T.

The prayer of monks robbeth, and holpeth not. W. T.

thy body laboureth, do pray and trust in God that he will assist thee, and through thee to save me. An hypocrite, that will put neither body nor goods in peril for to help me at my need, loveth me not, neither hath compassion on me; and therefore his heart cannot pray, though he wag his lips never so much. It is written, "If a man be a worshipper of God, and do his will," which is the true worship, "him God heareth." Now the will of God is, that we love one another, to help at need: and such lovers he heareth, and not subtle hypocrites. As love maketh thee help me at my need; so when it is past thy power to help, it maketh thee pray to God. Even so where is no love, to make thee take bodily pain with me, there is no love that maketh thee pray for me; but thy prayer is indeed for thy belly, which thou lovest.

John ix.

Love prayeth. W. T.

What were the scribes and Pharisees? The scribes, besides that they were Pharisees, as I suppose, were also officers; as our bishops, chancellors, commissaries, archdeacons, and officials. And the Pharisees were religious men[1], which had professed, not as now, one Dominick's, the other Francis', another Bernard's rules, but even to hold the very law of God, with prayer, fasting, and alms-deeds; and were the flower and perfection of all the Jews: as St Paul rejoiceth of himself, saying, "I was an Hebrew, and concerning the law a Pharisee, and concerning the righteousness of the law I was faultless." They were more honourable than any sect of the monks with us, whether Observant, or Ancre[2], or whatsoever other be had in price.

Scribes and Pharisees, what they were. W. T.

Phil. iii.

These might much better have rejoiced to have been the true church, and to have had the Spirit of God, and that they could not have erred, than they whom all the world seeth

The Pharisees might better have proved themselves the true church, than our spiritualty may. W. T.

[1 Religious men, or men of religion, having become equivalent to members of some monastic order, Tyndale uses the word here to taunt the monks.]

[2 Ancre, i.e. anchorite: a name derived from the profession of *retiring* entirely out of the world into some solitude. Tria sunt in Ægypto genera monachorum. Primum cœnobitæ, quod illi *sauses* gentili lingua vocant, nos in commune viventes possumus appellare. Secundum anachoritæ, quia soli habitant per deserta, et ab eo quod procul ab hominibus recesserint, nuncupantur. Tertium genus est, quod *remoboth* dicunt, deterrimum atque neglectum, et quod in nostra provincia (the country about Bethlehem) aut solum, aut primum est. —Hieron. Ep. ad Eustochium. De Cust. Virg.]

neither to keep God's laws nor man's, nor yet that devil's law of their own making. For God had made them of the old testament as great promises, that he would be their God, and that his Spirit and all grace should be with them if they kept his laws, as he hath made to us. Now seeing they kept the uttermost jot of the law, in the sight of the world, and were faultless; and seeing thereto that God hath promised neither us nor them aught at all, but upon the profession of keeping his laws; whether were more like to be the right church, and to be taught of the Spirit of God that they could not err, those Pharisees or ours? Might not the general councils of those, and the things there decreed without scripture, seem to be of as great authority as the general councils of ours, and the things there ordained and decreed both clean without, and also against, God's word? Might not the ceremonies which those had added to the ceremonies of Moses, seem to be as holy and well to please God as the ceremonies of ours? The things which they added to the ceremonics of Moses, were of the same kind as those ceremonies were; and no more to be rebuked than the ceremonies of Moses: as for an ensample, if Moses bade wash a table or dish, when an unclean worm had crept thereon, the Pharisees did wash the table with a wet clout before every refection, lest any unclean thing had touched them unawares to all men, as we put unto our tithes a mortuary for all forgotten tithes. What was then the wickedness of the Pharisees? Verily the leaven of their glosses to the moral laws, by which they corrupted the commandments, and made them no more God's; and their false faith in the ceremonies, that the bare work was a sacrifice and a service to God, the significations lost; and the opinion of false righteousness in their prayers, fastings, and alms-deeds, that such works did justify a man before God, and not that God forgiveth sin of his mere mercy, if a man believe, repent, and promise to do his uttermost to sin no more.

The promises are made upon the profession of the keeping of the law of God, so that the church that will not keep God's law, hath no promise that they cannot err. W. T.

The wickedness of the Pharisees, what it was. W. T.

When these thus sat in the hearts of the people, with the opinion of virtue, holiness, and righteousness, and their law the law of God; their works, works commanded by God, and confirmed by all his prophets, as prayer, fasting, and alms-deeds, and they looked upon as the church of God that could not err; and finally, they themselves either every where were the chief rulers, or so sat in the hearts of the rulers,

Why the true preacher is accused of treason and heresy. W. T.

that their word was believed to be the word of God; what other thing could it be, to preach against all such, and to condemn their righteousness for the most damnable sin that can be, than to seem to go about to destroy the law and the prophets? What other thing can such a preacher seem to be, before the blind world, than an heretic, schismatic, seditious, possessed with the devil, and worthy of shame most vile and death most cruel? And yet these must be first rebuked, and their false righteousness detected, ere thou mayest preach against open sinners. Or else, if thou shouldest convert an open sinner from his evil living, thou shouldest make him nine hundred times worse than before: for he would at once be one of these sort, even an Observant, or of some like sect, of which, among an hundred thousand, thou shalt never bring one to believe in Christ; where among open sinners many believe at the hour of death, fall flat upon Christ, and believe in him only, without all other righteousness. It were an hundred thousand times better never to pray, than to pray such lip-prayers; and never to fast or do alms, than to fast, and to do alms, with a mind thereby to be made righteous, and to make satisfaction for the fore sins.

Why hypocrisy must be first rebuked, though it be jeopardy to preach against it. W. T.

Ye have heard how that it was said to them of old time, Kill not, for whosoever killeth shall be in danger of judgment. But I say unto you, Whosoever is angry with his brother shall be in danger of judgment: and whosoever saith unto his brother Racha, shall be in danger of a council: but whosoever saith to his brother, Thou fool, shall be in danger of hell fire.

The law is restored W. T.

Here Christ beginneth, not to destroy the law (as the Pharisees had falsely accused him), but to restore it again to the right understanding, and to purge it from the glosses of the Pharisees. He that slayeth shall be guilty, or in danger of judgment: that is to say, if a man murder, his deed testifieth against him; there is no more to do than to pronounce sentence of death against him. This text did the Pharisees extend no farther than to kill with the hand and outward members: but hate, envy, malice, churlishness, and to withdraw help at need, to beguile and circumvent with wiles and subtle bargaining, was no sin at all. No; to bring him whom thou hatest to death with craft and falsehood, so thou didst

The Pharisees did extend their doings or acts to the outward shew or deed, and nothing to the heart.

not put thine hand thereto, was no sin at all: as when they had brought Christ to death wrongfully, and compelled Pilate with subtilty to slay him, they thought themselves pure; insomuch that they would not go into the hall, for defiling themselves, and being partakers with Pilate in his blood. And they said to the apostles, "Ye would bring this man's blood upon us:" as who would say, we slew him not. And Saul (in the first book of the Kings in the eighteenth chapter), being so wrath with David that he would gladly have had him slain, determined yet that he would not defile himself; but to thrust him into the hands of the Philistines, that they might slay him, and he himself abide pure. And as our spiritualty now offer a man mercy once, though he have spoken against holy church; only if he will but perjure, and bear a fagot: but if he will not, they do but diet him a season, to win him, and make him tell more; and deliver him to the lay power, saying, He hath deserved death by our laws, and ye ought to kill him, howbeit we desire it not.

Acts v.

1 Sam. xviii.

But Christ restoreth the law again; and saith, to be angry with thy neighbour is to slay him, and to deserve death. For the law goeth as well on the heart as on the hand. "He that hateth his brother is a murderer." If then the blind hand deserve death, how much more those parts which have the sight of reason! And he that saith Racha[1], 'Lewd,' or whatsoever sign of wrath it be, or that provoketh to wrath, hath not only deserved that men should immediately pronounce sentence of death upon him; but also that, when death is pronounced, they should gather a council, to decree what horrible death he should suffer. And he that calleth his brother fool hath sinned down to hell.

The law of God goeth as well on the heart as the hand.

1 John iii.

Racha.

Shall then a man not be angry at all, nor rebuke or punish? Yes, if thou be a father or a mother, master or mistress, husband, lord, or ruler; yet with love and mercy, that the anger, rebuke, or punishment, exceed not the fault or trespass. May a man be angry with love? Yea, mothers can be so with their children. It is a loving anger, that hateth only the vice, and studieth to mend the person. But

How a man may be angry without sinning. W. T.

[1 'ריקה *Raka;* a word expressive of the greatest contempt; very much used by the rabbinical writers, and very common in the mouth of their people.'—Lightfoot Hor. Hebr. in Matt. v. 22.]

here is forbidden not only wrath against father, mother, and all that have governance over thee, which is to be angry, and to grudge against God himself, and that the ruler shall not be wrath without a cause against the subject; but also all private wrath against thy neighbour, over whom thou hast no rule, nor he over thee, no, though he do thee wrong. For he that doth wrong lacketh wit and discretion; and cannot amend, till he be informed and taught lovingly. Therefore thou must refrain thy wrath, and tell him his fault lovingly, and with kindness win him to thy Father: for he is thy brother, as well made and as dear bought as thou, and as well beloved, though he be yet childish and lack discretion.

Love is the keeping of the law. W. T.

But some will say, I will not hate my neighbour, nor yet love him or do him good. Yes, thou must love him: for the first commandment, out of which all other flow, is, "Thou shalt love the Lord thy God with all thine heart, with all thy soul, and with all thy might:" that is, thou must keep all his commandments with love. Love must keep thee from killing or hurting thy neighbour, and from coveting in thine heart whatsoever is his. And "this commandment have we of him, that he which loveth God love his brother also." And again, "He that hath the substance of this world, and seeth his brother have necessity, and shutteth up his compassion from him, how is the love of God in him?" He then that helpeth not at need, loveth not God, but breaketh the first commandment. "Let us love," therefore, saith St John, "not with word and tongue, but in deed and truth." And again, St John saith in the said place, "He that loveth not his brother abideth yet still in death." And of love hath Moses texts enough: but the Pharisees glossed them out, saying, they were but good counsels, if a man desired to be perfect, but not precepts. "If thou meet thine enemy's ox or ass going astray, thou shalt in any wise bring them to him again." And, "If thou see thine enemy's ass fall down under his burden, thou shalt help him up again." And, "Thou shalt not hate thy brother in thine heart, but shalt in any wise rebuke thy neighbour, that thou bear no sin for his sake[1]."

1 John iv. 1 John iii. Exod. xxiii. Lev. xix.

He that helpeth not to amend sinners, must suffer with them when they be punished. W. T.

[[1] The authorised version has, 'that thou bear not sin for him,' in its margin.]

For if thou study not to amend thy neighbour, when he sinneth, so art thou partaker of his sins; and therefore, when God taketh vengeance and sendeth whatsoever plague it be, to punish open sinners, thou must perish with them. For thou didst sin in the sight of God as deep as they; because thou didst not love the law of God, to maintain it with all thine heart, soul, power, and might. Is not he that seeth his neighbour's house in jeopardy to be set on fire, and warneth not, nor helpeth in time, to avoid the peril, worthy (if his neighbour's house be burnt up) that his be burnt also; seeing it was in his power to have kept all out of jeopardy, if he had would; as he would, no doubt, if he had loved his neighbour? Even so, when God sendeth a general pestilence or war to thy city, to punish the sin thereof; art thou not worthy that thine house should be infected or perish, if thou mightest have kept it from sinning, and thou hadst been willing thereto? But if thou do thy best to further the law of God, and to keep thy land or neighbours from sinning against God; then (though it help not) thou shalt bear no sin for their sakes when they be punished. He therefore that loveth the law of God, may be bold in time of pestilence and all jeopardy to believe in God. And again in the same place, "Thou shalt not avenge thyself, nor bear hate in mind against the children of thy people; but shalt love thy fellow as thyself. I am the Lord." As who should say, For my sake shalt thou do it. And, "The Lord your God is the God of gods and Lord of lords, a great God, mighty and terrible, which regardeth no man's person or degree, nor taketh gifts; but doth right to the fatherless and the widow, and loveth the stranger, to give him raiment and food. Love therefore the stranger, for ye were strangers in the land of Egypt." And, "If a stranger sojourn by thee in your land, see that ye vex him not. But let the stranger, that dwelleth among you, be as one of yourselves, and love him as thyself: for ye were strangers in the land of Egypt. I am the Lord." As who should say, Love him for my sake.

In doing our best to further our neighbour in virtue (although we prevail not) we are excused.

Deut. x.

Lev. xix.

Notwithstanding, when thy neighbour hath shewed thee more unkindness than God hath love, then mayest thou hate him, and not before; but must love him for God's sake, till he fight against God, to destroy the name and glory of God.

When a man may hate his neighbour. W. T.

Therefore when thou offerest thy gift at the altar, and there rememberest that thy brother hath aught against thee; leave there thy gift before the altar, and go first and reconcile thyself unto thy brother, and then come and offer thy gift. Agree with thine adversary at once, while thou art in the way with him; lest thine adversary deliver thee to the judge, and the judge deliver thee to the minister, and thou be cast into prison. Verily I say unto thee, thou shalt not come out thence, till thou have paid the uttermost farthing.

This text, with the similitude, is somewhat subtle; and bindeth both him that hath offended to reconcile himself as much as in him is, and him that is offended to forgive and be at one. The offerings were signs, and did certify a man that God was at one with him, and was his friend and loved him. For the fat of beasts was offered, and wine thereto, as though God had sat and eaten and drunk with them; and the rest they and their households did eat before God, as though they had ate and drunk with God; and were commanded to be merry and to make good cheer, fully certified that God was at one with them, and had forgot all old offences, and now loved them, that he would fulfil all his promises of mercy with them.

Offerings or sacrifices, what they meant. W. T.

Now will God receive no sacrifice (that is to wit, neither forgive, nor fulfil any of his promises), except we be first reconciled unto our brethren, whether we have offended or be offended. In the chapter following thou readest, "If ye forgive, your Father shall forgive you." And, Hos. vi. "I love mercy and not sacrifice, and the knowledge of God more than I do burnt offerings:" that is to say, the knowledge of the appointments made between God and us; what he will have us to do first, and then what he will do for us again. And God refuseth fasting, and punishing of the body, that was coupled with cruelty, and saith, that he desired no such fast; but saith, This fast require I, that ye be merciful and forgive, and clothe the naked, and feed the hungry, &c. "Then call (saith he), and the Lord shall answer: cry, and he shall say, See, here I am."

Matt. vi. Hos. vi. Isai. lviii. The fast that God requireth.

And that similitude will, that as a man here, if he will no otherwise agree, must suffer the extremity of the law, if he be brought before a judge, (for the judge hath no power to forgive or to remit, but to condemn him in the uttermost of the law;) even so, if we will not forgive one another here, we shall have judgment of God without all mercy.

And that some make purgatory of the last farthing, they shew their deep ignorance. For first, no similitude holdeth every word and syllable of the similitude. Furthermore, when they dispute, Till he pay the last farthing; *ergo,* he shall pay: but not in hell; *ergo,* in purgatory: a wise reason! Joseph knew not Mary till she had borne her first son; *ergo,* she bare the second; or, he knew her after. I will not forgive thee till I be dead or while I live; *ergo,* I will do it after my death: and a thousand like.

Last farthing. W. T.

Ye have heard how it was said to them of old time, Commit not adultery. But I say to you, that whosoever looketh on a wife, lusting after her, hath committed advoutry with her already in his heart.

This commandment, 'Commit none adultery,' had the Pharisees blinded and corrupt with their sophistry and leaven, interpreting the concupiscence of the heart, lewd toys, filthy gestures, unclean words, clipping, kissing, and so forth, not to be imputed for sin; but even the act and deed alone: though Moses say in the text, 'Thou shalt not covet thy neighbour's wife,' &c. But Christ putteth to light and salt; and bringeth the precept to his true understanding and natural taste[1] again; and condemneth the root of sin, the concupiscence and consent of the heart. Before the world I am no murderer, till I have killed with mine hand: but before God I kill, if I hate; yea, if I love not, and of love keep me both from doing hurt, and also be ready and prepared to help at need. Even so the consent of the heart, with all other means that follow thereof, be as well advoutry before God as the deed itself.

How corruptly the Pharisees did attribute all evil to the deed only.

Finally, I am an advouterer before God, if I so love not my neighbour, that very love forbid me to covet his wife. "Love is the fulfilling of all commandments." And without love it is impossible to abstain from sinning against my neighbour in any precept, if occasion be given.

Love is the fulfilling of the law. W. T.

Carnal love will not suffer a mother to rob her child; no, it maketh her rob herself to make it rich. A natural father shall never lust after his son's wife; no, he careth more for

[[1] So L., but D. has *cast.*]

her chastity than his son doth himself. Even so would love to my neighbour keep me from sinning against him.

Advoutry. W. T.

Advoutry is a damnable thing in the sight of God, and much mischief followeth thereof. David, to save his honour, was driven to commit grievous murder also. It is unright, in the sight of God and man, that thy child should be at another man's cost, and be another man's heir: neither canst thou or the mother have lightly a quiet conscience to God, or a merry heart, as long as it so is. Moreover what greater shame canst thou do thy neighbour, or what greater displeasure? What if it never be known, nor come any child thereof? The preciousest gift that a man hath of God in this world is the true heart of his wife, to abide by him in wealth and woe, and to bear all fortunes with him. Of that hast thou robbed him; for after she hath once coupled herself to thee, she shall not lightly love him any more so truly; but haply hate him, and procure his death. Moreover thou hast untaught her to fear God, and hast made her to sin against God: for to God promised she, and not to man only; for the law of matrimony is God's ordinance. For it is written, when Potiphar's wife would have Joseph to lie with her, he answered: "How could I do this wickedness and sin against God?" Yea, verily; it is impossible to sin against man, except thou sin against God first. Finally, read chronicles and stories, and see what hath followed of adultery.

Gen. xxxix.

Some doctors have doubted in that which Christ hath flatly condemned.

What shall we say, that some doctors have disputed and doubted whether single fornication should be sin, when it is condemned both by Christ and Moses too? And Paul testifieth, that no fornicator, or whorekeeper, shall possess the kingdom of God. It is right that all men, that hope in God, should bring up their fruit in the fear and knowledge of God; and not to leave his seed where he careth not what come thereof.

1 Cor. vi.

Wherefore if thy right eye offend thee, pluck it out, and cast it from thee: for it is better for thee that one of thy members perish, than that thy whole body should be cast into hell. And even so if thy right hand offend thee, cut it off, and cast it from thee. For it is better for thee that one of thy members perish, than that thy whole body should be cast into hell.

This is not meant of the outward members. For then we must cut off nose, ears, hand and foot; yea, we must procure to destroy the seeing, hearing, smelling, tasting, and feeling, and so every man kill himself. But it is a phrase or speech of the Hebrew tongue, and will that we cut off occasions, dancing, kissing, riotous eating and drinking, and the lust of the heart, and filthy imaginations, that move a man to concupiscence. Let every man have his wife, and think her the fairest and the best-conditioned, and every woman her husband so too. For God hath blessed thy wife, and made her without sin to thee, which ought to seem a beautiful fairness. And all that ye suffer together, the one with the other, is blessed also, and made the very cross of Christ, and pleasant in the sight of God. Why should she then be loathsome to thee, because of a little suffering, that thou shouldest lust after another, that should defile thy soul, and slay thy conscience, and make thee suffer everlastingly?

Filthy. W. T.

A wife, how good a thing. W. T.

It is said, whosoever putteth away his wife, let him give her a testimonial of the divorcement. But I say unto you, whosoever putteth away his wife (except it be for fornication) maketh her to break wedlock; and whosoever marrieth the divorced, breaketh wedlock.

Moses permitted his Israelites in extreme necessity, as when they so hated their wives that they abhorred the company of them, then to put them away, to avoid a worse inconvenience; whereof ye read also Matt. xix. And he knit thereto, that they might not receive them again, after they had been known of any other persons. Which licence the Jews abused, and put away their wives for every light or feigned cause, and whensoever they lusted. But Christ calleth back again, and interpreteth the law after the first ordinance, and cutteth off all causes of divorcement, save fornication of the wife's party, when she breaketh her matrimony; in which case Moses's law pronounceth her dead, and so do the laws of many other countries: which laws, where they be used, there is a man free without all question. Now where they be let live, there the man (if he see sign of repentance and amendment) may forgive for once. If he may not find in his heart (as Joseph, as holy as he was, could not find in his heart to take Christ's mother to him, when he spied her with child), he is free no doubt to take another, while the law interpreteth her dead: for her sin ought of no right to bind him.

Deut. xxiv

Matt. xix.

What shall the woman do, if she repent and be so tempted in her flesh that she cannot live chaste? Verily I can shew you nothing out of the scripture. The office of the preacher is, to preach the ten commandments, which are the law natural; and to promise them which submit themselves to keep them, of love and fear of God, everlasting life for their labour through faith in Christ; and to threaten the disobedient with everlasting pain in hell. And his[1] punishment is, if any man have offended through frailty, and when he is rebuked turn and repent, to receive him unto grace, and absolve him; and if any man will not amend when he is rebuked, to cast him out among the infidels. This I say, if the temporal power shut her up as a convict person, appointing her a sober living, to make satisfaction to the congregation for her damnable example, they did not amiss. It is better that one misdoer suffer, than that a commonwealth be corrupt.

The office of a preacher. W. T.

Where the officers be negligent, and the woman not able to put herself to penance, if she went where she is not known, and there marry, God is the God of mercy. If any man in the same place where she trespasseth pitied her, and married her, I could suffer it; were it not that the liberty would be the next way to provoke all other that were once weary of their husbands to commit adultery, for to be divorced from them, that they might marry other which they loved better. Let the temporal sword take heed to their charge therefore. For this is truth: all the temporal blessings set in the law of Moses for keeping their laws, as wealth and prosperity, long life, the upper hand of their enemies, plenteousness of fruits, and cheap of all things, and to be without pestilence, war and famishment, and all manner other abominable diseases and plagues, pertain to us as well as to them, if we keep our temporal laws.

What followeth the keeping of the law. W. T.

And all the curses and terrible plagues which are threatened throughout the law of Moses, as hunger, dearth, war and dissension, pestilence, fevers, and wonderful and strange fearful diseases, as the sweat, plague, and falling sickness, shortening of days, that the sword, hunger, and such diseases shall eat them up in their youth, that their enemies should have the upper hand, that the people of the land should be minished, and the towns decayed, and the land brought unto

What followeth the breaking of the law. W. T.

[1 So D., but L. *this*.]

a wilderness, and that a plenteous land should be made barren, or so ordered that dearth should devour the inhabiters, and wealth be among few that should oppress the rest, with a thousand such like, so that nothing they begin should have a prosperous end; all those curses (I say) pertain to us as well as to them, if we break our temporal laws.

Let England look about them, and mark what hath chanced them, since they slew their right king whom God had anointed over them, king Richard the Second. Their people, towns, and villages are minished by the third part; and of their noble blood remaineth not the third, nor I believe the sixth, yea, and if I durst be bold, I wene I might safely swear that there remaineth not the sixteenth part. Their own sword hath eaten them up. And though pastures be enlarged above all measure, yet rot of sheep, murrain of beasts, with parks and warrens, with raising of fines and rent, make all things twice so dear as they were. And our own commodities are so abused, that they be the destruction of our own realm.

The enormities that hath chanced since the slaughter of king Richard the second unto this realm of England.

And right: for if we will not know God to keep his laws, how should God know us, to keep us, and to care for us, and to fulfil his promises of mercy unto us? Saith not Paul, (Rom. i.) of the heathen, *Sicut non probaverunt habere Deum in notitia, ita tradidit illos Deus;* As it seemed them not good, or as they had no lust, or as they admitted it not, nor allowed for right in their hearts to know God as God, to give him the honour of God, that is, to fear him as God, and as avenger of all evil, and to seek his will; even so God gave them up to follow their own blindness; and took his Spirit and his grace from them, and would no longer rule their wits? Even so if we cast off us the yoke of our temporal laws, which are the laws of God, and drawn out of the ten commandments and law natural, and out of "Love thy neighbour as thyself;" God shall cast us off and let us slip, to follow our own wit. And then shall all go against us, whatsoever we take in hand: insomuch that when we gather a parliament to reform or amend aught, that we there determine shall be our own snare, confusion, and utter destruction, so that all the enemies we have under heaven could not wish us so great mischief as our own counsel shall do us; God shall so blind the wisdom of the wise. If any man have any godly counsel, it shall

Tyrants: why God giveth us up, and leaveth us in the hands of tyrants and in all misery. W. T.

Rom. i.

have none audience: error, madness, and dasing[1] shall have the upper hand.

An admonition. W. T.

And let the spiritualty take heed and look well about them, and see whether they walk as they have promised God, and in the steps of his Son Christ, and of his apostles, whose offices they bear. For I promise them, all the devils in hell, if God had let them loose, could not have given them worse counsel than they have given themselves this twenty year long. God gave up his Israelites oftentime, when they would not be ruled, nor know themselves and their duty to God; and brought them into captivity under their enemies, to prove and feel (saith the text) whether were better service, either to serve God, and willingly to obey his law coupled with so manifold blessings; or to serve their enemies, and to obey their cruelness and tyranny (spite of their heads) in need and necessity. And let the temporalty remember, that because those nations, under which the Isralites were in captivity, did deal cruelly with them, not to punish them for their idolatry and sin, which they had committed against God, but to have their lands, and goods, and service only, rejoicing to make them worse and more out of their Father's favour; therefore when God had scourged his children enough, he did beat the other for their labour.

What rulers ought to do, touching such as run and fly from their wives without just cause.

But to our purpose: what if the man run from his wife and leave her desolate? Verily, the rulers ought to make a law, if any do so and come not again by a certain day, as within the space of a year or so, that then he be banished the country; and if he come again, to come on his head, and let the wife be free to marry where she will. For what right is it that a lewd wretch should take his goods, and run from his wife without a cause, and sit by a whore, yea, and come again after a year or two (as I have known it) and rob his wife of that she hath gotten in the mean time, and go again to his whore? Paul saith to the Corinthians, that if a man or woman be coupled with an infidel, and the infidel depart, the other is free to marry where they lust. And he saith:

Tim. v.

"If there be any man that provideth not for his, and namely for them of his own household, the same denieth the faith, and is worse than an infidel." And even so is this man much more to be interpreted for an infidel, that causeless

[1 So D., but L. *daunsyng.*]

runneth from his wife. Let, I say, the governors take heed how they let sin be unpunished, and how they bring the wrath of God upon their realms. For God will be avenged of all iniquity, and punish it with plagues from heaven.

In like manner, if the woman depart causeless and will not be reconciled, though she commit none adultery, the man ought of right to be free to marry again. And in all other causes, if they separate themselves of impatience that the one cannot suffer the other's infirmities, they must remain unmarried.

If any part burn, let the same suffer the pain or infirmities of the other. And the temporalty ought to make laws to bridle the unruly party.

Again, ye have heard how it was said to them of old time, foreswear not thyself, but pay thine oaths unto the Lord. But I say unto you, swear not at all, neither by heaven, for it is the seat of God; neither by the earth, for it is his footstool; neither by Jerusalem, for it is the city of the great king; neither shalt thou swear by thine head, for thou canst not make a white hair or a black. But your communication shall be, Yea, yea, nay, nay. For if aught be above that, it proceedeth of evil.

As to hate in the heart, or to covet another man's wife, was no sin with the Pharisees; no more was it to hide one thing in the heart, and to speak another with the mouth, to deceive a man's neighbour, if it were not bound with an oath. And though Moses say, 'Lie not, nor deceive any man his neighbour' or one another; yet they interpreted it but good counsel, if a man desired to be perfect; but no precept, to bind under pain of sin: and so by that means, not only they that spake true, but also they that lied to deceive, were compelled to swear and to confirm their words with oaths, if they would be believed.

Swearing. W. T.

Levit. xix.

But Christ bringeth light and salt to the text, which the Pharisees had darkened and corrupt with the stinking mist of their sophistry, and forbiddeth to swear at all, either by God or any creature of God's; for thou canst swear by none other at all, except the dishonour shall redound unto the name of God. If thou swear 'By God it is so,' or 'By God I will do this or that;' the meaning is, that thou makest God judge, to avenge it of thee, if it be not as thou sayest, or if thou shalt not do as thou promisest. Now if truth be not in thy

To swear by God. W. T.

words, thou shamest thine heavenly Father, and testifiest that thou believest that he is no righteous judge, nor will avenge unrighteousness; but that he is wicked as thou art, and consenteth and laugheth at thee, while thou deceivest thy brother, as well created after the likeness of God, and as dear bought with the precious blood of Christ, as thou. And thus through thee, a wicked son, is the name of thy Father dishonoured, and his law not feared, nor his promises believed. And when thou swearest by the gospel book, or bible, the meaning is, that God, if thou lie, shall not fulfil unto thee the promises of mercy therein written; but contrariwise to bring unto thee all the curses, plagues and vengeance therein threatened unto the disobedient and evil doers. And even so when thou swearest by any creature, as by bread or salt, the meaning is, that thou desirest, that the creator thereof shall avenge it of thee, if thou lie, &c. Wherefore our dealing ought to be so substantial, that our words might be believed without an oath. Our words are the signs of the truth of our hearts, in which ought to be pure and single love toward thy brother; for whatsoever proceedeth not of love is damnable. Now falsehood to deceive him, and pure love, cannot stand together. It cannot therefore be but damnable sin to deceive thy brother with lying, though thou add no oath to thy words. Much more damnable is it then to deceive, and to add an oath thereto, &c.

Men ought so to deal that their words may be credited without any oaths.

Swearing, in what sort it is lawful.

Howbeit all manner of swearing is not here forbidden, no more than all manner of killing, when the commandment saith, "Kill not;" for judges and rulers must kill. Even so ought they, when they put any man in office, to take an oath of him that he shall be true and faithful and diligent therein; and of their subjects it is lawful to take oaths, and of all that offer themselves to bear witness. But if the superior would compel the inferior to swear that [which] should be to the dishonour of God, or hurting of an innocent, the inferior ought rather to die than to swear: neither ought a judge to compel a man to swear against himself, that he make him not sin and forswear; whereof it is enough spoken in another place. But here is forbidden swearing between neighbour aud neighbour, and in all our private business and daily communication. For customable swearing, though we lied not, doth rob the name of God of his due reverence and fear. And in our daily communication and business one with the other is so much vanity of words, that we cannot but in many things lie; which to confirm with an oath, though we beguile not, is to take the name of God in vain, and unreverently, against the second precept. Now to lie for the intent to beguile is damnable of itself: how much more then to abuse the holy name of God thereto, and to call to God for vengeance upon thine own self!

Many cases yet there chance daily between man and man, in which charity compelleth to swear: as if I know that my neighbour is falsely slandered, I am bound to report the truth, and may lawfully swear, yea, and am bound if it need, and that though not before a judge. And unto the weak, where yea and nay have lost their credence through the multitude of liars, a man may lawfully swear to put them out of doubt: which yet cometh of the evil of them that abuse their language to deceive withal. Finally, to swear to do evil is damnable; and to perform that is double damnation. Herod's oath made him not innocent and guiltless of the death of John the baptist; though the hypocrite had not known what his wife's daughter would have asked. And when men say a king's word must stand; that is truth, if his oath or promise be lawful and expedient.

Charity moderateth the law. W. T.

Oath.

To perform an evil oath is double sin. W. T.

In all our promises it is to be added, "If God will," and, "If there be no lawful let." And though it be not added, it is to be interpreted, as added. As if I borrow thy sword, and by the hour I promise to bring it thee again, thou be beside thyself: if I promise to pay by a certain day, and be in the mean time robbed or decayed by chance, that I cannot perform it: I am not forsworn if mine heart meant truly when I promised. And many like cases there be, of which are touched in other places. To lie also, and to dissemble, is not alway sin. David told king Achish, the Philistine, that he had robbed his own people the Jews, when he had been a roving among the Amalekites, and had slain man, woman, and child for telling tales; and yet was that lie no more sin, than it was to destroy the Amalekites, those deadly enemies of the faith of one almighty God. Neither sinned Hushai, David's trusty friend, in feigning and beguiling Absalom, but pleased God highly. To bear a sick man in hand that wholesome bitter medicine is sweet, to make him drink it, it is the duty of charity, and no sin. To persuade him that pursueth his

He is not forsworn, whose heart meant truly when he promised.

To lie or dissemble in some causes not culpable. 1 Sam. xxvii.

2 Sam. xvii.

neighbour to hurt him or slay him, that his neighbour is gone another contrary way, is the duty of every Christian man by the law of charity, and no sin; no, though I confirmed it with an oath[1]. But to lie for to deceive and hurt, that is damnable only, &c.

Ye have heard, how it is said, An eye for an eye, a tooth for a tooth. But I say unto you, that ye withstand not wrong. But if a man give thee a blow on the right cheek, turn to him the other also. And if any man will go to law with thee and take away thy coat, let him have thy cloak thereto. And if any man compel thee to go a mile, go with him twain. Give to him that asketh, and from him that would borrow turn not away.

Christ here intended not to disannul the temporal regiment, and to forbid rulers to punish evil doers, no more than he meant to destroy matrimony when he forbade to lust and to covet another man's wife in the[2] heart. But as he there forbade that which defileth matrimony, even so he forbiddeth here that which troubleth, unquieteth, and destroyeth the temporal regiment, and that thing which to forbid the temporal regiment was ordained; which is, that no man avenge himself. Christ meddleth not with the temporal regiment; but in all this long sermon fighteth against the Pharisees' false doctrine, and salteth the law, to purge it of the corruption of their filthy glosses, and to bring it unto the right taste and true understanding again.

For the Pharisees had so interpreted that law of Moses, which pertained only unto the rulers, that every private person might avenge himself, and do his adversary as much harm again as he had received of him.

Now if he that is angry have deserved that men pronounce death upon him; and he that saith Racha, hath deserved that men should gather a council to determine some sundry and cruel death for so heinous a crime; and if he that calleth his brother fool have deserved hell, what deserveth he that smiteth or avengeth himself with his own hand? Here is forbidden therefore private wrath only, and that a man avenge himself.

To turn the other cheek; what it is. W. T.

To turn the other cheek, is a manner of speaking, and not to be understood as the words sound; as was to cut off

[1 The apostle says that they who should say, 'Let us do evil, that good may come,' would justly be condemned.]

[2 So D., but L. *thy*.]

the hand, and to pluck out the eye; and as we command our children not only not to come nigh a brook or water, but also not so hardy as once to look that way, either to look on fire, or once to think on fire; which are impossible to be observed. More is spoken than meant, to fear them; and to make them perceive that it is earnest that we command. Even so is the meaning here, that we in no wise avenge; but be prepared ever to suffer as much more, and never to think it lawful to avenge, how great soever the injury be: for he himself turned not the other cheek, when he was smitten before the bishop; nor yet Paul, when he was buffeted before the bishop also. But ye have had a little above, "Blessed are the meek, for they shall possess the earth." Meekness.
Let all the world study to do thee wrong, yea, let them do thee wrong; and yet if thou be meek, thou shalt have food and raiment enough for thee and thine. And moreover, if the worst come, God shall yet set such a tyrant over thee, that (if thou be meek and canst be content that he poll thee properly, and even as thou mayest bear) shall defend thee from all other. Who is polled intolerably, that his life is Polling, how to avoid it. W. T.
bitter and even death to him, but he that is impatient and cannot suffer to be polled? Yea, poll thyself and prevent other; and give the bailiff or like officer now a capon, now a pig, now a goose, and so to thy landlord likewise; or if thou have a great farm, now a lamb, now a calf; and let thy wife visit thy landlady three or four times in the year with spiced cakes, and apples, pears, cherries, and such like. And be thou ready with thine oxen or horses, three or four, or half a dozen days in the year, to fetch home their wood, or to plough their land: yea, and if thou have a good horse, let them have him good cheap[3], or take a worse for him; and they shall be thy shield and defend thee, though they be tyrants and care not for God, that no man else shall dare poll thee. And thereto thou mayest with wisdom get of them that [which] shall recompense all that thou doest to them. All this I mean, if thou be patient, and wise, and fear God thereto, and love thine neighbour, and do none evil. For if thou keep thyself in favour with hurting thy neighbour, thine end will be evil, and at the last desperation in this world, and hell after.

[3 See Vol. I. p. 122.]

But and if thou canst not poll thyself with wisdom, and laugh, and bear a good countenance, as though thou rejoicest while such persons poll thee, every man shall poll thee; and they shall maintain them, and not defend thee. Let this therefore be a common proverb—'Be contented to be polled of some man; or to be polled of every man.'

Two manner states and degrees of regiments. W. T.

Ye must understand that there be two states or degrees in this world: the kingdom of heaven, which is the regiment of the gospel; and the kingdom of this world, which is the temporal regiment. In the first state there is neither father, mother, son, daughter; neither master, mistress, maid, manservant, nor husband, nor wife, nor lord, nor subject, nor man, nor woman: but Christ is all; and each to other is Christ himself. There is none better than other; but all like good, all brethren, and Christ only is Lord over all. Neither is there any other thing to do, or other law, save to love one another as Christ loved us. In the temporal regiment is husband, wife, father, mother, son, daughter, master, mistress, maid, manservant, lord, and subject.

Every man is of the spiritualty, and of the temporalty, both. W. T.

Now is every person a double person; and under both the regiments. In the first regiment, thou art a person for thine own self, under Christ and his doctrine, and mayest neither hate nor be angry, and much less fight or avenge; but must after the ensample of Christ humble thyself, forsake and deny thyself, and hate thyself, and cast thyself away, and be meek and patient, and let every man go over thee, and tread thee under foot and do thee wrong; and yet love them, and pray for them, as Christ did for his crucifiers. For love is all; and what is not of love, that is damnable, and cast out of that kingdom.

He that loveth not his neighbour hath not the true faith of Christ. W. T.

For that kingdom is the knowledge of God and Christ. But he that loveth not, knoweth neither God nor Christ; therefore he that loveth not, is not of that kingdom. The minor is on this wise proved: he that knoweth God and Christ, seeth light, for Christ is light; but "he that hateth his
1 John ii. brother is in darkness, and walketh in darkness, and wotteth not whither he goeth, for darkness hath blinded his eyes:" *ergo*, he that hateth his brother knoweth not what Christ hath done for him; and therefore hath no true faith; nor is of the spiritual kingdom of God.

To hate thyself, that shalt thou get, if thou considerest

thine own sins, and the deep damnation that long[1] thereto, with due repentance. And to love, that thou shalt obtain, if thou behold the great and infinite mercy of God with strong faith; that there is none so great an enemy to thee in this world, but thou shalt lightly[2] love him, if thou look well on the love that God shewed thee in Christ.

The temporal regiment.

In the temporal regiment, thou art a person in respect of other; thou art an husband, father, mother, master, mistress, lord, ruler, or wife, son, daughter, servant, subject, &c. And there thou must do according to thine office. If thou be a father, thou must do the office of a father, and rule, or else thou damnest thyself. Thou must bring all under obedience, whether by fair means or foul. Thou must have obedience of thy wife, of thy servants, and of thy subjects; and the other must obey. If they will not obey with love, thou must chide and fight, as far as the law of God and the law of the land will suffer thee. And when thou canst not rule them, thou art bound in many cases to deliver them unto the higher officer, of whom thou didst take the charge over them.

Not to resist violence, how it is understood. W T.

Now to our purpose, whether a man may resist violence, and defend or avenge himself. I say nay, in the first state, where thou art a person for thyself alone, and Christ's disciple. There thou must love, and of love do, study, and enforce; yea, and suffer all things (as Christ did) to make peace, that the blessing of God may come upon thee, which saith: "Blessed be the peace-makers, for they shall be the children of God." If thou suffer and keepest peace in thyself only, thy blessing is the possession of this world. But if thou so love the peace of thy brethren, that thou leave nothing undone or unsuffered to further it, thy blessing is, thou shalt be God's son, and consequently possess heaven.

But in the worldly state, where thou art no private man, but a person in respect of other, thou not only mayest, but also must, and art bound under pain of damnation to execute thine office. Where thou art a father, thou must have obedience by fair means or by foul; and to whom thou art an husband, of her thou must require obedience and chastity, and, to get that, attempt all that the law of the land commandeth and will. And of thy servants thou must exact

[1 That is, belongs.]
[2 Without difficulty.]

obedience and fear, and mayest not suffer thyself to be despised. And where thou art a ruler thereto appointed, thou must take, prison, and slay too; not of malice and hate, to avenge thyself, but to defend thy subjects, and to maintain thine office.

Rulers must punish, not for malice, but for defence of the people, and maintenance of the laws.

Concerning thyself, oppress not thy subjects with rent, fines, or custom at all, neither pill them with taxes and such like, to maintain thine own lusts: but be loving and kind to them, as Christ was to thee; for they be his, and the price of his blood. But those that are evil doers among them and vex their brethren, and will not know thee for their judge and fear thy law, them smite, and upon them draw thy sword, and put it not up until thou hast done thine office; yet without hate to the person, for his master's sake, and because he is in the first regiment thy brother, but to amend him only; or if it cannot be but that thou must lose one to save many, then execute thine office with such affection, with such compassion and sorrow of heart, as thou wouldest cut off thine own arm to save the rest of the body.

An example of the two regiments.

Take an example: thou art in thy father's house among thy brethren and sisters. There if one fight with another, or if any do thee wrong, thou mayest not avenge nor smite; for that pertaineth to thy father only. But if thy father give thee authority in his absence, and command thee to smite if they will not be ruled, now thou art another person. Notwithstanding yet thou hast not put off the first person, but art a brother still, and must ever love, and prove all thing to rule with love: but if love will not serve, then thou must use the office of the other person, or sin against thy father. Even so, when thou art a temporal person, thou puttest not off the spiritual. Therefore thou must ever love; but when love will not help, thou must with love execute the office of the temporal person, or sin against God. A mother can smite and love: and so mayest thou with love execute the office of thy second state. And the wife, son, servant, and subject are brethren in the first state, and put not that person off by reason of the second degree; and therefore must they love ever, and with love pay custom, tribute, fear, honour and obedience to whom they belong, as Paul teacheth, Rom. xiii. And though the other do not his duty and love thee, but rule thee with rigorousness, and deal unkindly with thee, thou not deserving; yet cleave thou to

Whatsoever thou art bound to do, do it with love. Rom. xiii.

Christ, and love still; and let not his evil overcome thy goodness and make thee evil also.

And as, after the example above, thy father hath power over thee, to command thee to use his power over thy brethren, even so hath thy master, to give thee his authority over thy fellows: which when thou hast, thou must remember that thou art a fellow still, and bound to love still; but if love alone will not help, then put thy master's authority unto thy love. And so hath the ruler power over thee, to send thee to use violence upon thy neighbour, to take him, to prison him, and haply to kill him too. And thou must ever love thy neighbour in thine heart, by the reason that he is thy brother in the first state; and yet obey thy ruler and go with the constable or like officer, and break open thy neighbour's door, if he will not open it in the king's name: yea, and if he will not yield in the king's name, thou must lay on, and smite him to the ground till he be subdued. And look, what harm he getteth, yea, though he be slain, that be on his own head. For thine heart loved him; and thou desiredst him lovingly to obey, and hast not avenged thyself in that state where thou art a brother: but in the worldly state, where thou art another manner person, in this case thou hast executed the authority of him that hath such power of God to command thee; and where thou wert damned of God, if thou didst not obey.

How to be a warrior. W. T.

And like is it, if thy lord or prince send thee a warfare into another land; thou must obey at God's commandment, and go, and avenge thy prince's quarrel, which thou knowest not but that it is right. And when thou comest thither, remember what thou art in the first state with them against whom thou must fight, how that they be thy brethren, and as deeply bought with Christ's blood as thou, and for Christ's sake to be beloved in thine heart. And see that thou desire neither their life or goods, save to avenge thy prince's quarrel, and to bring them under thy prince's power. And be content with thy prince's wages, and with such part of the spoil (when thou hast won) as thy prince or his deputy appointeth thee. For if thou hate them in thine heart, and covet their goods, and art glad that an occasion is found (thou carest not whether it be right or wrong) that thou mayest go a robbing and murdering unpunished; then art thou a murderer in the

Thou mayest fight with, or slay thine enemies, and yet love them.

sight of God, and thy blood will be shed again for it, either in the same war following; or when thou art come home, as thou there didst in thine heart, so shalt thou rob and steal, and be hanged for thy labour, or slain by some other mischief.

Goods. W. T. Now concerning the goods of this world, it is easy to judge. In the first state or degree thou oughtest to be thankful to Christ, and to love, to give, and to lend to them that are bought with his precious blood, all that thou art able. For all that thou owest to Christ, whose servant thou art to
Matt. xxv. do his will, that must [thou] pay them. And that thou doest to them, that same thou doest to Christ; and that thou art not ready to do for them, that deniest thou to do for Christ. But and any of thy brethren will withhold, or take away by force above that thou mayest spare, by the reason of some office that thou hast in the second state; or invade thee violently, and lay more on thy back than thou canst bear; then hold thine heart and hand, that thou neither hate or smite, and speak fair and lovingly, and let neighbours go between. And when thou hast proved all means of love in vain, then complain to the law and the officer, that is set to be thy father and defend thee, and to judge between thee and thy brother.

To go to law. W. T. Thou wilt say, 'The text forbiddeth me to go to law;' for it saith, "If a man will law with thee and take thy coat, thou must let him have gown and all." 'If I must suffer myself to be robbed by the law,' wilt thou say, 'by what right can I with law recover mine own?' I answer: Behold the text diligently. For by no right of law can a man take thy coat from thee; for the law was ordained of God, to maintain thee in thy right, and to forbid that wrong should be done thee. Wherefore the text meaneth thus, that where the law is unjustly ministered, and the governors and judges corrupt, and take bribes, and be partial, there be patient, and ready to suffer ever as much more, whatsoever unright be done thee, rather than of impatience thou shouldest avenge thyself on thy neighbour, or rail, or make insurrection against the superiors which God hath set over thee. For to rise against them is to rebel against God and against thy Father, when he scourgeth thee for thine offence, and a thousand times more sin than to avenge thee on thy neighbour. And

To rise against the judge or magistrate is to resist God.

to rail on them is to rail on God; as though thou wouldest blaspheme him, if he made thee sick, poor, or of low degree, or otherwise than thou wouldest be made thyself.

Thou wilt haply say: 'The subjects ever choose the ruler, and make him swear to keep their law, and to maintain their privileges and liberties, and upon that submit their selves unto him: *ergo*, if he rule amiss, they are not bound to obey; but may resist him, and put him down again.' I answer: Your argument is naught. For the husband sweareth to his wife; yet though he forswear himself, she hath no power to compel him. Also though a master keep not covenant with his servant, or one neighbour with another, yet hath neither servant, no, nor yet neighbour (though he be under none obedience) power to avenge; but the vengeance pertaineth ever to an higher officer, to whom thou must complain.

Princes, whether they may be resisted or put down of their subjects in any case. W. T.

'Yea, but,' you will say, 'it is not like. For the whole body of the subjects choose the ruler. Now *cujus est ligare, ejus est solvere*[1]: *ergo*, if he rule amiss, they that set him up may put him down again.' I answer: God, and not the common people, chooseth the prince; though he choose him by them. For God commandeth to choose and set up officers; and therefore is God the chief chooser and setter up of them: and so must he be the chief putter down of them again; so that without his special commandment they may not be put down again. Now hath God given no commandment to put them down again: but contrariwise, when we have anointed a king over us at his commandment, he saith, "Touch not mine anointed." And what jeopardy it is to rise against the prince that is anointed over thee, how evil soever he be, see in the story of king David, and throughout all the books of the Kings[2]. The authority of the king is the authority of God; and all the subjects, compared to the king, are but subjects still, though the king be never so evil; as a thousand sons gathered together are but sons still, and the commandment, 'Obey your fathers,' goeth over all as well as over one. Even so goeth the commandment over all the subjects: obey your prince and the higher power, and he that resisteth him, resisteth God, and getteth him damnation. And unto your

Deut. xvi.

The king hath God's authority.

[[1] Whose office it is to bind, to the same belongs to loosen.]

[[2] In this expression the two books of Samuel are to be understood as included.]

An answer to the former argument.

argument, *Cujus est ligare, ejus est solvere,* I answer: He that bindeth with absolute power, and without any higher authority, his is the might to loose again; but he that bindeth at another man's commandment, may not loose again without the commandment of the same. As they of London choose them a mayor; but may not put him down again, how evil soever he be, without the authority of him with whose licence they chose him. As long as the powers or officers be one under another, if the inferior do thee wrong, complain to the higher. But if the highest of all do thee wrong, thou must complain to God only. Wherefore the only remedy against evil rulers is, that thou turn thine eyes to thyself, and thine own sin, and then look up to God and say: 'O Father, for our sin, and the sin of our fathers, is this misery come upon us: we know not thee as our Father, to obey thee and to walk in thy ways; and therefore thou knowest not us as thy sons, to set loving schoolmasters over us. We hate thy law, and therefore hast thou, through the wickedness of unrighteous judges, made that law that was for our defence to be a tyrant most cruel, and to oppress us, and do us injury above all other kinds of violence and robbing.' And amend thy living, and be meek and patient; and let them rob as much as they will, yet shall God give thee food and raiment, and an honest possession in the earth, to maintain thee and thine withal.

Goods.

The king, as he is lord of thy body, so is he of thy goods.

Moreover concerning thy goods, thou must remember how that thou art a person in the temporal regiment; and the king, as he is over thy body, even so is he lord of thy goods, and of him thou holdest them, not for thyself only, but for to maintain thy wife, children, and servants, and to maintain the king, the realm, and the country, and town or city where thou dwellest. Wherefore thou mayest not suffer them to be wasted, that thou were not able to do thy duty; no more than a servant may suffer his master's goods to go to wrack negligently. "For he that provideth not for his, and namely for them of his own household," saith Paul, "denieth the faith, and is worse than an infidel." But every man is bound to labour diligently and truly, and therewith so soberly to live, that he may have enough for him and his, and somewhat above for them that cannot labour, or by chance are fallen into necessity: and of that give and lend, and look not for it again; and if that suffice not thy neighbour's necessity, then speak and make labour to thy brethren, to help also. For it is a common proverb, "Many hands make light work;" and many may bear that that one alone cannot.

And thy wife, thy children, and servants, art thou bound to defend. If any man would force thy wife, thy daughter, or thy maid, it is not enough for thee to look on, and say, 'God amend you.' Nay, thou must execute thine office and authority which the king giveth thee. And by the way thou must defend thy master and his goods, and the king's goods, which thou hast to maintain thy wife and household withal, and thine neighbour that goeth with thee, against thieves and murderers. And against all such persons lay about thee, and do as thou wouldest do if thou were under the king's standard against his enemies which had invaded the realm. For all such persons are mortal enemies to the realm; and seek to put down the king, and law, and all together, and to make that it might be lawful to sin unpunished. And of this manner, if thou mark well the difference of these two states and regiments, thou mayest soil all like doubts that shall be laid against thee.

Regiments.

Moreover when I say, there be two regiments, the spiritual and the temporal; even so I say that every person, baptized to keep the law of God and to believe in Christ, is under both the regiments, and is both a spiritual person and also a temporal, and under the officers of both the regiments; so that the king is as deep under the spiritual officer, to hear out of God's word what he ought to believe, and how to live, and how to rule, as is the poorest beggar in the realm. And even so the spiritual officer, if he sin against his neighbour, or teach false doctrine, is under the king's or temporal correction, how high soever he be. And look, how damnable it is for the king to withdraw himself from the obedience of the spiritual officer, that is to say, from hearing his duty to do it, and from hearing his vices rebuked to amend them; so damnable is it for the spiritual officer, how high soever he be, to withdraw himself from under the king's correction, if he teach false, or sin against any temporal law.

Every man is under both regiments. W. T.

As the spirituality may rebuke kings' vices, so may kings use temporal correction against the spiritualty.

Finally, ye must consider that Christ here teacheth his disciples, and them that should be the light and salt in living and doctrine, to shine in the weak and feeble eyes of the

A preacher of the gospel may use no violence. W. T.

world, diseased with the megrim[1], and accustomed to darkness, that without great pain they can behold no light; and to salt their old festered sores, and to fret out the rotten flesh, even to the hard quick, that it smart again; and spare no degree, but tell all men, high and low, their faults, and warn them of the jeopardy, and exhort them to the right way. Now such schoolmasters shall find small favour and friendship with the rulers of this world, or defence in their laws: as Christ warneth them, saying, "I send you out as sheep among wolves. Beware therefore of men; for they shall deliver you up to their councils, and shall scourge you in their synagogues" or council-houses, "and ye shall be brought before the chief rulers and kings, for my sake;" and there teacheth them, as here, to arm themselves with patience, and to go forth boldly with a strong faith, and trust in the succour and assistance of God only, and to plant the gospel with all love and meekness, and to water it with their own blood, as Christ did. Thou mayest not, in that state, come with a sword, to defend either thyself or thy gospel, and to compel men to worship thee as God, and to believe what thou wilt. Nay, ye sheep, use no such regiment among wolves. If thou be a sheep, thou art not in evil taking, if thou canst bring to pass that the wolf be content with thy fleece only, and to shear thee yearly.

Rulers do repine to hear of their faults. Matt. x.

"Give to him that asketh, and from him that would borrow turn not away." Luke saith, "Give to whosoever asketh thee:" that is to say, wheresover thou seest need, or seest not the contrary but there may be need; to the uttermost of thy power there open thine heart, and be merciful only. And of mercifulness, set God thy father, and Christ thy lord and master, for an ensample: and enforce to be as like them as thou canst. If thou be merciful, God hath bound himself to be merciful to thee again. Lo, is not this an exceeding great thing, that God, which of no right ought to be bound to his creatures, hath yet put it whole in thine own hands, to bind him against the day of thy tribulation, then to shew thee mercy?

In lending, we must follow the rule of mercy.

Concerning lending, proceed by the foresaid rule of mercy. Many, in extreme need, yet ashamed to beg, shall desire thee to lend. Unto such, instead of lending, give; or

[1 Old editions *mygrim.*]

say thus, 'Lo, here is as much as ye require. If ye can pay it again well, do, and ye shall find me ready against another time, to lend or give (if need be) as much more. But and if ye shall not be able to pay it again, trouble not your conscience, I give it you. We be all one man's children: one man hath bought us all with his blood, and bound us to help one another.' And with so doing thou shalt win the heart of him to thy Father.

Concerning merchandise and chapmen, the less borrowing were among them, the better should the commonwealth be: if it were possible, I would it were, ware for ware; or money for ware; or part money and part ware. But if it will not be, but that a man, to get his living with, must needs lend, and call for it again, to find his household, and to pay his debts; then in the lending be first single and harmless as a dove, and then as wise as a serpent; and take heed to whom thou lendest. If when thou hast lent an honest man, God visit him, and take away his goods, with what chance it be, whether by sea or land, that he is not able to pay thee; then to prison him, or to sue him at the law, or once to speak an unkind word, were against the law of love, and contrary to shewing mercy. There thou must suffer with thy neighbour and brother, as Christ did with thee, and as God doth daily. If an unthrift have beguiled thee, and spent thy goods away, and hath not to pay, then hold thine hand and heart, that thou avenge not thyself; but love him, and pray for him, and remember how God hath promised to bless the patient and meek. Nevertheless, because such persons corrupt the common manners, and cause the name of God the less to be feared, men ought to complain upon such persons to the officer that is ordained of God to punish evil doers, and the officer is bound to punish them. If thou have lent a fox, which with cavillation will keep thy goods from thee; then if the ruler and the law will not help thee to thy right, do as it is above said of him that will go to law with thee, and take thy coat from thee; that is to say, be content to lose that and as much more to it, rather than thou wouldest avenge thyself. Let not the wickedness of other men pluck thee from God; but abide by God and his blessings, and tarry his judgment. Liberality is mercifulness, that bindeth God to be merciful again. Covetousness (the root of all evil,

We must not revenge ourselves upon our evil debtors, but refer our cause to God, and his officers.

Covetousness is the root of all evil. James ii. and father of all false prophets, and the schoolmaster that teaches the messengers of Satan to disguise themselves like to the messengers of Christ) is merciless, that shall have judgment without mercy; and therefore exhorteth Christ all his so diligently, and above all thing, to be liberal and to beware of covetousness.

Ye have heard, how it is said, Thou shalt love thy neighbour, and hate thine enemy. But I say unto you, Love your enemies. Bless them that curse you, do good to them that hate you. Pray for them which do you wrong, and persecute you: that ye may be the children of your heavenly Father. For he maketh his sun to arise over the evil, and over the good, and sendeth rain upon the righteous and unrighteous. For if ye love them that love you, what reward shall ye have? do not the publicans so? And if ye be friendly to your brethren only, what singular thing do ye? do not the publicans likewise? Ye shall therefore be perfect, as your Father, which is in heaven, is perfect.

This text, of hating a man's enemy, standeth not in any one place of the bible; but is gathered of many places, in which God commandeth the children of Israel to destroy their enemies, the Canaanites, the Amorites, the Amalekites, and other heathen people, as the Moabites, and Ammonites, which sought to bring them out of the favour of God, and to destroy the name of God. The Amalekites came behind them, and slew all that were faint and weary by the way, as they came out of Egypt. The Moabites and Ammonites hired Balaam to curse them, and beguiled them with their women, and made a great plague among them. These and like nations were perpetual enemies to their land which God had given them, and also of the name of God and of their faith: for which cause they not only might lawfully, but were also bound to hate them, and to study their destruction again; howbeit they might not yet hate, of the said nations, such as were converted to their faith.

The enemies of God and his word are to be hated.

Now by the reason of such texts as commanded to hate the common enemies of their country, and of God and his law, and of their faith, the Pharisees' doctrine was, that a man might lawfully hate all his private enemies, without exception, nor was bound to do them good. And yet Moses saith, "Thou shalt not hate thy brother in thine heart." And again, "Thou shalt not avenge thyself, nor bear hate

Lev. xix. Exod. xxiii.

in thy mind against the children of thy people." And, "If thine enemy's ass sink under his burden, help to lift him up again. And if his ox or ass go astray, bring them home again:" which all, no doubt, the Pharisees did interpret for good counsel, but for no precepts; wherefore Christ salteth their doctrine, and proveth that a man is bound both to love and to do good to his enemy; and as a natural son, though his brethren be never so evil, yet to love them, and shew them kindness for his father's sake, and to study to amend them. What hast thou to rejoice of, if thy religion be no better than the religion of thieves? For thieves love among themselves: and so do the covetous of the world, as the usurers and publicans, which bought in great the emperor's tribute, and, to make their most advantage, did overset the people[1]. Nay, it is not enough for thee to love thy benefactors only, as monks and friars do, and them of thine own coat and order, or the brethren of thine own abbey only; for among some their love stretcheth no farther, and that shall he that is removed out of another cloister thither well find: yea, and in some places charity reacheth not to all the cells of the same cloister, and to all the monks that were professed in the same place. But lift up thine eyes unto thy heavenly Father, and as thy Father doth, so do thou love all thy Father's children. He ministereth sun and rain to good and bad; by which two understand all his benefits: for of the heat and dryth of the sun, and cold and moist of the rain, spring all things that are necessary to the life of man. Even so provoke thou and draw thine evil brethren to goodness, with patience, with love in word and deed; and pray for them to him that is able to make them better and to convert them. And so thou shalt be thy Father's natural son, and perfect, as he is perfect. The text saith not, Ye shall be as perfect as God; but perfect after his example. To be perfect, in the scripture, is not to be a monk or a friar, or never to sin. For Christ teacheth not here monks or friars, but his disciples and every christian man and woman. And to be in this life altogether without sin is impossible. But to be perfect is to have pure doctrine without false opinions, and that thine heart be to follow that learning.

Publicans, what they were. W. T.

As our heavenly Father bestoweth his benefits upon good and bad, so ought we to love both friend and foe.

To be perfect, what it meaneth. W. T.

[[1] That is, they bought the gross produce of the tribute; and overcharged the people in the collection of it.]

AN EXPOSITION OF THE SIXTH CHAPTER.

Take heed to your alms, that ye do it not before men, to be seen of them, or else ye get no reward of your Father which is in heaven. Therefore when thou givest alms, make not a trumpet to be blown before thee, as the hypocrites do in the synagogues and in the streets, to be praised of men. Verily I say unto you, they have their reward. But thou, when thou givest alms, let not thy left hand know what thy right hand doth, that thine alms may be in secret. And then thy Father, which seeth in secret, shall reward thee openly.

Alms.

Deeds commanded by the scripture, done to any other end than they ought, are no good deeds.

As he rebuked their doctrine above, even so here he rebuketh their works; for out of devilish doctrine can spring no godly works. But what works rebuketh he? Verily such as God in the scripture commandeth, and without which no man can be a christian man; even prayer, fasting, and alms-deed. For as the scripture, corrupt with glosses, is no more God's word, even so the deeds commanded in the scripture (when the intent of them is perverted) are no more godly deeds. What said the scribes and Pharisees of him (think ye) when he rebuked such manner of works? No doubt, as they said, when he rebuked their false glosses, how he destroyed the law and the prophets, interpreting the scripture after the literal sense which killeth, and after his own brain, clean contrary to the common faith of holy church, and minds of great clerks, and authentic expositions of old holy doctors; even so here what other could they say than, 'Behold the heretic! and, Did not we tell you before whereto he would come, and that he kept some mischief behind, and spewed not out all his venom at once? see to what all his godly new doctrine that sounded so sweetly is come! He preached all of love, and would have the people saved by faith, so long till that now, at the last, he preacheth clean against all deeds of mercy, as prayer, fasting, and alms-deed, and destroyeth all good works. His disciples fast no more than dogs, they despise their divine service, and come not to church; yea, and if the holiest of all St Francis' order ask them alms, they bid him labour with his hands, and get his living, and say that he that laboureth not is not worthy to eat, and that God bade that no such strong lubbers should loiter, and go a begging, and be chargeable to the congregation, and eat up that other poor men get with the sweat of their bodies: yea, and at the last ye shall see, if we resist him not betimes, that he shall move the people to insurrection, as Caiphas said, and the Romans shall come and take our land from us.' As ye see in the text, Luke xxiii. how, when they could not drive the people from him with those pursuasions, they accused him to Pilate, saying: "We have found this fellow perverting the people, and forbidding to pay tribute to Cæsar, and saying that he is Christ, a king." Wherefore "thou canst not be Cæsar's friend, if thou let him escape." But after all these blasphemies, yet must the Holy Ghost rebuke the world of their righteousness, yea, of their false righteousness and false holiness, which are neither righteousness nor holiness, but colour of hypocrisy.

Luke xxiii.

John xix.

Christ here destroyeth not prayer, fasting, and alms-deed, but preacheth against the false purpose and intent of such works, and perverting the true use; that is to say, their seeking of glory, and that they esteemed themselves righteous thereby, and better than other men, and so despised and condemned their brethren. With our alms (which is as much to say as deeds of mercy), or compassion, we ought to seek our Father's glory only, even the wealth of our brethren, and to win them to the knowledge of our Father and keeping of his law. He that seeketh the glory of his good works, seeketh the glory that belongeth to God, and maketh himself God. Is it not a blind thing of the world, that either they will do no good works at all, or will be God for their good works, and have the glory themselves?

It is the purpose and intent of our deeds that make or mar.

Concerning blowing of trumpets, and ringing of bells, or making a cry, to call men to fetch alms, (though the right way be, that we should know in every parish all our poor, and have a common coffer for them; and that strangers should bring a letter of recommendation with them of their necessity, and that we had a common place to receive them into for the time; and though also we ought to flee all occasions of vain-glory,) yet while the world is out of order, it is not damnable to do it. So that the very meaning, both that we blow no trumpets, and that the left hand know not what the right hand doth, is, that we do as secretly as we can, and in no wise seek glory, or to receive it if it were proffered; but to do our deeds in singleness of conscience to God, because it is his commandment, and even of pure compassion and love

To blow trumpets, what. W. T.

Left hand. W. T.

to our brethren; and not that our good deeds, through standing in our own conceit, should cause us to despise them. If thou be tempted to vain-glory for thy good deeds, then look on thine evil thereto, and put the one in the one balance, and the other in the other. And then, if thou understand the law of God any thing at all, tell me, whether weigheth heavier. If that that thou doest do tempt thee, then consider what thou doest not. If it move thee to set up thy comb, when thou givest thy brother a farthing or a halfpenny, ponder in thine heart how far thou art off from loving him as well as thyself, and caring for him as much as for thyself. And be sure how much thou lackest of that, so much thou art in sin, and that in damnable sin, if God for Christ's sake did not pardon thee, because thine heart mourneth therefore, and thou fightest with thyself to come to such perfection. If a peacock did look well on his feet, and mark the evil-favoured shrieking of his voice, he would not be so proud of the beauty of his tail.

Vain-glory, a good remedy against it. W. T.

Finally, that many dispute, Because God hath promised to reward our deeds in heaven, that our deeds deserve heaven; and because he promiseth to shew mercy to the merciful, that with our deeds we deserve mercy; and because he promiseth forgiveness of sins to them that forgive, that our deeds deserve forgiveness of sin, and so justify us: I answer, first, there is enough spoken thereof in other places; so that to them that have read that it is superfluous to rehearse the matter again. Furthermore, the argument is naught, and holdeth by no rule. See ye not that the father and mother have more right to the child and to all it can do, than to an ox or a cow? It is their flesh and blood, nourished up with their labour and cost. The life of it, and the maintenance and continuance thereof, is their benefit; so that it is not able to recompense that it oweth to father and mother by a thousand parts. And though it be not able to do his duty, nor for blindness to know his duty, yet the father and mother promise more gifts still without ceasing, and that such as they think should most make it to see love, and to provoke it to be willing to do part of his duty. And when it hath done amiss, though it have no power to do satisfaction, nor lust or corage[1] to come to the right way again, yet their love

Works justify not from sin, neither deserve the reward promised.

[[1] Used as in Vol. I. p. 417, not for bravery, but for the inclination of the heart.]

and mercy abideth still so great to it, that upon appointment of mending they not only forgive that is past, and fulfil their promise nevertheless[2], but promise greater gifts than ever before, and to be better father and mother to it than ever they were. Now when it cannot do that thousandth part of his duty, how could it deserve such promises of the father and mother, as a labourer doth his hire? The reward thereof cometh of the love, mercy, and truth of the father and mother, as well when the child keepeth the appointment, as when they fulfil their promise when it hath broken the appointment; and not of the deserving of the child.

Our reward cometh not of our deserts, but through the love that God beareth us through faith in Jesus Christ.

Even so, if we were not thus drowned in blindness, we should easily see that we cannot do the thousandth part of our duty to God: no, though there were no life to come. If there were no life to come, it were not right that I should touch any creature of God otherwise than he hath appointed. Though there were no life to come, it had nevertheless been right that Adam had abstained from the forbidden apple-tree, and from all other too, if they had been forbid. Yea, and though there were no life to come, it were not the less right that I loved my brother, and forgave him to-day, seeing I shall sin against him to-morrow. Because a father cannot give his children heaven, hath he no power to charge them to love one another, and to forgive, and not to avenge one another? And hath he not right to beat them if they smite each other, because he cannot give them heaven? A bondman that hath a master more cruel than a reasonable man would be to a dog, if there were no heaven, might this bond-servant accuse God of unrighteousness, because he hath not made him a master? Now, then, when we cannot do our duty by a thousand parts, though there were no such promises, and that the thing commanded is no less our duty though no such promise were; it is easy to perceive that the reward promised cometh of the goodness, mercy, and truth of the promiser, to make us the gladder to do our duty, and not of the deserving of the receiver. When we have done all we can, we ought to say in our heart, that it was our duty, and that we ought to do a thousand times more; and that God (if he had not promised us mercy, of his goodness in Christ,) he might yet of right damn us for that we have left undone.

[[2] L., *not the later.*]

We may not challenge the promise by our merits, but by Christ's blood. Phil. iii.

And as touching forgiveness of sin: though forgiveness of sin be promised unto thee, yet challenge it not by thy merits, but by the merits of Christ's blood; and hear what Paul saith: "Concerning the righteousness of the law I was faultless," or such as no man could rebuke; "but the things that were to vantage, I thought damage for Christ's sake; yea, I think all thing to be damage, or loss, for the excellent knowledge's sake of Christ Jesus my Lord; for whose sake I let all go to loss, and count them as chaff or refuse," (that is to say, as things which are purged out, and refused, when a thing is tried and made perfect,) "that I might win Christ, and might be found in him, not having my righteousness that cometh of the law, but that which cometh of faith in Christ Jesus; which righteousness cometh of God through faith, and is to know him and the power of his resurrection," (how he is Lord over all sin, and the only thing that slayeth and vanquisheth sin), "and to know also the fellowship of his passions, that I might be made like unto his death."

Cross. W. T.

Works, what they do. W. T.

So that when righteousness and true merits be tried, we must be content that ours be the chaff, and Christ's the pure corn; ours the scum and refuse, and Christ's the pure gold. And we must fashion ourselves like unto Christ, and take every man his cross, and slay and mortify the sin in the flesh; or else we cannot be partakers of his passion. The sin we do before our conversion is forgiven clearly through faith, if we repent, and submit ourselves to a new life. And the sin we do against our wills, (I mean the will of the Spirit; for after our conversion we have two wills, fighting one against the other,) that sin is also forgiven us through faith, if we repent and submit ourselves to amend. And our diligence in working keepeth us from sinning again, and minisheth the sin that remaineth in the flesh, and maketh us pure and less apt and disposed to sin; and it maketh us merry in adversities, and strong in temptations, and bold to go unto God with a strong and fervent faith in our prayers, and sure that we shall be heard when we cry for help at need, either for ourselves or our brethren. Now, they that be negligent and sin, are brought in temptation unto the point of desperation, and feel the very pains of hell; so that they stand in doubt whether God hath cast them away or no: and in adversity

Negligence in doing good bringeth us to desperation.

they be sorrowful and discouraged, and think that God is angry, and punisheth them for their sins. When a child taketh pain to do his father's pleasure, and is sure that he shall have thank and a reward for his labour, he is merry, and rejoiceth in work and pain that he suffereth; and so is the adversity of them that keep themselves from sinning. But a child, when he is beaten for his fault, or when he thinketh his father is angry, and loveth him not, is anon desperate and discouraged: so is the adversity of them that are weak, and sin oft. A child that never displeaseth his father is bold in his father's presence, to speak for himself or his friend: but he that oft offendeth, and is correct or chid, though the peace be made again, yet the remembrance of his offences maketh him fearful, and to mistrust, and to think his father would not hear him; so is the faith of the weak, that sin oft. But as for them that profess not a new living, however so much they dream of faith, they have no faith at all; for they have no promise, except they be converted to a new life. And therefore in adversities, temptation and death, they utterly despair of all mercy, and perish.

Two apt similitudes of well and evil doings.

Promise. He that professeth not a new life, hath no promise of mercy in Christ. W. T.

And when thou prayest, thou shalt not be like the hypocrites. For they love to stand and pray in the synagogues, and in corners of the streets, that they might be seen of men. Verily, I say unto you, they have their reward. Thou therefore, when thou prayest, go into thy chamber, and shut thy door, and pray to thy Father which is in secret. And thy Father, which seeth in secret, shall reward thee openly.

After alms followeth prayer. For as it is a christian man's part to help his neighbour, and to bear with him when he is overcharged, and suffer with him, and to stand one by another, as long as we live here on this earth; even so, because we be ever in such peril and cumbrance that we cannot rid ourselves out, we must daily and hourly cry to God for aid and succour, as well for our neighbours as for ourselves.

Prayer.

To give alms, to pray, to fast, or to do any thing at all, whether between thee and God, or between thee and thy neighbour, canst thou never do to please God therewith, except thou have the true knowledge of God's word to season thy deeds withal. For God hath put a rule in the scripture, without which thou canst not move an hair of thine head, but

Works must be seasoned with God's word, if they shall please God.

that it is damnable in the sight of God. As it is of the Jews, though (as Paul beareth them record) they have a fervent zeal to God, yea, and have the scripture thereto; yet because they have not the true understanding, all is damnable that they do. Hypocrites with scraps of alms get an hundredfold. And with prayer they get praise, (as thou seest here); and pray thereto, and rob widows' houses, as thou readest
Matt. xxiii. Matt. xxiii. And with fasting they get fat bellies, full dishes, and ever more than enough. And yet there is none alms, praying, or fasting among them, in the sight of God. With their prayers they exclude all true prayers, and make it impossible that there should be any among them. For prayer is either a longing for the honour and name of God, that all men should fear him, and keep his precepts, and believe in him; and contrary to that, they seek their own honour, that men should fear them and keep their ordinances, and believe in their sweet blessings, prayers, pardons, and whatsoever they promise: if they bid fast, thou must do it or be damned, and be an heretic and rebellious to holy church: if they dispense, and give thee clean remission for to eat flesh on Good Friday, though thou be never so lusty, thou must obey, or else thou art damned, and an heretic, because thou dost not believe in holy church. Either prayer is, to give God thanks for the benefits received: contrary to which, they will first have thanks of the world for their prayers, and rob not only widows' houses, but also lord, prince, emperor, and all the world, of house and land; yea, and of their wits too. And then they bind God to thank them, and to give them (beside the thanks which they have gotten in the world) not only heaven and a higher place, but that he give heaven to no other man, save through their merits. Either prayer is a complaining and a shewing of thine own misery and necessity, or of thy neighbour's before God; desiring him, with all the power of thine heart, to have compassion and to succour. Contrary to this, they have excluded with their prayers all necessity and misery from among them. They be lords over all, and do what they will through the whole world. King and emperor are their servants; they need but say the word, and their will is fulfilled. And as for their neighbours, they have no compassion upon them, to bring their complaints before God; but with

Prayer, what it is. W. T.

their prayers rob them of that little they have, and so make them more miserable.

Of entering into the chamber and shutting the door to, I say as above, (of that the left hand should not know what the right hand doth,) the meaning is, that we should avoid all worldly praise and profit, and pray with a single eye and true intent according to God's word; and [it] is not forbidden thereby to pray openly. For we must have a place to come together, to pray in general, to thank and to cry to God for the common necessities, as well as to preach the word of God in: where the priest ought to pray in the mother tongue, that the name of God may be hallowed, and his word faithfully taught and truly understood, and faith and godly living increased; and for the king and rulers, that God will give them his Spirit, to love the commonwealth; and for peace, that God will defend us from all enemies; for wedering[1] and fruits, that God will keep away pestilence and all plagues. And the priest should be an example to the people how they should pray. There be, of such things as the priests and other babble (and not pray), many good collects, that should much edify the people, if they were spoken in the mother tongue. And then, while the priests sing psalms, let every man pray privately, and give God thanks for such benefits as his heart knoweth he hath received of God, and commend to God his private necessities, and the private necessities of his neighbours which he knoweth, and is privy to. Neither is there, in all such, any jeopardy of vain-glory. But and if God hath given any man the spirit of praying, as all men have not like gifts, that he pray oft and when other do not; then to have a secret place to pray in, both for the avoiding of vain-glory and speech of people, and that thou mayest be free to use thy words as thou lustest, and whatsoever gestures and behaviours do move thee most to devotion, is necessary and good.

To shut thy chamber door, what it meaneth. W. T.

And, finally: whatsoever necessity thou hast, though thou feel thyself a great sinner, yet if thine heart be to amend, let not that discourage thee: but go boldly to thy Father, seeing thou hast his commandment ever to pray, and promise that he will hear thee, not for thy goodness, but of his goodness, and for his truth.

God's commandment and promise should move us to pray.

[[1] Saxon; pæðeɲunʒ, inclement weather.]

Moreover, when ye pray, babble not much as the heathen do. For they think that they shall be heard for their much babbling's sake. Be not, therefore, like unto them. For your Father knoweth of what things ye have need, before ye ask him. Of this manner, therefore, pray ye:

The Paternoster.

O! Our Father, which art in heaven, honoured be thy name, thy kingdom come. Thy will be fulfilled, even in earth, as it is in heaven. Give us this day our daily bread. And forgive us our trespasses as we forgive our trespassers. And lead us not into temptation, but deliver us from evil. For thine is the kingdom, the power and the glory for ever. Amen.

As before he rebuked their false intent in praying, that they sought praise and profit of that work, which ought to be direct to God alone, either to give him thanks, that is to say, to be aknowen, and to confess in the heart that all we have cometh of him; or to call upon him for aid and succour in temptations and all necessity: even so here he rebuketh a false kind of praying, wherein the tongue and lips labour, and all the body is pained, but the heart talketh not with God, nor feeleth any sweetness at all, nor hath any confidence in the promises of God; but trusteth in the multitude of words, and in the pain and tediousness of the length of the prayer; as a conjuror doth in his circles, characters, and superstitious words of his conjuration: as ye see now to be among our friars, monks, canons and nuns, and even throughout all the spiritualty; which (as I have proved above) have, with their false intent of praying, excluded all occasions and the whole matter of true prayer, and have turned it into a bodily labour, to vex the tongue, lips, eyes, and throat with roaring, and to weary all the members; so that they say (and may truly swear it) that there is no greater labour in the world than prayer; for no labour, whatsoever it be, when the body is compelled, and the heart unwilling, can be other than grievous and painful. But true prayer (if they complained and sought help either for themselves, or for their neighbours, and trusted in the promise of God) would so comfort the soul and courage the heart, that the body, though it were half dead and more, would revive and be lusty again, and the labour would be short and easy: as for an ensample; if thou were so oppressed that thou were weary of thy life, and wentest to the king for help, and haddest sped, thy spirits would so rejoice, that thy body would receive her

That prayer is vain wherein the heart is not joined with the tongue.

False prayer is painful.

True prayer is pleasant.

strength again, and be as lusty as ever it was; even so the promises of God work joy above all measure, where they be believed in the heart.

But our hirelings have no God's word, but trust in the multitude of words, length of babbling, and pain of body, as bond servants: neither know they any other virtue to be in prayer; as ye may see by the ordinances of all foundations. King Henry the Fifth built Sion, and the Charterhouse of Shene[1] on the other side of the water, of such a manner that lip-labour may never cease. For when the friars of Sion ring out, the nuns begin; and when the nuns ring out of service, the monks on the other side begin; and when they ring out, the friars begin again, and vex themselves night and day, and take pain for God's sake; for which God must give them heaven. Yea, and I have known of some ere this, that for very pain and tediousness have bidden the devil take their founders. They call Lent the holiest time of the year: but wherein is that holiness? Verily, in multitude of words, and the tedious length of service. For let them begin at six, and it will be twelve or they can end; in which time they be so wearied, that by the time they have dined, they have lust to nothing save to sleep. And in the end of all they think no farther, than that God must reward their pain. And if you ask how they know it? they will answer: He must reward it, or be unrighteous. Now, God looketh not on the pain of the prayer, but on thy faith in his promise and goodness; neither yet on the multitude of thy words, or long babbling: for he knoweth thy matter better than thou thyself. And though the Jews and the heathen were so foolish, through their unbelief, to babble many words, yet were they never so mad as to mumble and buz out words that they understood not. Thou wilt say, What matter maketh it if I speak words which I understand not, or if I pray not at all, seeing God knoweth my matter already? I answer: He will have thee to open thine heart to him, to inform and edify thine ownself, (that thou mightest know how all goodness is of him,) to put thy trust and confidence in him, and to fly to him in time of need, and to be thankful, and to love him and obey his commandments, and turn and

Sion.

Shene.

Not the multitude of thy words, but thy faith in praying, God doth respect.

[[1] Shene; whose name Henry VII. changed to Richmond, his own early title.]

be converted unto thy Lord God; and not to run wild as the ungodly do, which know not the benefits of God, and therefore be unthankful to obey his commandments.

And that thou mayest know how, and what to pray, he giveth thee a short instruction and ensample, saying, After this manner pray:

Our Father, which art in heaven.

The Paternoster is expounded. W. T.

First, thou must go to him as a merciful Father; which of his own goodness and fatherly love, that he beareth to thee, is ready to do more for thee than thou canst desire, though thou have no merits, but because he is thy Father, only if thou wilt turn, and henceforth submit thyself to learn to do his will.

Honoured be thy name.

To honour God's name, what it is. W. T.

Honoured and praised be thy name; or honoured and praised be thou: for to honour God, and to honour the name of God, is all one. And to honour the name of God is to dread him, to love him, and to keep his commandments. For when a child obeyeth his father, he honoureth and praiseth his father: and when he is rebellious and disobedient, he dishonoureth his father. This is, then, the understanding and meaning of it. O Father, seeing thou art Father over all, pour out thy Spirit upon all flesh, and make all men to fear, and dread, and love thee as their Father, and in keeping thy commandments to honour thee and thy holy name.

Thy kingdom come.

Kings must command nothing, nor forbid to do any thing, contrary to God's word.

That is, seeing thou art king over all, make all to know thee; and make the kings and rulers, which are but thy substitutes, to command nothing but according to thy word, and to them make all subjects obey.

Thy will be fulfilled in earth as it is in heaven.

This is all one with that goeth before. Forasmuch, then, as thou art Father and king over all, and all we thy children and brethren among ourselves, make us all as obedient to seek and to do thy will, as the angels do in heaven. Make that no man seek his own will, but all thine. But and if thou withdraw thine hand, to tempt thy children, that the rulers command ought contrary to thy will, then make the subjects to stand fast by thy word, and to offer themselves to suffer all extremity rather than to obey. Finally, when we pray to thee in our temptations and adversities, desiring thee of whatsoever thing it be, and mean truly; yet if thou, which knowest all, seest a better way to thy glory and our profit, then thy will be, and not ours: as thy son Jesus gave us an ensample, when he desired (if it had been possible) that that cup of bitter death might have departed from him, saying, "Yet not as I will, but as thou wilt."

When we request anything at God's hand, we must pray that his will be done, and not ours.

Give us our daily bread.

By bread is understood all manner of sustenance, in the Hebrew speech; yea, and here is understood thereby all that pertaineth unto the necessity of this life. If we have bread, there is dearth of nothing that can pinch, namely[1] in that land. Give us our daily bread. Give us all that the necessity of this life daily requireth. Give us it day by day as we need it. We desire not to have store for many years, to exclude all necessity of praying to thee, and to be, as it were, out of thy danger, and to forget thee: but minister it day by day, that we may daily feel thy benefits, and never forget thee. Or if thou give us abundance above that we desire, then give us an heart to use it, and to bestow it for that purpose thou gavest it, and to deal[2] with our neighbours, and not to love it inordinately; but to think that it is thine, and that thou mayest take it away every hour, and that we be content that thou so do at thy pleasure; and so ever to have it but for daily bread.

Daily bread, whereby is understood all that pertaineth to the necessity of this life.

Forgive us our trespasses, as we forgive our trespassers.

Because he knoweth that our nature is so weak that we cannot but sin daily; therefore he teacheth us daily to repent, and to reconcile ourselves together, and daily to ask God forgiveness. Seeing he commandeth us to ask, we may be bold so to do, and to believe that he will forgive us. No man, therefore, needeth to despair, that can repent and ask forgiveness, however so deep he hath sinned. And, methinketh, if we looked somewhat nearer to this text, we needed not make

[1 Namely, i. e. *especially* in the land of Canaan, where Christ was when he spoke this prayer.]

[2 Deal, i. e. divide.]

the pope so great a god, for his pardons. For Christ (which is a man to be believed) sheweth us here a more sure way; yea, and that a sensible way, by which we may feel that we be pardoned, and our sins forgiven. We can have no experience of the pope's things, whether they be so or no. He can with all his pardons deliver no man of any purgatory that God putteth us unto in this world. He cannot bless, or heal any man so much as of a poor ague, or tooth-ache; which diseases yet (by his own confession) God putteth on us to purge us from sin. But where we cannot see, feel, or have any experience at all, that it so is, there is he mighty. If I were come home out of a land where never man was before, and were sure never man should come, I might tell as many wonders as Master More doth of Utopia, and no man could rebuke me.

A surer way than pardons.

But here Christ maketh thee sure of pardon; for if thou canst forgive thy brother, God hath bound himself to forgive thee. What if no man have sinned against me? That were hard in this life; nevertheless yet, if that profession be in thine heart, that thou knowest that it is thy duty to forgive thy brother for thy Father's sake, and art obedient to thy Father's ordinance, and wouldest forgive, if any of thy brethren had offended thee, and did ask thee forgiveness; then hast thou that same spirit which God desireth to be in thee. Mark what Christ saith above, in the beginning of the fifth chapter: "Blessed be the merciful, for they shall have mercy." Dost thou pity thy brethren that sin, and dost thy best to amend them, that thy Father's name may be honoured? Then hast thou that, whereby thou art sure of mercy as soon as thou desirest it. And again: "Blessed be the peace-makers, for they shall be God's children." Lo, if there be any variance among thy brethren, that one have offended the other, do thy best to set them at one, and thou hast the same thing that God desireth of thee, and for which he hath bound himself to forgive thee.

How thou mayest be sure of pardon for thy sins.

Matt. v.

Lead us not into temptation.

That is, let us not slip out of thy lease[1], but hold us fast; give us not up, nor cease to govern us, nor take thy Spirit

[[1] Lease, or Leash; a cord or thong, by which the huntsman held one or more dogs.]

from us. For as a hound cannot but follow his game when he seeth it before him, if he be loose; so can we not but fall into sin when occasion is given us, if thou withdraw thine hand from us. Lead us not into temptation. Let no temptation fall upon us greater than thine help in us; but be thou stronger in us than the temptation thou sendest, or lettest come upon us. Lead us not into temptations. Father, though we be negligent, yea, and unthankful and disobedient to thy true prophets; yet let not the devil loose upon us to deceive us, with his false prophets, and to harden us in the way in which we gladly walk, as thou diddest Pharaoh with the false miracles of his sorcerers; as thine apostle Paul threateneth us. A little thread holdeth a strong man, where he gladly is. A little pulling draweth a man, whither he gladly goeth. A little wind driveth a great ship, with the stream. A light persuasion is enough to make a lecherous man believe that fornication is no sin; and an angry man, that it is lawful to avenge himself, and so forth, by all the corrupt nature of man. A little miracle is able to confirm and harden a man in that opinion and faith which his blind reason believeth already. A few false miracles were sufficient to persuade the covetousness of Pharaoh, and his greediness to hold the children of Israel in bondage for their service, that thy true miracles, shewed by Moses for their deliverance, were not of thee, but of the same kind, and done by the same craft, as were the miracles of his sorcerers, and so to harden his heart.

We cannot of ouselves but fall into sin.

2 Thess. ii.

Small occasions draw us to sin, whereunto we are naturally prone.

Even so, Father, if thou give us over for our unkindness, seeing the blind nature of man delighteth in evil, and is ready to believe lies, a little thing is enough to make them that love not to walk in thy truth, (and therefore never able to understand thy Son's doctrine, John vii.) for to believe the feignings of our most holy father, all his superstitious popery and invisible blessings, and to harden them therein. As a stone cast up into the air can neither go any higher, neither yet there abide, when the power of the hurler ceaseth to drive it; even so, Father, seeing our corrupt nature can but go downward only, and the devil and the world driveth thereto that same way, how can we proceed further in virtue or stand therein, if thy power cease in us? Lead us not therefore, O merciful Father, into temptation, nor cease at any time to govern us.

John vii.

Now, seeing the God of all mercy, which knoweth thine

infirmity, commandeth thee to pray in all temptation and adversity, and hath promised to help, if thou trust in him; what excuse is it to say, when thou hast sinned, I could not stand of myself; when his power was ready to help thee, if thou haddest asked?

But deliver us from evil.

First, as above, let us not fall into temptation. Secondarily, if we be fallen (as who liveth and falleth never? For never to fall were enough to make a man as evil as Lucifer, and to believe that he stood by his own power: if therefore we be fallen) even to the bottom, howsoever deep it be, put in thine arm after, (for it is long and strong enough,) and pluck us out again.

Who should think himself to be without sin, were as evil as Lucifer.

Thirdly, deliver us from evil, and pluck us out of the flesh, and the world, and the power of the devil; and place us in thy kingdom, where we be past all jeopardy, and where we cannot sin any more.

For the kingdom, and the power and the glory, is thine for ever. Amen.

Because that thou only art the king, and all other but substitutes. And because all power is thine, and all other men's power but borrowed of thee; therefore ought all honour and obedience to be thine of right, as chief Lord; and none to be given other men, but only for the office they hold of thee. Neither ought any creature to seek any more in this world than to be a brother, till thou have put him in office; then (if brotherliness will not help, which he ought first to prove) let him execute thy power. Neither may any man take authority of himself, till God have chosen him; that is to wit, till he be chosen by the ordinance that God hath set in the world, to rule it. Finally, no king, lord, master, or what ruler he be, hath absolute power in this world, and is the very thing which he is called; for then they ceased to be brethren still, neither could they sin, whatsoever they commanded. But now their authority is but a limited power, which when they transgress, they sin against their brethren, and ought to reconcile themselves to their brethren, and to ask forgiveness; and they are bound to forgive.

Kings and subjects are all one afore God.

Finally, let kings, rulers, and officers remember that God is the very king, and refer the honour that is given to them for their offices' sake to him, and humble themselves to him, and knowledge and confess in their hearts, that they be but brethren, and even no better before God, than the worst of their subjects. So be it[1].

For if ye forgive men their faults, your heavenly Father shall forgive you also. But and if ye do not forgive men their faults, no more shall your Father forgive your faults.

This is God's covenant with us, and a confirmation of the petition above rehearsed in the Pater-noster: "Forgive us our trespasses, as we forgive our trespassers." If thou wilt enter into the covenant of thy Lord God, and forgive thy brother; then whatsoever thou hast committed against God, if thou repent and ask him forgiveness, thou art sure that thou art so absolved by these words, that none in heaven nor earth can bind thee; no, though our most holy father curse thee as black as coals, seven foot under the earth, and seven foot above, and cast all his lightning upon thee, to burn thee to powder. Keep the covenant of the Lord thy God therefore, and fear no bugs. But and if thou wilt not come within the covenant of God, or if, when thou hast professed it, and received the sign thereof, thou cast the yoke of the Lord from off thy neck, be thou sure thou art bound by these words so fast that none in heaven or in earth can loose thee; no, though our earthish god whisper all his absolutions over thee, and claw thee, and stroke thine head with all his sweet blessings.

A covenant wherewith God is bound to forgive us, and we to forgive each other. W. T.

God's covenant is a sure absolution to all that keep it. W. T.

Furthermore, though forgiveness of thy sins be annexed to thy work and forgiving thy brother; yet do not (as I said) thy works justify thee before God. But the faith in Christ's blood, and in the promises made to us for his sake, doth bring righteousness into the heart. And the righteousness of the heart by faith is felt and known by the work: as Peter, in the first of his second epistle, commandeth to do good works, for to make our vocation and election sure; that we might feel our faith, and be certified that it is right. For except a man be proved and tried, it cannot be known, neither to himself or other men, that he is righteous and in the true faith. Take an example, lest thou be beguiled with sophistry. Christ saith, "The kingdom of heaven is like leaven which a woman taketh and hideth in three pecks of meal till all be leavened," or sour. Leaven is sometimes taken in an evil

2 Pet. i.

Matt. xiii.

Leaven, how many ways is taken.

[1 Thus L., but D. Amen.]

sense, for the doctrine of the Pharisees, which corrupted the sweetness of the word of God with the leaven of their glosses; and sometime in a good sense, for the kingdom of heaven, that is to say, the gospel and glad tidings of Christ. For as leaven altereth the nature of dough, and maketh it thorough sour; even so the gospel turneth a man into a new life, and altereth him a little and a little, first the heart, and then the members.

Faith, what power it is of, and the fruits that spring thereof.

Faith in Christ first certifieth the conscience of the forgiveness of sins, and delivereth us from the fear of everlasting damnation; and then bringeth the love of God and of his law into the heart, which love is the righteousness of the heart. Love bringeth good works into the members; which works are the outward righteousness, and the righteousness of the members. To hate the will of God is the unrighteousness of the heart; and causeth evil works, which are the unrighteousness of the members: as when I hated my brother, my tongue spake evil, my hands smote, and so forth. To love is the righteousness of the heart; and causeth good works, which are the righteousness of the members: as if I love my brother, and he have need of me, and be in poverty, love will make me put mine hand into my purse, or almonry, and to give him somewhat to refresh him, &c. That the love of God and of his commandments is the righteousness of the heart, doth no man doubt, save he that is heartless. And that love springeth of faith, thou mayest evidently see, 1 John ii.: "He that loveth his brother dwelleth in the light. But he that hateth his brother, is in darkness, and walketh in darkness, and wotteth not whither he goeth; for darkness hath blinded his eyes." Why is he that hateth in darkness? Verily, because he seeth not the love of God in Christ: for if he saw that, he could not but love his brother for so kind a father's sake. If any man hate his brother, be thou sure that the same man is in darkness, and hath not the light of true faith, nor seeth what Christ hath done. If a man so love that he can forgive his brother, assure thyself that he is in the light of the true faith, and seeth what mercy is shewed him in Christ.

Love is righteousness. W. T.

Faith bringeth love. W. T. 1 John ii.

Works.

This is then the sum of all together: works are the outward righteousness before the world, and may be called the righteousness of the members, and spring of inward love. Love is the righteousness of the heart, and springeth of faith. Faith is the trust in Christ's blood, and is the gift of God;

Love. Faith. Eph. ii.

whereunto a man is drawn of the goodness of God, and driven through true knowledge of the law, and of beholding his deeds in the lust and desire of the members unto the request of the law, and with seeing his own damnation in the glass of the law. For if a man saw his own damnation in the law, he should immediately hate God and his works, and utterly despair, except God offered him Christ, and forgave all that were past, and made him his son, and took the damnation of the law away, and promised that if he would submit himself to learn and to do his best, that he should be accept as well as an angel in heaven; and thereto, if he fell of frailty, and not of malice and stubbornness, it should be forgiven upon amendment, and that God would ever take him for his son, and only chastise him at home when he did amiss, after the most fatherliest manner, and as easily as his disease would suffer, but never bring him forth to be judged after the rigorousness of the law. And as thou couldest not see leaven, though thou brakest up a loaf, except thou smelledst or tastedst the sourness, even so couldest thou never see true faith or love, except thou sawest works; and also sawest the intent and meaning of the worker, lest hypocrisy deceive thee.

As leaven cannot be seen in a loaf without smell or taste, so cannot faith in us without good works, and the intent of the same, be seen or appear.

Our deeds are the effect of righteousness, and thereto an outward testimony and certifying of the inward righteousness, as sourness is of leaven. And when I say faith justifieth, the understanding is, that faith receiveth the justifying. God promiseth to forgive us our sins, and to impute us for full righteous. And God justifieth us actively: that is to say, forgiveth us, and reckoneth us for full righteous. And Christ's blood deserveth it; and faith in the promise receiveth it, and certifieth the conscience thereof. Faith challengeth it for Christ's sake, which hath deserved all that is promised; and cleaveth ever to the promise, and truth of the promiser; and pretendeth not the goodness of her work, but knowledgeth that our works deserve it not, but are crowned and rewarded with the deservings of Christ. Take an ensample of young children, when the father promiseth them a good thing for the doing of some trifle, and, when they come for their reward, dallieth[1] with them, saying: 'What, that thou hast done is not worth half so much: should I give thee so great thing for so little a trifle?' they will answer: 'Ye did promise me: ye said, I

That faith justifieth, what it meaneth. W. T.

[[1] So L., but D. *delayeth.*]

should have it: why did ye promise, and why then did ye say so?' And let him say what he will to drive them off, they will ever say again, 'Ye did promise me, so ye did: ye said I should have it, so ye did.' But hirelings will pretend[1] their work, and say, 'I have deserved it: I have done so much, and so much, and my labour is worth it.'

Faith.

Now at the first covenant-making with God, and as oft as we be reconciled, after we have sinned, the righteousness cometh of God altogether. But after the atonement is made and we reconciled, then we be partly righteous in ourselves and unrighteous; righteous as far as we love, and unrighteous as far as the love is unperfect. And faith in the promise of God, that he doth reckon us for full righteous, doth ever supply that unrighteousness and imperfectness, as it is our whole righteousness at the beginning.

Works are sacraments. W. T.

Finally, our works which God commandeth, and unto which he annexed his promises that he will reward them, are as it were very sacraments, and visible and sensible signs, tokens, earnest obligations, witnesses, testimonies, and a sure certifying of our souls, that God hath and will do according to his promise, to strength our weak faith, and to keep the promise in mind. But they justify us not, no more than the visible works of the sacraments do. As for example, the work of baptism, that outward washing, which is the visible sacrament or sign, justifieth us not. But God only justifieth us actively, as cause efficient or workman. God promiseth to justify whosoever is baptized to believe in Christ, and to keep the law of God; that is to say, to forgive them their fore sins, and to impute righteousness unto them, to take them for his sons, and to love them as well as though they were full righteous. Christ hath deserved us that promise, and that righteousness. And faith doth receive it; and God doth give it and impute it to faith, and not to the washing. And the washing doth testify it, and certify us of it, as the pope's letters do certify the believers of the pope's pardons. Now the letters help not or hinder, but that the pardons were as good without them, as with them[2], save only to stablish weak souls, that could not believe except

Baptism. W. T.

Christ.

Faith.

[[1] Allege as giving a legal claim; from the use of the word *prætendo* in law Latin. So Gesner's Thesaurus, Barbaris *prætendere* est postulare tanquam jure sibi suo debitum.]

[[2] So L., but the last three words are not in D.]

they read the letters, looked on the seal, and saw the print of St Peter's keys.

O a merciful God, and a most loving Father, how careth he for us! First, above all and beside all his other benefits, to give us his own Son Jesus, and with him to give us himself and all; and not content therewith, but to give us so many sacraments, or visible signs, to provoke us and to help our weak faith, and to keep his mercy in mind: as baptism, the sacrament of his body and blood, and as many other sacraments as they will have, if they put significations to them (for we destroy none, but they destroy which have put out the significations, or feigned some without), as wedlock, to signify that Christ is the husband and we his wife and partakers with him, as the wife with her husband, of all his riches, &c. And beyond all those visible sacraments, to give us yet more sensible and surer sacraments, and surances of his goodness, even in our ownselves: as if we love and give alms to our neighbour, if we have compassion and pray for him, if we be merciful and forgive him, if we deny ourselves, and fast, and withdraw all pleasures from the flesh, for love of the life to come, and to keep the commandments of God. For when such things being before impossible, and now are easy and natural, we feel and are sure that we be altered, and[3] a new creature, shapen in righteousness after the image of Christ and God our Father, seeing his laws of righteousness are written in our hearts.

When ye fast, be not sad as the hypocrites are. For they fashion them a new countenance, that it might appear unto men how they fast. Verily, I say unto you, they have their reward. Thou therefore, when thou fastest, anoint thine head, and wash thy face, that it appear not unto men how thou fastest; but unto thy Father which is in secret: and thy Father which seeth in secret, shall reward thee openly. Fast.

As above of alms and prayer, even so here Christ rebuketh the false intent and hypocrisy of fasting; that they sought praise of that work that was ordained for to tame the flesh, and used such fashions, that all the world might know that they fasted, to praise them, and to say, 'O what holy men are these; how pale and pitiful look they, even like death, hanging down their heads, and beholding the earth, as men clean out of the world! If these come not to heaven, what shall become of us poor wretches of the world? If these be not great in the

If fasting be used to any other end, than to tame the flesh, that thereby we may be the more prone to serve God, it is abused.

[3 So L., but in D. *and of a new*, &c.]

favour of God, and their prayers be heard whatsoever they ask, in what case are we lay people? Happy is he that may be a brother among them, and partaker of their prayers and fastings, and other holy living. In an unhappy (in an happy, I would say) hour was he born that buildeth them a cell or a cloister, or giveth them a portion of his land to comfort them good men in this painful living, and strait penance which they have taken upon them. Blessed were he that might kiss the edge of the coat of one of them. Oh, he that might have his body wrapped in one of their old coats at the hour of death, it were as good to him as his christendom[1], &c.' It appeareth also by that they asked Christ, why his disciples fasted not as well as the Pharisees, that they oft fasted when the common people fasted not, and all to appear holy; as ours fast advent, and begin before lent at Septuagesima, when *Laus tibi Domine*[2] cometh in.

To anoint the head, what it meaneth. W. T.

And concerning the anointing of thy head, &c. is meant, as afore of turning the other cheek, and of that the left hand should not know what the right did: that is, that they should avoid all vain-glory, and fast to God, and for the intent that God ordained it for, and that with a merry heart and cheerful countenance, thereby to feel the working of God, and to be sure of his favour. Such is the meaning, and not to bind them that will fast to anoint their heads and wash their faces. And the manner or phrase of speaking cometh of an usage, that was among the Jews, to anoint themselves with sweet and odoriferous anointments, when they were disposed to be merry and to make good cheer, as ye see how Mary of Bethany poured a box of precious ointment upon Christ's head at supper.

Fasting.

As concerning fasting, it were good, that kings and rulers did set an order of soberness among their subjects, to avoid dearth, innumerable diseases, and the great heap of vices that spring of intemperancy; and that they forbid not only riot and excess, but also all manner wanton, delicious, and customable eating and drinking of such things as corrupt the people, and

[1 Christening.]

[2 Praise to thee, O Lord. From Septuagesima to Palm Sunday the Roman breviary directs the omission of Te Deum in the Sunday service; and *Laus tibi Domine* is then added as a ninth responsorium in its stead.]

make the men more effeminate than the women, so that there remaineth no more tokens of a man in them save their beards. Our fashions of eating make us slothful, and unlusty to labour and study; unstable, inconstant, and light-mannered; full of wits, after-witted (as we call it), incircumspect, inconsiderate, heady, rash, and hasty to begin unadvisedly, and without casting of perils, the end not considered what may follow, nor the means well looked upon, how and by what way the matter might be brought to pass, triflers, mockers, rude, unsavoury jesters[3] without all manner of salt, and even very apes and marmosets, and full of wanton and ribaldish communication and lewd gestures. It corrupteth the wit with false judgment, and infecteth the body with lust, and maketh the whole man so unquiet in himself, that the body cannot sit still and rest in one place, and continue in his work, nor the mind persevere and endure in one purpose.

The heap of inconveniences that spring by intemperate and superfluous eating and drinking

Let them provide that there be diligent fishing in the sea, and command the sea coast, and towns whither fish may easily come, to fast Friday, Saturday, and Wednesday too, if need be, and on the Friday to eat no white meat. And let the countries which have none abundance of fish, yet have white meat enough, fast Friday and Saturday from flesh only. And let those countries where scarcity of both is, fast Friday from flesh only, and eat flesh Wednesday and Saturday; but abstain from supper, or from dinner, or eat soberly those days. And let them so moderate their fasts that the people may bear it, a provision made for the old, the sick, and feeble, &c.: which fast shall be a temporal thing, for a temporal commonwealth only, and not a service to God.

Fasting days, or days of abstinence, are to be ordained for commonweal's sake.

Then let the priests preach first the law truly, and teach the people to see their sins, and so bring them to repentance; and secondarily, the faith of Christ, and the forgiveness of sin through faith; and thirdly, alms, prayer, and fasting, which are the whole life of a christian man, and without which there is no christian man alive. And let them preach the true use of their alms, which is to help thy neighbour with counsel, with body and goods, and all that is in thy power; and the true use of prayer, which is to bring his necessity and thine own before God, with a strong faith in his promises; and the true use of fasting, which is to tame the flesh

Alms. **Prayer.** **Fasting.**

[3 So L., but D. *unsavoury jesture.*]

unto the spirit, that the soul may attend to the word of God and pray through faith.

Alms, prayer, and fasting, how necessary. W. T.

By these three we keep the Spirit of God; and both continue, and also grow in righteousness, and wax perfecter and perfecter in soul and body. And if these fail, or that we understand not the right intent, we lose the Spirit again, and the righteousness of faith, and the true understanding of the scripture, and all our learning shall be but pure darkness. And then what a blindness is that, when the darkness of hell is called the light of heaven!

Alms, prayer, and fasting, are inseparable. W. T.

As it is of alms and prayer, so it is of fasting: judge like[1] of all three. Where any one of them is, there are they all three: and where any one is away, there is none at all. We must have the profession of all three ever written in our hearts. I must ever love my neighbour and be ready to help, and when occasion is offered, then do it. I ought to consider and know that all cometh of God; and to knowledge that same to him in mine heart. And whatsoever we need, we ought to know that we must receive that of God, and therefore to call ever to him with a strong faith. Even so I must ever fight against my flesh, and therefore ever withdraw from it all that moveth it to rebel against the Spirit.

Fasting is not in eating and drinking only. W. T.

So now fasting standeth not in eating and drinking only, and much less in flesh alone; but in abstinence of all that moveth the flesh against the Spirit, as long sleeping, idleness, and filthy communication, and all worldly talking, as of covetousness and promotion and such like, and wanton company, soft clothes, and soft beds, and so forth; which are that right hand and right eye, that must be cut off and plucked out, that the whole man perish not. And as ye can put no general rule of alms or prayer, no more can ye of fasting. But I must be always ready to cut off whatsoever I perceive to strength the flesh against the Spirit. And I must have a diligent eye to the flesh and his complexion; and, if aught escape me in word or deed, seek whence the occasion came, and at once cut off that right hand, and pluck out that eye.

Works make hypocrites, if the true intent be away. W. T.

If this fast be truly preached, then is fasting good, and not afore, for making of hypocrites: as Christ would not let his disciples fast before they were learned, lest they should

[[1] So D., but in L. *like* is wanting.]

thereby have been no better than the Pharisees. And then the outward fasting, ordained by the temporal rulers, helpeth much for the weak's sake. Yea, and though the land were so plenteous, that it needed not to command such fast for to avoid dearth, yet they ought to set such up, because of them that cannot rule themselves; for whose sakes they ought to forbid excesses of taverns, and alehouses, and rioting out of season. For if the people could rule themselves, what need rulers? Moreover, if any man privately shew the priest his infirmities, and the priest see any manner of abstinence or chastising apt for the person, that let him counsel him to do for the subduing of the flesh; and not command as a tyrant, under pain of damnation, and to make satisfaction. Thuswise let him say: 'Brother or sister, ye be bound under pain of deadly sin to tame your flesh by some manner of way, that ye sin not against God; and I know no better than this: My counsel and my desire therefore is, that ye use this, till either ye have no more need, or till God shew you some better,' &c. And let elders consider diligently the course of their youth, and with wisdom, counsel, and discreet governance help the younger to avoid the perils and jeopardies which they have learned, by their own experience, to be in that dangerous journey.

Rulers be ordained for them that cannot rule themselves. W. T.

Moreover, when the people be fallen from their profession, and from the law; as it shall be impossible for the preacher to keep the great multitude together, if the temporal sword be slack and negligent in punishing open offences (as they ever have and will be, save in those points only wherein lieth the pith of their own profit and advantage, and the weight of their honour and maintenance of their dignities); and when God also (as his promise is) hath brought upon them the curses of the law, hunger, death, battle, pestilence and all manner of plagues, with all misfortune and evil luck; then let the true preachers be importune, and shew the people the causes of their misery and wretched adversity; and expound the law to them, and bring them to knowledge of their sins; and so bind their consciences, and draw them to repentance, and to the appointment and covenant of the Lord again: as many holy prophets, priests, and kings in the old Testament did call the people back, and brought them again in time of adversity unto the appointment of the Lord; and the priest, prophet, or king,

The office of a true preacher. W. T.

Note this well, ye temporal magistrates.

Prophets, priests, yea, and kings of the old Testament, zealous preachers.

in God's stead smote hands with them, and took an oath of them, to be the Lord's people, and to turn again to the Lord's covenant, for to keep his law and to believe in his promises: and God immediately withdrew his hand, and rid them out of all captivity and danger, and became as merciful as ever before.

Papists have often called to the pope's covenant, but seldom to the Lord's.

But we Christians have been very seldom, or never, called again to the covenant of the Lord, the law of God, and faith of Christ; but to the covenant of the pope often: as he now clucketh apace for his chickens, and will both prove all his old policies, and seek and imagine new practices. And if the people come again, let the priest or bishop, after the ensample of the prophets and high priests of the Israelites, take an oath, in God's stead, of the king and lords. And let the king and lords receive an oath of the people, and follow the ensample of the Ninevites in fasting and praying.

Objection.

Some men will say, Seeing fasting is to withdraw all pleasures from the body and to punish the flesh, then God delighteth in our pain-taking, &c.

Solution.

I answer: God delighteth in true obedience, and in all that we do at his commandment, and for the intent that he commandeth it for. If thou love and pity thy neighbour, and help him, thy alms is acceptable. If thou do it of vain-glory, to have the praise that belongeth to God, or for a greater profit only, or to make satisfaction for thy sins past, and to dishonour Christ's blood, which hath made it already; then is thine alms abominable. If thy prayer be thanks in heart, or calling to God for help, with trust in him according to his promise, then thy prayer pleaseth. If thou believe in Christ's blood for the remission of sins, and henceforth hatest sin, that thou punishest thy body to slay[1] thy lusts, and to keep them under, that thou sin not again; then it pleaseth God exceedingly. But and if thou think that God delighteth in the work for the work itself, the true intent away, and in thy pain for thy pain itself, thou art as far out of the way as from heaven to the earth.

How God delighteth in our pain-taking. W. T.

If thou wouldest kill thy body, or, when it is tame enough, pain him further that thou wert not able to serve God and thy neighbour according to the room and estate thou art in; thy sacrifice were clean without salt, and altogether unsavoury in the taste of God, and thou mad and out

[1 So L., but D. *flee*]

of thy wit. But and if thou trust in thy work, then art thou abominable.

Now let us look on the pope's fast. First, the intent should be to tame thy lusts, not lechery only, but pride chiefly, wrath, malice, hate, envy, and covetousness, and to keep the law of God; and therefore standeth not in meat and drink only. But how they keep God's law, compare it to their deeds, and thou shalt see. Secondarily, the fast of the old law was, to put on mourning clothes, as hair or sack, and neither to eat nor drink until night, and all the while to pray, and to do alms-deeds and shew mercy: and at even they ate flesh, and what God gave, soberly; as little as would sustain the body, &c. The pope's fast is commonly only to eat no flesh. I say not, look how lean they be; but, consider what a taming of the flesh it is, to eat ten or twenty manner of fishes, dressed after the costliest manner, and to sit a couple of hours, and to pour in of the best wine and ale that may be gotten; and at night to banquet with dew (as they say) of all manner of fruits and confections, marmalade, succade, green ginger, comfits, sugarplate with malmsey and romney burnt with sugar, cinnamon and cloves, with bastado, muscadell and ipocrass, &c. Think ye not that a piece of salt fish or pickerel, with drinking and such dews, doth not tame the body exceedingly?

The intent of fasting, what it is. W. T.

How the Jews did fast. W. T.

The pope's fast. W. T.

A feasting fast.

Furthermore, that the true intent is away, both of their fasting and prayers, it is evident; first, by the multiplying of them: for when the Jews had lost the understanding of their sacrifices, and did believe in the work, then they were mad upon them, that well was he that could rob himself to offer most; insomuch that the prophets cried out against them, that their offerings stank in the nose of God. And ours had so multiplied their fasting, that they could no longer bear them: at the beginning they were tolerable, for the vantage, *quia levis est labor cum lucro*[2]; but when they had purchased enough and enough again, they became intolerable. And therefore all our monks, whose profession was never to eat flesh, set up the pope, and took dispensations, both for that fast, and also for their strait rules, and made their strait rules as wide as the hoods of their cowls. And

The true intent is away from the pope's fasting.

Monks made the pope a god for his dispensations.

[2 Because lucrative labour is light.]

as for the hypocrisy of the fratry[1], where they eat but invisible flesh, or that is interpret to be no flesh[2], [it] is spoken of in other places. Another proof is that they so long a time have given pardons, of the merits of their fasting, as though they had done more than enough for themselves; and of that merchandise have gotten all they have, and have brought the knowledge of Christ's blood clean into darkness. And last of all, what shall I say of the open idolatry of innumerable fasts; of St Brandon's fast[3], St Patrick's fast, of four holy Fridays[4], of St Anthony's between St Mary's days[5], of our Lady fast, either seven year the same day that her day falleth on in March, and then begin, or one year with bread and water[6], and all for what purposes, ye know well enough; and

[1 The fratry, or refectory, was the dining-room of a monastery. Fosbroke has devoted his thirty-fifth chapter to a description of its usages and luxuries.—Brit. Monachism.]

[2 The flesh of the otter came under this description; being counted no flesh, and therefore lawful food on fast days, because the otter was supposed to live exclusively on fish.—Fosbroke, ch. XXXV. p. 218. n. d. Third edition, 1843.]

[3 The wild legend, which tells the tale of this imaginary British abbot and bishop must have been peculiarly offensive to Tyndale, from the glaring way in which it teaches that works of charity will be rewarded, irrespective of faith in Christ. For it describes Brandon as deserting the duties of his office to search the ocean for the terrestrial paradise; and as finding Judas Iscariot in the midst of the sea, upheld from drowning by sitting on a stone, which he said that he remembered having put down in a muddy part of Jerusalem to save passengers from falling into the dirt.—Catalogus sanctorum; editus a Rev.[ssimo] Petro de Natalibus; episc. Equilino. MDXIII. fol. CV.—See also Legenda aurea, CCXXX.]

[4 The Fridays of the fasts Quatuor temporum; of which Bingham says, "Some think Gregory VII." (pope Hildebrand) "was the first who ordered that the ordination fasts should concur with them."—Origin. Eccles. B. XXI. ch. II. § 1 and 7, Vol. VII. pp. 236 and 243. Lond. 1840.]

[5 Antony, an Egyptian monk of the third century, was so popular a saint, that it would seem that the fast of his vigil, kept on the sixteenth of January, was of more note than any other occurring between the vigils preceding the festival of the Virgin's conception, on the eighth of December, and that preceding the festival of the purification on the second of February.—See Vol. I. p. 91.]

[6 The Lady fast here described seems to have been a species of penance, whether voluntary or enjoined, in which the penitent had the

of such like, I trow, ten thousand in the world? And who hath rebuked them?

See that ye gather not treasure upon the earth, where rust and moths corrupt, and where thieves break up and steal: But gather you treasure in heaven, where neither rust nor moths corrupt, and where thieves neither break up nor steal. For where your treasure is, there will be your hearts also.

Note the goodly order of Christ's preaching. First he restored the true understanding of the law, then the true intent of the works. And here, consequently, he rebuketh the mortal foe and sworn enemy both of true doctrine and true living, which is covetousness; the root of all evil, saith Paul, (1 Tim. vi.) Covetousness is image-service, (Col. iii.) It maketh men to err from the faith, (1 Tim. vi). It hath no part in the kingdom of Christ and God, (Eph. v). Covetousness hardened the heart of Pharaoh, that the faith of the miracles of God could not sink into it. Covetousness did make Balaam, which knew all the truth of God, to hate it, and to give the most pestilent and poisonful[7] counsel against it that heart could imagine, even for to destroy it, if it had been possible. Covetousness taught the false prophets in the old Testament to interpret the law of God falsely, and to pervert the meaning and intent of all the sacrifices and ceremonies, and to slay the true preachers that rebuked them. And with their false persuasions they did lead all the kings of Israel out of the right way, and the most part of the kings of Judah also. And Peter, in the second chapter of his second epistle, prophesieth that there should be false teachers among us, that should follow the way of Balaam (that is to say, for covetousness persecute the truth), and through covetousness with feigned words to make merchandise of the people, and to bring in damnable sects too. And here ye have an infallible rule, that where covetousness is, there is no truth; no, though they call themselves the church, and say thereto that they cannot err. Covetousness kept Judas still in un-

Covetousness, what a pestilence it is. W. T.

1 Tim. vi.
Col. iii.
Eph. v.

2 Pet. ii.

Covetousness cannot but err. W. T.

choice of either fasting once a week for seven years, on that day of the week on which Lady-day happened to fall, beginning his course from that day, or of finishing his penance sooner by taking as many fasting-days together, which would obviously amount to one whole year.]

[7 So D., but L. has *poison counsel.*—See Vol. I. p. 17, n. 4.]

belief, though he saw and did also many miracles in the name of Christ, and compelled him to sell him to the scribes and Pharisees; for covetousness is a thing merciless. Covetousness made the Pharisees to lie on Christ, to persecute him, and falsely to accuse him. And it made Pilate, though he found him an innocent, yet to slay him. It caused Herod to persecute Christ, yet in his cradle. Covetousness maketh hypocrites to persecute the truth, against their own consciences; and to lie to princes, that the true preachers move sedition and make their subjects to rise against them: and the said covetousness maketh the princes to believe their wicked persuasions, and to lend their swords to shed innocent blood.

Finally, covetousness maketh many, whom the truth pleaseth at the beginning, to cast it up again, and to be afterward the most cruel enemies thereof, after the ensample of Simon Magus; yea, and after the ensample of sir Thomas More, Kt, which knew the truth, and for covetousness forsook it again, and conspired first with the cardinal to deceive the king, and to lead him in darkness: and afterward, when the light was sprung upon them, and had driven them clean out of the scripture, and had delivered it out of their tyranny, and had expelled the dark stinking mist of their devilish glosses, and had wiped away the cobwebs, which those poisoned spiders had spread upon the face of the clear text, so that the spiritualty (as they call themselves) were ashamed of their part, as shameless as they be; yet for all that, covetousness blinded the eyes of that gleering fox more and more, and hardened his heart against the truth, with the confidence of his painted poetry, babbling eloquence, and juggling arguments of subtle sophistry, grounded on his "unwritten verities[1]," as true and as authentic as his story of Utopia. Paul therefore biddeth Timothy to charge the rich

Acts viii.

More. W. T.

Covetousness blinded the eyes, and hardened the heart of sir Thomas More.

[[1] "When they (the Romanists) be not able to prove any of these doctrines by the word of God written, then they fly to their *unwritten verities;* that is, to certain things delivered, as they say, from the apostles by word of mouth, without writing.... Whatsoever pleaseth them and maketh for their purpose, profit, and lordly ambition, that is *an unwritten verity*, not to be gainsaid or denied."—The translator's preface to "A Confutation of Unwritten Verities," in Archbishop Cranmer's Remains, Vol. VI. p. 153. Jenkyn's ed. Oxf. 1833. Vol. II. p. 10, Park. Soc.]

to believe in the living God, and not in their uncertain riches; for it is impossible for a covetous idolater, or image-server, that trusteth in the dead god of his riches, to put his trust in the living God.

One misery is, that they which here gather and lay up, cannot tell for whom. Another is rust, canker, moths, and a thousand misfortunes besides; thieves, extortioners, oppressors, and mighty tyrants, to the which the rich be ever a prey. And though they prosper to the end outwardly, yet fear ever gnaweth their hearts inwardly. And at the hour of death they know and feel that they have gathered nought; and then sorrow they, and are like one that dreameth of riches, and in the morning, when he findeth nought, is heavy and sorry for the remembrance of the pleasant dream. And finally, when they be most loth to die, and hope to live long, then they perish suddenly; after the ensample of that rich man, which intended to make him larger barns and store-houses. Happy therefore is he that layeth up treasure in heaven, and is rich in faith and good works; for the reward thereto promised shall God keep sure for him: no man can take it away. Here is not forbidden to have riches; but to love it, to trust in it, and to be careful for it. For God hath promised to care for us, and to give us enough, and to keep that which is gotten, if we will care to keep his commandments. Whatsoever office or degree thou art in in this world, do the duty of thine office diligently, and trust in God, and let him care. If thou be an husbandman, ear[2] and sow, and husband thy ground, and let God alone for the rest; he will care to make it grow plenteously, and to send seasonable weather to have it in, and will provide thee a good market to sell, &c.

The commodities that follow covetous and worldly rich men.

Luke xii.

In like manner, if thou be a king, do the office of a king, and receive the duties of the king, and let God care to keep thee in thy kingdom. His favour shall do more for thee than a thousand millions of gold. And so of all other: he that hath but a little, and is sure that God shall keep both him and it, is richer than he which hath thousands, and hath none other hope than that he and it must be kept with his own care and policy.

And, finally, mark one point in Luke xiv: "None of them, that refuseth not all that he possesseth, can be my disciple;"

Luke xiv.

[[2] Ear: to plow; as in 1 Sam. viii. 12. Author. version.]

that is, he that casteth not away the love of all worldly things, can be no scholar of Christ's to learn his doctrine. Then he addeth that "salt is good; but, if the salt be unsavoury," or hath lost his virtue, "what can be seasoned therewith?" Verily, nothing. Now, by salt is understood the doctrine; and the meaning is, if ye be covetous and love worldly things, it will corrupt the salt of your doctrine, so that whatsoever you powder therewith, it shall be more unsavoury than before.

Covetousness maketh the salt of God's word unsavoury.

"Where your treasure is, there are your hearts." If your treasure be in the world, so is the love of your hearts. And if ye love the world, and the things of the world, the love of God is not in you; and the love of God is the love of his commandments: and he that loveth not God's commandments shall never preach them truly, because he loveth them not; but shall corrupt them with glosses, that they may stand with that which his heart loveth, and until they have another sense than ever God gave them. Ergo, no covetous person can be a true prophet. It is not for nought, then, that Christ so oft and so diligently warneth his disciples to beware of covetousness, as of that thing which, he wist well, had ever corrupt the word of God, and ever should.

Covetousness maketh a false prophet.

The light of thy body is thine eye: wherefore, if thine eye be single, all thy body shall be full of light; but and if thine eye be wicked, then shall thy whole body be dark. If therefore the light that is in thee be darkness, how great is that darkness!

Darkness. W. T.

Note the conclusion with a proper similitude. The eye is the light of the body; and by the light of the eye all other members see and are governed. As long as the eye seeth, hand and foot do their duties; neither is there any fear that a man should stumble, or fall into fire or water. But if the eye be blind, all the body is blind; and that so blind, that there is no remedy at all: set a candle before him, he seeth not; give him a lantern in his hand, and yet he goeth not straight: bring him out into the sun, and point him unto that which thou wouldest have him see; it booteth not. Even so, if covetousness have blinded the spiritual eye, and perverted the right intent of the law of God, and of the works commanded by God, and of the sacrifice, ceremonies, and sacraments, and of all other ordinances of God, (which intent is the spiritual eye,) then is all the doctrine dark, and very

Covetousness causeth darkness. W. T.

blindness: yea, and then how dark is the darkness, when that which is pure blindness is believed to be light! How dark is the doctrine of them that teach that a man may compel God, with the works of free-will, to give him his favour and grace; or make God unrighteous! How dark is the doctrine of them which (to the rebuke of Christ's blood) teach that works do justify before God, and make satisfaction for sins! How blind are they which think prayer to be the pattering of many words; and will therefore not only be praised and paid of the world, but also by the title thereof challenge heaven, and not by the merits of Christ's blood! How dark is the doctrine of them whose faith is only and altogether in appointments which they themselves have feigned between them and God, unto which yet God never subscribed: in which also they assign what work, and how much they will do, and what reward, and how great, God must give them, or choose whether he will be unrighteous.

How dark is the doctrine of them that say stiffly, that the work of the sacraments in itself (not referring it to stir up the faith of the promises annexed to them) doth justify; and affirm, that bodily pain, for the pain itself, (not referring it either to the love of the law of God or of their neighbour,) doth please God! How dark, damnable, and devilish, is the doctrine of them, which not only think lucre to be the service of God, but also are so far past all shame, that they affirm they be the holy church, and cannot err; and all that they decree must be an article of our faith, and that it is damnable once to doubt, or search the scripture whether their doctrine will thereto agree or no; but say their decrees must be believed as they sound, how contrary soever the scripture be, and the scripture must be expounded and made agree to them. They need not to regard the scripture, but to do and say as their Holy Ghost moveth them; and if the scripture be contrary, then make it a nose of wax, and wrest it this way and that way, till it agree.

Darkness.

The darkness of the pope's doctrine here plainly appeareth.

Faith of works was the darkness of the false prophets, out of the which the true could not draw them. Faith of works was the blindness of the Pharisees, out of the which neither John Baptist nor Christ could bring them. And though John Baptist piped to them with reasons of the scripture invincible, and Christ thereto added miracles, yet the

Faith in works is darkness. W. T.

Pharisees would not dance. For John Baptist, as they thought, was too mad, to live so strait a life, and to refuse to be justified thereby: and as for Christ and his disciples, the Pharisees were much holier themselves, fasted oftener, and prayed thicker; yea, and uttered many more words in their prayer than they. Faith of works is that belief of the Turks and Jews, which driveth them ever away from Christ. Faith of works hath been that light of darkness in which a great part of us Christen[1] have walked ever since Pelagius and Faustus[2], well about twelve hundred years, and ever more and more; and in which all our religious have walked all, and more too, this four or five hundred year; and in which the priests also have walked a long season: the Lord bring them out again!

Darkness. Finally: how dark is the darkness, when a Pharisee and a very Pelagian standeth up, and preacheth against the Pharisees and the Pelagians, and is allowed of all the audience! And, in conclusion, when the world, ever since it began, hath and doth of natural blindness believe in their own works; then, if the scripture be perverted to confirm that error, how sore are their hearts hardened, and how deep is that darkness!

No man can serve two masters: for he shall either hate the one, and love the other; or cleave to the one, and despise the other. Ye cannot serve God and mammon.

Mammon, what it is. W. T. Mammon is riches, or abundance of goods. And Christ concludeth with a plain similitude, that as it is impossible to serve two contrary masters, and as it is impossible to be retained unto two divers lords, which are enemies one to the other, so is it impossible to serve God and mammon. Two masters of one mind and one will might a man serve: for if one will, one mind, and one accord be in twenty, then are they all but one master. And two masters, where one is under the other and a substitute, may a man serve: for the service of the inferior is the commandment of the superior; as to serve and obey father, mother, husband, master, and lord, is God's commandment. But and if the inferior be of a contrary will to the superior, and command any contrary thing, then

[1 A plural, equivalent to *Christians*.]

[2 Pelagius, the noted author of the heresy which bears his name, and Faustus, a defender of Manichæism, were propagators of error at the close of the fourth century.]

mayest thou not obey: for now they be two contrary masters. So God and mammon are two contrary masters: yea, two contrary gods, and of contrary commandments. Mammon is a god.

God saith: "I thy Lord God am but one, and me shalt thou serve alone:" that is, thou shalt love me with all thine heart, or with thine whole heart, with all thy soul, and with all thy might. Thou shalt neither serve, obey, or love any thing save me, and that I bid thee; and that as far, and no farther than I bid thee.

And mammon saith the same: for mammon will be a god also, and served and loved alone.

God saith: 'See thou love thy neighbour; that thou labour with thine hands to get thy living, and somewhat above, to help him.'

Mammon saith: 'He is called thy neighbour, because he is nigh thee. Now who is so nigh thee as thyself? Ergo, *proximus esto tibi*[3]: that is, love thyself, and make lewd[4] and vile wretches to labour diligently to get thee as much as thou mayest, and some scraps above for themselves. Or wilt thou be perfect? Then disguise thyself, and put on a grey coat, a black or a pied[5], and give thyself to devotion; despise the world, and take a covetous (I would say a contemplative) life upon thee. Tell the people how hot purgatory is, and what pains there must be suffered for small faults. And then give mercifully a thousand fold for one, spiritual for temporal: give heaven, and take but house and land, and foolish temporal things.' Mammon maketh men disguise themselves. W. T.

God saith :'Judge truly between thy brethren, and therefore take no gifts.'

Mammon saith: 'It is good manners, and a point of courtesy to take that is offered. And he that giveth thee, loveth thee better than such a churl that giveth thee nought; yea, and thou art more bound to favour his cause.'

God saith : 'Sell and give alms.'

Mammon saith: 'Lay up, to have enough to maintain thine estate, and to defend thee from thine enemies, and to serve thee in thine age, &c.'

[[3] Count thyself thy nearest neighbour.]

[[4] Ignorant.]

[[5] Alluding to the different vestments by which different monastic orders were distinguished from the laity, and from each other.]

The servants of mammon are not of Christ's church. W.T.

Forasmuch then as God and mammon be two so contrary masters, that whosoever will serve God must give up mammon, and all that will serve mammon must forsake God; it followeth that they which are the sworn servants of mammon, and have his holy spirit, and are his faithful church, are not the true servants of God, nor have his Spirit of truth in them, or can be his true church.

The servant of mammon is no true preacher. W. T.

Moreover, seeing that God and mammon be so contrary, that God's word is death in mammon's ear, and his doctrine poison in mammon's mouth; it followeth that if the ministers of God's word do favour mammon, they will so fashion their speech, and so sound their words, that they may be pleasant in the ears of mammon.

To be mammon's servant, what it is. W. T.

Finally, alonely to have riches is not to be the servant of mammon; but to love it, and cleave to it in thine heart. For if thou have goods only to maintain the office which God hath put thee in, and of the rest to help thy neighbour's need, so art thou lord over thy mammon, and not his servant.

Mammon's servant, how he is known. W. T.

Of them that be rich, how shalt thou know the master of mammon from the servant? Verily, first by the getting: secondarily, when his poor neighbour complaineth, if he be mammon's servant, mammon will shut up his heart and make him without compassion. Thirdly, the cross of Christ will try them, the one from the other: for when persecution ariseth for the word, then will the true servant of Christ bid mammon adieu; and the faithful servant of mammon will utter his hypocrisy, and not only renounce the doctrine of Christ, but also be a cruel and a sharp persecutor thereof, to put away all surmise, and that his fidelity, which he hath in his master mammon, may openly appear.

Therefore I say unto you, Care not for your lives what ye shall eat, or what ye shall drink; neither for your bodies what ye shall put on. Is not the life more than meat, and the body more than the raiment?

The goodness of God towards mankind.

He that buildeth a costly house even to the tiling, will not leave there, and lose so great cost for so small a trifle more. No more will he that gave thee so precious a soul, and so beautiful a body, let either of them perish again before the day, for so small a thing as food or raiment. God never made mouth, but he made meat for it; nor body, but he made raiment also. Howbeit, mammon blindeth our eyes, so that we can neither see nor judge aright.

Behold the fowls of the air, how they sow not, neither reap, nor gather into store-houses; and yet your heavenly Father feedeth them. And are not ye far better than they? Which of you with taking thought is able to put one cubit unto his stature?

He that careth for the least of his creatures will much more care for the greatest. The birds of the air and beasts preach all to us, that we should leave caring, and put our trust in our Father. But mammon hath made us so dull and so clean without capacity, that none ensample or argument, be it never so vehement, can enter the wits of us, to make us see or judge aright. Finally, what a madness it is to take so great thought for food or raiment, when the wealth, health, life of thy body, and all together is out of thy power! If all the world were thine, thou couldest not make thyself one inch longer, nor that thy stomach shall digest the meat that thou puttest into it. No, thou art not sure that that which thou puttest into thy mouth shall go through thee, or whether it shall choke thee. Thou canst not make, when thou liest or sittest down, that thou shalt arise again; or when thou sleepest, that thou shalt awake again, or that thou shouldest live one hour longer. So that he which cared for thee, when thou couldest not care, must care for thee still, or else thou shouldest perish. And he will not care for thee to thy soul's profit, if thou mistrust him and care for thyself. Birds and beasts teach us to put away care. W. T.

And for raiment why take ye thought? Behold the lilies of the field, how they grow: they labour not, neither spin. And yet I say to you, that even Salomon in all his glory was not apparelled like one of them. Wherefore, if the grass, which is to day in the fields, and to-morrow shall be cast into the furnace, God so clothe, how much more shall he do the same unto you, O ye of little faith!

Not only fowl and beast, but also tree, herb, and all the flowers of the earth do cry unto us, to trust God; and to cast away care, that is coupled with covetousness of more than sufficient to bear the charges which we have in our hands by the reason of the state we be in the world, and all care that is annexed with mistrust, that God should not minister enough to bear all our charges, if we endeavour ourselves to keep his commandments, and to do every man his craft or office he Care.

is in truly, and (when God, to prove us, suffereth us to have need of our neighbours) we first complain to God, and desire him to prepare the hearts of our neighbours, against we come to desire their help.

Mammon. But mammon pipeth another song, saying: 'If thou shouldest make no other manner of labour for a benefice, than as if thou caredst not whether thou hadst it or hadst it not, it would be long ere thou gattest one; all would be taken out of thine hand.' I answer: As thy labour was to get it, such shall be thy behaviour in it; as thou flatteredst to have it, so shalt thou in it; and as thou boughtest and soldest to get it, so shall thou sell in it, to buy favour and to be set by in the world. If thy principal intent, that thou seekest a benefice for, be lucre, then take heed to the example of thy forefather Simon Magus. (Acts viii.) Let thy care therefore be to do the office that God putteth thee in truly; and the blessing, that he coupleth thereto, that take with thanks, and neither care nor covet farther.

Take no thought therefore, saying, What shall we eat, or what shall we drink, or what shall we put on? All these things the heathen seek. Yea, and your heavenly Father knoweth that ye need all these things. But seek first the kingdom of God and the righteousness thereof, and all these things shall be ministered unto you.

Be not like the heathen, which have no trust in God nor his word, nor believe any life to come. Let them vex themselves, and each be a devil to another, for worldly things. (Keep covenant with God, and he shall keep promise with thee. W. T.) But comfort thou thyself with the hope of a better life in another world, ever assured that thou shalt have here sufficient, only if thou keep covenant with the Lord thy God, and seek his kingdom and the righteousness thereof above all things. (Kingdom of heaven, what. W. T.) The kingdom of God is the gospel and doctrine of Christ. (Righteousness of the kingdom of heaven, what it is. W. T.) And the righteousness thereof is to believe in Christ's blood, for the remission of sins: out of which righteousness springeth love to God, and thy neighbour, for his sake; which is also righteousness, as I have said afore, so far as it is perfect, and that which lacketh is supplied by faith in God's word, in that he hath promised to accept that, till more come. Then followeth the outward righteousness of works, by the which, and diligent recording[1] of God's word together, we

[[1] Calling to mind; meditating upon.]

grow and wax perfect, and keep ourselves from going back and losing the Spirit again.

And these have our spiritualty with their corrupt doctrine mingled together, (that is to say, the righteousness of the kingdom of God, which is faith in Christ's blood, and the outward righteousness of the members,) that we ascribe to the one that pertaineth to the other. Seek the kingdom of heaven therefore, and the righteousness of the same; and be sure thou shalt ever have sufficient, and these things shall be ministered unto thee, that is to say, shall come of their own accord, by the promise of God; yea, Christ promiseth thee an hundred fold, even in this life, of all that thou leavest for his sake. If that were true, would some say, who would not rather serve him than mammon? Yet is it true: for first, if thou be servant of mammon, thou must keep thy god, and thy god not thee; and every man, that is stronger than thou, will take thy god from thee. Moreover, God will take either thee from thy mammon, or thy mammon from thee, ere thou wouldest; to avenge himself of thy blind unkindness, that when he hath made thee, and given thee all, thou forsakest him and servest his mortal enemy. But if thou follow Christ, all the world (and let them take all the devils in hell to them) shall not be able to disappoint thee of a sufficient living. And though they persecute thee from house to house a thousand times, yet shall God provide thee of another, with all things sufficient to live by. Now compare the surety of this with the uncertainty of the other; and then the blessed end of this (that heaven is promised thee also) with the miserable departing from the other so sore against thy will, and then the desperation that thy heart feeleth that thou art already in hell. And then may not this be well called a thousand fold more than the other?

If thou follow Christ, thou canst not lack a sufficient living.

Care not then for the day following; but let the day following care for itself. For the day that is present hath ever enough of his own trouble.

Care.

If thou look well on the covenant that is between thee and thy Lord God, on the one side, and the temptations of the world, the flesh, and Satan on the other, thou shalt soon perceive that the day present hath ever enough to be cared for, and for which thou must cry instantly to God for help also, though thou do thy best. Now then, seeing the day present is overcharged with her own care, what madness is it to lade upon her also the care of the day following, yea, the care of a year, yea, of twenty years, or as though thou never intendest to die, and to torment and vex the soul through mistrust and unbelief, and to make thy life sour and bitter, and as unquiet as the life of the devils in hell!

What we ought chiefliest to care for.

Therefore care day by day and hour by hour earnestly to keep the covenant of the Lord thy God, and to record therein day and night, and to do thy part unto the uttermost of thy power. And as for God's part, let him care for it himself; and believe thou his words stedfastly, and be sure that heaven and earth shall sooner perish, than one jot bide behind of that he hath promised. And for thine own part also, care not of that manner as though thou shouldest do all alone: nay, God hath first promised to help thee; secondarily, to accept thine heart, and that little that thou art able to do, be it never so imperfect; thirdly, though wind, weather, and the stream carry thee clean contrary to thy purpose, yet, because thou bidest still in thy profession, ready to turn the right course as soon as the tempest is a little overblown, God promiseth to forgive that, and not the less to fulfil his promises of one jot.

Why God letteth his children be tempted with adversity. W. T.

Doth Christ so defend his, that they never come in danger of trouble? Yes; they come into such straits oft, that no wit nor reason can see any way out, save faith only is sure that God hath, and will make a way through. But that temptation is but for an hour, to teach them, and to make them feel the goodness of their Father, and the passions[1] of their brethren, and of their master Christ also. It is but as a loving mother, to make her child to perceive and feel her kindness, to love her again and be thankful, letteth it hunger in a morning; and when it calleth for his breakfast, maketh as she heard it not, till for pain and impatience it beginneth to cry agood: and then she stilleth it, and giveth it all it asketh, and more too, to please it; and when it is peaced[2] and beginneth to eat, and rejoiceth and is glad and fain, she asketh, 'Who gave thee that, thy mother?' and it saith, 'Yea.' Then saith she, 'Am not I a good mother, that

[1 Passions: sufferings.]
[2 Caused to be at peace.]

give thee all things?' And it answereth, 'Yea.' And she asketh, 'Wilt thou love thy mother?' &c. And it saith, 'Yea.' And so cometh it to the knowledge of his mother's kindness, and is thankful. Such is the temptation of Christ's elect, and otherwise not.

Here is not forbidden all manner of care, but that worldly and devilish care, that springeth of an inordinate love to worldly things and of mistrust in God. As for an ensample: I covet inordinately more than sufficient, or but even that I have need of; and it (because I mistrust God, and have no hope in him, and therefore pray not to him) cometh not. Then I mourn, sorrow, and pine away, and am whole unquiet in mine heart. Or whether I have too much, or but sufficient, and love it inordinately, then I care for the keeping: and because I mistrust God, and have no hope in him that he will help me; therefore, when I have locked doors, chambers, and coffers, I am never the nearer at rest, but care still; and cast a thousand perils, of which the most part were not in my might to avoid, though I never slept. And where this care is, there can the word of God have no resting-place; but is choked up, as soon as it is sown.

What care is forbidden. W. T.

There is another care, that springeth out of the love of God (for every love hath her care), and is a care to keep God's commandments. This care must every man have. For a man liveth not by bread only, but much more by every word that proceedeth out of the mouth of God. The keeping of God's commandment is the life of a man, as well in this world as in the world to come. As, "Child, obey father and mother; that thou mayest long live on the earth." And by father and mother is understood all rulers; which if thou obey, thy blessing shall be long life; and contrary, if thou disobey, short life, and shalt either perish by the sword, or by some other plague, and that shortly. And even so shall the ruler, if he rule not as God hath commanded. "Oppress thou a widow and fatherless children (saith God), and they shall cry to me, and I will hear their voice; and then will my wrath wax hot; so I will smite you with sword, and your wives shall be widows, and your children fatherless."

What care every man ought to have. W. T.

God's commandment is man's life. W. T.

Exod. xxii.

Some will say, 'I see none more prosper, or longer continue, than those that be most cruel tyrants.' What then? Yet say I that God abideth ever true: for where he setteth

Why God suffereth tyrants to prosper. W. T.

up a tyrant, and continueth him in prosperity, it is to be a scourge to wicked subjects, that have forsaken the covenant of the Lord their God; and unto them his good promises pertain not, save his curses only. But if the subjects would turn and repent, and follow the ways of God, he would shortly deliver them. Howbeit yet, where the superior corrupteth the inferior, which else is disposed enough to goodness, God will not let them long continue.

AN EXPOSITION OF THE SEVENTH CHAPTER.

Judge not, that ye be not judged. For as ye judge, so shall ye be judged; and with what measure ye mete, with the same shall it be measured to you again. Why lookest thou on the mote that is in thy brother's eye, and markest not the beam that is in thine own eye? Or how canst thou say to thy brother, Let me pluck out the mote out of thine eye, and, behold, there is a beam in thine own eye? Thou hypocrite, pluck first the beam out of thine own eye; and then thou shalt see clearly to pluck the mote out of thy brother's eye.

Judging.

THIS is not meant of the temporal judgments; for Christ forbade not that, but oft did stablish it; as do Peter and Paul in their epistles also. Nor here is it not forbidden to judge those deeds which are manifest against the law of God; for those ought every Christian man to persecute, yet must they do it after the order that Christ hath set. But when he saith, "Hypocrite, cast out first the beam that is in thine own eye," it is easy to understand of what manner of judging he meaneth.

What judging is rebuked. W. T.

The hypocrites will have fastings, prayings, kneeling, crouching, ducking, and a thousand ceremonies of their own invention; and whosoever do not as they do, him they count a damned soul by and by. To Christ they say, "Why fast not thy disciples, as the Pharisees do? Why pluck they the ears of corn, and rub them in their hands, (though they did it compelled with pure hunger,) and do that is not lawful on the sabbath-day? Why break ye the traditions of our elders, and wash not when ye sit down to meat? Yea, and why dost thou thyself heal the people upon the holy day? Why didst thou not only heal him that was bedrid thirty-eight years, but also badest him bear his bed away upon the sabbath-day? Be there not working days sufficient to do good deeds to the praise of God, and profit of thy neighbour, but that thou must break thy sabbath-day? He cannot be but a damned person, that breaketh the holy day, and despiseth the ordinance of the holy church.'

All days are indifferent to do good deeds, to the praise of God, and the profit of our neighbour.

'He eateth butter on Fridays, without a dispensation of our holy father the pope; yea, and cake-bread, made with milk and eggs too, and white meat in the Lent; he taketh no holy water when he cometh to the church; he heareth no mass from Sunday to Sunday. And either he hath no beads at all, or else you shall not hear a stone clink[1] in the hand of him, nor yet his lips wag all the mass and matins while,' &c. "O hypocrite! Cast out first the beam that is in thine own eye, and then thou shalt see" better. Thou understandest all God's laws falsely, and therefore thou keepest none of them truly: his laws require mercy, and not sacrifice. Moreover, thou hast a false intent in all the works that thou doest, and therefore are they all damnable in the sight of God. "Hypocrite! cast out the beam that is in thine own eye;" learn to understand the law of God truly, and to do thy works aright, and for the intent that God ordained them: and then thou shalt see whether thy brother have a mote in his eye or not; and if he have, how to pluck it out, and else not.

The beam. W. T.

For he that knoweth the intent of the law and of works, though he observe a thousand ceremonies for his own exercise, he shall never condemn his brother, or break unity with him, in those things which Christ never commanded, but left indifferent. Or if he see a mote in his brother's eye, that he observeth not with his brethren some certain ordinance made for a good purpose, because he knoweth not the intent; he will pluck it out fair and softly, and instruct him lovingly, and make him well content. Which thing if our spiritualty would do, men would not so abhor to obey their tyranny: but they be hypocrites, and do and command all their works for a false purpose; and therefore judge, slay, and shed their brethren's blood mercilessly. God is the father

Ceremonies: he that breaketh unity for zeal of ceremonies understandeth not God's law. W. T.

Ceremonies.

[[1] Alluding to the custom of measuring the number of aves or paternosters uttered, by dropping at the close of each one stone of the string of beads.]

of all mercy, and therefore gave not hypocrites such absolute power to compel their brethren to obey what they list, or to slay them without pity, shewing either no cause of their commandments at all, but 'So will we have it!' or else assigning an intent damnable and contrary to all scripture. Paul
Rom. xiv. (Rom. xiv.) saith to them that observed ceremonies, that they should not judge them that did not; for he that observeth, and knoweth not the intent, judgeth at once: and to them that observed not, that they should not despise them that observed; he that observeth not ought not to despise the weakness or ignorance of his brother, till he perceive that he is obstinate and will not learn.

Measures. Moreover, such measure as thou givest, thou shalt receive again: that is, if thou judge thy neighbour, God shall judge thee; for if thou judge thy neighbour in such things, thou knowest not the law of God, nor the intent of works, and art therefore condemned of God, &c.

Give not that holy thing unto dogs, neither cast your pearls before the swine, lest they tread them under their feet, and the other turn again and all-to[1] tear you.

Dogs, who they be, and what is signified thereby. The dogs are those obstinate and indurate, which for the blind zeal of their leaven, wherewith they have soured both the doctrine and also the works, maliciously resist the truth, and persecute the ministers thereof; and are those wolves among which Christ sendeth his sheep, warning them not only to be single and pure in their doctrine, but also wise and circumspect, and to beware of men: for they should bring them before judges and kings, and slay them, thinking to do God service therein; that is, as Paul (to the Romans) testifieth of the Jews, for blind zeal to their own false and feigned righteousness, persecute the righteousness of God.

Swine truly described. The swine are they, which, for all they have received the pure gospel of Christ, will yet continue still in sin, and roll themselves in the puddle and mire of their old filthy conversation, and both before the ignorant, and also the weak, use the uttermost of their liberty; interpreting it after the largest fashion and most favour of the flesh, as it were the pope's pardon; and therewith make that truth evil spoken of,

[[1] An old idiom, which also occurs in Judges ix. 53, Author. Vers., as equivalent to *entirely* or utterly.]

that thousands, which else might have been easily won, will now not once hear thereof; and stir up cruel persecution, which else would be much easier, yea, and sometimes none at all. And yet will those swine, when it cometh to the point, abide no persecution at all; but offer themselves willing, even at the first chop, for to deny all, ere they be scarcely apposed of their doctrine. Therefore, lay first the law of God before them, and call them to repentance: and if thou see no hope of mending in them, cease there, and go no farther; for they be swine.

But, alas! it ever was, and shall be, that the greater number receive the words for a newness and curiosity (as they say); and to seem to be somewhat, and that they have not gone to school in vain, they will forthwith, ere they have felt any change of living in themselves, be schoolmasters, and begin at liberty, and practise openly before their disciples. And when the Pharisees see their traditions broken, they rage and persecute immediately. And then our new schoolmasters be neither grounded in the doctrine, to defend their doings; nor rooted in the profession of a new life, to suffer with Christ, &c.

Ask, and it shall be given you; seek, and ye shall find; knock, and it shall be opened unto you. For all that ask receive; and he that seeketh findeth; and to him that knocketh it shall be opened. For what man is there among you, if his son ask him bread, that would proffer him a stone? Or if he asked him fish, would he offer him a serpent? If ye then, which are evil, know to give good gifts to your children, how much more shall your Father which is in heaven give good things to them that ask him!

First, note of these words, that to pray is God's commandment, as it is to believe in God, to love God, or to love thy neighbour; and so are alms and fasting also. Neither is it possible to believe in God, to love him, or to love thy neighbour, but that prayer will spring out there-hence immediately. For to believe in God is to be sure that all thou hast is of him, and all thou needest must come of him: which if thou do, thou canst not but continually thank him for his benefits, which thou continually, without ceasing, receivest of his hand; and thereto ever cry for help, for thou art ever in need, and canst no whence else be holpen. And thy neighbour is in such necessity also: wherefore, if thou love him, it

Prayer is a commandment. W. T.

To believe in God, what W. T.

will compel thee to pity him, and to cry to God for him continually, and to thank as well for him as thyself.

Secondarily, this heaping of so many words together, "ask, seek, and knock," signify that the prayer must be continual; and so doth the parable of the widow, that sued to the wicked judge: and the cause is, that we are ever in continual necessity, as I said; and all our life [is] but even a warfare and a perpetual battle; in which we prevail as long as we pray, and be overcome as soon as we cease praying: as Israel overcame the Amalekites, as long as Moses held up his hands in prayer; and as soon as he had let down his hands for weariness, the Amalekites prevailed and had the better. Christ warned his disciples at his last supper, to have peace in him; affirming that they should have none in the world. The false prophets shall ever impugn the faith in Christ's blood, and enforce to quench the true understanding of the law, and the right meaning and intent of all the works commanded by God; which fight is a fight above all fights. First, they shall be in such number, that Christ's true disciples shall be but a small flock in respect of them. They shall have works like Christ's; so that fasting, prayer, poverty, obedience, and chastity, shall be the names of their profession. For, as Paul saith to the Corinthians, the angels or messengers of Satan shall change themselves into angels or messengers of light and truth. They shall come in Christ's name, and that with signs and miracles; and have the upper hand also, even to deceive the very elect, if it were possible. Yea, and beyond all this, if thou get the victory of the false prophets, and pluck a multitude out of their hands, there shall immediately rise of the same, and set up a new false sect against thee. And against all these Amalekites the only remedy is to lift up the hands of thy heart to God in continual prayer: which hands if thou for weariness once let fall, thou goest to the worst immediately. Then, beside the fight and conflict of the subtle sophistry, false miracles, disguised and hypocritish works of these false prophets, cometh the dogs and wolves of their disciples, with the servants of mammon, and the swine of thine own scholars: against which all thou hast no other shield or defence but prayer. Then the sins and lusts of thine own flesh, Satan, and a thousand temptations unto evil in the world, will either drive thee to

Luke xviii.

By prayer we win the victory only, and therefore is it of all things the most necessary. W. T.

Exod. xvii.

False prophets, what their wickedness is. W. T.

Mark xiii.

Matt. xxiv.

Thy heart must be joined with thy prayer.

the castle and refuge of prayer, or take thee prisoner undoubtedly.

Last of all, thy neighbour's necessity and thine own will compel thee to cry, "Father, which art in heaven, give us our daily bread;" though thou wert as rich as king Salomon. For Christ commandeth the rich, as well as the poor, to cry to God continually for their daily bread; and if they have no such need, then is Christ a deceiver and a mocker. What need I to pray thee to give, or lend me, that is in mine own possession already? Is not the first commandment, that there is but one God, and that thou put thy whole trust in him? Which if it were written in thine heart, thou shouldest easily perceive, and though thou hadst as many thousands as David left behind him, and Salomon heaped more to them, that thou hadst no more than the poor beggar that goeth from door to door; yea, and that the beggar (if that commandment be written in his heart) is sure that he is as rich as thou.

The rich must pray for daily bread. W. T.

For first, thou must knowledge that thou hast received that great treasure of the hand of God. Wherefore, when thou fetchest an halfpenny thereof, thou oughtest to give God thanks in thine heart for the gift thereof.

Thou must confess, also, that God only hath kept it and thee that same night, and ever before; or else be an idolater, and put thy trust in some other thing than God. And thou must confess, that God only must keep it and thee, the day and night following, and so continually after; and not thine own wit or power, or the wit or power of any other creature or creatures. For if God kept it not for thee, it would be thine own destruction, and they that help thee to keep it would cut thy throat for it. There is no king in christendom so well beloved, but he hath enow of his own evil subjects (if God kept them not down with fear) that would at one hour rise upon him and slay him, to make havoc of all he hath. Who is so well beloved throughout all England, but that there be enow in the same parish, or nigh about, that would, for his good, wish him to hell if they could, and would with their hands destroy him, if God kept him not, and did[1] cast fear on the other?

To think ourselves saved, or preserved, by any other means than by God's, is idolatry.

Now, then, if God must ever keep it for thee, and thou

[[1] That is, did not keep him and cast fear, &c.]

must daily receive it of his hand (as a poor man doth receive his alms of another man), thou art in no more surety of thy daily bread, no, though thou were a cardinal, than the poorest is. Wherefore, howsoever rich thou be, yet must thou ever cry to God for thy daily bread. So now it is a commandment to pray, and that continually; short, thick, and oft, as the psalms be, and all the prayers of the bible.

Faith must be joined to our prayer. W. T.

Finally, the third is, that we be commanded to pray with faith and trust; and that we believe in the Lord our God, and doubt not in his promises, unto which Christ induceth us with an apt similitude, saying, "If ye being evil can give good things unto your children, how much more shall God fulfil his promises of mercy unto his children, if they cry unto him!" He is better and more merciful than all men. Wherefore, seeing God commandeth thee to pray, and forasmuch as thou hast so great necessity so to do, and because he is merciful, and hath promised and is true, and cannot deny his own words; therefore pray; and when thou prayest, look not on thine unworthiness, but on his commandment, mercy, and goodness, and on his truth and faithfulness, and believe stedfastly in him. Moreover, whatsoever thou hast done, yet if thou repent and will amend, he promiseth that he will not think on thy sins. And though he defer thee, think it not long, nor faint not in thy faith, or be slack in thy prayer: for he will surely come and give thee more than thou desirest, though he defer for thy profit, or change thy request into a better thing.

Though God defer thy request, yet must thou not faint.

All things, therefore, whatsoever ye would men should do to you, so do ye to them. This is, verily, the law and the prophets.

This is a short sermon, that no man need complain that he cannot, for the length, bear it away. It is so nigh thee, that thou needest not to send over sea for it. It is with thee, that thou needest not to be importune upon master doctor, saying, 'Sir, I pray you, what say ye to this case and to that; and is not this lawful, and may I not so do, and so, well enough?' Ask thine own conscience, what thou mayest or oughtest to do. Wouldest thou men did so with thee? then do it. Wouldest thou not be so dealt with? then do it

Doubts. How to soil doubts. W. T.

not. Thou wouldest not that men should do thee wrong and oppress thee: thou wouldest not that men should do thee shame and rebuke, lie on[1] thee, kill thee, hire thine house from thee, or tice thy servant away, or take against thy will aught that is thine. Thou wouldest not that men should sell thee false ware, when thou puttest them in trust to make it ready, or lay it out for thee; nor thou wouldest not that men should deceive thee with great oaths, swearing that to be good which indeed is very naught: thou wouldest not, also, that men should sell thee ware that is naught and too dear, to undo thee. Do no such things, then, to thy neighbour. But as loth as thou wouldest be to buy false ware, or too dear, for undoing thyself, so loth be thou to sell false ware, or too dear, for undoing thy neighbour. And in all thy needs how glad thou wouldest be to be holpen, so glad be to help thy neighbour. And so, in all cases, examine thy conscience, and ask her what is to be done, in all doubts between thy neighbour and thee; and she will teach thee, except thou be more filthy than a swine, and altogether beastly.

Note.

He saith here, "This is the law and the prophets." And he saith, "Thou shalt love thy Lord God with all thine heart, with all thy soul, and with all thy mind:" and, as Mark addeth, "with all thy might, and thy neighbour as thyself. In these two commandments hangeth the whole law and the prophets." And Paul (Rom. xiii. and Gal. v.) saith, that "love is the fulfilling of the law." And it is written, that "Christ is" the fulfilling or "end of the law." To make all these agree, this thou must understand; that to love God purely is the final and uttermost end of all the law and the prophets. To love thy neighbour is the end of all laws that is between man and man; as are, kill not, steal not, bear no false witness, commit none adultery, covet not thy neighbour's wife, his house, ox, ass, maid, man-servant, nor aught that is his, &c. Christ is the fulfilling of the law for us, where we be imperfect; and when we break and repent, his fulfilling is imputed unto us. And this text, "This is the law and the prophets," mayest thou understand as when Paul saith, "Love is the fulfilling of the law:" that is, to

Note. Matt. xxii.

Law, what the fulfilling thereof is. W. T.

The end of all laws between man and man is to love thy neighbour as thyself.

[[1] *On* is used for *of* or *against*.]

do as thou wouldest be done to, is all the law that is between thee and thy neighbour; and that according to the true understanding and interpreting of all true prophets.

Enter in at the strait gate: for wide is the gate, and broad is the way, that leadeth to destruction, and many they be that go in thereat. But strait is the gate, and narrow is the way, that leadeth unto life, and few they be that find it.

Strait gate. W. T.

The strait gate is the true knowledge and understanding of the law, and of the true intent of works: which whosoever understandeth, the same shall be driven to Christ, to fetch of his fulness, and to take him for his righteousness and fulfilling of the law, altogether at the beginning, and as oft as we fall afterward, and for more than the thousandth part of our fulfilling of the law and righteousness of our best works all our life long. For except the righteousness of Christ be knit to the best deed we do, it will be too short to reach to heaven.

The narrow way. W. T.

And the narrow way is to live after this knowledge. He that will enter in at this gate must be made anew: his head will else be too great; he must be untaught all that he hath learned, to be made less for to enter in; and disused in all things to which he hath been accustomed, to be made less, to walk through that narrow way; where he shall find such an heap of temptations, and so continual, that it shall be impossible to endure or to stand, but by prayer of strong faith.

Few find the narrow way, and why. W. T.

And note another; that few find the way. Why? For their own wisdom, their own power, and the reasons of their own sophistry, blind them utterly: that is to say, the light of their own doctrine which is in them, is so extreme darkness that they cannot see. 'Should God let his church err,' say they? 'Should our elders have gone out of the way? Should God have let the devil do these miracles,' and so forth? And when Christ saith, "Few shall find the gate;" 'Yea,' say they, 'in respect of the Turks and Saracens, which are the greater multitude.' Yea, but yet hear a little: the scribes and Pharisees, which had all the authority over the people, and taught out of the scripture, and the Sadducees, with all other false prophets that were when Christ came, were no Turks nor Saracens; neither had God any other church than was among them. And St Peter prophesieth that it shall be so among us; and that we shall be drawn with false sects, of covetousness to deny Christ; as we now do, and believe no more in him. And Paul and Christ confirm the same; that the elect should be deceived, if it were possible. Moreover, if it were enough to say, I will believe and do as mine elders have done, as though they could not err; then was Christ to blame for to say, that except thou forsake father, mother, and thine elders, thou couldest not be his disciple. Christ must be thy master, and thou must be taught of God; and therefore oughtest thou to examine the doctrine of thine elders by the word of God. For the great multitude, that Christ meaneth, are the false prophets and them that follow them: as it shall better appear hereafter.

Peter. Paul. Christ.

Beware of false prophets, which come to you in sheep's clothing; but are within ravening wolves. By their fruits ye shall know them. Do men gather grapes of thorns, either figs of briers? Even so every good tree bringeth forth good fruit; but a corrupt tree bringeth forth evil fruit. A good tree cannot bring forth evil fruit, nor a corrupt tree bring forth good fruit. Every tree that bringeth not forth good fruit, is to be hewn down and to be cast into the fire. Wherefore by their fruits ye shall know them.

Here Christ warneth thee, and describeth unto thee those captains that should so blind the great multitude that they should not find the strait gate, and lead them the broad way to perdition. Note first, that though they be false, yet he calleth them prophets; which word in the new testament is taken for an expounder and an interpreter of scripture. And he saith, "They shall come to you," my disciples. Then they must be our preachers and our doctors. Yea, verily, they must be those our false preachers, which Peter prophesied should be among us, and bring in damnable sects, for to fulfil and satisfy their covetousness, and follow the way and steps of their father Balaam. And they shall come thereto in sheep's clothings: ergo, they be neither the Turks nor yet Saracens. For they come clothed in iron and steel; and will thereto suffer us to keep our faith, if we will submit ourselves to them, as the Greeks do. And as for the Jews,

The false prophets, who. W. T.

they be an hundred times fewer than we, and are everywhere in bondage, yea, and for the great part captives unto us. They also be not clothed in sheep's skins; but maintain openly their faith, clean contrary to ours.

Sheep's clothing, what it meaneth. W. T. Matt. xxiv.

But what are these sheep's clothings? Truly the very name of Christ. For saith Christ, "There shall come many in my name, and deceive many." And besides that, they shall do miracles in Christ's name; as it followeth in the text, that they shall call Christ, Master, Master, and begin their sermon, saying: 'Our master Christ saith in such a chapter, Whatsoever ye bind upon earth shall be bound in heaven; see, friends, these be not our words, but our master Christ's.' And they shall do miracles in Christ's name thereto, to confirm the false doctrine which they preach in his name. O fearful and terrible judgment of Almighty God, and sentence of extreme rigorousness upon all that love not the truth, when it is preached them, that God, to avenge himself of their unkindness, shall send them so strong delusions, that doctrine should be preached unto them in the name of Christ, and made seem to follow out of his words, and be confirmed with miracles done in calling upon the name of Christ, to harden their hearts in the faith of lies, according to the prophecy of Paul to the Thessalonians, in the second epistle! (Thess. ii.)

Sheep's clothing. W. T.

Another of their sheep's coats is, that they shall in every sermon preach mightily against the scribes and Pharisees, against Faustus and Pelagius, with such like heretics; which yet never preached other doctrine than they themselves do. And more of their clothing is, they shall preach that Christ preached alms, prayer, and fasting; and profess obedience, poverty, and chastity; works that our Saviour Christ both preached and did. Finally, they be holy church, and cannot err.

Ravening wolves. W.T.

But they be within ravening wolves. They preach to other, "Steal not;" yet they themselves rob God of his honour, and take from him the praise and profit of all their doctrine and of all their works. They rob the law of God of her mighty power, wherewith she driveth all men to Christ; and make her so weak, that the feeble free-will of man is not able to wrestle with her, without calling to Christ for help.

They have robbed Christ of all his merits, and clothed

themselves therewith. They have robbed the soul of man of the bread of her life, the faith and trust in Christ's blood; and have fed her with the shales[1] and cods of the hope in their merits and confidence in their good works.

They have robbed the works commanded by God of the intent and purpose that they were ordained for. And with their obedience they have drawn themselves from under the obedience of all princes and temporal laws. With their poverty they have robbed all nations and kingdoms; and so with their wilful poverty have enriched themselves, and have made the commons poor. With their chastity they have filled all the world full of whores and sodomites, thinking to please God more highly with keeping of a whore than an honest chaste wife. If they say it is not truth, then all the world knoweth they lie; for if a priest marry an honest wife, they punish him immediately, and say he is an heinous heretic, as though matrimony were abominable: but if he keep a whore, then is he a good chaste child of their holy father the pope, whose ensample they follow; and I warrant him sing mass on the next day after, as well as he did before, without either persecution or excommunication: such are the laws of their unchaste (I would say their own chaste) father.

The obedience, poverty, and wilful chastity of our spiritualty. W. T.

If thou profess obedience, why runnest thou from father, mother, master, and ruler, which God biddeth thee to obey, to be a friar? If thou obey, why obeyest thou not the king and his law, by whom God defendeth thee both in life and goods, and all thy great possessions?

Obedience.

If thou profess poverty, what doest thou with the lands of gentlemen, squires, knights, barons, earls, and dukes? What, should a lord's brother be a beggar's servant? Or what, should a beggar ride with three or four score horses waiting on him? Is it meet that a man of noble birth, and the right heir of the lands which thou possessest, should be thine horsekeeper, thou being a beggar?

Poverty.

If ye profess chastity, why desire ye above all other men the company of women? What do ye with whores openly in many countries, and with secret dispensations to keep con-

Chastity.

[[1] It appears from a sentence which presently follows, where he uses the expression *shales without kernels*, that this word is equivalent to *shells*.]

cubines? Why corrupt ye so much other men's wives? And why be there so many sodomites among you?

Charity. Your charity is merciless to the rest of the world, to whom ye may give nought again; and only liberal to yourselves (as is the charity of thieves) thirty or forty of you together in one den: among which yet are not many that love three of his neighbours heartily.

Fasting. Your fasting maketh you as full and as fat as your hides can hold; beside that ye have a dispensation of your holy father for your fasting.

Prayer. Your prayer is but pattering without all affection; your singing is but roaring to stretch out your maws (as do your other gestures and rising at midnight), to make the meat sink to the bottom of the stomach, that he may have perfect digestion, and be ready to devour afresh against the next refection.

Thorns bear no figs. W. T. "Ye shall know them by their fruits." First, thorns bear no grapes, nor briers figs. Also, if thou see goodly blossoms in them, and thinkest there to have figs, grapes, or any fruit for the sustenance or comfort of man, go to them in time of need, and thou shalt find nought at all. Thou shalt find, 'Forsooth I have no goods, nor any thing proper, or that is mine own. It is the convent's. I were a thief if I gave it my father, whatsoever need he had. It is St Edmund's patrimony, St Alban's patrimony, St Edward's patrimony, the goods of holy church; it may not be minished, nor occupied upon lay and profane uses.' The king of the realm, for all that he defendeth them above all other, yet getteth he nought, what need soever he have, save then only when he must spend on their causes all that they give, with all that he can get beside of his poor commons. If the king will attempt to take aught from them, by the authority of his office, for the defence of the realm; or if any man will entreat them otherwise than they lust themselves, by what law or right it be, they turn to thorns and briers, and wax at once rougher than a hedgehog; and will sprinkle them with the holy water of their maledictions as thick as hail, and breathe out the lightning of excommunication upon them, and so consume them to powder.

The answer of cloisterers to such as shall desire relief at their hands.

A corrupt tree beareth no good fruit. W. T. Moreover "a corrupt tree can bear no good fruit:" that is, where they have fruit that seemeth to be good, go to and prove it, and thou shalt find it rotten, or the kernel eaten out, and that it is but as a hollow nut. For faith in Christ (that we and all our works, done within the compass of the law of God, be accepted to God for his sake) is the kernel, the sweetness, and the pleasant beauty of all our works in the sight of God; as it is written, "This is the work of God, that ye believe in him whom he hath sent." This faith is a work which God not only worketh in us, but also hath therein pleasure and delectation, and in all other for that faith's sake.

Faith is the kernel of all our good fruits. W. T.

John vi.

Faith is the life of man, as it is written, *Justus ex fide vivit*[1]; out of which life the pleasantness of all his works spring. As for an ensample, thou art a shoe-maker; which is a work within the laws of God; and sayest in thine heart, 'Lo, God, here I make a shoe as truly as I would for myself, to do my neighbour service, and to get my living in truth with the labour of mine hands, as thou commandest; and thank thee that thou hast given me this craft, and makest it lucky, that I get my living therewith; and am surely persuaded that both I and my work please thee, O Father, for thy Son Jesus' sake.' Lo, now this faith hath made this simple work pleasant in the sight of God.

Faith maketh the work good and acceptable. W. T.

Another ensample: thou takest a wife, and sayest, 'O Father, thou not only permittest this, but also commandest all that burn, and have their minds unquieted, to marry for fear of fornication, and so forth. And, Father, I promise thee to love this woman truly; and to care for her, and govern her after thy laws; and to be true to her, and to stand by her in all adversities; and to take in worth as well the evil as the good, and to bring up the fruit, that thou shalt give me of her, in thy fear, and teach it to know thee.'[2]

An example how thy work or deed may be pleasant, and acceptable before God.

The will that Abraham had to slay Isaac, and all that he did till he came at the very point to slay him, were good works; and so had been the slaying also. And Abraham was sure that he pleased God highly, and as well as in any other work, and had as deeply sinned if he had been disobedient therein, as though he had done any other cruel deed, forbidden by God. 'Yea, but shoe-making is not commanded

[1 The just liveth by faith.]

[2 The next illustration has been omitted; as turning upon a subject too indelicate for profitable contemplation.]

Handycrafts are the commandment of God. W. T.

by God.' Yes; and hath the promise of God annexed thereto. For God hath commanded me, for the avoiding of sin, to do my brethren service, and to live thereby, and to choose one estate or other. For if thou wouldest receive only of thy brethren, and do nought again, thou were a thief, and an extortioner, and a tyrant. And I choose shoe-making; or receive it at the obedience of mine elders. Now have I God's commandment to work therein truly; and his promise annexed thereto, that he will bless mine occupation, and make it lucky and fruitful, to bring me an honest living. Work I not now at God's commandment, and have his promise that it pleaseth him?

Note this also: First, my craft is God's commandment. Secondarily, I believe, and am sure, that my work pleaseth God for Christ's sake. Thirdly, my work is profitable unto my neighbour, and helpeth his necessity. Fourthly, I receive my reward of the hand of God with thanks; and work, surely certified that I please God in my work through Christ, and that God will give me my daily bread thereby.

But if thou examine their doctrine, thou shalt find that this faith is away in all their fruits; and therefore are they worm-eaten, and shales without kernels.

The Jews and Turks give alms as we do, yet for lack of faith it is abominable.

Note again: the Turks and Jews give alms as well as we, and as much, and yet abominable, for lack of faith and knowledge of the true intent. What saith the text? "He that receiveth a prophet in the name of a prophet, shall have the reward of a prophet." That is, because thou aidest him in preaching of Christ's word, thou shalt be partaker with him and have the same reward. And, "He that receiveth a disciple in the name of a disciple, shall have," &c. And, "He that giveth one of these little ones but a cup of cold water for my name's sake, shall have his reward." If a king minister his kingdom in the faith of this name, because his subjects be his brethren and the price of Christ's blood, he pleaseth God highly; and if this faith be not there, it pleaseth him not. And if I sew a shoe truly, in the faith of his name, to do my brother service, because he is the price of Christ's blood, it pleaseth God. Thus is faith the goodness of all works.

God is as well pleased when we thankfully receive

Finally, when God giveth, and I receive with thanks, is not God as well pleased as when I give for his sake, and he receiveth? A true friend is as glad to do his friend a good turn, as to receive a good turn. When the father giveth his son a new coat, and saith, 'Am not I a good father, and wilt not thou love me again, and do what I bid thee?' and the boy receiveth it with thanks, and saith, 'Yea;' and is glad and proud thereof; doth not the father rejoice as much now in the lad, as another time when the lad doth whatsoever it be at his father's commandment? But the false prophets do well to paint God after the likeness of their own visenomy[1]: glad when he receiveth, yea, when they receive in his name; but sour, grudging, and evil content when he giveth again. But thou pleasest God when thou askest in faith, and when thou receivest with thanks, and when thou rejoicest in his gifts, and lovest him again, to keep his commandments, and the appointment and covenant made between him and thee.

his benefits, as when we do give for his sake.

And for a conclusion, besides that they expel faith, which is the goodness of all works, they set up works of their own making; to destroy the works of God, and to be holier than God's works, to the despising of God's works, and to make God's works vile.

Hypocrites extol their own works, to destroy the works of God.

With their chastity they destroy the chastity that God ordained, and only requireth. With their obedience they destroy the obedience that God ordained in this world, and desireth no other. With their poverty they destroy the poverty of the spirit, which Christ taught only; which is, only not to love worldly goods. With their fast they destroy the fast which God commandeth, that is, a perpetual soberness to tame the flesh. With their pattering prayer they destroy the prayer taught by God, which is either thanks, or desiring help, with faith and trust that God heareth me.

Their holiness is to forbid that God ordained to be received with thanksgiving, as meat and matrimony. And their own works they maintain, and let God's decay. Break theirs, and they persecute to the death: but break God's, and they either look through the fingers, or else give thee a flap with a fox-tail, for a little money. There is none order among them that is so perfect, but that they have a prison more cruel than any jail of thieves and murderers. And if one of

The holiness of hypocrites, wherein it is. W. T.

[1 Physiognomy.]

their brethren commit fornication or adultery in the world, he finisheth his penance therein in three weeks or a month; and then is sent to another place of the same religion[1]. But if he attempt to put off the holy habit, he cometh never out, and is so straitly dieted thereto, that it is marvel if he live a year; beside other cruel murder that hath been found among them: and yet is this shameful dieting of theirs murder cruel enough.

Ask the Austin Friars, why they murdered one of their fellows at London. W. T.

Be not deceived with visors[2], nor yet with miracles. But go to, and judge their works; for "the spiritual judgeth all things," saith Paul. Who is that spiritual? Not such as we now call men of holy church; but all that have the true interpretation of the law written in their hearts, the right faith of Christ, and the true intent of works, which God biddeth us work: he is spiritual, and judgeth all things, and is judged of no man.

1 Cor. ii. Who is the spiritualty.

Not all that say to me, Lord, Lord, shall enter into the kingdom of heaven; but he that fulfilleth the will of my Father which is in heaven. Many will say unto me at that day, Lord, did we not prophesy in thy name? and in thy name cast out devils? and did we not in thy name many miracles? Then will I confess unto them, I never knew you; depart from me, ye workers of iniquity.

This doubling of "Lord" hath vehemency; and betokeneth that they which shall be excluded are such as think themselves better and perfecter than other men, and to deserve heaven with holy works, not for themselves only, but also for other. And by that[3] they prophesied, by which thou mayest understand the interpreting of scripture; and by that they cast out devils, and did miracles in Christ's name, (and for all that, they are yet workers of wickedness, and do not the will of the Father which is in heaven,) it is plain that they be false prophets; and even the same of which Christ warned before.

And now, forasmuch as Christ and his apostles warn us

[1 Monastic order.]

[2 L. has *visures*, i.e. *visors*, and this agrees with what follows below: but D. has *visions*.]

[3 *By that*, or as we should say, *Inasmuch as*. The same idiom occurs in our 13th Article, "For that they are not done."]

that such shall come, and describe us the fashions of their visors, (Christ's name, holy church, holy fathers, and fifteen hundred years, with scripture and miracles,) and command us to turn our eyes from their visors, and consider their fruits, and cut them up, and look within whether they be found in the core and kernel or no, and give us a rule to try them by; is it excuse good enough to say, 'God will not let so great a multitude err; I will follow the most part, and believe as my fathers did, and as the preachers teach, and will not busy myself: choose they, the fault is theirs, and not ours; God shall not lay it to our charge if we err?'

Ignorance excuseth not, if we will not see. W. T.

Where such words be, there are the false prophets already. For where no love to the truth is, there are the false prophets. And where such words be, there to be no love to the truth, is plain; ergo, where such words be, there be the false prophets in their full swing, by Paul's rule (2 Thess. ii.). Another conclusion: where no love to the truth is, there be false prophets; the greatest of the world have least love to the truth: ergo, the false prophets be the chaplains of the greatest, which may with the sword compel the rest; as the kings of Israel compelled to worship the golden calves. And by false prophets understand false teachers, as Peter calleth them, and wicked expounders of the scripture.

False prophets, how to know where they be. W. T.

2 Thess. ii.

Whosoever heareth these words of me and doeth them, I will liken him unto a wise man that built his house upon a rock: and there fell a rain, and the floods came, and the winds blew, and beat upon that house; but it fell not, for it was grounded upon a rock. And all that hear of me these words, and do them not, shall be likened unto a foolish man, that built his house upon the sand: and there fell a rain, and the floods came, and the winds blew, and dashed upon that house, and it fell; and the fall thereof was great.

Christ hath two sorts of hearers, of which neither nother[4] do thereafter. The one will be saved by faith of their own making, without works; the other with works of their own making, without faith. The first are those voluptuous, which have yielded themselves up to sin, saying, 'Tush, God is merciful, and Christ died for us; that must save us only,

Believers without works, and workers without faith, are built on sand. W. T.

[[4] D. has *neither of them;* but L. and a small octavo edition, without date (probably by Copland, about 1540), have *neither nother;* i. e. *neither the one nor the other.*]

for we cannot but sin without resistance.' The second are the hypocrites; which will deserve all with their own imagined works only. And of faith they have no other experience, save that it is a little meritorious where it is painful to be believed: as that Christ was born of a virgin, and that he came not out the way that other children do;—fie, no, that were a great inconvenience: but above, under her arm, and yet made no hole, though he had a very natural body, and as other men have;—and that there is no bread in the sacrament, nor wine, though the five wits say all yea. And the meritorious pain of this belief is so heavy to them, that except they had feigned them a thousand wise similitudes and lousy likenesses, and as many mad reasons to stay them withal, and to help to captivate their understanding, they were like to cast all off their backs. And the only refuge of a great many, to keep in that faith, is to cast it out of their minds, and not to think upon it: as though they forgive not, yet if they put the displeasure out of their minds, and think not of it till a good occasion be given to avenge it, they think they love their neighbour well enough all the while, and be in good charity.

The papists have that faith in their own works which they should have in Jesus Christ.

And the faith of the best of them is but like their faith in other worldly stories. But the faith, which is trust and confidence to be saved, and to have their sins forgiven by Christ, which was so born, have they not at all: that faith have they in their own works only. But the true hearers understand the law as Christ interpreteth it here, and feel thereby their righteous damnation; and run to Christ for succour, and for remission of all their sins that are past, and for all the sin which chance, through infirmities, shall compel them to do, and for remission of that the law is too strong for their weak nature.

Faith, what it breedeth.

Love.

And upon that they consent to the law, love it, and profess it, to fulfil it to the uttermost of their power, and then go to and work. Faith, or confidence in Christ's blood, without help, and before the works of the law, bringeth all manner of remission of sins, and satisfaction. Faith is mother of love; faith accompanieth love in all her works, to fulfil as much as there lacketh, in our doing the law, of that perfect love which Christ had to his Father and us, in his fulfilling of the law for us. Now, when we be reconciled, then is love and faith together our righteousness, our keeping the law, our continuing, our proceeding forward in the grace which we stand in, and our bringing to the everlasting saving and everlasting life. And the works be esteemed of God according to the love of the heart. If the works be great, and love little and cold, then the works be regarded thereafter of God. If the works be small, and love much and fervent, the works be taken for great of God.

And it came to pass, that when Jesus had ended these sayings, the people were astonished at his doctrine: for he taught them as one having power, and not as the scribes.

The scribes and Pharisees had thrust up the sword of the word of God into a scabbard or sheath of glosses, and therein had knit it fast, that it could neither stick[1] nor cut; teaching dead works without faith and love, which are the life and the whole goodness of all works, and the only thing why they please God. And therefore their audience abode ever carnal and fleshly-minded, without faith to God and love to their neighbours.

Christ's words were spirit and life: that is to say, they ministered spirit and life, and entered into the heart, and grated on the conscience; and, through preaching the law, made the hearers perceive their duties; even what love they owed to God, and what to man, and the right damnation of all them that had not the love of God and man written in their hearts; and, through preaching of faith, made all that consented to the law of God feel the mercy of God in Christ, and certified them of their salvation. For "the word of God is a two-edged sword, that pierceth and divideth the spirit and soul of man asunder." A man before the preaching of God's word is but one man, all flesh; the soul consenting unto the lusts of the flesh, to follow them. But the sword of the word of God, where it taketh effect, divideth a man in two, and setteth him at variance against his own self; the flesh haling one way, and the spirit drawing another; the flesh raging to follow lusts, and the spirit calling back again, to follow the law and will of God. A man, all the while

John vi.

Heb. iv.

The word of God, where it taketh effect, divideth a man into two parts; that is, causeth the flesh to hold one way, and the spirit to draw another.

[1 Old English for *pierce*.]

he consenteth to the flesh, and before he be born again in Christ, is called soul[1] or carnal: but when he is renewed in Christ through the word of life, and hath the love of God and of his neighbour, and the faith of Christ written in his heart, he is called spirit or spiritual[2]. The Lord of all mercy send us preachers with power; that is to say, true expounders of the word of God, and speakers to the heart of man; and deliver us from scribes, Pharisees, hypocrites, and all false prophets! Amen.

[1 ψυχικόν. 1 Cor. xv. 46.]
[2 πνευματικόν. Id. ibid.]

THE

EXPOSITION

OF THE

FIRST EPISTLE OF SAINT JOHN,

SET FORTH BY

M. WILLIAM TYNDALE,

IN THE YEAR OF OUR LORD 1531. SEPTEMB.

EXPOSITION

OF

THE FIRST EPISTLE OF SAINT JOHN.

[An ancient edition of the following exposition is preserved in the library of St Paul's Cathedral, and has been collated for the present editor by George Offor, Esq. Its peculiar readings will be distinguished by the letters P. C. L.; whilst those found in Day's less ancient edition of Tyndale's works will be denoted by the letter D. In the former, Tyndale is found to have systematically avoided giving the Roman pontiff the title of pope; but in Day's reprint his editor John Foxe has with like regularity substituted *pope* for the words 'bishop of Rome,' or for any other periphrasis to the same purport. Another difference is, that in the older copy the relative pronoun *which* is frequently found with *the* prefixed; whilst Day has modernised this idiom by omitting *the*. In the present edition Tyndale's manner of designating the pope will be restored; but the obsolete idiom connected with *which* will be relinquished, after Day's example; and these two repeatedly recurring variations will not be farther noticed at the foot of the page.

But, besides these unimportant differences, the volume in the cathedral library contains an exposition of the second and third epistles of St John, printed on the same paper and in the same type, and followed by a table, or index, with references to the expositions of all the three, as to one work; whilst the want of a title-page prevents us from knowing whether its editor announced the whole as Tyndale's, or informed the public that the exposition of the two less epistles had been 'added by another hand.' Tyndale himself has said in his prologue, 'I have taken in hand to interpret *this* epistle,' as though he was not intending to expound the other two; and Sir Thomas More, in the preface to his 'Confutacyon' (date 1532), has said, 'Then have we from Tyndale the first epistle of St John, in such wise expounded that I dare say that blessed apostle, rather than his holy words were in such a sense believed of all Christian people, had lever his epistle had never been put in writing.' Day's edition of Tyndale was compiled rather more than 40 years after he and More had spoken thus; and in it the reprint of the exposition of the first epistle is unaccompanied by any notice of the existence of an exposition of the other two by Tyndale: so that Foxe either did not know of its existence, or did not believe it to be Tyndale's. Indeed every known averment of his having composed an exposition of all St John's epistles is traceable to bishop Bale's introducing the words *In epistolas Joannis* into his enumeration of Tyndale's works, in the *Scriptorum illustr. Maj. Britanniæ Catalogus*.

As however Tyndale might have composed a continuation of his exposition of the first epistle, between 1531 and his death, though he had not contemplated so doing; and as Bale's frequent inaccuracy ought not to prevent his testimony from having considerable weight, inasmuch as he was nearly 30 years of age when Tyndale suffered martyrdom; it has been the present editor's duty to give the exposition of the two less epistles a careful examination. But having done so, he would not think himself justified in reproducing it, either as Tyndale's work, or as too valuable to be left in obscurity. The text of those two epistles, incorporated into their exposition, is indeed nearly identical with Tyndale's, having only such occasional verbal changes as he has introduced into the text in his other expositions; and one of those changes, viz. that of *senior* into *elder*, is such as he had, in 1530, announced his intention of making. But when sir T. More's cavils drew from him that announcement, Tyndale added, 'He rebuketh me also that I render this Greek word *Agape* into *love*, and not rather into *charity*. Verily charity is no known English in that sense which *Agape* requireth.' These words are followed by a whole section of remarks on the impropriety of using the word *charity*, where there is occasion to speak of that *love* which the scriptures commend. (Answ. to sir T. More's Dial.). But the author of the exposition of the two less epistles does not get through his second paragraph before he uses *charity* twice for *love*, in the very manner to which Tyndale thus objected: and short as the whole exposition is, he does not conclude it without employing the same word three times more, where Tyndale would have considered the word *love* as more plain English, and sufficient for expressing what was meant to be said.

There are also such ungrammatical and ill-constructed sentences in the exposition of the two less epistles, as Tyndale was too skilful a writer to have penned. For example, in explaining verse 12 of epistle III, the expositor has expressed himself as follows: 'It must undoubtedly have been a man of marvellous integrity and unblameable, this Demetrius, unto whom all the congregation of good men, yea, and the truth also, beside that the apostle John, a man without guile, and that had not learned to flatter, gave such verdict.' But besides these discrepancies between his words and style, and those of Tyndale, this expositor has indulged in such fancies as are not at all in harmony with Tyndale's manner of commenting upon the scriptures. Thus on verse 1 of epistle II, he says, 'John calleth the church or congregation a lady, because she is the bride of the Lord Jesus; and the members of the church he calleth children, remaining so still, in comparing and alluding.' And in concluding his exposition, he says, of both epistles, 'The shortness hath a wondrous favour; and the briefness hath also mysteries.' If Tyndale had written upon these epistles, and so thought, he would have told his readers why he imagined there was a mystery in the brevity, and what he supposed that mystery to mean. In another place, on ver. 10 of Epist. III, the expositor has said that 'it is the duty of true herdsmen, to forgive nought.' It is incredible that Tyndale would have expressed himself so rashly, or inculcated a rule of proceeding so contrary to plain scripture.]

THE PROLOGUE.

¶ Except a man have the profession of his baptism in his heart, he cannot understand the scripture.

We must first learn the profession of our baptism. Ant. ed.

As a man can by no means read, except he be first taught the letters of the cross row, even so it is unpossible for a man, of whatsoever degree or name he be of, to understand aught in the scripture unto the honour of God and health of his soul, except he be first taught the profession of his baptism, and have it also written in his heart.

The profession of our baptism, what it is.

Which profession standeth in two things: the one is the knowledge of the law[1] of God, understanding it spiritually, as Christ expoundeth it Matt. v. vi. and vii. chapters, so that the root and life of all laws is[2] this: Love thy Lord God with all thine heart, all thy soul, and all thy might; and thy neighbour as thyself, for his sake: and that love only is the fulfilling of the law (as Paul teacheth); and that whatsoever deed we do, and not of that love, that same fulfilleth no law in the sight of God.

Gospel.

And the other is, to know the promises of mercy which are in our Saviour Christ; understanding them also purely without all leaven, after the mercifullest fashion as scripture expresseth[3] them, and after all fatherly love and kindness of God, unto all that repent toward the law, and believe in Christ.

All our sins for Jesus Christ's sake, and for his death and passion, are clearly forgiven. Ant. ed.

And to have this profession written in thine heart is to consent unto the law that it is righteous and good, and to love it in thine heart, and to submit thyself thereunto for to learn it, and to rule and square all thy deeds thereby; and then to believe in Christ, that for his sake all thy sins, which thou diddest before the knowledge of this profession, are forgiven thee clearly, both *a pœna et culpa*[4], to use the Romish[5]

[1 So P. C. L., in D. the words *of the law* are wanting.]
[2 So P. C. L., D. has *be.*]
[3 So P. C. L., but D. has *soundeth.*]
[4 From the penalty and guilt.]
[5 So P. C. L., but D. has *pope's.*]

terms; and that for none other satisfaction to God-ward than Christ's blood; and even so, that all the sin which we do after this knowledge, either of chance, ignorance, infirmity, negligence, or provoked and overcome of the flesh, is forgiven us likewise, both *pœna et culpa,* through repentance and faith in Christ, without our satisfaction of works to God-ward.

Every Christian man must reconcile himself unto his brother. Ant. ed.

Notwithstanding we, being all sons of one God, and servants of one Christ, must agree among ourselves; and he that hath offended must meekly knowledge his fault, and offer himself to make amends unto the utmost of his power; and if he have not wherewith, ask forgiveness for Christ's sake, and[6] the other is bound to forgive him. Neither, without reconciling himself unto his brother, may any man be at the first received unto the profession of Christ's faith, nor continue therein, nor be received in again, if he be for his open offences put thereout. For how can a man love his neighbour as well as himself, and be sorry that he hath hurt him, except he should offer himself to make amends?

The right penance is repentance of sin and amendment of life. Ant. ed.

All our life must tend to this end, to tame our flesh and serve our neighbour. Ant. ed.

And we must from henceforth walk in the life of penance, (if ye will have it so called,) and after the doctrine of Christ every man tame his flesh with prayer, fasting, and the continual meditations of Christ's penance and passions for us, and of the holy saints, and with such abstinence, and kind of living, as every man thinketh most meet for his complexion; the younger confessing their infirmities to the elder, discreeter, and better learned, and asking their advice and wholesome counsel for the repressing of their diseases; but all to tame the flesh, and to serve thy neighbour, without any superstitious mind.

Faith in Christ's blood, with a repentant heart, is the only satisfaction that we can make towards God. Ant. ed.

But to God-ward is there no satisfaction, save faith in Christ's blood out of a repenting heart. For our outward deeds cannot be referred unto God, to do him service in his own person, and to help him, or make him better therewith. We can do no more with them, were they never so perfect, and done with all love, than satisfy the law for the present time, and do our duty unto our neighbours, and tame our own flesh; but not to make satisfaction to God for sin that is once past. The sin that is once committed must God forgive freely, of a fatherly love, for Christ's sake.

[6 So P. C. L., in D. *and* is wanting.]

When God visiteth us with sickness, poverty, or whatsoever adversity it be, he doth it not of a tyrannous mind, to satisfy his lust in our suffering of evil, to make satisfaction for the sin that is past, of which we repent and be sorry; but of a fatherly love, to make us know ourselves and feel his mercy, and to tame our[1] flesh, and to keep us from sinning again: as no natural father punisheth his child because he delighteth in tormenting of him, to take satisfaction for the sin that is past; but first teacheth kindly, and suffereth, and forgiveth once or twice; and then at the last, when he seeth the body so wanton, that the child cannot continue in the right way for the rage of wild lusts, he beateth him[2], to subdue the flesh only, and to tame it, that the doctrine of the father may have her due course in the heart of the child, and should not be choked with lusts and concupiscences of our wicked nature[3].

The father of love correcteth the child. Ant. ed.

Even so is it of God: if any of his children, that have professed his law and the faith of our Saviour, be negligent to tame his flesh with prayer, fasting, and good deeds after the doctrine of Christ, he will surely scourge him, to bring him into the right way again, and to keep him, that the doctrine of his soul's health perish not in him. But he taketh not his mercy from us, nor thinketh on the sin that is past, after that we repent and be full converted; but absolveth us both *a pœna et culpa* for Christ's sake; and is as mighty and as merciful to do it for Christ's sake, as the bishop of Rome for money; besides that he hath promised mercifully so to do.

God as a loving father careth for us, and gently correcteth us to keep us in the right way. Ant. ed.

¶ The knowledge of our baptism is the key and the light of the scripture.

And again, as he which knoweth his letters well, and can spell perfectly, cannot but read if he be diligent; and as he which hath clear eyes without impediment or let, and walketh thereto in the light and open day, cannot but see, if he attend and take heed; even so whosoever hath the profession of baptism written in his heart, cannot but understand the scripture, if he exercise himself therein, and compare one

To understand our baptism is to understand the law and the gospel. Ant. ed.

[[1] So D., but P. C. L. has *the* instead of *our*.]
[[2] So P. C. L., in D. *him* is wanting.]
[[3] The last six words are in P. C. L., but not in D.]

place to another, and mark the manner of speech, and ask here and there the meaning of a sentence of them that be better exercised[4].

For as the doctrine which we should be taught before we were baptized, and for lack of age is deferred unto the years of discretion, is the key that bindeth and looseth, locketh and unlocketh, the conscience of all sinners; even so that lesson, where it is understood, is only the key that openeth all the scripture, and even the whole scripture in itself, gathered together in a narrow compass, and brought into a compendiousness. And till thou be taught that lesson, that thine heart feel the sweetness of it, the scripture is locked and shut up from thee, and so dark that thou couldest not understand it, though Peter, Paul, or Christ himself did expound it unto thee; no more than a blind man can see, though thou set a candle before him, or shewedst him the sun, or pointedst with thy finger unto that thou wouldest have him look upon.

The key and light of the scripture W. T.

How the scripture is locked up from our understanding. W. T.

Now we be all baptized; but, alas! not one, from the highest to the lowest, ever taught the profession or meaning thereof. And therefore we remain all blind generally, as well our great rabbins for all their high learning which they seem to have, as the lay people. Yea, and so much the more blind are our great clerks, that where the lay people, for a great number of them, are taught nothing[5] at all, they be all wrong taught, and the doctrine of their baptism is all corrupt unto them with the leaven of false glosses, ere they come to read the scripture; so that the light which they bring with them, to understand the scripture withal, is utter darkness, and as contrary unto the scripture as the devil unto Christ: by reason whereof the scripture is locked up and become so dark unto them, that they grope for the door, and can find no way in; and is become a maze unto them, in which they wander as in a mist, or (as we say) led by Robin Goodfellow, that they cannot come to the right way, no, though they turn their caps; and the brightness thereof hath blinded their eyes with malice, so that though they believe not the scripture to be false, yet they persecute the right understanding thereof, and cannot believe it true in the plain sense, which it speaketh

If we be not taught by God, we do but wander clean out of the way. W. T.

[[4] In P. C. L. the words *than he is* are added here.]
[[5] So P. C. L., but D. has *naught.*]

to them in. It is become a turn-again lane unto them, which they cannot go through, nor make three lines agree together. And finally, the sentences of the scripture are nothing but very riddles unto them, at the which they cast as the blind man doth at the crow, and expound by guess, an hundred doctors an hundred ways; and one man in twenty sermons alleging one text after twenty fashions, having no sure doctrine to cleave unto; and all for lack of the right knowledge of the profession of our baptism.

¶ He that hath the profession of his baptism written in his heart can be no heretic.

He that understandeth the profession of his baptism can be no heretic. Ant. ed.

Another conclusion is this: as he which ever creepeth along by the ground, and never climbeth, cannot fall from on[1] high; even so no man, that hath the profession of his baptism written in his heart, can stumble in the scripture, and fall unto heresies, or become a maker of division and sects, and a defender of wild and vain opinions. For the whole and only cause of heresies and sects is pride. Now the law of God, truly interpreted, robbeth all them in whose hearts it is written, and maketh them as bare as Job, of all things whereof a man can or may[2] be moved to pride. And on the other side, they have utterly forsaken themselves, with all their high learning and wisdom, and are become the servants of Christ only, which hath bought them with his blood; and have promised in their hearts unfeignedly to follow him, and to take him only for the author of their religion, and his doctrine only for their wisdom and learning, and to maintain it in word and deed, and to[3] keep it pure, and to build no strange doctrine thereupon, and to be at the highest never, but fellow with their brethren, and in that fellowship to wax ever lower and lower, and every day more servant than another[4] unto his weaker brethren, after the example and image of Christ, and after his commandment and ordinance, and not in feigned words of the pope.

The scripture teacheth lowliness, and hateth pride. Ant. ed.

The scripture maketh no heretics. W. T.

This be[5] said because of them that say that the scripture maketh men heretics, and corrupteth with false opinions,

[1 So P. C. L., but D. has *an*.]
[2 So P. C. L., but in D. *or may* is wanting.]
[3 P. C. L. has *to*, but Day *so*.]
[4 So P. C. L., but D. has *other*.]
[5 So P. C. L.: D. has *he said*.]

contrary unto the profession of their baptism; and the light wherewith they should expound the scripture is turned into darkness in their hearts, and the door of the scripture locked, and the wells stopped up ere they come at it.

And therefore, because their darkness cannot comprehend the light of scripture, as it is written, "The light shined in darkness, but the darkness could not comprehend it;" they turn it into blind riddles, and read it without understanding, as lay-men do our lady matins, or as it were Merlin's prophecies, having[6] ever their minds upon their heresies. And when they come to a place that soundeth like, there they wrest, and wring out wonderful expositions, to stablish their heresies withal[7]. Is it not a great blindness to say in the beginning of all together, that the whole scripture is false in the literal sense, and killeth the soul? Which pestilent heresy to prove, they abuse the text of Paul saying, "The letter killeth;" because that text was become a riddle unto them, and they understood it not: when Paul by this word *letter* understood the law given by Moses to condemn all consciences, and to rob them of all righteousness, to compel them unto the promises of mercy that are in Christ.

John i.

If God lighten not our hearts, we read the scripture in vain. Ant. ed.

The law condemneth, to drive us to faith in Christ's death. Ant. ed.

Heresy springeth not of the scripture, no more than darkness of the sun; but it[8] is a dark cloud that springeth out of the blind hearts of hypocrites, and covereth the face of the scripture, and blindeth their eyes, that they cannot behold the bright beams of the scripture.

Heresy springeth out of the hearts of hypocrites. Ant. ed.

The whole[9] sum then of all together is this: If our hearts were taught the appointment made between God and us in Christ's blood, when we were baptized, we had the key to open the scripture, and light to see and perceive the true meaning of it, and the scripture should be easy to understand. And because we be not taught that profession, is the cause why the scripture is so dark, and so far passing our capacity. And the cause why our expositions are heresies, is because we be wrong taught, and corrupt with false opinions beforehand, and made heretics ere we come at the scripture, and have

[6 So P. C. L., but D. wants *having*, and has *are* after minds.]

[7 In D. Tyndale's last remark is followed by a jocular illustration, for which there is no authority in the older edition.]

[8 So P. C. L.: in D. *it* is wanting]

[9 So P. C. L., but D. interposes *and.*]

corrupt it, and it not us; as the taste of the sick maketh wholesome and well-seasoned meat bitter, wearish, and unsavoury. Nevertheless yet the scripture abideth pure in herself and bright, so that he which is sound in the faith shall at once perceive that the judgment of the heretics is corrupt in their expositions, as an whole man doth feel at once, even with smelling to the meat, that the taste of the sick is infected. And with the scripture shall they ever improve heresies and false expositions: for the scripture purgeth herself, even as the water once in the year casteth all filthiness unto the sides of it[1]. Which to be true ye see by the authority of Paul, saying, "All the scripture was given of God by inspiration, and is good to teach withal, to improve," and so forth; and by the example of Christ and the apostles, how they confounded the Jews with the same scripture which they had corrupt, and understood them amiss after their own darkness; and as ye see by the example of us now also, how we have manifestly improved the hypocrites in an hundred texts which they had corrupt to prove their false opinion brought in besides the scripture, and have driven them off; and they be fled, and openly confess unto their shame, that they have no scripture, and sing another song, and say they received them by the mouth of the apostles. Unto which stopping of theirs[2], I answer here grossly, seeing they are answered before; that as he were a fool, which would trust him to tell his money in his absence, that hath picked his purse before his face; even so, sith ye have corrupt the open scripture before our eyes, and are[3] taken with the maner[4], that ye cannot deny, we

He that is sound in faith shall easily attain to the true sense of the scripture. Ant. ed.

Tim. iii.

The papists' unwritten verities are not to be credited. Ant. ed.

[1 So P. C. L. edition: D. wants *of it.*]

[2 So P. C. L., but D. has *oyster* instead of *of theirs.*]

[3 So P. C. L., but D. wants *are.*]

[4 In Numbers v. 13, our authorised version has introduced the words 'with the manner,' in italics, to fill out the brief Hebrew expression 'she be taken.' Todd observes (Johnson's Dictionary), that in our old law-books *manner* is written *mainour* in this phrase, from the French *manier*, to seize with the hand. He adds that in our old Norman statutes it is written according to some, 'Pris ove manour,' and explained, 'taken with the goods in the hand.' But Burn, enlarging on 3 Ed. I. c. 15, says, 'Taken with the mainer, i. e. with the thing stolen, as it were, in his hand.' Burn's Justice, vol. I. p. 138. In Day's edition of Tyndale it is spelt *maner;* but so also is the word *manner*, when used in its ordinary sense.]

were mad to believe that which hath lien fifteen hundred years, as ye say, in your rotten maws, should now be wholesome for us; ye have chewed and mingled it with your poison spittle. Can ye bear us in hand, and persuade us, think ye, with your sophistry, to believe that ye should minister your secret traditions without ground truly, when we see you minister the open scripture falsely? Can ye bewitch our wits with your poetry, to believe that ye should minister your secret traditions for our profit, when we see you corrupt the open scripture to the loss of our souls for your profit? Nay, it is an hundred times more likely that ye should be falser in secret things than in open. And therefore in the very sacraments, which the scripture testifieth that Christ himself ordained them, we must have an eye unto your hand, how ye minister them. And as we restore the scripture unto her right understanding from your false glosses, even so deliver we the sacraments and ceremonies unto their right use from your abuse. And that must we do with the scripture; which can corrupt no man that cometh thereto with a meek spirit, seeking there only to fashion himself like Christ, according to the profession and vow of our baptism: but contrariwise, he shall there find the mighty power of God, to alter him, and change him in the inner man, a little and little in process, until he be full shapen after the image of our Saviour, in knowledge, and love of all truth, and power to work thereafter.

The papists have corrupted the scripture, and abused the sacraments. Ant. ed.

Finally then, forasmuch as the scripture is the light and life of God's elect, and that mighty power wherewith God createth them, and shapeth them, after the similitude, likeness, and very fashion of Christ; and therefore sustenance, comfort, and strength to courage them, that they may stand fast, and endure, and merrily bear their souls' health, wherewith the lusts of the flesh are[5] subdued and killed, and the spirit mollified and made soft, to receive the print of the image of our Saviour Jesus: and forasmuch[6] as the scripture is so pure of itself, that it can corrupt no man, but the wicked only, which are infect beforehand, and, ere they come at it, corrupt it with the heresies that[7] they bring with them:

The scripture is the life of God's elect. Ant. ed.

[5 So P. C. L., but D. wants *are*.]
[6 So P. C. L., but D. wants *for*.]
[7 So P. C. L., but D. wants *that*.]

Hypocrites say that the scripture maketh heretics. Ant. ed.

and forasmuch as the complaint of the hypocrites, that the scripture maketh heretics, is vain and feigned; and the reasons wherewith they would prove that the lay people ought not to read the scripture, are[1] false, wicked, and the fruit of rotten trees: therefore are they faithful servants of Christ, and faithful ministers and dispensers of his doctrine, and true-hearted toward their brethren, which have given themselves up into the hand of God, and put themselves in jeopardy of all persecution, their very life despised, and have translated the scripture purely and with good conscience, submitting themselves, and desiring them that can to amend their translation, or (if it please them) to translate it themselves after their best manner, yea, and let them sew to their glosses, as many as they think they can make cleave thereto, and then put other men's translation out of the way.

The translation of the scripture is not sufficient only, but it must be well taught, that the people may have the true sense. Ant. ed.

Howbeit, though God hath so wrought with them that a great part is translated; yet, as it is not enough that the father and the mother have both begotten the child and brought it into this world, except they care for it and bring it up, till it can help itself; even so it is not enough to have translated, though it were the whole scripture into the vulgar and common tongue, except we also brought again the light to understand it by, and expel that dark cloud which the hypocrites have spread over the face of the scripture, to blind the right sense and true meaning thereof. And therefore are there[2] divers introductions ordained for you, to teach you the profession of your baptism, the only light of the scripture; one upon the epistle of Paul to the Romans, and another called "The Pathway into the Scripture." And for the same cause have I taken in hand to interpret this epistle of St John the evangelist to edify the layman, and to teach him how to read the scripture, and what to seek therein; and that he may have to answer the hypocrites, and to stop their mouths withal.

Introductions made to bring you to the true understanding of the scripture. Ant. ed.

And first, understand that all the epistles that the apostles wrote are the gospel of Christ, though all that is the gospel be not an epistle. It is called a gospel, that is to say, glad tidings, because it is an open preaching of Christ; and an epistle, because it is sent as a letter, or a bill, to them that are absent.

[1 P. C. L. has *is*.] [2 So P. C. L. Day has *at their*.]

THE EXPOSITION

OF THE

FIRST EPISTLE OF ST JOHN.

Here beginneth the first epistle of St John.

THE FIRST CHAPTER.

THAT which was from the beginning declare we unto you, which we have heard, which we have seen with our eyes, which we looked upon, and our hands have handled of the word of life. For the life appeared, and we have seen, and bear witness, and shew unto you that everlasting life, which was with the Father, and appeared unto us. 1 John i.

IN that St John saith, "The thing which was from the beginning," and "the everlasting life that was with the Father," he witnesseth that Christ is very God; as he doth in the beginning of his gospel, saying: "The word," or the thing[3], "was at the beginning, and the thing was with God, and that thing was God, and all things were made by it." St John witnesseth that Christ is very God. Ant. ed.

And when he saith, "Which we heard, and saw with our eyes, and our hands handled" him; he testifieth that Christ is very man also; as he doth in the beginning of his gospel, saying: "The word," or that thing, "was made flesh," that is, became man. And thus we have in plain and open words a manifest article of our faith, that our Saviour Christ is very God and very man. That Christ is very man. Ant. ed.

Which article whosoever not only believeth, but also believeth in it, the same is the son of God, and hath everlasting life in him, and shall never come into condemnation: as it is written, John i. "He gave them power to be the sons of God, in that they believed in his name[4];" and John iii., "He that believeth in the Son hath everlasting life;" and a little before in the said chapter, "He that believeth in him shall not be condemned." And to believe in the words of this article is that eating of Christ's flesh, and drinking his blood, He that believeth that Christ is the son of God, and also very man, hath everlasting life. Ant ed. John i. John iii. John vi.

[3 As the Hebrew word דָּבָר means alike *word* and *thing*, Tyndale was led to consider the apostle as using λόγος for its equivalent.]

[4 So Tyndale's translation of John i. 12.]

of which is spoken, John vi. "The words which I speak are spirit and life, and the flesh profiteth not at all;" meaning of the fleshly eating of his body, and fleshly drinking of his blood. There is therefore great difference between believing that there is a God, and that Christ is God and man; and to believe in God and Christ, God and man, and in the promises of mercy that are in him. The first is common to good and bad, and unto the devils also, and is called an historical faith and belief[1]. The second is proper unto the sons of God, and is their life, as it is written, "The righteous liveth by faith;" that is, in putting his trust, confidence, and whole hope in the goodness, mercy and help of God, in all adversities, bodily and ghostly, and all temptations, and even in sin and hell[2], how deep soever he be fallen therein.

To believe in Christ. W. T.

To believe that Christ is God and man is to put all our trust, hope, and confidence in him. Ant. ed.

But as he which feeleth not his disease can long for no health, even so it is impossible for any man to believe in Christ's blood, except Moses have had him first in cure, and with his law have robbed him of his righteousness, and condemned him unto everlasting death, and have shewed him under what damnation they are in by birth in Adam, and how all their deeds (appear they never so holy) are yet but damnable sin, because they can refer nothing unto the glory of God, but seek themselves, their own profit, honour and glory: so that repentance toward the law must go before this belief; and he which repenteth not, but consenteth unto the life of sin, hath no part in this faith.

Moses.

And when John calleth Christ the everlasting life that was with the Father, he signifieth that Christ is our life; as after in the epistle, and in the first also of his gospel, saying, "In him was life." For until we receive life of Christ by faith, we are dead, and can be but dead, as saith John iii., "He that believeth not in the Son, can see no life, but the wrath of God abideth upon him." Of which wrath we are heirs by birth, saith Paul, (Eph. ii.) Of which wrath we are ignorant, until the law be published; and walk quietly after our lusts, and love God wickedly, that he should be content therewith, and maintain us therein, contrary unto his godly and righteous nature. But as soon as the law (whose nature is to utter sin, Rom. iii.,

Christ is our life. W.T.

John iii.

By nature we are the children of wrath. Ant. ed. Eph. ii.

Rom. iii.

[1 So P. C. L., but D. has *devils thereto, and is called the faith and belief of the history.*]

[2 Tyndale probably adverted to Ps. xlix. 15, or lxxxvi. 13.]

and to set man at variance with God) is preached; then we first awake out of our dream, and see our damnation, and have[3] the law which is so contrary unto our nature, and grudge against God thereto, as young children do against their elders when they first command, and count God a cruel tyrant because of his law, in that he condemneth us for that thing which we cannot love, nor of love fulfil.

The law condemneth us. Ant. ed.

But when Christ is preached, how that God for his sake receiveth us to mercy, and forgiveth us all that is past, and henceforth reckoneth not unto us our corrupt and poisoned nature, and taketh us as his sons, and putteth us under grace and mercy, and promiseth that he will not judge us by the rigorousness[4] of the law, but nurture us with all mercy and patience, as a father most merciful, only if we will submit ourselves unto his doctrine and learn to keep his laws; yea, and he will thereto consider our weakness[5], and, whatsoever chanceth, never taketh away his mercy, till we cast off the yoke of our profession first, and run away with utter defiance, that we will never come more at school; then our stubborn and hard hearts mollify and wax soft; and in the confidence and hope that we have in Christ, and his kindness, we go to God boldly as unto our father, and receive life, that is to say, love unto God and unto the law also.

Christ.

If we submit ourselves to Christ, and knowledge our weakness, he will of his great mercy receive us. Ant. ed.

That which we have seen and heard we declare unto you, that ye may have fellowship with us, and that our fellowship may be with the Father, and with his Son Jesus Christ. And these things we write unto you, that your joy may be full.

To bring unto the fellowship of God and Christ, and of them that believe in Christ, is the final intent of all the scripture, why it was given of God unto man, and the only thing which all true preachers seek; and whereby ye shall ever know and discern the true word of God from all false and counterfeited doctrine of vain traditions, and the true preacher from the wily hypocrite. We preach unto you, saith St[6] John, that everlasting life which we have heard, and in hearing received through faith, and are sure of it, to draw you to us out of the fellowship that ye have with the

The touchstone of all true doctrine and preachers. W. T.

[3 Probably a typographical error for *hate*.]
[4 So D., but P. C. L. has *righteousness*.]
[5 So P. C. L., but D. has *meekness*.]
[6 So P. C. L.; but here and where Paul occurs, D. omits *St.*]

damned devils in sinful lusts and ignorance of God; for we
2 Cor. xii. "seek you and not yours," as saith saint Paul, 2 Cor. xii. We love you as ourselves in God, and therefore would have you fellows and equal with us, and build you upon the foundation laid of the apostles and prophets, which is Christ Jesus, and make you of the household of God for ever; that ye and we, fellows and brethren, and coupled together in one spirit, in one faith, and in one hope, might have our fellowship thereby with God, and become his sons and heirs, and with Jesus Christ, being his brethren and co-heirs, and to make your joy full through that glad tidings, as the angel said unto the shepherds, Luke ii. "Behold, I shew you great joy that shall be unto all the people, how that there is a Saviour born unto you this day, which is Christ the Lord." And these tidings we bring you with the word of God only, which we received of his Spirit, and out of the mouth of his Son, as true messengers.

The modest and charitable manner of St Paul's doctrine. Ant. ed.

Luke ii.

"We preach not ourselves, but Christ our Lord, and us your servants for his sake:" we do not love ourselves, to seek yours unto us, that after we had with wiles robbed you of all ye have, we should exalt ourselves over you, and separate ourselves from you, and make ourselves a several kingdom, free and frank[1], reigning over you as heathen tyrants, and holding you in bondage to serve for[2] our lucre and lusts, tangling your conscience with doctrine of man, which draweth from God and Christ, and fearing[3] you with the bug of excommunication, against God's word; or, if that served not, shaking a sword at you.

St Paul preached Christ, and not himself. Ant. ed.

And this is the tidings which we have heard of him, and declare unto you, that God is light, and in him is no darkness at all. If we say that we have fellowship with him, and yet walk in darkness, we lie, and do not the truth. But and if we walk in light, as he is in light,

[1 Frank. He alludes to the expression Frank-almoigne: "Tenure in Frank-almoign, in libera eleemosyna, or free alms, is that whereby a religious corporation, aggregate or sole, holdeth lands of the donor to them and their successors for ever. The service which they were bound to render for these lands was not certainly defined, but only in general, to pray for the souls of the donor and his heirs, dead or alive; and therefore they did no fealty (which is incident to all other services but this), because this divine service was of a higher and more exalted nature." Blackstone's Comm. Vol. II. p. 101.]

[2 So P. C. L., but D. omits *our*.] [3 P. C. L. has *fraying*.]

then have we fellowship together, and the blood of Christ his Son cleanseth us from all sin.

As the devil is darkness and lies, so is God light and truth only; and there is no darkness of falsehead and consenting to wickedness in him. And the brightness of his light is his word and doctrine, as the hundred and eighteenth[4] Psalm saith, "Thy word is a lantern unto my feet, and a light to my paths." And Christ is "the light that lighteneth all men." And the apostles are called "the light of the world," because of the doctrine. And all that know truth are light: "Ye were once darkness," saith Paul, "but now light in the Lord; walk therefore as the children of light." And good works are called the fruits of light. And all that live in ignorance are called darkness; as he saith afterwards, "He that hateth his brother walketh in darkness." For if the light of the glorious gospel of Christ did shine in his heart, he could not hate his brother.

As God is light, so the devil is darkness. Ant. ed.

Psal. cxix.

Christ and his words are the light. W. T.

Eph. v.

Good works are the fruits of light. Ant. ed.

By walking understand consenting, doing, and working. If then we walk in darkness, that is, consent and work wickedness, and say we have fellowship with God, we lie: for to have fellowship with him is to know, and consent, and profess his doctrine in our hearts. Now if the commandments of God be written in our hearts, our members cannot but practise them, and shew the fruit of them[5]. So whether light or darkness be in the heart, it will appear in the walking. For though our members be never so dead unto virtue, yet if our souls knowledge the truth, and consent unto righteousness, we have the spirit of life in us. And therefore[6] Paul saith, "If the Spirit of him that raised up Jesus from death be in you, then will he that raised up Jesus from death quicken your mortal bodies by the reason of the Spirit that dwelleth in you." So that it is not possible for him that knoweth the truth, and consenteth thereto, to continue in sin. And then, finally, if we have the light in our hearts, and walk therein, then we have fellowship with God, and are his sons and heirs, and are purged from all sin through Christ's blood.

Walking in darkness or in light. W. T.

Rom. viii. If we have the Spirit of God in us, then will he raise us up with Jesus Christ. Ant. ed.

[4 The 118th of the vulgate, but the 119th of the Hebrew and of the English version. Day's edit. has, c and xix.]

[5 So P. C. L., but D. omits *of them*.]

[6 So P. C. L., though D. omits *therefore*.]

If we say we have no sin, we deceive ourselves, and the[1] truth is not in us.

He that saith he hath no sin deceiveth himself. Ant. ed.

If we think there is no sin in us, we are beguiled and blind, and the light of God's word is not in us; and either follow sin as beasts without conscience at all; or if we see the gross sins, as murder, theft, and adultery, yet we have hanged a vail of false glosses upon Moses's face, and see not[2] the brightness of the law, how that it requireth of us as pure a heart to God, and as great love unto our neighbours, as was in our Saviour Jesus, and ceaseth not before to condemn us as sinners.

If we knowledge our sins, he is faithful and just to forgive us our sins, and to cleanse us from all unrighteousness.

If we confess our sins to God with true faith and repentance, he will forgive us. Ant. ed.

If we confess our sins, not in the priest's ear, (though that tradition, restored unto the right use, were not damnable,) but in our hearts to God, with true repentance and fast belief; then is he faithful to forgive and to purge us, because of his merciful truth and promise. For he promised Abraham, that in his Seed all the world should be blessed from the curse of sin; and hath abundantly renewed his everlasting mercy unto us in the new Testament, promising that our sins shall be forgiven us in Christ's blood, if we repent, and trust thereto.

If we say we have not sinned, we make him a liar, and his word is not in us.

All men are sinners. Ant. ed. 1 Kings viii.

For his word testifieth against us, that we are all sinners; yea, and else Christ died in vain. Salomon saith, that "there is no man that sinneth not against God." And Paul proveth by the authority of the scripture unto the Romans, that we are all sinners without exception. And the scripture witnesseth that we are damnable sinners, and that our nature is to sin: which corrupt and poisoned nature, though it be begun to be healed[3], yet it is never thorough whole until the hour of death. For the which cause, with all our best fruits, there grow weeds among. Neither can there be any deed so perfect that could not be amended. When a blind bungler

[[1] So P. C. L., but D. and Tyndale's version have not *the*.]
[[2] So D., but P. C. L. has *do not see nor perceive*.]
[[3] P. C. L. has *cured and healed*.]

wondereth at his glorious works, a cunning workman, that hath a clear judgment, perceiveth that it is unpossible to make a work that could not be made better. Now the law requireth works of us in the highest degree of perfection, and ceaseth not to accuse us, until our works flow naturally as glorious in perfection as the works of Christ. And Christ teacheth us to pray in our pater-noster, "Forgive us our trespasses as we forgive our trespassers." Whereby ye may easily understand, that we sin daily one against another, and all against God. Christ taught also to pray, that our Father should not let us slip into temptation; signifying that our nature cannot but sin, if occasions be given, except that God of his special grace keep us back: which readiness[4] to sin is damnable sin in the law of God. David prayed, "Let not the tempest drown me, let me not fall into the bottom, and let not the pit shut her mouth upon me:" as who should say, First, keep me, O God, from sinning; then, if I shall chance to fall, as no flesh can escape, one time or other, then call me shortly back again, and let me not sink too deep therein: and though I yet fall never so deep, yet, Lord, let not the way of mercy be stopped: signifying that it is unpossible to stand of ourselves, and much less to rise again. Which impotency and feebleness is damnable in the law of God, except that we saw it and repented, and were fled to Christ for mercy; which he giveth abundantly unto them that require it with a faithful heart, and not wavering faith[5].

Nothing can be so well done, but it may be amended. Ant. ed

Psal. lxix.

All the nature of man is sinful. W. T.

[[4] So D., but P. C. L. has *pronyte,* i.e. *proneness.*]

[[5] In D. the chapter ends at the word *mercy*: what follows is found in the P. C. L. edition.]

CHAPTER. II.

My little children, I write these things unto you, that ye sin not. And though any man sin, yet we have an advocate with the Father, even Jesus Christ, which is righteous.

I write unto you on the one side, that God is light; and therefore that no man, which willingly walketh in the unfruitful works of darkness, hath any fellowship with that light, or part in the blood of his Son. And this I write and testify unto you, my dear children, that ye sin not: that is, that ye consent not unto sin, nor should sin of lust and purpose maliciously; but contrariwise that ye fear God, and resist sin with all your might and power according as ye have promised. For whosoever sinneth of purpose after the knowledge of the truth, the same sinneth against the Holy Ghost remediless.

We must resist sin with all our power and might. Ant. ed.

Heb. vi. x.

And on the other side, I testify unto you, that we be always sinners, though not of purpose and malice after the nature of damned devils, but of infirmity and frailty of our flesh; which flesh not only letteth us, that our works cannot be perfect, but also now and then, through manifold occasions and temptations, carrieth us clean out of the right way, spite of our hearts. Howbeit (I say) if, when the rage is past, we turn unto the right way again, and confess our sins unto our Father with a repenting heart, he hath promised us mercy, and is true to fulfil it. So that if we sin not devilishly against the Holy Ghost, refusing the doctrine which we cannot improve that it should not be true, but after the frailty of man, there is no cause to despair: for we have an advocate and an intercessor with the Father, even Jesus Christ that is righteous.

We sin daily by the frailty and weakness of our flesh. Ant. ed.

The name of our advocate is "Jesus," that is to say, a Saviour. "Call his name Jesus," said the angel to Joseph; "he shall save his people from their sins." And this advocate, and our Jesus, to save us from our sins, continueth ever, as it is written; and hath *sempiternum Sacerdotium*[1], an everlasting office, to make an atonement for sin: by the reason whereof, saith the text, "he is able ever to save them that come to God through him" with repentance and faith, and liveth ever to speak for us. And

Our advocate. W. T. Matt. i.

Heb. vii.

[1 An everlasting priesthood.]

besides that, our Jesus is God, and Almighty. He took our nature upon him, and felt all our infirmities and sicknesses, and in feeling learned to have compassion on us, and for compassion cried mightily in prayers to God the Father for us, and was heard. And the voice of the same blood that once cried, not for vengeance as Abel's, but for mercy only, and was heard, crieth now and ever, and is ever heard, as oft as we call unto remembrance with repenting faith, how that it was shed for our sins. He is also called *Christus*, that is to say, king *anointed* with all might and power over sin, death and hell, and over all sins; so that none that flieth unto him shall ever come into judgment of damnation. He is anointed with all fulness of grace, and hath all the treasure and riches of the Spirit of God in his hand, with which be blesseth all men, according to the promise made to Abraham; and is thereto merciful, to give[2] unto all that call on him. And how much he loveth us, I report me unto the ensamples of his deeds.

Jesus, that is God and man, calleth unto thee, O Father, for us. Ant. ed.

Christus. W. T.

By Jesus Christ we are made blessed. Ant. ed.

And he is "righteous," both toward God, in that he never sinned, and therefore hath obtained all his favour and grace; and also toward us, in that he is true to fulfil all the mercy that he hath promised us, even unto the uttermost jot.

And he is the satisfaction for our sins; and not for ours only, but also for all the world's[3].

That I call *satisfaction*, the Greek calleth *Ilasmos*, and the Hebrew *Copar*[4]: and it is first taken for the suaging of

Satisfaction, what it is. W. T.

[2 So P. C. L. but D. has *forgive*.]

[3 In this exposition, as well as in that upon the Sermon in the Mount, Tyndale translates as the subject proceeds, without appearing to have had his own previous translation before him. In his first published version he had rendered the first clause, "He it is that obtaineth grace for our sins;" and this inaccurate rendering is found in the latest editions of his new Testament, in Coverdale's Bible, in Cranmer's, and in the Genevan Bible of 1557, notwithstanding the obviously greater correctness of the rendering which Tyndale had here given.]

[4 Ἱλασμὸς, "A propitiation, or rather a propitiatory victim, or sacrifice for sin." Parkhurst, Lex. If Tyndale's explanation is to be understood to belong to כָּפַר, lexicographers have not confirmed his opinion respecting the primary meaning of this word, which they declare to be that of *covering by smearing with somewhat*. It first occurs Gen. vi. 14, where Noah is directed to cover the ark with a smearing

wounds, sores, and swellings, and the taking away of pain and smart of them; and thence is borrowed for the pacifying and suaging of wrath and anger, and for an amends-making, a contenting, satisfaction, a ransom, and making at one, as it is to see abundantly in the bible. So that Christ is a full contenting, satisfaction and ransom for our sins: and not for ours only, which are apostles and disciples of Christ while he was yet here; or for ours which are Jews, or Israelites, and the seed of Abraham; or for ours that now believe at this present time, but for all men's sins, both for their sins which went before and believed the promises to come, and for ours which have seen them fulfilled, and also for all them which shall afterward believe unto the world's end, of whatsoever nation or degree they be. For Paul commandeth, 1 Tim. ii. "to pray for all men and all degrees," saying that to be "acceptable unto our Saviour God, which will have all men saved and come to the knowledge of the truth;" that is, some of all nations and all degrees, and not the Jews only. "For," saith he, "there is one God, and one Mediator between God and man, the man Christ Jesus, which gave himself a redemption" and full satisfaction "for all men." David also said in the eighteenth[1] Psalm: "Their sound is gone throughout all the earth, so that the benefit stretched on all men[2]."

Christ's blood is the satisfaction for our sins. Ant. ed.

Tim. ii.

Christ gave himself for the redemption and salvation of all the world. Ant. ed.

Let this therefore be an undoubted article of thy faith: not of a history faith, as thou believest a gest of Alexander, or of the old Romans, but of a lively faith and belief, to put thy trust and confidence in, and to buy and sell thereon, as we say; and to have thy sins taken away, and thy soul saved thereby, if thou hold it fast; and to continue ever in sin, and to have thy soul damned, if thou let it slip; that our Jesus, our Saviour, that saveth his people from their sins, and our Christ, that is our king over all sin, death and hell, anointed with fulness of all grace and with the Spirit of God, to distribute unto all men, hath, according unto the epistle to

Christ is king over death, hell, and sin. Ant. ed.

of pitch. Hence its secondary meaning is 'to blot out;' and, where sin is spoken of, 'to obliterate sin by covering it with expiatory blood; to atone, expiate; or appease him from whose indignation the sin is thus covered.' See Robertson's *Clavis Pentateuchi*, on Exod. xxix. 33.]

[1 The nineteenth of the Hebrew and of the English version.]

[2 So P. C. L.; in Day's edition the last two sentences are omitted.]

the Hebrews and all the scripture, in the days of his mortal flesh, with fasting, praying, suffering, and crying to God mightily for us, and with shedding his blood, made full satisfaction both *a pœna et a culpa* (with our holy father's leave) for all the sins of the world; both of theirs that went before, and of theirs that come after in the faith; whether it be original sin or actual: and not only the sins committed with consent to evil in time of ignorance, before the knowledge of the truth, but also the sins done of frailty after we have forsaken evil and consented to the laws of God in our hearts, promising to follow Christ and walk in the light of his doctrine.

Christ only is our Saviour. W. T. Matt. i. Acts iv. Acts x. Eph. ii. iii. Rom. v. John x.

He saveth his people from their sins, Matth. i., and that he only: so that there is no other name to be saved by. Acts iv. And "unto him bear all the prophets record, that all that believe in him shall receive remission of their sins in his name." Acts x. And by him only we have an entering in unto the Father, and unto all grace. Eph. ii. and iii. and Rom. v. And as many as come before him are thieves and murderers, John x.; that is, whosoever preacheth any other forgiveness of sin than through faith in his name, the same slayeth the soul.

Christ forgiveth all our sins freely for his mercy sake. Ant. ed. John viii. John v. Acts ii.

This to be true, not only of original but also[3] of actual [sin], and as well of that we commit after our profession as before, mayest thou evidently see by the ensamples of the scripture. Christ forgave the woman taken in adultery, John viii. and another whom he healed, John v. And he forgave publicans and open sinners, and put none to do penance, as they call it, for to make satisfaction for the sin which he forgave through repentance and faith; but enjoined them the life of penance, the profession of their baptism, to tame the flesh in keeping the commandments, and that they should sin no more. And those sinners were for the most part Jews, and had their original sin forgiven them before through faith in the testament of God. Christ forgave his apostles their actual sins after their profession, which they committed in denying him, and put none to do penance for satisfaction. Peter (Acts ii.) absolveth the Jews, through repentance and faith, from their actual sins, which they did in consenting unto Christ's death; and enjoined them no penance to make satisfaction. Paul

[3 So P. C. L., but D. omits *also*.]

also had his actual sins forgiven him freely, through repentance and faith, without mention of satisfaction. Acts ix. So that, according unto this present text of John, if it chance us to sin of frailty, let us not despair; for we have an advocate and intercessor, a true attorney with the Father, Jesus Christ, righteous towards God and man, and [he] is the reconciling and satisfaction for our sins.

Christ only is our advocate. Ant. ed. Acts ix.

For Christ's works are perfect; so that he hath obtained us all mercy, and hath set us in the full state of grace and favour of God, and hath made us as well beloved as the angels of heaven, though we be yet weak: as the young children, though they can do no good at all, are yet as tenderly beloved as the old. And God, for Christ's sake, hath promised that whatsoever evil we shall do, yet if we turn and repent, he will never more think on our sins.

Popish forgiveness. W. T.

Thou wilt say, God forgiveth the displeasure, but we must suffer pain to satisfy the righteousness of God. Ah,[1] then God hath a righteousness which may not forgive pain and all, that the poor sinner might[2] go scot free without aught at all! God was unrighteous to forgive the thief his pain, and all through repentance and faith; unto whom for lack of leisure was no penance enjoined! And my faith is, that whatsoever ensample of mercy God hath shewed one, that same he hath promised all. Yea, will he peradventure forgive me, but I must make amends? If I owe you twenty pounds, ye will forgive me; that is, ye will no more be angry with me, but I shall pay you the twenty pounds! O popish forgiveness, with whom it goeth after the common proverb, No penny, no pardon! His fatherhood giveth pardon freely; but we must pay money abundantly.

The forgiveness that we have of God for Christ's sake is free. Ant. ed.

Rom. iv.

Paul's doctrine is, Rom. iv. If a man work, it ought not to be said that his hire was given him of grace or of favour, but of duty: "But to him that worketh not, but believeth in him that justifieth the ungodly, his faith" (he saith not, his works, although he commandeth us diligently to work, and despiseth none that God commandeth), "his faith" (saith he) "is reckoned him for his righteousness:" confirming his saying with the testimony of the prophet David in the thirty-second Psalm, saying, "Blessed is the man unto whom God

Faith in Christ is accounted to us for righteousness.

[1 Old editions *A*, an ancient mode of writing this interjection.]
[2 So P. C. L., but D. has *should*.]

imputeth" or reckoneth "not his sin;" that is to say, which man, although he be a sinner, yet God layeth it not to his charge, for his faith's sake. And in the eleventh he saith, "If it come of grace, then it cometh not of works; for then were grace no grace," saith he. For it was a very strange speaking in Paul's ears, to call that grace that came of deserving of works; or that deserving of works which came by grace; for he reckoned works and grace to be contrary, in such manner of speech. But our holy father hath coupled them together, of pure liberality, I dare say, and not for covetousness. For as his holiness, if he have a cause against any man, immediately breatheth out an excommunication upon him, and will have satisfaction for the uttermost farthing, and somewhat above, to teach them to beware against another time, ere he will bless again from the terrible sentence of his heavy curse; even so of that blessed complexion he describeth the nature of the mercy of God, that God will remit his anger to us upon the appointment of our satisfaction: whereas[3] the scripture saith, Christ is our righteousness, our justifying, our redemption, our atonement, that hath appeased God, and cleanseth us from our sins, and all in his blood, so that his blood is the satisfaction only.

We are saved by grace, and not by works of the law. Ant. ed.

Rom. xi.

The pope, when any man offendeth him, falleth to cursing. Ant. ed.

And that thou mayest the better perceive the falsehead of our holy father's fleshly imagination, call to mind how that the scripture saith, (John iv.) "God is a Spirit, and must be worshipped in the spirit:" that is, repentance, faith, hope, and love towards his law, and our neighbour for his sake, is his worship in the spirit. And therefore whosoever worshippeth God with works, and referreth his works to God, to be a sacrifice unto him, to appease him, as though he delighted in the work for the work's sake, the same maketh of God an image or idol, and is an image-server, and as wicked an idolater as ever was any blind heathen, and serveth God after the imagination of his own heart, and is abominable unto God: as thou seest in how many places God defieth[4] the sacrifice of the children of Israel, for the said imagination. So that whosoever supposeth that his candle-sticking before an image, his putting a penny in the box, his going a pil-

Works can be no satisfaction for sin to Godward. Ant. ed.

John iv. God is a Spirit, and must be worshipped in the spirit. Ant. ed.

Popish works. Ant. ed.

[3 So P. C. L., but D. has *when*.]

[4 Disdaineth: expresseth scorn against. So in Auth. version, Numbers xxiii. 7 and 8, where defy is the rendering of זעם.]

grimage, his fasting, his woolward going, barefoot going, his crouching, kneeling, and pain-taking, be sacrifices unto God, as though he delighted in them as we in the gestures of Jack Napes, is as blind as he that gropeth for his way at noon. God's worship is to love him for his mercy; and of love to bestow all our works upon our neighbour for his sake, and upon the taming of our flesh, that we sin not again, which should be the chiefest care of a christian man; whilst Christ careth for that that is once past and committed already, whether before our profession or after. For the conditions of the peace that is made between God and us in Christ's blood are these: The law is set before us, unto which if we consent and submit ourselves to be scholars thereof, then are not only all our fore sins forgiven, both *pœna et culpa* (with our holy father's licence ever); but also all our infirmities, weakness, proneness[1], readiness, and motions unto sin, are pardoned, and taken aworth[2], and we translated from under the damnation of the law, which damneth as well those infirmities as the sin that springeth of them, and putteth us under grace, (Rom. vii.): so that we shall not henceforth, as long as we forsake not our profession, be judged by the rigorousness[3] of the law; but chastised, if we do amiss, as children that are under no law. Now then if God in Christ pardon our infirmities, by reason of which we cannot escape but that we shall now and then sin; it followeth that he must likewise pardon the actual sin which we do, compelled of those infirmities in spite of our hearts, and against the will of the Spirit. For if thou pardon the sickness of the sick, then must thou pardon the deeds which he doth, or leaveth undone, by the reason of his sickness. If the madness of a madman be pardoned, and under no law, then if he murder in his madness, he may not be slain again. If children within a certain age are not under the law that slayeth thieves, then can ye not of right hang them, though they steal. What popish pardoning were that! This doth Paul (Rom. vii.) so confirm, that all the world cannot quitch against it, saying: "I consent unto the law of God that it is good," and fain would I do it, and yet have I not always power so to do, but find another

God's worship. W. T.

God doth pardon and forgive all our sins, whatsoever they are, for Christ's sake. Ant. ed.

Rom. vii.

[1 *Pronite* in P. C. L.]
[2 See Vol. I. p. 463.]
[3 So Day, but P. C. L. has *righteousness*.]

thing in my flesh, rebelling against the will of my mind, and leading me captive into sin, so that I cannot do that I would do, but am compelled to do that I would not: "If," saith he, "I do that I would not, then I do it not, but the sin that dwelleth in me doth it." And then saith he, "Who shall deliver me from this body of death," in which I am bound prisoner against my will? "Thanks be to God," saith he, "through Jesus Christ our Lord," which hath conquered and overcome sin, death, and hell, and hath put the damnation of the law out of the way unto all that profess the law, and believe in him.

Christ's victory. W. T.

We be under the law to learn it, and to fashion our deeds as like as we can; but not under the damnation of the law, that we should be damned, though our deeds were not[4] perfect as the law requireth, or though of frailty we at a time break it: as children are under the law, that they steal not; but not under the damnation, though they steal. So that all they that are grafted into Christ to follow his doctrine, are under the law to learn it only, but are delivered from fear of everlasting death and hell, and all the threatenings of the law, and from conscience of sin, which feared us from God. And we are come in to God through the confidence that we have in Jesus Christ; and are as familiar and bold with him as young innocent children, which have no conscience of sin, are with their fathers and mothers, or them that nourish them: which were unpossible, if God now (as the bishop of Rome painteth him) did shake a rod at us of seven years' punishment, as sharp as the pains of hell, for every trespass we do; which trespasses for the number of them were like to make our purgatory almost as long as hell, seeing we have no God's word that we shall be delivered thence, until we have paid the last farthing. And therefore could our conscience never be at rest, nor be bold and familiar with God.

The pope's purgatory is terrible. Ant. ed.

If ye say, the bishop of Rome can deliver my conscience from fear of purgatory (as his poetry only putteth me in fear), and that by this text, "Whatsoever thou bindest on earth, &c.;" if thou this way understand the text, "Whatsoever thou, being in earth, loosest any where;" then might he loose in hell, and bind in heaven. But why may not I take the text

Bind and loose. W. T.

[4 So D., but P. C. L. has *as* after *not*.]

John xvi. Note this text. W. T. Binding and loosing is by the true preaching of God's word. Ant. ed.

of Christ, John xvi. "Whatsoever ye ask my Father in my name, he will give it you;" and desire forgiveness of all together in Christ's name, both *a pœna et culpa;* and then remaineth no such purgatory at all? Howbeit the text of binding and loosing is but borrowed speech, how that after the similitude of worldly binding and loosing, locking and unlocking, the word of God truly preached doth bind and loose the conscience.

Jer. i.

God saith to Jeremiah the prophet in his first chapter[1], "Behold, I give thee power over nations and kingdoms to pluck up by the roots, and to shiver in pieces, to destroy and cast down, and to build and plant." How did he destroy nations and kingdoms, and how did he build them? Verily, by preaching and prophesying. What nation, kingdom, or city he prophesied to be overthrown, was so; and what city he prophesied to be built again, was so; and what nation, after they were brought into captivity, he prophesied to be restored again, were so; and whom he prophesied to perish, perished; and whom he prophesied to be saved, was saved. Even so, whomsoever a true preacher of God's word saith shall be damned for his sin, because he will not repent and believe in Christ, the same is damned: and whomsoever a true preacher of God's word saith shall be saved, because he repenteth and believeth in Christ's blood, the same is saved. And this is the binding and loosing that Christ meant.

Notwithstanding, ye must understand, that when we have sinned, though our hearts were not to sin, and though we repent ere the deed be done, yet the body, in sinning, hath overcome the spirit, and hath gotten the mastery: so that the spirit is now weaker and feebler to virtue, and to follow the law of God and doctrine of Christ, and the flesh stronger to follow vice and sin. Wherefore as, when an old sore is broken forth again, we begin, as it were, a new cure with greater diligence and more care than before; even so here we must renew our old battle against the flesh, and more strongly go to work, to subdue it, [and to quench the lusts thereof, which are waxen so rank, that they bud out openly,][2] according to the profession of our baptism, which is the very

We must struggle and strive with sin. Ant. ed.

[1 So P. C. L., but Day, to Hieremias, cap. I.]

[2 The passage between brackets is not in the P. C. L. ed.]

sacrament or sign of repentance, (or, if they will so have it called, penance,) by the interpretation of Paul (Rom. vi). For the plunging into the water, as it betokeneth on the one part that Christ hath washed our souls with his blood; even so on the other part it signifieth that we have promised to quench and slay the lusts of the flesh with prayer, fasting, and holy meditation, after the doctrine of Christ, and with all godly exercise, that tame the flesh, and kill not the man.

How penance came up, and purgatory. Ant. ed.

Whereupon the bishops that succeeded the apostles, when men had done any open sins, enjoined them penance, as they call it, by the authority of the congregation and governors thereof, and advice of the most wise and discreet, and with the willing consent of the trespassers, to tame the flesh; as to go woolward, to wear shirts of hair, to go bare-foot, and bare-head, to pray, to fast bread and water, some once in the week, some twice, or all the week, an whole year, two years, three years, eight years, twenty years, and some all their lives long; and to go in pilgrimage, to visit the memorial of saints[3], to strength them the better to follow their ensample, and such like, and all to slay the worldly mind of the flesh: which manner, when it was once received of the people by custom, it became a law. And the bishops by little and little gat it whole into their own hands.

How the pope and his shavelings have abused penance. Ant. ed.

When the bishops saw that, how they had gotten the simple people under them in such humble obedience, they began to set up their crests, and to reign over them as princes, and to enjoin sore penance for small trifles, namely if aught were done against their pleasure; and beat some sore, and spared other, and sold their penance to the rich, and overladed the poor, until the tyranny was waxen so grievous that the people would bear it no longer. For by

[[3] Augustine tells us that Paulinus, bishop of Nola, wrote to him, 'quærens a me utrum prosit cuique post mortem, quod corpus ejus apud sancti alicujus memoriam sepelitur.' In reply he composed his treatise *De cura agenda pro mortuis;* in which he explains the origin of the name *memoria* or memorial, as follows: Non ob aliud vel memoriæ vel monumenta dicuntur ea quæ insignita fiunt sepulcra mortuorum, nisi quia eos qui viventium oculis morte subtracti sunt, ne oblivione etiam cordibus subtrahantur, in memoriam revocant, et admonendo faciunt cogitari; nam et memoriæ nomen id apertissime ostendit, et monumentum eo quod moneat mentem, id est admoneat, nuncupatur.—Op. Tom. VI. col. 515, 519, C.]

this time, what with the multitude of ceremonies, and heap of men's constitutions, whose right use was thereto clean forgotten, and partly because our shepherds were busied to seek themselves and their high authority, and exalted every man his throne, and were become wolves unto the flock, the cause why the people were disobedient unto wholesome counsel was, that[1] the word of God was sore darkened, and no where purely preached. And therefore the prelates, loath to lose their high authority, and to let the people go free of their yoke, began to turn their tale, and sing a new song, how that this penance was enjoined to make satisfaction to God for the sin that was committed; robbing our souls of the fruit of Christ's blood, and making us image-servants; referring our deeds unto the person of God, and worshipping him, as an image of our own imagination, with bodily work: saying moreover, if we would not do such penance here at their injunctions, we must do it in another world; and so feigned purgatory, where we must suffer seven years for every sin. And when the kingdom of antichrist was so enlarged that it must have a head, they set up our holy father of Rome, or he rather usurped the realm[2] with violence; and to him was given this prerogative, to sell whom he would from purgatory[3].

Here was purgatory kindled. W. T.

And the sacrament of penance they thus describe: contrition, confession, and satisfaction: contrition; sorrow for thy sins: confession; not to God and them whom thou hast offended, but tell thy sins in the priest's ear: satisfaction, to do certain deeds enjoined of them, to buy out thy sins. And in their description they have clean excluded the faith in the satisfaction of Christ's blood; which only bringeth life, and the spirit of life, and righteousness, and without the which it is impossible to please God: in whose stead they have put in the presumption of our own works. And for lack of trust in Christ's blood, our contrition is but a fruitless sorrow in the respect of hell, which maketh us hate the law still, and consequently God that made it: where true contrition, annexed with faith, is sorrow in respect of the law, unto which we consent that it is good, and

The definition of penance made by the papists. Ant. ed.

Heb. xi. Faith is the chiefest part of penance. Ant. ed.

[1 So P. C. L. Day wants, *was that.*]

[2 So P. C. L. but Day has *or rather usurped that Rome.*]

[3 That is, to take a price for making over the merits of the saints to a soul in purgatory, that it might be released.]

love it, and therefore mourn, partly because we have offended it, and partly because we lack power to fulfil it as we would.

These things to be true our prelates know by open histories, as well as that[4] when it is noon the sun is flat south. But it delighteth them to resist the Holy Ghost, and to persecute the preachers of the things which, if they as well loved them as they know them[5] to be true, they would preach the same themselves and live thereafter. Hereof ye may see our works are but to tame the flesh only; and can be no satisfaction to God, except we make him an image, and ourselves image-servants. And hereof ye may see how out of this open penance came the ear-confession, satisfaction of works, purgatory and pardons. For when they had put the satisfaction of Christ's blood out of the way, then as they compelled men to confess open sins, and to take open penance, even so they compelled them[6] to confess secret sins, and to take secret penance. And as they made merchandise of open penance, so did they of secret. And for them that would not receive such pardons feigned they purgatory, and for them that received them feigned they pardon, turning binding and loosing, with preaching God's word, unto buying and selling sin for money. And since that time hitherto, the worse the people were, the better were the prelates content, ever resisting that they should be made better, through their blessed covetousness and proud desire of honour.

Our works can make no satisfaction, but only faith in Christ's blood. Ant. ed.

The practice and merchandise of the pope and his clergy. Ant. ed.

And out of this false presumption of works sprang the wicked vows of religion; which they vow to make satisfaction for sin, and to be higher in heaven, instead of the life of penance which Christ taught us in the gospel, to tame the flesh, and to crucify the members withal, that we henceforth should walk in the ways of God's law, and sin no more.

Vows of religion. Ant. ed.

And to speak of worshipping of saints, and praying unto them, and of that we make them our advocates well nigh above Christ, or altogether, though it require a long disputation, yet it is as bright as the day to all that know the truth; how that our fasting of their evens, and keeping their holy days, going bare-foot, sticking up of candles in the bright day, in the wor-

Worshipping of saints. Ant. ed.

[4 So P. C. L.: in D., *that* is omitted.]

[5 The two *thems* are wanting in D., but found in P. C. L.]

[6 The *them* here also, and *men* in the preceding clause are in P. C. L. but not in D.]

shipping of them to obtain their favour, our giving them so costly jewels, offering into their boxes, clothing their images, shoeing them with silver shoes with an ouch of crystal in the midst, to stroke the lips and eyes of the ignorant, as a man would stroke young children's heads to entice them and bring them in, and rock them asleep in ignorance, are with all like service plain idolatry, that is, in English, image-service. For the saints are spirits, and can have no delectation in bodily things. And because those bodily deeds can be no service unto the spiritual saints, and we do them not to be a service to ourselves or our neighbours; we serve the work and the false imagination of our fleshly wit, after the doctrine of man, and not of God, and are image-servants. And this is it that Paul calleth *servire elementis mundi*[1], to be in captivity under dumb ceremonies and vain traditions of men's doctrine, and to do the work for the work itself; as though God delighted therein, for the deed itself, without all other respect.

The pope and his clergy setteth up idolatry. Ant. ed.

But and ye will know the true worshipping of saints, hearken unto Paul, where he saith, "Ye shine as lights in the world, holding fast the word of life unto my glory, (or worship,) against the day of Jesus Christ, that I have not run nor laboured in vain." That is to wete, the worship which all true saints now seek, and the worship that all the true messengers of God seek this day, or ever shall seek, is to draw all to Christ with preaching the true word of God, and with the ensample of pure living fashioned thereafter. Will ye therefore worship saints truly? Then ask[2] what they preached, and believe their doctrine; and as they followed that doctrine, so conform your living like unto theirs: and that shall be unto their high worship in the coming again of Christ (when all men's deeds shall appear, and every man shall be judged, and receive his reward, according unto his deeds), how that they not only, while they here lived, but also after their death, with the ensample of their doctrine and living, left behind in writing and other memorials, unto the ensample of them that should follow them[3] unto Christ, that were born five hundred, yea, a thousand years after their death. This was their worship in the spirit at the beginning, as they were spirits; and

The true worshipping of saints. Ant. ed.

Phil. ii.

Good lessons are to be learned of the saints. Ant. ed.

The true worshipping of saints is to follow their life and doctrine. Ant. ed.

[1 To be in bondage to the elements of the world.]

[2 So P. C. L., but Day has *hear*.]

[3 So Day; in P. C. L. *them* follows *Christ*.]

lights were sticked before their memorials at the beginning, to be a ceremony to put us in remembrance that we so praised the saints, and boasted their livings, that we followed their ensamples in our deeds; as Christ saith, "Let your light so shine before men that they see your good works, and glorify your Father that is in heaven." For preaching of the doctrine, which is light, hath but small effect to move the heart, if the ensample of living do disagree.

The sticking up of candles before images. W. T.

Matt v.

And that we worship saints for fear, lest they should be displeased and angry with us, and plague us or hurt us, (as who is not afraid of St Laurence? who dare deny St Anthony a fleece of wool, for fear of his terrible fire, or lest he send the pox among our sheep?) is heathen image-service, and clean against the first commandment, which is, "Hear, Israel, the Lord thy God is one God." Now God in the Hebrew is called *El*, or *Elohim* in the plural number, *strength* or *might*. So that the commandment is, Hear, Israel, he that is thy power and might, thy sword and shield, is but one; that is, there is none of might to help or hurt thee, save one, which is altogether thine, and at thy commandment, if thou wilt hear his voice. And all other might in the world is borrowed of him: and he will lend no might against thee contrary to his promises. Keep therefore his commandments, and he shall keep thee: and if thou have broken them, and he have lent of his power against thee, repent and come again unto thy profession; and he will return again unto his mercy, and fetch his power home again, which he lent to vex thee, because thou forsookest him and brakest his commandments. And fear no other creature; for false fear is the cause of all idolatry.

Note this for the first commandment. W. T.

If we hearken to the voice of God, he is mighty and of power to help us. Ant. ed.

Moreover all we, that are baptized in Christ, have professed to do good for evil, and not to avenge ourselves. And many of us come unto such perfection, that we can be provoked by no temptation to desire vengeance, but have compassion, and meekly pray for them that slay us.

We must do good for evil. Ant. ed.

How wicked a thing then is it to think that the saints trouble and[4] plague us, because we do them not such superstitious honour, which is their dishonour and our shame? It is verily a popish imagination, and even to describe the saints after the nature of our prelates, which be meek and lowly till they be where they would be; but when they be once aloft,

A popish imagination. Ant. ed.

[[4] So P. C. L., but Day omits *trouble and*.]

they play the tormentors if we will not honour them, and do whatsoever they command more earnestly than that which God himself hath commanded, and fear them above God himself.

And it can be but like abomination also, that we choose of a fleshly mind every man his several saint, or rather several gods, to be our advocates, attornies, mediators (when there is but one, 1 Tim. ii.) and intercessors; and call them our advouries, when we might better call them our adulterers[1]; and serve them, or rather a painted post in their stead, with our image-service, therewith to bind them for to help us, whensoever and for whatsoever we call unto them, and to save our souls thereto with their prayers and merits; and will yet neither hear the doctrine, nor follow the ensample of living (which is their only honour) in the spirit of any saint, whose doctrine and living is authentic.

1 Tim. ii.

Advouries. W. T.

Idolatry. Ant. ed.

For first, God, which alone hath power to help or hurt, hath made appointment betwixt him and us, in Christ's blood; and hath bound himself to give us whatsoever we ask in his name, testifying thereto that there is no other name to be saved by; and that he will be a father unto us, and save us both in this life and in the life to come, and take us from under the damnation of the law, and set us under grace and mercy, to be scholars only to learn the law; and that our unperfect deeds shall be taken in worth, yea, and though at a time we mar all through our infirmity, yet, if we turn again, that shall be forgiven us mercifully, so that we shall be under no damnation: which testament is confirmed with signs and wonders wrought through the Holy Ghost. Now, this indented obligation laid apart, we make another, of our own imagination, between the saints and us, in their merits for our image-service: which can be but a false faith; seeing it hath not God's word, unto which alone we ought to cleave, but is also clean contrary thereto.

God hath promised to give us whatsoever we ask in Christ's name, and for Christ's sake. Ant. ed.

Saints cannot help us. Ant. ed.

And again, the saints were not saved through their own merits, but through Christ's. Neither were their deeds, which

The saints were not saved by

[[1] Advouryes: protectors. In Chaucer's Jacke Upland's questions to the freres, the 29th is, 'Why clepe ye hem your patrons and avowries?' In French *avouerie* is protection. Tyndale writing the word advoury makes it differ by but one letter from advoutry, which is with him a synonym for adultery. See Vol. I. p. 17.]

they did after they were received under grace, sufficient in themselves to fulfil the law for the present time, save as Christ's merits did supply the imperfectness of them, and that which was lacking on their part through their infirmities. And therefore as the saints' holy works made no satisfaction for the sin they did before they were received under mercy, even so made they none for the deadly sins which they did under mercy; seeing the deeds were unperfect, and had sin annexed unto them by reason of the flesh, and were insufficient to excuse their own masters. What merits have they in store for us then, seeing by all men's confession they now merit not? If the most obedient child in the world disobey his father's commandments, his fore good deeds cannot make that disobedience no sin, or to be a satisfaction, that the child should presume in the confidence of his old deeds, and think his father should do him wrong to punish him: but he must knowledge his fault, and that he hath deserved punishment, and desire forgiveness, unto the glory of his father's mercifulness, and not of his old deeds, though his old obedience be a great presumption that he sinned of frailty, and not of purpose. Even so if I, being as holy as ever was Paul in his most holiness, sin this day through the frailty of my flesh, mine old deeds can be no satisfaction: but I must knowledge my sin unto my Father, and grant that I have deserved damnation, and meekly desire forgiveness, and challenge it by the obligation wherein God hath bound himself to me, unto the glory of the mercy of God, and not to the glory of my holy deeds: for if my deeds save me, it is my glory; but if he forgive us freely, without respect of my deeds, then it is the glory of his mercy, by Paul's doctrine unto the Romans.

their own merits, but by Christ's merits. Ant. ed.

Of the meritings of saints. W. T.

We must humble ourselves to the mercy of almighty God. W. T.

Moreover if the saints be in heaven, then can they be there in none other case than the angels; in which state Christ testifieth they shall be in the resurrection. Now the angels are ministers sent of God to do service unto the elect, which shall be saved. And God hath bound himself, that if I come in the right way, by the door of Christ's blood, and ask help, that he will send me, if need be, an hundred legions of angels or saints. But when God hath bound himself to send me angels or saints, or an angel or saint, he hath not promised to send this angel or that, or this or that saint. And therefore, when I appoint God whom he shall send, and bind

The angels serve us. W. T.

Heb. i.

him, where he hath not bound himself, to send me what saint I will, I tempt God. And thus this choosing of several saints is but tempting of God. And yet we do worse than this: for we leave the way of Christ's blood, and go not to God through him; but run to the saints, in a testament of our own making, and will that they either save us themselves for our image-service, or compel God for their[1] merit's sake to save us. Why goest thou not unto thy father thine ownself? 'I am a sinner,' will they say, 'and dare not.' If thou go in the right way, thou hast no sin. Christ hath taken all thy sins from thee; and God hath no rod in his hand, nor looketh sour, but merrily, that it is a lust to behold his cheerful countenance, and offereth thee his hand. But this way is stopped up through unbelief; and therefore we seek another, which is no way to life, but unto everlasting death. We will not look on the law with open eyes, and therefore have we no due repentance, and so no lust to hearken unto the gospel of glad tidings in Christ's blood. And where the right way is set before us, and we of malice will not walk therein, God cannot but let the devil play with us, and juggle our eyes to confirm us in blindness.

To choose saints to be our advocates is mere idolatry. Ant. ed.

Christ is the way, and life, that leadeth us to salvation. Ant. ed.

But after what manner doth Christ pray for us? Verily Christ in the days of his mortal flesh suffered and prayed for all that shall be saved, and obtained and was heard, and had his petitions granted. And he made satisfaction, and purged, and purchased forgiveness, even then, for all the sin that ever shall be forgiven. And his praying for us, and being a mediator now, is that the remembrance of all that he did for us is present in the sight of God the Father, as fresh as the hour he did them; yea, the same hour is yet present, and not past, in the sight of God. And Christ is now a king, and reigneth; and hath received power of all that he prayed for, to do it himself; and that, whensoever the elect call for aught in his name, he sendeth help, even of the power which he hath received: yea, ere they ask, he sendeth his Spirit into their hearts to move them to ask: so that it is his gift that we desire aught in his name. And in all that we do or think well, he preventeth us with his grace: yea, he careth for us ere we care for ourselves, and when we be[2] yet evil

How Christ prayeth for us. W. T.

Christ is a king, and hath power himself to forgive us, and to receive us unto himself. Ant. ed.

[[1] So P. C. L. but D. omits *their*.]
[[2] So P. C. L. but D. has *were*.]

he sendeth to call us, and draweth us with such power that our hearts cannot but consent and come, and the angels stand by, and behold the testament of the elect, how we shall be received into their fellowship, and see all the grace that Christ shall pour out upon us. And they rejoice, and praise God for his infinite mercy; and are glad, and long for us; and of very love are ready against all hours, when we shall call for help in Christ's name, to come and help. And Christ sendeth them, when we call in his name; and ere we call, even while we be yet evil, and haply persecute the truth of ignorance, as Paul did, the angels wait upon us to keep that the devils slay us not before the time of our calling be come.

All the blessed company of heaven rejoice, and are glad, to have us to be with them, that we might joy together. Ant. ed.

Now if an angel should appear unto thee, what wouldest thou say unto him? If thou prayedst him to help, he would answer: 'I do. Christ hath sent me to help thee; and believe that the angels be ever about thee to help.' If thou desiredst him to pray for thee, to obtain this or that; he would say: 'Christ hath prayed, and his prayer is heard for whatsoever thou askest in his name;' and would shew thee all that God would do to thee, and what he would also have thee to do: and if thou believest so, then[3] wert thou safe. If thou desiredst him to save thee with his merits, he would answer that he had no merits, but that Christ only is Lord of all merits; nor salvation, but that Christ is Lord of salvation. 'Wilt thou therefore be saved by merits?' would the angel say; 'then pray to God in Christ's name, and thou shalt be saved by the merits of him, and have me, or some other, thy servant immediately to help thee unto the uttermost of our power, and to keep thee, and bring thee unto the reward of his merits.' If thou wouldest promise him to worship him with image-service, that is, to stick up a candle before his image, or such an image as he appeared to thee in; he would answer that he were a spirit, and delighted in no candle-light; but would bid thee give a candle to thy neighbour that lacketh, if thou hadst too many. And so would he answer thee, if thou wouldest put money in a box for him, or clothe his image in cloth of gold, or put golden shoes upon his image's feet. If thou saidst that thou wouldest build a chapel in his name, he would answer that he dwelt in no house made

Christ prayeth for us, and his prayer is heard. Ant. ed.

Image-service is abhorred of God. Ant. ed.

God hateth superstition. Ant. ed.

[[3] So P. C. L. but in D. *believest, so wert, &c.*]

with stones, but would bid thee go to the churches that are made already, and learn of the preachers there how to believe, and how to live, and honour God in the spirit; for the which cause churches were chiefly builded, and for quietness to pray: and if there be no church, then to give of that thou mayest spare, to help that one were builded to be a preaching and a praying house, and of worshipping God in the spirit, and not of image-service.

Churches were ordained for preaching, and calling on the name of God. W. T.

And if Paul appeared unto thee, what other thing could he answer also, than that he were a spirit, and would refuse all thy image-service? And if thou speak to Paul of his merits, he can none otherwise answer thee than he answered his Corinthians: That he died for no man's sins, and that no man was baptized in his name, to trust in his merits. He would say, 'I builded all men upon Christ's merits; preaching that all that repented, and believed in his name, should be saved, and taken from under the wrath, vengeance, and damnation of the law, and be put under mercy and grace. And by this faith was I saved from damnation, and put under mercy and grace, and made one with Christ, to have my part with him, and he with me; or rather to make a change, that he should have all my sins, and I his mercy and the gifts of his grace, and become glorious with the ornaments of his riches. And of my Saviour Christ I received this law, that I should love my brethren, all God's elect, as tenderly as he loved them. And I consented unto this law, for it seemed right; and became a scholar, to learn it. And as I profited in the knowledge, faith, and love of Christ, so I grew in the love of my brethren, and suffered all things for their sakes, and at the last waxed so perfect, that I wished myself damned (if it might have been) to save my brethren. And all my brethren, that received Christ, received the same commandment, and grew therein. And they that were perfect loved me, and all their other brethren, no less than I loved them. And look, with what love I ministered the gifts of grace, which I received of Christ for the edifying of his congregation, upon my brethren, with the same love did they minister their gifts again on me, which they had and I lacked; and so love made all common. And moreover, if they call my works my merits, I bestowed all my works upon my brethren to teach them; and reaped the fruit thereof, even my brethren's

Christ hath made a change with us, for he hath taken upon him all our sins, and granted us his mercy and gifts of grace. Ant. ed.

Love maketh all things common. Ant. ed.

edifying and soul's health; yea, and reap daily, in that I left my doctrine and ensample of living behind me, by which many are converted unto Christ daily. If thou desire therefore to enjoy part of my merit, go and read in my gospel; and thou shalt find the fruit of my labour, the knowledge of Christ, the health of the soul and everlasting life.

'And as I loved my brethren when I lived, so I love them still, and now more perfectly. Howbeit my love then was painful: for the more I loved, the more I sorrowed, feared, and cared for them, to bring them into the knowledge of the truth, and to keep them in unity of faith, lest the false prophets should deceive them, or their own infirmities should break peace and unity, or cause them to fall into any sin. But now my love is without pain. For I see the will and providence of God, and how the end of all things shall be unto his glory and profit of the elect. And though I see the elect shall sometime fall; yet I see how they shall arise again, and how that their fall shall be unto the glory of God and their own profit. And we, that are in heaven, love you all alike: neither love we one more and another less. And therefore if ye love us more one than another, that is fleshly; as mine old Corinthians once loved, and I rebuked them. Neither can we be moved to come more to help one than another; but we wait when God will send any of us unto the elect, that call for help in Christ's name. Wherefore, if thou wilt be holpen of any of us, pray in Christ's name: and God shall send one of us, an angel or a saint, to keep the power of the devils from you; but not whom thou wouldest choose, tempting God, but whom it pleaseth God to send.

St Paul was a loving and careful preacher. Ant. ed.

A good saying of St Paul. Ant. ed.

'And if your preachers love you not after the same manner, to edify you with the true doctrine of Christ and ensample of living thereafter, and to keep you in unity of faith and charity, they be not of Christ's disciples, but antichrists, which, under the name of Christ, seek to reign over you as temporal tyrants. And in like manner, if this be not written in your hearts, that ye ought to love one another as Christ loved you, and as ye had ensample of us his apostles, ye go astray in vanities, and are not in the right way.'

And hereby are we sure that we know him, if we keep his commandments.

The state of grace. W. T.

This is clean against the doctrine of them which say, that we cannot know whether we be in the state of grace or no. John saith, If we keep his commandments, then we be sure that we know Christ is everlasting life. Then, contrary to the bishop of Rome, christian men have doctrine to know whether they be in grace or no.

They that keep the commandments are in the state of grace. Ant. ed.

The keeping of God's commandments certifieth us that we be in the state of grace. But our pharisaical[1] doctors have no doctrine to know when a man is in a state of grace: wherefore it is manifest that they keep not God's commandments, nor be in state of grace, but of all ungraciousness.

When we do good to our neighbour, then we may be assured that we are in the state of grace. Ant. ed.

Neither know such[2] doctors whether they be in state of grace, but[3] keep men's commandments: ergo, men's commandments certify not that we be in state of grace. Though thou have a devotion to stick up a candle before a post, and so forth, yet thou canst never be sure thereby, that thou art in the favour of God. But if thou have devotion to help thy brother in all his misfortunes, because he is the image of God and price of Christ's blood, then thy devotion certifieth thee that thou art in the favour of God, or state of grace.

He that saith, I know him, and yet keepeth not his commandments, is a liar, and the truth is not in him.

A sure argument to know false prophets by. W. T.

When our Pharisees say, 'Do as we bid you, and not as we do;' they testify that they keep not God's commandments: unto which testimony our eyes also bear record. And they that keep not God's commandments, be liars and have no truth in them: and then, when they preach, they cannot but preach lies; and then, though they preach Christ, they preach him falsely, unto their fleshly vantage, and not our souls' health.
1 Cor. v.
And forasmuch as we may have no fellowship with them that keep not God's commandments, and inasmuch as all such are false prophets, void of all truth; it followeth that we ought to give our doctors no[4] audience, though their defenders stood by them with their swords drawn; but rather to lay down our heads, and stretch forth our necks to be slain.

[1 So P. C. L., but D. omits *pharisaical.*]
[2 So P. C. L., but in D. *our doctors know not.*]
[3 So P. C. L., but D. *our doctors keep, &c.*]
[4 So P. C. L., but D. has *none.*]

He that keepeth his word, in him verily is the love of God perfect, and hereby know we that we are in him.

That is, he that keepeth his commandments, loveth unfeignedly; and is thereby sure that he is in God. For to be in God is to believe in the mercy of God; and to believe in mercy is cause of love, and love cause of working. And therefore he that worketh for God's sake, is sure that he loveth and that he trusteth in God; which is to be in God or in Christ. And as by wilful keeping of the commandments we be sure that we love God, and believe in God; even so through wilful breaking of them, we may be sure that we neither love nor believe in him, and therefore that we be not in him.

To be in God is to believe in the mercy of God Ant. ed.

A rule to know whether we love God, or love him not. W. T.

He that saith he abideth in him, ought to walk as he walked.

All that be baptized in Christ are washed in him, to put off pride, wrath, hate and envy, with all their old conversation, by which they oppressed their neighbours; and have promised to become, every man even as Christ himself unto his brethren, in love and kindness both in word and deed. They therefore which resist Christ's testament, and will not let it be known, and walk in the testament of the arch-priest of Rome[5], with unions, pluralities and totquots, some one of them robbing ten parishes of the tenth of all their yearly increase, and withdrawing from them God's word, the food of their souls, and from the poor their daily sustenance, which ought to have their part in the tithes and other rents, when the preacher and other necessary ministers have out their parts, (a due and lawful stipend,) are not in Christ: for Christ neither so walked nor so taught.

Look upon the bishop of Rome's own decrees. Causa XII. quæst. ii. and other places[5]. W. T.

[[5] In D. the marginal note to this passage is, "They that be enemies to the testament of Christ, and are teachers of man's inventions, are not in Christ." The marginal note given above is that found in the P. C. L. ed. Qu. ii. of causa XII contains no less than 75 capitula, the 26th of which, or *Concesso*, professes to be an extract from a rescript of pope Gelasius, Clero et ordini et plebi Brundusii; in which he says, Reditus et oblationes fidelium in quatuor partes dividat [antistes]; quarum unam episcopus sibi ipsi retineat; alteram clericis pro officiorum suorum sedulitate distribuat; fabricis tertiam; quartam pauperibus et peregrinis habeat fideliter erogandam; quarum rationem divino est redditurus examini. The five next capitula are made up of decrees or affirmations, by popes and others, to the same effect. Corp. Jur. Can. Decr. 2[da] pars, Thielman Kerver. 1516.]

Brethren, I write no new commandment unto you, but an old commandment which ye had at the beginning: for an old commandment is the word which ye heard from the beginning.

An old commandment is the word which ye heard from the beginning. Ant. ed.

I write no new precept, but only put you in remembrance of that old, which was taught you when you were first baptized in Christ, to love each other as he did you: which is an old commandment, and was given at the beginning of the world, and hath ever since been written in the heart of all that put their hope in God.

Again, a new commandment I write unto you, which is true in him, and also in you; for the darkness is past, and the true light now shineth.

The devil hath sown his darkness in the field where this commandment should grow; and the weeds of men's traditions had overgrown the corn of this old commandment; so that it was antiquate[1], and clean out of knowledge. But Christ, the light of all true doctrine, now shineth; and hath scattered the darkness, and plucked up the weeds by the roots, and restored this old commandment again. And in him it is a true commandment; for he loved truly. And in you it is a true commandment; for ye, for his sake, love one another truly also. And by the reason of this renewing it is called a new commandment, as it is now called a new learning, and may well so be; for it hath lain long in darkness, and that in such darkness, that many be shrined for holy saints, whose deeds and living (when thou lookest upon them, conferring them to the light of this old doctrine, that now shineth again out of darkness) are abominable blasphemies to God's doctrine, the which they have sworn to teach and follow[2].

He that saith he is in the light, and yet hateth his brother, is in darkness.

He that hateth his brother is

For whosoever feeleth his own damnation under the law, and believeth in the mercy that is in Christ, the same cannot but love Christ, and his neighbour for his sake. And therefore he that hateth his brother for any offence done to him, the

[1 So D. but in P. C. L. *waxen old.*]

[2 Such is the conclusion of this paragraph in the P. C. L. edition; but in Day's edition a contemptuous account of Cardinal Wolsey's death has been substituted for it.]

same seeth not what Christ hath done for him, but is in darkness still.

in darkness, and seeth not Christ. Ant. ed.

He that loveth his brother, abideth in the light, and there is none offending in him.

Abideth in the light; that is, continueth in the knowledge of Christ. And there is none offending in him; that is, first, he will willingly do nothing, either in word or in deed, that shall offend his brother: for love will not let him. And secondarily, if aught be done or said, that may be well done or said, he taketh it to the best, and is not offended. And thus ye see that the knowledge of Christ is cause of all goodness, and the ignorance of Christ cause of all evil. And so the doctrine of them is not false, which say that faith in Christ is root of all godly virtue, and the cause of keeping the commandments; and where faith is, thereto be no sin nor damnation; and that say unbelief to be the mother of all vice, and cause of breaking the commandments, and to keep men in sin and damnation only, as faith only looseth us thence.

To abide in the light is to abide in the knowledge of Christ. Ant. ed.

Faith in Christ is the root of all goodness. Ant. ed.

And he that hateth his brother is in darkness; and walketh in darkness, and knoweth not whither he goeth: for darkness hath blinded his eyes.

He that hateth his brother is in the ignorance of Christ and of his own sin, and without repentance and faith that his sins be forgiven him in Christ; and therefore is merciless unto his brother, whom Christ commandeth him to pity and love. And in that ignorance he walketh, that is, worketh evil, and loveth the things of the world, and seeketh in them the lusts of the flesh, which are the quenching of the Spirit and death of the soul, and for love of them hateth his brother. And this ignorance of Christ, which is unbelief, is the cause of all the wickedness that we do unto our brethren.

He that hateth his brother is in ignorance. Ant. ed.

Ignorance. Ant. ed.

I write unto you, little children, that your sins are forgiven you for his name's sake. I write unto you, fathers, that ye know him that was from the beginning. I write unto you, young men, how that ye have overcome the wicked.

I write unto you, that are young in the faith and yet weak, and therefore fall now and then, how that your sins are forgiven you, as soon as ye repent and reconcile yourselves unto your brethren whom ye have offended, even for his

When we have offended our brother, if we reconcile ourselves unto him again, then are our sins forgiven. Ant. ed.

name's sake only, and not for our own deeds, whether afore or after, or for any other man's deeds or satisfaction, save for his only.

I write unto you, that are fathers in the doctrine of God, to teach other how that ye know him that was from the beginning, and is no new thing, though he newly received our nature. And through knowledge of him which is the only light, and the door unto the knowledge of God, ye are become fathers in the scriptures. Or else ye had never understood it, though ye had studied never so much: as it appeareth by the indurate Jews, and also by our own[1] new Pharisees; which persecute the scripture, and the true sense thereof, because they be drowned in the ignorance of Christ, as their deeds and contrary living well testify.

I write unto you, young men, that are strong in suffering persecutions, and fight for your profession, not with the sword, but with suffering, how that ye have overcome that wicked which poisoned the world at the beginning, and yet worketh in the children of darkness and unbelief; and that in believing the word of truth, as it followeth anon after.

I write unto you, young children, how that ye know the Father. I write unto you, fathers, how that ye know him that was from the beginning. I write unto you, young men, that ye be strong, and the word of God dwelleth in you, and that ye have overcome the wicked.

We cannot know the Father, but by the Son. Ant. ed.

I write unto you, young children, how that ye know the Father, whom ye love through knowledge of the Son; or else you had never known him as a Father, but as a judge and a tyrant, and had hated him. I write unto you, fathers, as before, how ye are fathers of all truth, in knowing the Son: or else ye had ever continued in darkness remediless.

Faith in Christ overcometh the world. Ant. ed. Chap. v.

I write unto you, young men, how that ye are strong, and that your strength is the word of God, which dwelleth in your breast through faith, in which ye have overcome the wicked devil, and all his pomps; as it followeth: "This is the victory that overcometh the world, even our faith."

Love not the world, nor the things that are in the world. If a man love the world, the love of the Father is not in him. For all that is in the world, as the lust of the flesh, the lust of the eyes, and the pride of good, are not of the Father, but are of the world. And the world

[[1] In P. C. L *own* is wanting.]

vanisheth away, and the lust thereof: but he that doeth the will of God abideth ever.

The love of the world quencheth the love of God. Balaam, for the love of the world, closed his eyes at the clear light which he well saw. For love of the world the old Pharisees blasphemed the Holy Ghost, and persecuted the manifest truth, which they could not improve. For love of the world many are this day fallen away; and many which stood on the truth's side, and defended it awhile, for love of the world have gotten them unto the contrary part, and are become the antichrist of Rome's mamelukes, and are waxen the most wicked enemies unto the truth, and most cruel against it. They know the truth, but they love the world: and when they espied that the truth could not stand with the honours which they sought in the world, they hated it deadly, and both wittingly and willingly persecuted it, sinning against the Holy Ghost: which sin shall not escape here unpunished; as it shall not be without damnation in the world to come; but shall have an end here with confusion and shame, as had Judas Iscariot, the traitor[3].

Avarice or covetousness. W. T.

The love of the world draweth many from Christ. Ant. ed.

By the lust of the flesh is understood lechery, which maketh a man altogether a swine; and by the lust of the eyes is understood covetousness, which is the root of all evil, and maketh to err from the faith. And then followeth pride: which three are the world, and captains over all other vices, and occasions of all mischief.

The lust of the flesh and of the eyes. W. T.

1 Tim. vi. Pride.

And if pride, covetousness, and lechery be the world, as St John saith, then turn your eyes unto the spiritualty, unto the Roman bishop, cardinals, bishops, abbots, and all other prelates, and see whether such dignities be not the world, and whether the way to them be not also the world! To get the old abbot's treasure, I think it be the readiest way to be the new. How few come by promotion, except they buy it, or serve long for it, or both! To be skilled in war and in polling, to maintain war and lusts, and to be a good ambassador, is the only way to a bishoprick, or to pay truly for it. See whether pluralities, unions, totquots, and changing the less benefice and bishoprick for the greater (for the contrary change I trow was never seen), may be without covetousness and pride. And then, if such things be the world, and the world not of God,

Compare the world to the pope, cardinals, &c., and you shall find them to be the world. Ant. ed.

[3 So P. C. L. ed., in D. there is another notice of Wolsey's death.]

Pride. Ant. ed. John v. Covetousness. W. T.

how is our spiritualty of God? If pride be seeking of glory, and they that seek glory cannot believe, how can our spiritualty believe in Christ? If covetousness turn men from the faith, how are our spiritualty in the faith? If Christ, when the devil proffered him the kingdoms of the world and the glory thereof, refused them, as things impossible to stand with his kingdom, which is not of the world; of whom are our spiritualty, which have received them? If covetousness be a traitor, and taught Judas to sell his master; how should he not in so long time teach our spiritualty the same craft?—namely when they be of all kings' secrets, and the ambassadors of their secrets, and have thereto throughout all Christendom a secret council of their own, of the which never lay-man was partaker, and with which they turn the end of all appointments unto their own honour and profit? Covetousness hath taught them to bring in damnable sects, according unto the prophecy of Peter, and to corrupt the scripture with false glosses, and to turn every good ordinance, that had a virtuous beginning, unto a vicious end. The promotions of the spiritualty corrupt their minds, while they be yet in the shell and unhatched: for they come thither but for covetousness, and to avoid the cross of Christ in the world; except them that be compelled of their friends, or be so simple that they mark not their falsehood beforehand. Who, knowing the truth and loving it, would put his head in the Romish bishop's halter, that so muzzleth men's mouths that they cannot open them to defend any truth at all? When temporal kings were in their high authority, then the general council repressed the enormities of the spiritualty. But since the antichrist of Rome, cardinals and bishops, were exalted, and the emperor and kings became their servants, they would suffer nought to be determined in their councils that should reform the world of their devilish pride, insatiable covetousness, and stinking lechery, which may stand with no godly virtue. But the world, which is not of God, shall at the last have an end with confusion; and they only abide that do the will of the Father, which will is, that we believe in the Son, and love one another. Let them therefore that have the world's good (I might say the world's god) use it, but not love it; that they may be ready to bestow it at the pleasure of God. And let them which have it not, desire it not, for it blindeth the eyes of the seeing; (Deut. xvi.):

Note. Ant. ed. The promotions of the spiritualty corrupt their minds. Ant. ed.

Popes and bishops will suffer nothing that shall restrain their pride and covetousness. Ant. ed.

Riches and covetousness blindeth the eyes of the seeing. Ant. ed. Deut. xvi.

but let them put their trust in God, which shall not fail them, nor leave them destitute of raiment and food, which Paul counselleth to be content with. The rich (as James saith) persecute the true believers. The rich will never stand forth openly for the word of God. If of ten thousand there spring one Nicodemus, it is a great thing.

Little children, it is now the last hour: and as ye have heard that antichrist should come, even so now are many antichrists come already; whereby we know that it is the last hour. They went out of us, but were none of us; for had they been of us, they had continued with us. But that fortuned that it might appear, how they were not all of us.

Hour is here taken for time; the last hour is as much to say as the last time. Though the apostles might not know when the last day shall be, and how long the world should endure, yet this was shewed them, and us by them, that antichrist should first come; and not only come, but also prevail, and be received after a worldly manner, and reign over all; and set up a long continuing kingdom, with damnable sects and wonderful kinds of hypocrisy, that is to say, falsehood cloaked under a contrary pretence, as testifieth Paul and also Peter. Which antichrist began with the apostles, and sowed his doctrine among the doctrine of the apostles; preaching many things as the apostles did, and adding ever somewhat of his own, that the weeds might ever grow up together with the corn. Of which John gathered a sign, that the last day drew nigh; though he could not be sure how long it were thereto.

What the last hour is. W. T.

Antichrist. W. T.

Antichrist is one of the first that seeth the light, and cometh and preacheth Christ awhile, and seeketh his glory in Christ's gospel. But when he espieth that there will no glory cleave unto that preaching, then he getteth him to the contrary part, and professeth himself an open enemy, if he cannot disguise himself, and hide the angle of his poisoned heresy under a bait of true doctrine.

The worldlings love the gospel so long as it bringeth gain. Ant. ed.

The apostles were clear-eyed, and espied antichrist at once, and put him to flight, and weeded out his doctrine quickly. But when charity waxed cold, and the preachers began to seek themselves, and to admit glory and honour of riches; then antichrist disguised himself after the fashion of a true apostle, and preached Christ wilily, bringing in now this

The papists powdered the doctrine of Christ with their dregs. Ant. ed.

tradition, and now that, to darken the doctrine of Christ; and set up innumerable ceremonies, and sacraments, and imagery, giving them significations at the first; but at the last, the significations laid apart, preached the work as an holy deed, to justify and to put away sin, and to save the soul, that men should put their trust in works, and in whatsoever was unto his glory and profit; and under the name of Christ ministered[1] Christ out of all together[2], and became head of the congregation himself.

The pope hath put Christ from his rule and government. Ant. ed.

The bishop of Rome made a law of his own, to rule his church by, and put Christ's out of the way. All the bishops swear unto the bishop of Rome, and all curates unto the bishops; but all forswear Christ and his doctrine.

But seeing John took a sign of the last day, that he saw antichrist begin, how nigh ought we to think that it is, which, after eight hundred years reigning in prosperity, see it decay again, and his falsehood to be disclosed, and him to be slain with the spirit of the mouth of Christ; that is, with that old doctrine that proceeded out of Christ's mouth: for Paul saith, when antichrist is uttered[3], then cometh the end.

Antichrist hath been long among us. W. T.

But ye have anointing of that holy, and know all things. I write not unto you as though ye knew not the truth, but as unto them that know it, and know that no lie is of truth.

The holy. W. T.

Christ in the scripture is called The Holy; because he only sanctifieth, and halloweth us. And he is called Christ, that is to say, anointed; because he anointeth our souls with the Holy Ghost, and with all the gifts of the same. Ye are not anointed with oil in your bodies, but with the Spirit of Christ in your souls: which Spirit teacheth you all truth in Christ, and maketh you to judge what is a lie, and what truth, and to know Christ from antichrist. For except he taught your souls within, the pouring in of words at your ears were in vain. For they must be all taught of God: and the things of God no man knoweth, save the Spirit of God; and the carnal man knoweth not the things of the Spirit of God; when contrary, the spiritual, that is anointed

Anointed. W. T.

John vi.

The carnal man knoweth not the things of the Spirit of God. Ant. ed.

[1 So D., but P. C. L. has *mustered.*]

[2 That is, so served Christ as to turn him out of the possession of every thing.]

[3 Made conspicuous. See Vol. I. p. 12.]

with the Spirit, judgeth all things. And therefore we are forbidden to call us any master upon earth; seeing we have all one master now in heaven, which only teacheth us with his Spirit, though by the administration and office of a faithful preacher: which preacher yet cannot make his preaching spring in the heart, no more than a sower can make his corn grow, nor can say, 'This man shall receive the word[4], and this not;' but soweth the word only, and committeth the growing to God, whose Spirit breatheth where he listeth, and maketh the ground of whose heart he lusteth fruitful, and chooseth whom he will at his own pleasure, and for no other cause known unto any man.

1 Cor. ii.
Matt. xxiii.

Who is a liar, but he that denieth that Jesus is Christ? The same is antichrist, that denieth the Father and the Son.

'Forasmuch as antichrist and Christ are two contraries, and the study of antichrist is to quench the name of Christ, how can the Romish bishop and his sects be antichrist, when they all preach Christ?' 'How was,' say I again to thee, 'Pelagius, whose doctrine the bishop of Rome defendeth in the highest degree, antichrist, and all other heretics?' Verily, sir, the bishop of Rome seeketh himself, as all heretics did; and abuseth the name of Christ, to gather offerings, tithes and rents in his name, to bestow them unto his own honour and not Christ's, and to bring the conscience of the people into captivity under him through superstitious fear, as though he had such authority given him of Christ. And every syllable, that hath a sound as though it made for his purpose, that he expoundeth falsely and fleshly; and therewith juggleth and bewitcheth the ears of the people, and maketh them his own possession, to believe what him listeth[5], as though it made no matter to them whether he preached true or false, so they believe and do as he biddeth them. But all the texts that shew him to do his duty[6], he putteth out of the way; and all the texts thereto, that set the consciences at liberty in Christ, and prove our salvation to be in Christ only. And, with Pelagius, he preacheth the justifying of works; which is the denying of

Antichrist, who it is. Ant. ed.

The pope captivateth the understanding of all men with his superstitious rites and ceremonies. Ant. ed.

The bishop of Rome and Pelagius agree. W. T.

[4 So P. C. L., in D. *the word* is wanting.]
[5 D. has *lusteth.*]
[6 So P. C. L., but in D. *shew his duty to do.*]

Christ. He preacheth a false binding and loosing with ear-confession, which is not in the trust and confidence of Christ's blood-shedding. He preacheth the false penance of deeds; not to tame the flesh that we sin no more, but to make satisfaction, and to redeem the sin that is past: which what other can it be, save the denying of Christ, which is the only redemption of sin? He maketh of the works of the ceremonies, which were wont to be signs and remembrances of things to be believed or done, image-service unto God and his saints, which are spirits, to purchase with the merits of them whatsoever the blind soul imagineth; which all are the denying of Christ. For if thou wilt receive any anointing of grace or mercy any whence, save of him, he is no longer Christ unto thee. Christ is called Jesus, a Saviour; he is called Christus, king anointed over all men, of whom they must hold, and whose benefit must all they have. He is called Emmanuel, God is with us: for he only maketh God our God, our strength, power, sword and shield, and shortly our Father. He is called Sanctus, that is, holy, that halloweth, sanctifieth and blesseth all nations. And these be his names for ever, and be no names of hypocrisy: as we sometimes call him Thomas Curteis[1], which is but a churl; and as we call them curates, which care for their parishes as the wolf for the flock; and them bishops, that are overseers, which will so oversee, that they will suffer nought to be prosperous save their own commonwealth; and as some call themselves dead, which live in all voluptuousness; and as some call themselves poor, without having any thing proper[2], and yet live in all abundance; and as they shave and disguise themselves with garments and ornaments, to signify ever a contrary thing than that they be.

Jesus. Christus. Emmanuel. Sanctus. Thomas Curteis, a churl. Ant. ed. Dead men. Poor men.

Nay, Christ is no hypocrite, or disguised, that playeth a part in a play, and representeth a person, or state, which he is not; but is alway that his name signifieth, he is ever a Saviour, and ever anointeth[3] with grace, and ever maketh

Christ is no disguised person. Ant. ed.

[1 Archdeacon Todd in his edition of Johnson's Dictionary traces the word *courteous* to the gothic *Kurteis*, as its earliest known form.]

[2 That is, *of their own:* he alludes to the vow of mortification made by all monastic orders; and that of poverty made by the mendicant friars.]

[3 So D., but P. C. L. has *anointed.*]

God with us, and ever sanctifieth. Neither is there any other to save and sanctify from sin, or anoint with grace, or to set God at one with men. And these things, which his name signify, doth he ever unto all that have trust and confidence in his blood, as soon as they repent of the sin which they desire to be saved and sanctified from.

Now though the bishop of Rome and his sects give Christ these names, yet in that they rob him of the effect, and take the significations of his names unto themselves, and make of him but an hypocrite, as they themselves be, they be the right antichrists, and deny both the Father and Son. For they deny the witness that the Father bare unto his Son, and deprive the Son of all the power and glory that his Father gave him.

The pope and his shavelings are right antichrists. Ant. ed.

Whosoever denieth the Son, the same hath not the Father.

For no man knoweth the Father, but the Son, and to whom the Son sheweth him. Moreover, if thou know not the mercy that God hath shewed thee in Christ, thou canst not know him as a Father. Thou mayest well, besides[4] Christ, know him as a tyrant. And thou mayest know him by his works, as the old philosophers did, that there is a God; but thou canst neither believe in his mercy, nor love his laws, which is his only worship in the spirit, save by Christ.

To know God. Ant. ed. Matt. xi.

Let therefore abide in you that which ye heard at the beginning. If that which ye heard at the beginning shall remain in you, then shall ye continue in the Son, and in the Father. And this is the promise that he hath promised us, everlasting life.

If we abide in the old doctrine which the apostles taught, and hearken to no new learning[5]; then abide we in the Son (for upon the Son build they us), and in the Father through confidence in the Son; and are heirs of everlasting life.

The apostles' doctrine ought we to abide by. W. T.

These things have I written unto you, because of them that deceive you. And the anointing that ye received of him dwelleth in you, and ye need not that any man teach you; but as that anointing teacheth you of all things, and is true, and is no lie, even as it hath taught you, so abide therein.

When a true preacher preacheth, the Spirit entereth the hearts of the elect, and maketh them feel the righteousness

[4 That is, *apart from.*]

[5 In D. *learning* is omitted.]

of the law of God, and by the law the poison of their corrupt nature; and thence leadeth them, through repentance, unto the mercy that is in Christ's blood; and as an ointment healeth the body, even so the Spirit, through confidence and trust in Christ's blood, healeth the soul, and maketh her love the law of God; and therefore is it called anointing or an ointment, and may well be signified by the oil of our sacrament. But outward oil can neither heal the soul, nor make her feel, save as a sign, or as a bush at a tavern door quencheth a man's thirst, neither is it a thing to put trust in. Let us therefore follow the teaching of the Spirit; which we have received as (Paul saith) an earnest, to certify our hearts, and to make us feel the things of God, and not cleave unto the traditions of men; in which is no feeling, but that one saith so, and another thus, confirming their assertions with glorious persuasions of wisdom, but not after the wisdom of God: which reasons another denieth with contrary sophisms; and so riseth brawling about vain words, without certainty[1].

Anointing. W. T.

Outward oil availeth nothing. Ant. ed.

And now, little children, abide in him, that when he shall appear, we may have confidence, and not be made ashamed of him at his coming.

We must cleave to the doctrine of the apostles. Ant. ed.

Here are two things to be marked: one, if we cleave unto Christ after the doctrine of the apostles, and as they built us upon him, we shall be bold and sure of ourselves at his coming; as a servant, which in his master's absence doth only his master's commandments, cannot be confounded at his coming home again. But and if we follow men's doctrine, how can we be bold, yea, how should we not be ashamed with our teachers, unto whom he shall then[2] say (when they boast themselves how that they have been his vicars), 'I know you not; depart from me, ye that have wrought wickedness, and under my name have brought in damnable sects, and have taught your disciples to believe in other things than in me.' Now the sum of all that the apostles taught, and how they built us upon Christ, is the new Testament. But the bishop of Rome's doctrine is not there found, but improved[3]. Confounded there-

A sore saying to all hypocrites and teachers of false doctrine. Ant. ed.

[1 In Day, without *all* certainty.]

[2 So P. C. L., but D. *then he should.*]

[3 So D., but P. C. L. has *founded, but even improved.* The reader will remember that by *improved* T. means *reproved.*]

fore shall he be, which, witting and willing, shutteth his eyes at the true light, and openeth them to believe his lies.

Another thing is this: all the scripture maketh mention of the resurrection and coming again of Christ, and that all men, both they that go before, and they that come after, shall then receive their rewards together; and we are commanded to look every hour for that day. And what is done with the souls, from the departing of[4] their bodies unto that day, doth the scripture make no mention; save only that they rest in the Lord, and in their faith. Wherefore he that determineth aught of the state of them that be departed, doth but teach the presumptuous imaginations of his own brain; neither can his doctrine be any article of our faith. What God doth with them is a secret laid up in the treasury of God: and we ought to be patient, being certified of the scripture, that they which die in the faith are at rest, and ought no more to search that secret, than to search the hour of the resurrection, which God hath put only in his own power. But this remember, that the whole nature of man is poisoned and infected with sin. And the whole life of sin must be mortified. Now the root of all sin, and first vice that[5] we were infect with, is, that we would be wise where God hath not taught us; as ye see how Eve would have been as God, in the knowledge of good and bad. And therefore hath God hid many things in his power; and commanded that we shall search none of his secrets further than he hath opened them in his scripture, to mortify this poison of all poisons, the desire to appear wise, and that we be ashamed to be ignorant in any thing at all. Wherefore they that violently make articles of the faith, without God's word, are yet alive in the root of all sin and vice, and grow out of the devil, and not out of Christ. And their articles are of the blindness of the devil, and not of the light of Christ; for Christ's light hath testimony of the scripture everywhere.

We must believe the resurrection, and not to be curious to understand the state of the souls departed, where they are, nor what they do. Ant. ed.

If ye know that he is righteous, know that all that work righteousness are born of him.

Our nature is to work wickedness, and so blind thereto that it can see no righteousness. And then it followeth that

[4 So P. C. L., but D. has *their departing*.]
[5 So P. C. L., but D. has *and* for *now*, and omits *that*.]

we must be born anew in Christ, ere we[1] can either do or yet know what is righteous. And in him we must first be made righteous ourselves, ere we can work righteous works; which conclusion is contrary unto the bishop of Rome: for he saith, that the works do make the man righteous; and Christ's doctrine saith, that the man maketh the works righteous. A righteous man springeth out of righteous works, saith the bishop of Rome's doctrine: righteous works spring out of a righteous man, and a righteous man springeth out of Christ, saith Christ's doctrine: the works make the man righteous, which before was wicked, saith the bishop of Rome: the works declare that the man is righteous, saith Christ's doctrine: but the man was first made righteous, in Christ; and the Spirit of Christ taught him what righteousness was, and healed his heart, and made him consent thereto, and to have his lust in righteousness, and to work righteously.

The doctrine of the pope is clean contrary to Christ's doctrine. Ant. ed.

THE THIRD CHAPTER.

BEHOLD, what love the Father hath shewed us, that we should be called the sons of God. For this cause the world knoweth you not, because it knoweth not him. Dearly beloved, now we are the sons of God, though yet it appeareth not what we shall be: but we know that when he shall appear we shall be like him; for we shall see him as he is.

The love of God to us-ward is exceeding great, in that he hath made us his sons, without all deserving of us; and hath given us his Spirit through Christ, to certify our hearts thereof, in that we feel that our trust is in God, and that our souls have received health and power to love the law of God; which is a sure testimony that we are sons, and under no damnation. Neither ought it to discourage us, or to make us think we were less beloved, because the world hateth us, and persecuteth us; for the world knoweth us not. Neither let[2] any marvel; for the world could not know Christ himself, for all his glorious coming with miracles and benefits, in healing the sick and raising the dead. But for all the oppression of the world, we are yet sure that we are God's sons. And in

The world could not know Christ. W. T.

[[1] In P. C. L., *ere we be, or can.*]
[[2] So P. C. L., but D. wants *let.*]

like manner, though the glory, that we shall be in, appear not, yet we are sure that we shall be like him, when he appeareth. As darkness vanisheth away at the coming of the sun, and the world receiveth a new fashion, and is turned into light, and suddenly made glorious; even so when he appeareth, and we shall see him as he is, we shall, with the sight[3] of him, be changed into the glory of his image, and made like him. And then shall the world both know him and us, unto their shame and confusion.

The world shall know Christ. W. T.

And all that have this hope in him purge themselves as he is pure.

The faith and hope of a christian man are no dead, idle, or barren things; but lively, working, and fruitful. For when the law through conscience of sin hath slain the soul, then hope and trust in Christ's blood, through certifying of the conscience that the damnation of the law is taken away, quickeneth her again; and maketh her to love the law, which is the purifying of the soul, and her life, and serving the law in the inner man. And then the said gifts, of hope and faith, stretch themselves forth unto the members, dead with natural lust, consent, and custom to sin; and quicken them, and purge them with the wholesome penance of Christ's doctrine; and make them serve the law outward, and bear wholesome fruit of love unto the profit of their neighbours, according to Christ's love unto us. For if the Spirit of Christ, with which God anointeth us and maketh us kings, and sealeth us and maketh us his sure and several kingdom, and which he giveth us in earnest (2 Cor. i.), and with which he changeth us into the image of Christ (2 Cor. iii.), dwell in our souls through faith, the same Spirit cannot but quicken the members also, and make them fruitful, (Rom. viii.) Wherefore the faith and hope of the Roman bishop, which by their own confession may stand with all wickedness, and consent unto all evil, and be without repentance toward God's law (as it appeareth by their three capital sins, touched of John a little above, pride, covetousness and lechery), are no true faith and hope, but vain words and visors only, according to his other disguising and names of hypocrisy.

A christian man's faith and hope are not idle. Ant. ed.

The faith of a christian man. W. T.

2 Cor i.

2 Cor. iii.

Rom. viii.

The pope's faith. W. T.

[3 So D., but P. C. L. has *light*.]

All that commit sin commit unrighteousness; for sin is unrighteousness.

What sin is. W. T.

That the English calleth here unrighteousness, the Greek calleth *anomia*, unlawfulness or breaking the law: so that all sin is breaking of God's law; and only the transgression of God's law is sin. Now all God's laws are contained in these two points; believe in Christ, and love thy neighbour. And these two points are the interpreting and expounding of all laws: so that whatsoever edifieth in faith and love, is to be kept as long as it so doth; and whatsoever hurteth faith or love, is to be broken immediately, though bishop[1], king, emperor, or an angel command it. And all indifferent things, that neither help nor hurt faith and love, are whole in the hands of father, mother, master, lord and prince. So that if they will sin against God, and overlade our backs, we may well run away, if we can escape; but not avenge ourselves. But and if they will break into thy conscience, as the bishop of Rome doth with his dumb traditions, and saith, 'To do this saveth thy soul, and to leave it undone loseth thy soul;' then defy them as the works of antichrist, for they make thee sin against the faith that is in Christ's blood, by which only thy soul is saved, and for lack of that only damned. And how love breaketh the law, take an example. It is a good law that men come to the church on the Sundays, to hear God's word, and to receive the sacrament of the body and blood of Christ, in remembrance of his benefits, and so to strengthen thy soul for to walk in his love, and in the love of our neighbour for his sake, &c.; yet if my father, mother, or any other that requireth my help be sick, I break that good commandment, to do my duty to my elders or my neighbour. And thus all laws are under love, and give room to love: and love interpreteth them, yea and breaketh them at a time, though God himself command them. For love is lord over all laws, and the thing that Christ commanded above all others[2].

The sum of God's law. W. T.

Love breaketh the law. Ant. ed.

And ye know that he appeared to take away our sins; and there is no sin in him.

Christ died not alone to purchase pardon for our fore-sins,

[1 So P. C. L., but D. has *king, emperor, pope.*]
[2 So P. C. L., but this last clause is not found in D.]

but also to slay all sin and the life of sin in our members. For all we that are baptized in the name of Christ, saith Paul (Rom. vi.), are baptized to die with him concerning sin; and that, as he after his resurrection dieth no more, so we after our baptism should walk in a new life, and sin no more. Our members are crucified with him, in all that pertaineth unto the life of sin. And if in Christ be no sin, then how can there be wilful sin in the faith that is in him, or in the quick members, that through faith grow out of him? Every man therefore that hath the true faith of Christ, purgeth himself, as he is pure.

Rom. vi. The signification of our baptism. W. T.

All that abide in him sin not. And all that sin have neither seen him nor known him.

As there is no sin in Christ the stock, so can there be none in the quick members, that live and grow in him by faith. And they that give themselves to sin, have neither seen, known, or felt by faith, the mercy that is in him. Our holy father then, which forbiddeth matrimony, and giveth his disciples licences, with his holy blessing, to keep whores, and pluralities, unions, and totquots, to rob the parishens[3], hath neither seen nor known Christ; no more have his disciples, that consent unto his iniquity. And if they know him not, they cannot truly describe him unto us. It followeth then, that their preaching is but hypocrisy.

The filthiness of the pope's doctrine.

Little children, let no man beguile you. He that worketh righteousness is righteous, as he is righteous.

Judge men by their deeds. For whosoever hath the light of God in his soul, he will let his light shine, that men shall see his good works. And therefore where ye see not the righteousness of works in the members outward, there, be sure, is no righteousness of faith in the heart inward. Let no man mock you with vain words. Whosoever preacheth Christ in word and deed, him take for Christ's vicar. And them that would prove themselves his vicars with sophistry, and, when it is come to the point, make a sword only their mighty arguments, and live contrary to all his doctrine, and in all their preachings blaspheme and rail on his blessed blood, take for the vicars of antichrist.

Where true faith is, there proceedeth good works.

Christ's vicar. W. T.

[3 Parishioners: see Vol. I. p. 257.]

He that sinneth is of the devil; for the devil sinneth from the beginning. But for this cause appeared the Son of God, even to destroy the works of the devil. All that are born of God do no sin: for his seed abideth in them; and they cannot sin, because they be born of God: And hereby are the sons of God known, and also the sons of the devil.

God and the devil are two contrary fathers, two contrary fountains, and two contrary causes: the one of all goodness, the other of all evil. And they that do evil are born of the devil; and first evil by that birth, ere they do evil. For ere a man do any evil outward, of purpose, he conceived that evil first in his mind, and consented unto it, and so was evil in his heart ere he wrought evil; and ere he conceived evil in his heart, he was born of the devil, and had received of his seed and nature; by the reason of which nature, seed and birth, he worketh evil naturally, and can do no other: as Christ saith, (John viii.) "Ye are of your father the devil, and therefore will do the lusts of your father." For it is a common proverb, the child followeth his father's nature[1].

The man is first evil. W. T.

John viii.

And on the other side, they that do good are first born of God, and receive of his nature and seed; and, by the reason of that nature and seed, are first good ere they do good, by the same rule. And Christ, which is contrary to the devil, came to destroy the works of the devil in us, and to give us a new birth, a new nature, and to sow new seed in us, that we should, by the reason of that birth, sin no more. For the seed of that birth, that is to wete the Spirit of God and the lively seed of his word sown in our hearts, keepeth our hearts, that we cannot consent to sin; as the seed of the devil holdeth the hearts of his, that they cannot consent to good[2]. This is contrary unto the bishop of Rome in two points: in the one, that he saith, that our good deeds make us first good, and teacheth us not to believe in Christ's blood, there to be washed and made first good; and in another, that he saith, God chooseth us first for our good qualities and properties, and for the enforcement and good endeavour of our free-will. What good endeavour is there, where the devil possesseth the whole heart, that it can consent to no good?

The man is first good. W. T.

The pope's doctrine. Ant. ed.

[1 So P. C. L., but in D. the paragraph ends with the quotation from John viii.]

[2 So D., but P. C. L. has *God.*]

And, finally, there is great difference between the sin of them that believe in Christ unfeignedly, and the sin of them that believe not. For they that believe sin not of purpose and of consent to wickedness, that it is good, casting and compassing aforehand, without grudge of conscience, to bring their purpose about: as ye see our hypocrites have vexed all Christendom this twenty years, to bring a little lust to effect[3]. Their fathers conceived mischief these eight hundred years ago; and the sons consent unto the same, and have no power to depart therefrom: and therefore their sin is devilish, and under the damnation of the law. But if he that believeth sin, he doth it not of purpose, or that he consenteth unto the life of sin; but of infirmity, chance, and some great temptation that hath overcome him. And therefore his sin is venial, and under mercy and grace, though it be murder, theft, or adultery; and not under the damnation of the law: so that his father shall scourge him, but not cast him away, or damn him. Mark the sin of Saul and of David. Saul ever excused his sin, and could not but persecute the will of God; and David confessed his sin, with great repentance, at the first warning, whensoever he forgot himself.

The faithful and unfaithful sin diversly. W. T.

All that work not righteousness are not of God; nor he that loveth not his brother. For this is the tidings which ye heard at the beginning, that we should love one another, and not be as Cain, which was of the devil and slew his brother. And wherefore slew he him? For his deeds were evil, and his brother's righteous. Marvel not my brethren though the world hate you.

The law of righteousness is, that we love one another as Christ loved us; and he that hath not this love[4] living in his heart, and, when the time is, bringeth not forth the fruits thereof, the same is not of God, but of the devil; whose birth and properties of the same ye see described in Cain, how he resisted God, and persecuted the children of God for their belief and works thereof. And as ye see in Cain and his brother Abel, so shall it ever continue, between the children of God and of the devil, unto the world's end. Wonder not therefore, though the world hate you.

[[3] This sentence is not in P. C. L., but is found in D.: and the expression *their fathers*, in the next sentence, seems to require some such antecedent as *our hypocrites*.]

[[4] So P. C. L., but D. has *law*.]

We know that we are translated from death to life, because we love the brethren. He that loveth not his brother abideth in death. All that hate their brethren are murderers; and ye know that no murderer hath eternal life abiding in him.

If thou love thy brother in Christ, and art ready to do and to suffer for him, as Christ did for thee, then thou art sure thereby, that thou art the son of God, and heir of life, and delivered from death and damnation. So have Christian men signs, to know whether they be in the state of grace or no. And on the other side, he that hath no power to love his brethren, may be sure that he is in the state of death and damnation. Another is this, let every man look upon his heart, and be sure that he which hateth his brother hath slain him before God, and is a murderer. And murderers shall not obtain the kingdom of God, but are Cain's brethren and the devil's children, and are heirs of death, and ever under damnation. Compare the regiment of the spiritualty, which have had the temporal sword in their hands now above eight hundred years, unto this doctrine of John; and judge whether they have led us truly after the steps of Christ's doctrine, or no[1].

Gal. v.

Hereby we are assured of love, because he left his life for us; and therefore ought we to leave our lives for our brethren. He then that hath the substance of the world, and seeth his brother have need, and shutteth up his compassion from him, how dwelleth the love of God in him?

If we felt the love of Christ's death, it would sure set our heart on fire to love him again, and our brethren for his sake, and should never cease to slay our resisting members, until we could not only be well content that our brethren were in a more prosperous state than we, but also until we could bless them when they curse us, and pray for them when they persecute us, and to suffer death for them, to testify the word of their soul's health unto them, and with love to overcome them, and to win them unto Christ. If now every christian man ought to have this rule of his profession before his eyes to learn it, that he should love his brother as Christ did him, to depart with his life for his brother's example, how far are they off from good scholars, that cannot find in their hearts

We must recompense evil with goodness. W. T.

[[1] So P. C. L., but D. omits *or no.*]

to depart with a little of the abundance and superfluity of their temporal goods, to help their neighbour's need!

My little children, let us not love in word, nor with the tongue; but with the deed, and of a truth. For thereby we know that we be of the truth, and so shall we certify our hearts in his sight.

If we have power to work, then doth the work certify our hearts that our faith in Christ, and love to God and our neighbour for his sake, are unfeigned; and that we are true children, and no hypocrites. And then are we bold in our conscience before God. And this is it that Peter meaneth (2 Pet. i.), where he biddeth us minister in our faith virtue[2], godly living, and all manner of good works, and therewith to make our vocation and election, or our calling and choosing, sure. For the sight of the work doth certify us, that God hath called us and chosen us unto grace and mercy.

Good works declare where good faith is. Ant. ed.

2 Pet. i.

But and if, when the time of working is come, we fly and have no power to work, then will our conscience accuse us of sin and transgression within the heart before God; and so, for fear of the rod, we dare not be bold, but draw back and stand aloof.

Let a child have never so merciful a father, yet if he break his father's commandments, though he be not under damnation, yet is he ever chid and rebuked, and now and then lashed with the rod; by the reason whereof he is never bold in his father's presence. But the child that keepeth his father's commandments, is sure of himself, and bold in his father's presence, to speak and ask what he will. "They that minister well get them good degree, and great confidence in the faith that is in Christ Jesus," saith Paul[3]. He that worketh is bold before God and man: for his conscience accuseth him not within, neither have we ought to wite[4] him withal, or to cast in his teeth. And as without the sight of the works Jacob the apostle cannot see thy faith (James ii.), no more shalt thou ever be sure or bold before God or man.

1 Tim. iii.

James ii.

[2 So Tyndale has rendered Ἐπιχορηγήσατε ἐν τῇ πίστει ὑμῶν τὴν ἀρετὴν &c., in his translation of 2 Pet. i. 5: 'In your faith minister virtue, and in virtue knowledge, &c.']

[3 For they that minister well get themselves good degree, and great liberty in the faith which is in Christ Jesu. Tyndale's Trans.]

[4 Wite: blame. See Vol. I. p. 164.]

But if our hearts condemn us, God is greater than our heart, and knoweth all things.

If our conscience accuse us of sin, God is so great and so mighty that it cannot be hid.

Dearly beloved, if our hearts condemn us not, then we trust to God-ward. And whatsoever we ask, that shall we receive of him; because we keep his commandments, and do the things which are pleasant in his sight.

Keeping of the commandments maketh a man see his faith, and to be bold therein. And faith, when it is without conscience of sin, goeth in to God boldly; and is strong and mighty in prayer to conjure God by all his mercies, and therewith obtaineth whatsoever he asketh of all his promises. And the text saith, "because we keep his commandments." Yea, verily his commandments make us bold. But the keeping of men's traditions and dumb ceremonies make us not bold before God, nor certify our conscience that our faith is unfeigned. Thou shalt not know, by sprinkling thyself with holy water, nor kissing the pax[1], nor with taking ashes, or though thou were anointed with all the oil in Thames street, that thy faith is sure. But and if thou couldest find in thine heart to bestow both life and goods upon thy neighbour in a just cause, and hast proved it; then art thou sure, that thou lovest Christ, and feelest that thou hast thy trust in his blood.

And this is his commandment, That we believe in his Son Jesus Christ, and love one another, as he gave commandment.

Faith is the root of all commandments. W. T.

Faith is the first, and also the root, of all commandments: and out of faith springeth love; and out of love, works. And when I break any commandment, I sin against love; for had I loved, I had not done it: and when I sin against love, I sin against faith; for had I earnestly, and with a full trust, remembered the mercy that Christ hath shewed me, I must have loved. Wherefore when we have broken any commandment, there is no other way to be restored again, than to go through repentance unto our faith again, and ask mercy for Christ's sake. And as soon as we have received faith that our sin is forgiven, we shall immediately love the commandment again, and through love receive power to work.

[[1] See Vol. I. p. 279.]

And he that keepeth his commandments abideth in him, and he in him. And hereby we know that there dwelleth in us of his Spirit which he gave us.

Through the works we are sure that we continue in Christ, and Christ in us; and that his Spirit dwelleth in us. For his Spirit it is that keepeth us in faith, and through faith in love, and through love in works.

THE FOURTH CHAPTER.

Dearly beloved, believe not every spirit, but prove the spirits whether they be of God. For many false prophets are gone out into the world.

SPIRITS are taken here for preachers, because of the preaching or doctrine, which, if it be good, then is it[2] of the Spirit of God; and if it be evil, of the spirit of the devil. Now ought we not to believe every man's doctrine unadvisedly, or condemn any man's preaching ere it be heard and seen what it is: but a christian man's part is to examine, judge and try it, whether it be true or no. "Quench not the Spirit," saith Paul, "neither despise prophesyings; but prove all things, and keep that which is good." Destroy not the gifts of the Spirit of God; but try whether they be of God, and good for the edifying of his congregation: and keep that which is good, and refuse that which is evil. And suffer every person that hath any gift of God to serve God therein, in his degree and estate, after a christian manner and a due order. Why shall we try the doctrines? Verily, for there be many false prophets abroad already. We told you before that antichrist should come; as our master Christ told us that he should come: but now I certify you that antichrist's kingdom is begun already; and his disciples are gone out to preach. Try therefore all doctrine. Wherewith shall we try it? With the doctrine of the apostles, and with the scripture, which is the touchstone: yea, and because ye love compendiousness, ye shall have a short rule to try them withal.

Spirits. W. T.

We may not believe every doctrine that is taught and preached, but we must first examine it with the touch-stone of God's word, and so either receive it or reject it. Ant. ed. 1 Thess. v.

The trial of all doctrine. W. T.

[[2] So P. C. L., but D. omits *then* and *it*.]

Hereby know ye the Spirit of God. Every spirit that confesseth that Jesus Christ is come in the flesh, is of God. And every spirit that confesseth not that Jesus Christ is come in the flesh, is not of God. And the same is that spirit of antichrist, of whom ye have heard that he should come; and even now he is in the world already.

Antichrist will not confess that Christ is come in the flesh. Ant. ed.

Whatsoever opinion any member of antichrist holdeth, the ground of all his doctrine is, to destroy this article of our faith, that Christ is come in the flesh. For though the most part of all heretics confess that Christ is come in the flesh, after their manner, yet they deny that he is come as the scripture testifieth, and the apostles preached him to be come. The whole study of the devil and all his members is to destroy the hope and trust that we should have in Christ's flesh, and in those things which he suffered for us in his flesh, and in the testament and promises of mercy which are made us in his flesh. For the scripture testifieth that Christ hath taken away the sin of the world in his flesh; and that at the same hour that he yielded up his spirit into the hands of his Father, he had full purged, and made full satisfaction for all the sins of the world: so that all the sin of the world, both before his passion and after, must be put away through repentance toward the law, and faith and trust in his blood, without respect of any other satisfaction, sacrifice, or work. For if I once sin, the law rebuketh my conscience, and setteth variance between God and me: and I shall never be at peace with God again, until I have heard the voice of his mouth, how that my sin is forgiven me for Christ's blood sake. And as soon as I believe that, I am at peace with God, and love his law again, and of love work.

Rom. v.

And that Christ hath done this service in his flesh, deny all the members of antichrist. And hereby thou shalt know them. All doctrine that buildeth thee upon Christ to put thy trust and confidence in his blood, is of God, and true doctrine: and all doctrine that withdraweth thine hope and trust from Christ is of the devil, and the doctrine of antichrist. Examine the Romish bishop by this rule, and thou shalt find that all he doth is to the destruction of this article. He wresteth all the scriptures, and setteth them clean against the woll[1], to

The doctrine that is of God. W. T.

The doctrine that is of the devil. W. T.

[[1] So P. C. L. and Day. Woll was not an unusual way of spelling *will;* and seems equivalent here to *intent* or *purpose.*]

destroy this article. He ministereth the very sacraments of Christ unto the destruction of this article; and so doth he all other ceremonies, and his absolution, penance, purgatory, dispensations, pardons[2], vows, with all disguisings. The Romish bishop preacheth that Christ is come to do away sins, yet not in the flesh, but in water, salt, oil, candles, boughs[3], ashes, friars' coats, and monks' cowls; and in the vows of them that forswear matrimony to keep whores, and swear beggary to possess all the treasure, riches, wealth and pleasures of the world; and have vowed obedience, to disobey with authority all the laws both of God and man. For in these hypocritish and false sacrifices teacheth he us to trust for the forgiveness of sins, and not in Christ's flesh.

The bishop of Rome's doctrine of Christ. W. T.

Ye are of God, little children, and have overcome them. For greater is he that is in you than he that is in the world.

He that dwelleth in you, and worketh in you through faith, is greater than he which dwelleth and worketh in them through unbelief. And in his strength ye abide by your profession, and confess your Lord Jesus; how that he is come in the flesh, and hath purged the sin of all that believe in his flesh. And through that faith ye overcome them in the very torments of death: so that neither their jugglings, neither their pleasures, neither their threatenings, nor their torments, nor the very death wherewith they slay your bodies, can prevail against you.

God is the worker in us by faith that we have in him. Ant. ed.

They be of the world, and therefore they speak of the world, and the world attendeth unto them. We be of God, and he that knoweth God heareth us; and he that is not of God heareth us not. And hereby we know the spirit of truth, and the spirit of error.

There be, and ever shall be, two generations in the world: the one of the devil, which naturally hearken unto the false apostles of the devil, because they speak so agreeable unto their natural complexion; and another of God, which hearken unto the true apostles of God, and consent unto their doctrine. And this is a sure rule to judge spirits withal; that we judge them to have the spirit of truth which hearken unto the true

Two generations in the world. W. T.

[2 P. C. L. omits *pardons*.]
[3 P. C. L. omits *boughs*.]

doctrine of Christ's apostles, and them to have the spirit of error, which hearken unto worldly and devilish doctrine, abhorring the preaching of the apostles. And look whether the bishop of Rome's doctrine be worldly or no, if pride and covetousness be worldly, yea, and lechery too. For what other is all his doctrine, than of benefices, promotions, dignities, bishopricks, cardinalships, vicarages, parsonages, prebends, change of bishopricks and resigning of benefices, of unions, pluralities, totquots, and that which cometh once into their hands may not out again; yea, and of whores and concubines, and of captiving of consciences for covetousness? And all that hearken to that doctrine abhor the doctrine of the[1] apostles, and persecute it, and them that preach it.

The bishop of Rome's doctrine is worldly. W. T.

Dearly beloved, let us love one another; for love is of God: and all that love are born of God, and know God. And he that loveth not, knoweth not God; for God is love.

John singeth his old song again; and teacheth an infallible and sure token, which we may see and feel at our fingers' ends, and thereby be out of all doubt, that our faith is unfeigned, and that we know God, and be born of God, and that we hearken unto the doctrine of the apostles purely and godly, and not of any curiosity, to seek glory and honour therein unto ourselves, and to make a cloak thereof to cover our covetousness and filthy lusts: which token is, if we love one another. For the love of a man's neighbour unfeignedly springeth out of the unfeigned knowledge of God in Christ's blood: by which knowledge we be born of God, and love God and our neighbours for his sake. And so he that loveth his neighbour unfeignedly is sure of himself, that he knoweth God, and is of God unfeignedly: and contrariwise, he that loveth not, knoweth not God; for God in Christ's blood is such a love, that if a man saw it, it were impossible that he should not break out into the love of God again, and of his neighbour for his sake.

He that loveth God is born of God. Ant. ed.

The fountain of love. W. T.

Herein appeared the love of God unto us-ward, because God sent his only Son into the world, that we should live through him. Herein is love, not that we loved God, but that he loved us, and sent his Son a satisfaction for our sins.

[[1] In P. C. L. *doctrine of the* is wanting.]

If a man had once felt within in his conscience the fierce wrath of God toward sinners, and the terrible and most cruel damnation that the law threateneth; and then beheld with the eyes of a strong faith the mercy, favour and grace, the taking away of the damnation of the law, and restoring again of life, freely offered us in Christ's blood, he should perceive love, and so much the more, that it was shewed us when we were sinners and enemies to God; and that without all deservings, without our endeavouring, enforcing and preparing ourselves, and without all good motions, qualities and properties of our freewill; but when our hearts were as dead unto all good working as the members of him whose soul is departed. Which thing to prove, and to stop the blasphemous mouths of all our adversaries, I will, of innumerable texts, rehearse one, in the beginning of the second chapter to the Ephesians, where Paul saith thus: "Ye were dead in trespass and sin, in which ye walked according to the course of the world, and after the governor that ruleth in the air, the spirit that worketh in the children of unbelief; among which we also had our conversation in time past, in the lusts of our flesh, and fulfilled the lusts of the flesh and of the mind," (so that the flesh and mind were agreed both to sin, and the mind consented as well as the flesh,) "and were by nature the children of wrath as well as other. But God, being rich in mercy, through the great love wherewith he loved us, even when we were dead in sin, hath quickened us with Christ; for by grace are ye saved; and with him hath raised us up, and with him has made us sit in heavenly things, through Jesus Christ, for to shew in time to come the exceeding riches of his grace in kindness to us-ward in Jesus Christ. For by grace are ye saved through faith; and that not of yourselves; for it is the gift of God, and cometh not of works, lest any man should boast himself. But we are his workmanship, created in Christ Jesu unto good works; unto which God ordained us before, that we should walk in them." The text is plain: we were stone dead, and without life or power to do or consent to good. The whole nature of us was captive under the devil, and led at his will. And we were as wicked as the devil now is (except that he now sinneth against the Holy Ghost); and we consented unto sin with soul and body, and hated the law of God. But God, of his grace only, quickened us in Christ; and raised us out of

God first loved us, before we could love him. Ant. ed.

Rom. v.

Eph. ii.

Herein appeareth the great and loving mercy of almighty God toward us, when we were yet sinners. Ant. ed.

that death, and made us sit with Christ in heavenly things: that is, he set our hearts at rest, and made us sit fast in the life of Christ's doctrine, and unmoveable from the love of Christ. And finally we are, in this our second birth, God's workmanship and creation in Christ; so that, as he which is yet unmade hath no life nor power to work, no more had we, till we were made again in Christ. The preaching of mercy in Christ quickened our hearts through faith wrought by the Spirit of Christ, which God poured into our hearts, ere we wist.

Dearly beloved, if God so loved us, then ought we to love one another.

If we felt the love of God in Christ's blood, we could not but love again, not only God and Christ, but also all that are bought with Christ's blood. If we love God for the pleasures that we receive, then love we ourselves. But if we love him to do him pleasure again; that can we no otherwise do, than in loving our neighbours for his sake: them that are good, to continue them in their goodness; and them that are evil, to draw them to good. Love is the instrument wherewith faith maketh us God's sons, and fashioneth us like the image of God, and certifieth us that we so are. And therefore commandeth Christ, "Love your enemies, bless them that curse you, pray for them that persecute you, that ye may be the sons of your heavenly Father; which maketh his sun rise over good and bad, and sendeth his rain upon just and unjust:" yea, which made the sun of his mercy shine upon us, and sent the rain of the blood of his dear and only child upon our souls to quicken us, and to make us see love, to love again.

The use of love. W. T.

Love maketh us the sons of God. Ant. ed.

Matt. v.

No man hath at any time seen God. If we love one another, God dwelleth in us, and his love is perfect in us.

Though we cannot see God, yet if we love one another, we be sure that he abideth in us, and that his love is perfect in us; that is, that we love him unfeignedly. For to love God truly, and to give him thanks, is only to love our neighbour for his sake: for upon his person thou canst bestow no benefit. And forasmuch as we never saw God, let us make no image of him, nor do him any image-service after our own imagination; but let us go to the scripture, that hath seen him, and there wete what fashion he is of, and what service he will

No man hath seen God. W. T.

The scripture hath seen God. Ant. ed.

be served with. Blind reason saith, God is a carved post, and will be served with a candle: but scripture saith, "God is love," and will be served with love. If thou love thy neighbour, then art thou the image of God thyself; and he dwelleth in the living temple of thine heart. And thy loving of thy neighbour for his sake is his service and worship in the spirit, and a candle that burneth before him in thine heart, and casteth out the light of good works before the world, and draweth all to God, and maketh his enemies leave their evil, and come and worship him also.

Hereby we know that we abide in him, and he in us. For he hath given us of his Spirit.

He that hath not Christ's Spirit, the same is none of his. If we have the Spirit of God, then are we sure. But how shall we know whether we have the Spirit? Ask John, and he will say, 'If we love one another.'

By this badge of love we are known to have the Spirit of God. Ant. ed.

And we have seen and do testify, that the Father hath sent his Son, the Saviour of the world. Whosoever confesseth that Jesus is the Son of God, in him dwelleth God, and he in God. And we have known and believed the love that God hath to us.

First, the apostles taught no fables, but that they saw and received of God by the witness of his Spirit. Secondarily, John ascendeth up step higher, from love to faith; and saith, "He that believeth that Jesus is God's Son, hath God in him." And I doubt not but the bishop of Rome and his defenders will answer John, and say, 'Then the devil hath God in him, and is also in God:' for other faith, than such as the devil hath, felt they never any. But John preventeth them, saying[1], "We have known and believed the love that God hath to us:" that is, we believe not only with story faith, as men believe old chronicles, but we believe the love and mercy that God shewed us, and put our trust and confidence therein (and so taketh scripture belief); we believe that Jesus is the Son of God, became man and was slain[2] for our sins, which is a token of great love. And that love believe we, and trust thereto. Where Paul saith, No man can call Jesus Lord except the Holy Ghost have taught him, "but through the Holy Ghost;"

He that believeth that Jesus is God's Son, hath God in him. Ant. ed.

1 Cor. xii.

[1 So P. C. L., but D. omits *saying.*]
[2 So P. C. L., but in D. *made man and slain.*]

he meaneth, not with the mouth only, but in the heart, with unfeigned faith, putting his hope and trust in the lordship which he hath over sin, damnation, hell, and death. For so could no man call Jesus lord, except the Holy Ghost had taught him; as Christ saith, (Matt. xvi.) "Flesh and blood shewed thee not that."

Matt. xvi.

But yet how shall I see my faith? I must come down to love again, and thence to the works of love, ere I can see my faith. Not always, but sometimes, thou shalt feel thy faith without the outward deed; as in great adversity and persecution, when the devil assaulteth thee with desperation, and layeth thy sins before thee, and would bear thee in hand that God had cast thee away, and left thee succourless, for thy sins' sake: then cometh faith forth with her shield, and turneth back again the darts of the devil, and answereth: 'Nay; for Jesus is the Son of God, yea, and my very God and my very lord, and hath taken away my sins and all damnation. And this trouble and adversity which is come upon me, by setting on of thee and of thy limbs[1], is only to make me feel the mercy of my Father, and his power and help within in my soul, and to slay the rest of the poison which remaineth in the flesh.'

Faith taketh hold of Christ's death and deserving. Ant. ed.

God is love; and he that abideth in love abideth in God, and God in him.

This have we heard above, and it is easy to be understood.

Herefore[2] is love perfect with us, that we should have confidence in the day of judgment, [that as he is, even so are we in this world.]

Howsoever this text doth[3] sound, this methinketh should be the meaning: that we should provoke each other to love, and ever have those examples of edifying before our eyes that should most move us to love. For perfect love serveth to make a man bold, because it is the keeping of the commandments. And therefore he that is perfect in love, when he seeth himself, yet in this world, to be unto his neighbour as God is unto him, and to be like his heavenly Father in

Love maketh the faithful and christian man to be bold. Ant. ed.

[1 So P. C. L.: Day has, setting of thee and one of thy limbs.]

[2 So both P. C. L., and D.; but in Tyndale's translation of 1526 the word is *herein*. The clause in brackets is in that translation, but omitted in D.]

[3 D. omits *doth*.]

all example of kindness, is bold in the presence of God; yea, though he come to judge sinners: when, on the other side, they that continue ever in their wickedness, and grow not in love, fall often; and therefore their conscience ever accuseth them, and putteth them in fear, by the reason of the fresh memory of the offence, that they cannot at once be bold, though they have never so great promises of mercy.

There is no fear in love; but perfect love casteth out fear: for fear hath painfulness. He therefore that feareth, is not perfect in love.

Love is not painful; but maketh all things easy and pleasant: fear of punishment, for the trespass newly committed, is painful: therefore, where love is perfect, there is no such fear. Love is the fulfilling of all commandments: and therefore, where love is perfect, there is no sin; and where the conscience doth not accuse of sin, there is faith bold to go in to God and to stand before him and look him in the face, and to conjure him by all his mercies, and to ask the petitions of his desire. Lack of love is the breaking of the commandments, and cause of sin; and where the conscience accuseth of sin, their faith is abashed, dismayed, ashamed and afraid to go in, for fear of rebuke. Love therefore serveth to make a man bold in the day of judgment, and in all temptations. Love.

John speaketh not generally of all manner fear, but of that only which the conscience of sin putteth a man in. For divers fears there be that accompany love, and grow as she doth. The more a woman loveth her child, the more she careth for it; and feareth, lest aught should chance unto it amiss. Even so the more we love our brethren, the more we care for them, and fear lest any temptation should trouble them: as Paul saith, (2 Cor. xi.) "Who is sick, and I am not sick? Who is offended or hurt, and mine heart burneth not?" How cared he for Timothy, for Titus, and for all that were weak, and for the Corinthians, Galatians, and for all congregations! And how diligently wrote he to them in his absence! And the more we love God, the more diligent and circumspect are we, that we offend him not. And tell me, I pray thee, whosoever hast had experience, what a pain and grief, yea, and what a fretting corosy[4] is it, unto the Fear. If we love our brethren, then are we careful for them. Ant. ed. 2 Cor. xi. The more we love God, the more diligent we are to do his will. Ant. ed.

[4 Corrosive. In P. C. L., *corose.*]

heart of a true lover of God, to hear the poison generation of vipers, the pestilent sect of hypocritish Pharisees, wittingly and willingly to blaspheme and rail on the open and manifest truth of the Holy Ghost!

Exod. xxxii. Numb. xiv.

If ye will see how bold love is, go to Moses (Exod. the thirty-second chapter, and Numb. the fourteenth chapter); and there behold how he conjureth God, and among all saith: "Forgive this people; or put me out of the book that thou hast written." As who should say, 'They be thy people, and thou commandest me to love them; and for thy sake I love them, and teach them, and care for them, as a mother that had borne them, and love them no less than myself. Wherefore, if thou love me, as thou promisest me, then save them with me; or if not, then cast me away with them, and let me have such part as they take.' And Paul said as much, Rom. ix. Look upon worldly love, and see what pageants she playeth now and then, and how drunken a thing it is: and be sure, where the love of God is perfect, she will not only go between bodily death and her lover, but also between him and hell. If a man would take of this, that a man might be so perfect in this life that he might not be perfecter, it would not follow. For though the spirit at a time get the upper hand of the flesh, and winneth herself to God, that she cannot tell whether she be in the body or no; yet the flesh will pull her down again, and not let her continue, and now and then pluck off some of her feathers, for mounting so high again. For Moses fell through unbelief well enough after that ferventness.

Where perfect love is, there is no fear. Ant. ed.

Rom. ix.

We love him, because he loved us first.

We deserve not the love of God first; but he deserveth our love, and loveth us first, to win us, and to make us his friends of his enemies; and as soon as we believe his love we love again. And so faith is mother of all love: and as great as my faith is, so great is love, though faith cannot be perfectly seen, but through the works of love and in the fire of temptation.

Faith is the mother of love. W. T.

If a man say, I love God, and hateth his brother, he is a liar. For how can he, that loveth not his brother whom he seeth, love God whom he seeth not? And this commandment have we of him, that he which loveth God, love his brother also.

To love a man's neighbour in God is a sure rule to know that we love God: and not to love him is a sure token that we love not God; and to hate our neighbour is to hate God. For to love God is to do his commandments; as Christ saith, "Ye are my lovers, if ye do those things which I have commanded you." And the commandment is, to love our neighbours: then he that loveth not his neighbour loveth not God. And likewise to hate the commandment is to hate God that commanded it: and the commandment is to love our neighbours: he then that hateth his brother, whom God biddeth him love, hateth God.

A sure rule. Ant. ed.

John xv. If we love God, we must do his commandments, and his commandment is to love our neigbours. Ant. ed.

THE FIFTH CHAPTER.

All that believe that Jesus is Christ are born of God. And all that love him which begat, love him that is begotten of him. In this we know that we love the sons of God, when we love God and keep his commandments. For this is the love of God, that we keep his commandments.

THIS is a sure conclusion, that we be born of God through faith. And that faith maketh us God's sons, in that we believe that Jesus is Christ: as the first chapter of John also testifieth, "He gave them power to be the sons of God, in that they believed in his name."

Faith maketh us God's sons. W. T.

John i.

What it is to believe that Jesus is Christ, may be understood by that which is above rehearsed. It is a far other thing than as the devil believed it, against his will and to his great pain; or as they believe it, which, to fulfil their sin, envy the glory of Christ, and persecute his gospel, forbidding to preach it or to read in it. To believe that Jesus is Christ, is to believe in Christ: that is, to believe earnestly, and to put all thy trust therein, and to lay the price of thy soul thereupon; that the son of Mary, whom the angel commanded to be called Jesus, because he should save his people from their sins, is that Christ, that Messias, and that anointed, which God promised the fathers should come and bless all nations, and anoint them with the oil of his Spirit and with mercy and grace, and to deliver them from death of their souls, which is the consenting to sin, and to make them

What it is to believe that Jesus is Christ. W. T.

Jesus the true Messias, and the Saviour of the world from their sins. Ant. ed.

alive with consenting unto the law of God, and in certifying them that they be the sons of God; and to put thy whole trust in all that he suffered in his flesh for thy sake, and in all promises of mercy that are in him; and that thou be full persuaded that there is none other name under heaven, given unto men to be saved from sin by, or to purchase forgiveness of the least sin that ever was committed or ever shall be in this world[1].

All that love God love all that believe in him. Ant. ed.

Another conclusion is this, Whosoever loveth God loveth all that believe in God. For all that love him that begetteth, love them that are begotten of him: and all that believe in God are begotten of God through that belief, and made his sons: then all that love God love all that believe in God.

He that loveth God loveth also the sons of God. Ant. ed.

Another conclusion is this, When we love God and his law, then we love the sons of God. Which is this-wise proved: The love of God is to keep the law of God: by the text, before and after, the law of God is to love our neighbours; and therefore if we love God, in keeping his laws, we must needs love the sons of God.

But John should seem to be a very negligent disputer to many men, in that he here certifieth us of the love of our neighbours by the love of God, when above he certifieth us that we love God because we love our neighbours. He seemeth to do as I heard once a great clerk in Oxford stand half an hour in a pulpit, to prove that Christ was a true prophet by the testimony of John Baptist; and another half hour to prove John the Baptist a true prophet by the authority of Christ: as we say, Claw me, claw thee; and as every thief might lightly prove himself a true man, in bearing record to another as false as he, and taking record of the same again. Which kind of disputing schoolmen call *Petitio principii*, the proving of two certain things, each by the other; and is no proving at all: as our holy father proveth the authority of scripture by his decrees, (for the scripture is not authentic, but as his decrees admit it;) and to make his decrees shine and appear glorious, and to obtain authority, he allegeth the scripture, after his juggling manner, to make fools stark mad.

But it is not so here: for both the demonstrations are certain, both the proof of the love of God and his law by the love of my neighbour, and the proof of the love of my

[[1] So P. C. L., in D. the paragraph ends with *committed.*]

neighbour by the love of God and his law. For when two things are so joined together that they cannot be separated, then the presence of the one uttereth the presence of the other, whethersoever thou first seest: as if I see fire, I am sure that something doth burn; and if I smell burning, I am certified of fire. Even so the love of God is the cause why I love my neighbour; and my love toward my neighbour is the effect of the love of God. And these two loves are ever inseparable; so that whethersoever I feel first, the same certifieth me of the other.

The love of God is cause of my neighbour's love. W. T.

John calleth the love of a man's neighbour the deeds of love, after the Hebrew speech; as to help at need, though he were even an enemy to me; to give the best counsel I can; to visit and relieve him if he be sick and needy, yea, if need were, to bestow even my life for him[2]. For the deed declareth what the man is within: neither can my love to God, and faith, be seen to the world, save through the works: and by the works doth Christ command us to judge. So that, if a man have evil works, and continueth therein, he loveth not God, nor knoweth God, no, though he call himself master doctor or God's vicar: neither understandeth he God's word, for all his high divinity; but is in all his preaching an hypocrite, a false prophet, and a liar, though his preaching please the world never so well. Nevertheless, a man is certified that he loveth God, ere he come at the work, by the testimony of the Spirit, which is given him in earnest. "The Spirit," saith Paul, "testifieth unto our spirit, that we be the sons of God:" and then it testifieth that we believe in God; for through faith are we sons. And then it certifieth me that I love God; for faith and love are inseparable. The Spirit through faith certifieth my conscience that my sins are forgiven, and I received under grace, and made the very son of God, and beloved of God: and then naturally mine heart breaketh out into the love of God again, and I seek how to utter my love, and to do God some pleasure; and because I can neither do service nor pleasure unto his own person, my neighbour is set before me, to do God service and pleasure in him, and to be to him as Christ is to me, because he is my brother, bought with Christ's blood as I am. And I consent unto that law, and love it, ere I come at

Works set forth and declare faith. Ant. ed.

Rom. viii.

To do good to my neighbour is to do God good service. Ant. ed.

[[2] So P. C. L., but in D. this sentence concludes with *help at need.*]

the deed, and long after the deed. And then, when I love my neighbour in the deed, according to this law, I am sure that I love him truly. Or else, if I examined not my love by this law, I might be deceived. For some love their neighbours for pleasure, profit, glory, and for their doing service only, as our spiritualty love us, and of that blessed love do their busy cure[1] to keep us in darkness: which love is a sign that a man hateth God, and his neighbour thereto, and loveth himself only. But God's law is, that I should abstain from mine own pleasure and profit, and become my neighbour's servant, and bestow life and goods upon him, after the ensample of Christ. Wherefore if I love my neighbour out of the love of Christ, and after the example of his law, I am sure that I love him truly.

And his commandments are not grievous. For all that is born of God overcometh the world: and this is the victory that overcometh the world, even our faith.

To love is not painful: the commandments are but love, therefore they be not grievous; because love maketh the commandments easy. The service that a mother doth unto her child is not grievous, because she loveth it; but if she should do the tenth part unto one that she loved not, her heart would brast[2] for impatience. Unto a man that feeleth not the love of Christ it is as impossible to keep the commandments, as for a camel to enter through the eye of a needle. But impossible is possible, and easy too, where the love of Christ is believed. For it followeth: "All that are born of God overcome the world;" that is to wit, the devil, which is the ruler of the world, and his disciples, which have their lust in his governance, and consent to sin both in body and soul, and give themselves to follow their lusts without resistance, and their own flesh, which also consenteth to sin, do they overcome, with all that moveth to sin. By what victory? Verily, through faith. For if our souls be truly underset[3] with sure hope and trust, and continual meditations of Christ's love, shewed already, and of succour, help and assistance that is promised in his name, and with the continual

A goodly similitude of love. W. T.

All that are born of God overcome the world. Ant. ed.

[1 Do their office busily.]
[2 Burst.] [3 Underpropped.]

memory of their examples which in times past have fought through faith and overcome; then were it impossible for the world, with all his chivalry, to overthrow us with any assault, or with any ordnance that he could shoot against us. For if that faith and meditation were ever present in us, then love through that faith should easily overcome whatsoever peril thou couldest imagine. Read in the bible, and see what conquests faith hath made, both in doing and also suffering. The eleventh chapter unto the Hebrews ministereth unto thee examples abundantly. How mighty was David, when he came to fight; and how overcame he through faith! And how mightier was he when he came to suffering, as in the persecution of the king Saul! Insomuch that when he had his most mortal enemy, king Saul, (that twelve years persecuted him against all right,) in his hands[4], to have done what he would with him, through faith he touched him not, nor suffered any man else to do, though he was yet all his life a man of war, and accustomed to murder and shedding of blood: for he believed that God should avenge him on his unrighteous king, upon whom it was not lawful to avenge himself.

The conquests of faith. Ant. ed.

Who is it that overcometh the world, but he that believeth that Jesus is the Son of God?

If to believe that Jesus is God's Son be to overcome the world, then our prelates understand not what belief is; which affirm that the best belief and the worst man in the world may stand together.

This is he that came by water and blood, Jesus Christ; not by water only, but by water and blood. And it is the Spirit that testifieth, because the Spirit is truth. For there are three that bear witness in heaven, the Father, the Word, and the Holy Ghost; and these three are one. And there are three which bear record in earth, the Spirit, water, and blood; and these three are one.

Christ came with three witnesses, water, blood, and Spirit. He ordained the sacrament of baptism, to be his witness unto us. And he ordained the sacrament of his blood, to be his witness unto us. And he poureth his Spirit into the hearts of his, to testify and to make them feel that the testimony of those two sacraments are true. And the testimony of these

Christ had three witnesses. Ant. ed.

[[4] So D., but P. C. L. has *that when he had gotten him in*, &c.]

three is, as it after followeth, that we have everlasting life in the Son of God. And these three are one full witness; sufficient at the most that the law requireth, which saith two or three, at the most, is one full sufficient witness. But, alas! we are not taught to take the sacraments for witnesses, but for image-service, and to offer[1] the work of them to God with such a mind as the old heathen offered sacrifices of beasts unto their gods: so that whatsoever testifieth unto us that we have everlasting life in Christ, that mouth have they stopped with a leavened maunchet[2] of their pharisaical glosses.

The true doctrine of the sacraments is away from us. Ant. ed.

If we receive the witness of men, the witness of God is greater. For this is the witness that God hath borne of his Son.

If the witness of men, so[3] they be three, is to be received; much more is the witness of God to be received. Now the witness that these three, water, blood, and Spirit, bear, is the witness of God, and therefore the more to be believed.

He that believeth in the Son of God, hath witness in himself. And he that believeth not God, maketh him a liar, because he doth not believe the witness that God hath testified of his Son. And this is the witness, that God hath given us eternal life, and this life is in his Son. He that hath the Son hath life: and he that hath not the Son of God hath not life.

The faithful have the true witness of God in their hearts. Ant. ed.

The true believers have the testimony of God in their hearts, and they glorify God, witnessing that he is true. They have the kingdom of God within them; and the temple of God within them; and God in that temple; and have the Son of God, and life through him. And in that temple they seek God, and offer for their sins the sacrifice of Christ's blood, and the fat of his mercies in the fire of their prayers; and in the confidence of that sacrifice go in boldly to God their father.

The unfaithful worship God in image-ser-

But the unbelievers blaspheme God, and make him false, describing him after the complexion of their lying nature.

[1 So P. C. L., Day has, *to fore.*]

[2 Maunchet or manchet: a small loaf of fine bread. Tyndale presently gives the same name to the thin roll or wafer used in the mass.]

[3 Thus D., but P. C. L. has *when* instead of *so.*]

And because they be so full stuffed with lies that they can receive nothing else, they look for the kingdom of God in outward things, and seek God in a temple of stone, where they offer their image-service and the fat of their holy deeds; in confidence whereof they go in to God, and trust to have everlasting life. And though the text testifieth that this life is only in the Son, yet they will come at no son, nor sunshining[4]; but, as unclean birds, hate the light.

vice and outward popery. Ant. ed.

These things have I written unto you that believe in the name of the Son of God, that ye may know that ye have everlasting life, and that ye may believe in the Son of God.

They that have the faith of Christ's apostles know that they have eternal life. For the Spirit testifieth unto their spirits that they are the sons of God (Rom. viii.), and received under grace. Our doctors say they cannot know whether they be in the state of grace; therefore they have not the faith of the apostles. And that they know it not, is the cause why they rail on it.

The papists have not the faith of the apostles, neither do they know, and therefore they rail on it. Ant. ed.

This is the confidence that we have in him, that if we ask aught according to his will, he heareth us. And if we know that he heareth us, whatsoever we ask, we know that we have the petitions that we ask of him.

Christ saith (Matt. vii.), "Ask and it shall be given you;" and John (in chapter xvi.), "Whatsoever ye ask in my name, he shall give it you." To ask in the name of Jesus Christ, and according to his will, be both one; and are nothing else but to ask the things contained in the promises and testament of God to us-ward, that God will be our father, and care for us both in body and in soul; and, if we sin of frailty, and repent, forgive us; and minister us all things necessary unto this life, and keep us that we be not overcome of evil, &c. Now if they which believe in Christ are bold with God that he heareth them, and sure that he granteth their petitions, it followeth that they which are not bold that he heareth them, nor sure that he granteth their petitions, do not believe in Christ. They that go to dead saints, with which they never spake nor wot where they be, be not bold that God will hear

To ask in Christ's name. W. T. Matt. vii. John xvi.

[[4] Thus P. C. L., but D. omits *son, nor*. In Tyndale's time it was usual to write *sonne* alike for *son*, and for *sun:* and this is continued in Day's edition.]

Such as lack faith in Christ wander they wot not whither.

them, nor sure that he will grant them[1] their petitions; therefore they believe not in Christ. That they be neither bold nor sure, appeareth first by their deeds, and secondarily by their own confession; for they say, what should God hear them or grant them aught, seeing they be unworthy? yea, and they confirm it with a similitude of worldly wisdom, that they should be put back for their malapertness, and fare the worse; as if a rude fellow should break up into the king's privy chamber, and press unto his own person without knocking, or speaking to any other officer: so that they believe it an augmenting of sin to go to God themselves in the confidence of Christ's blood, as he bade them.

If a man see his brother sin a sin not unto death, let him ask; and he shall give him life for them that sin not unto death. There is a sin unto death; and for it I say not that thou shouldest pray. All unrighteousness is sin: and there is a sin not to death.

The sin to the death.

Whatsoever sin we see in the world, let us pray, and not despair; for God is the God of mercy. But for the sin to death, which is resisting grace, and fighting against mercy, and open blaspheming of the Holy Ghost, affirming that Christ's miracles are done in Beelzebub, and his doctrine to be of the devil, I think that no christian man, if he perceive it, can otherwise pray than as Paul prayed for Alexander the coppersmith, (the 2 Tim. the last,) "that God would reward him according unto his works." They that go back again after they know the truth, and give themselves willingly to sin for to follow it, and persecute the doctrine of truth by profession to maintain falsehood for their glory and vantage, are remediless: as ye may see Heb. vi. and x. Balaam sinned so; the false prophets in the old Testament sinned so; the Pharisees sinned so; Alexander sinned so; and now many sin so, following their pride and covetousness.

Tim. iv.

Heb. vi. x.

We know that all that are born of God, sin not; but he that is born of God keepeth himself; and the wicked toucheth him not.

All that are born of God cannot sin. Ant. ed.

As thou readest in the third chapter, they that are born of God cannot sin; for the seed of God keepeth them. They cannot cast off the yoke of Christ, and consent to continue in sin, nor defy his doctrine, nor persecute it, for to quench it, or to maintain any thing contrary unto it. But in whatsoever

[1 P. C. L. has *them*, omitted by D.]

captivity they be in the flesh, their hearts yield not; but imagine to break loose, and to escape, and fly away, unto the party and standard of their Lord Christ. And as men of war they ever keep watch and prepare themselves unto war, and put on the armour of God, the which is God's word, the shield of faith, the helmet of hope, and harness themselves with the meditation of those things which Christ suffered for us, and with the ensamples of all the saints that followed him, and think earnestly that it is their part to live as purely as the best, and come after as fast as they can. And yet, in all their works, they knowledge themselves sinners unfeignedly, as long as one jot of the perfectness, that was in the deeds of Christ, is lacking in theirs: so that the devil cannot touch the hearts of them, neither with pride, nor vain glory of pure living, neither to make them consenting unto the flesh in gross sins, if at a time they be taken tardy, and catch a fall. Whatsoever chance them, the devil can catch no hold of them, to keep them still in captivity; but they will break loose again, and repent and do penance, to chastise their flesh, that they come no more under the devil's claws.

The armour of a christian man. Ant. ed.

We know that we be of God, and that the whole world is set on mischief.

They that believe, that is to say, put their trust in Christ, see both their own glorious state in God, and also the wretched estate of the world in their wickedness. But the world, as they know not God, nor the glory of the sons of God, even so they see not their own miserable estate in wickedness, and damnation under the law of God; but the worse they are, the bolder they be, and the surer of themselves, the further from repentance, and the more standing in their own conceits, for the darkness that is in them. And therefore, say our doctors, a man cannot know whether he be in the state of grace or no; nor needeth to care therefore. And they be therefore the blind leaders of the blind.

The world seeth not the things that are of God. Ant. ed.

We know that the Son of God is come, and hath given us understanding to know him that is true: and we be in the truth through Jesus Christ. He is very God, and eternal life.

Christ is all, and the fountain of all; and of his fulness receive we all. And as he poureth the gifts of his grace upon them that believe in him, so he giveth them understanding to

Christ only is the fountain and fulness of all good gifts. Ant. ed.

know the very God, and that they be in the very God, and that they have obtained that through his purchasing; and leaveth not his sheep in darkness. And the same Jesus Christ is very God and eternal life: God and eternal life was he from the beginning, and became man for the great love he had to us, for to bring us unto his eternal life. And he that hath any other way thither, whether his own works, or other men's, or works of ceremonies, or sacraments, or merits of saints, or of aught save Jesus Christ only, shall never come thither. The world seeth the bishop of Rome, and seeth that they which be in him be lords in this world: and therefore they care to be in the bishop of Rome; but whether they be in God or not, they say, it is not necessary to know.

He that seeketh any other way to eternal salvation, than by Christ shall never come there. Ant. ed.

Little children, beware of images.

Idolatry.

Idolater. W. T.

Serve none image in your hearts. Idolatry is Greek, and the English is image-service: and an idolater is also Greek, and the English an image-servant. Be not idolaters nor commit idolatry; that is, be none image-servants, nor do any image-service, but beware of serving all manner images. And think it not enough to have put all the images of false gods out of the way, if ye now set up the image of very God and of his true saints in their rooms, to do the same service unto them which ye did unto the other. For ye may do as strong image-service unto the image of God and of his saints, as unto the images of false Gods: yea, thou mayest commit as great idolatry to God, and yet before none outward image, but before the image which thou hast feigned of God in thine heart, as thou mayest before an outward image of the devil. The Jews in the temple of God, where was none image of God, did as great image-service to God, as the heathen unto their false gods: yea, the Jews, in doing to God the things which God commanded them, did commit worse idolatry, and sinned more grievously against God, than the heathen did in offering unto their false gods; which thing to be true the prophets testify. For when the Jews did their ceremonies and sacrifices (the meaning and signification lost, and the cause forgotten, which God ordained them for) to flatter and please God with the gloriousness of the deed in itself, and to purchase aught of him for the costliness or properness of the present; what other made they of God in their imagination, than a child, whom, if

As great idolatry may be committed to the image of a saint, as was by the gentiles committed unto idols. Ant. ed.

he cry or be displeased, men still with a puppet, or if we will have him to do aught, make him an horse of a stick, or such like?

If thou bring a bowl of blood and set it before God to flatter him, to stroke him, and to curry and claw him, as he were an horse, and imaginest that he hath pleasure and delectation therein, what better makest thou of God than a butcher's dog? If thou bring the fat of thy beasts to God, for the same imagination, what makest thou of God, but one that had need of grease to grease shoes or smear boots? If thou burnest blood and fat together to please God, what other thing dost thou make of God, than one that had lust to smell to burnt flotess[1]?

Gross worshipping of God. Ant. ed.

God commanded a courtesy of all first ripe fruits to be offered: not to be an image-service, but a witness and testimony that he had made them grow, that the people should not forget God, but think on his benefits, and love him, and of love keep his commandments. And likewise, if any had sinned against God's law, God commanded that they should repent, and then bring a beast and flay it, and offer the blood and the fat of the inwards; not to make satisfaction, but to testify only that God was appeased[2], and had of his mercy at the repentance of the heart forgiven the sin. The sacrifices of blood were ordained partly to be a secret prophesying of Christ's blood-shedding, and partly to be a testimony and certifying of our hearts, that the sin was forgiven, and peace made between us and God; and not to be a satisfaction: for that were image-service, and to make an image of God.

Ceremonies. Ant. ed.

Sacrifices.

We read in the histories, that when a love-day[3], or a truce, was made between man and man, the covenants were rehearsed: and upon that they slew beasts, in a memorial and remembrance of the appointment only. And so were the sacrifices signs and memorials only, that God was at one with us. For the Jew could believe no words, though an angel had spoken, without a token; as we hold up our fingers, and clap hands. And likewise whatsoever they were bid to do, they must have had a token of remembrance, though it had been but a ring of a rush, as it is to be seen in the bible.

The Jews could believe nothing without tokens. Ant. ed.

[1 Flotess: scum.]

[2 So P. C. L., but D. has *pleased*.]

[3 See Vol. I. p. 440.]

Sacraments and ceremonies were ordained only for remembrances. Ant. ed.

Even so our images, relics, ceremonies and sacraments, were our memorials and signs of remembrance only; and he that giveth in his heart more to them than that, is an image-servant. But when God is a Spirit, and worshipped in the spirit, we for lack of faith, being spiritless, and having no power to desire of God any spiritual thing, serve God in the body with imagined service, for such wordly things as our profession is to defy. Who kisseth a relic, or beholdeth an image, for love of the saints' living, to follow their example? Nay, we will fast the saints' evens, and go barefoot unto their images, and take pain to obtain greater pleasure in the world, and to purchase worldly things; as to maintain the body in lusts, that the soul cannot once wish for power to live as the saints lived, or to long for the life to come. If we went in pilgrimage to keep the remembrance of the saints' living in mind, for our example, and fasted and went barefoot to tame the flesh, that it should not lust after such worldly things which we now desire of the saints; then did our fasting and pilgrimage-going serve us, yea, and the saint were yet our servant to edify us in Christ with the remembrance of his life left behind, to preach, and to provoke us to follow his example. For our bodily service can be no service unto the saint, which is a spirit, except we imagine him to be an image.

Idolatry.

St White must have a cheese once in a year, and that of the greatest sort; which yet eateth no cheese: it shall be given to the poor in her[1] name, say they. First, that to be false, we see with our eyes. Secondarily, Christ commandeth to care for the poor, and give them all that we may spare, in his name; saying, that what is given them, is given him, and what is denied them is denied him. If the law of Christ be written in thine heart, why distributest thou not unto thy brethren with thine own hands, in the name of thy Saviour

We ought to be frank, and to distribute to our poor brethren such as God hath sent us. Ant. ed.

[[1] It appears from the Britannia Sancta, a work published by Meighan, a Romish bookseller, Lond. 1745, that our countrymen were wont to venerate a St Witta, there said to have been 'a fellow-labourer of Boniface' (or Winfrid the Saxon) 'in Germany, and consecrated by him bishop of Buraburg near Fritzlar. Some authors call him Albuin, by changing his name, which signifies White, into a Latin name.' Brit. Sanc. par. II. p. 221. The apparently feminine termination of this saint's Saxon name was probably the cause of his being supposed to be a female by persons who did not know his history. In Bishop Hooper's works, Park. Soc. ed. p. 320, White is spoken of as a male saint.]

Jesus Christ, which died both for them and thee, as thou hast vowed and promised to him in thy baptism?

Moreover they say[2], 'It is given unto St White's chaplain.' St White's chaplain hath a stipend already, sufficient for a christian man, and ought to receive no more, but therewith to be content, and to be an example of despising covetousness. Moreover, that priest that would follow the living of Jesus Christ, as St White did, and teach his parishens to do so, were a right chaplain of Christ. And they have a promise to be fed and clothed, as well as ever was their master, in the name of Christ. And so be they, and ever were; so that they need not to beg in the name of St White.

Superstitious popery is idolatry.

What shall St White do for thee again for that great cheese? For I wot well it is not given for nought. Shall she give abundance of milk, to make butter and cheese? All we that believe in Christ are the sons of God, and God hath promised to care for us, forasmuch[3] as we care for the keeping of his commandments; and hath promised that we shall receive whatsoever we ask, to his honour and our need, of his hand. If we then be the natural sons of God, why run we from our father a begging to St White? St White sendeth no rain upon the earth, nor maketh the sun shine thereon, nor maketh the grass grow. Neither is there any God's word that he will now do so much for us at her request. But God hath promised, if we will keep his laws, to do so much for us at our own request, for the blood of his Son Jesus. What other thing then is thy serving of St White, than lack of faith and trust to God-ward in Christ's name; and a false faith of thy own feigning, to St White-ward, for thine image-service or serving her with cheese, as though she were a bodily thing? And like disputation is it of all other saints.

In all our needs we must call upon God in the name of Jesus Christ, and he will hear us. Ant. ed.

And as we worship the saints with image-service, to obtain temporal things, even so worship we God. And as the Jews turned their sacrifices unto image-service, which were given them of God to be signs to move them to serve God in the spirit, even so have we our sacraments. And for an example let us take the mass, which, after the Romish bishop's abuse of it, is the most damnable image-service that

The mass made an image-service. W. T.

[2 So P. C. L., but this introductory clause is omitted in D.]

[3 So P. C. L., but in D. *as much*, omitting *for*.]

ever was since it began. Christ, according to the testimony of the scripture, made in the days of his flesh satisfaction for all the sin of them that had believed[1], or should believe in his name; and obtained that they should be the sons of God, and taken from under the damnation of the law, and put under grace and mercy, and that God should henceforth deal with them as a merciful father dealeth with his children that run not away from him, no, though aught be at a time chanced amiss, but tarry ever still by their father and by his doctrine, and confess their trespass, and promise henceforth to enforce themselves, unto the uttermost of their power, that they do no more so negligently. And this purchase made he with the things which he suffered in his flesh, and with the strong prayers which he prayed. And to keep his testament ever fresh in mind, that it were not forgotten, he left with us the sacrament or sign[2] of his body and blood, to strength our faith, and to certify our conscience, that our sins were forgiven, as soon as we repented and had reconciled ourselves unto our brethren, and to arm our souls, through the continual remembrance of Christ's death, unto the despising of the world, mortifying of the flesh, and quenching of the lusts and thirst of worldly things: as they which have daily conversation with the sick and miserable, and are present at the deaths of men are moved to defy the world, and the lusts thereof.

We must ever cleave unto God, and submit ourselves to his mercy. Ant. ed.

And as Christ had institute the sacrament of his body and blood, so the bishops, in process of time, set signs of all the rest of Christ's passion in the ornaments and gestures of the mass; so that the whole passion was daily described before our eyes, as though we had presently looked upon it.

The mass at the first was a declaration of Christ's passion. Ant. ed.

And mark also[3], see for what cause they came unto the sacrament. They reconciled themselves each one to other, if any man had offended his brother, ere they were admitted into the congregation or body of Christ, to be members of each other, knit together in one faith and love to eat the Lord's supper (as Paul calleth it); for the congregation, thus gathered, is called Christ's body and Christ their head. And likewise, if a man had been taken in open sin, against the profession of his baptism, he was rebuked openly; and he confessed his

The right use of the mass. W. T. 1 Cor. xi. 1 Cor. x. and xii. Eph. i.

[[1] So P. C. L., but D. omits *believed*.]
[[2] So D., but P. C. L. omits *or sign*.]
[[3] So P. C. L., but D. has *that thou mayest*.]

sin openly, and asked forgiveness of God, and of the congregation, whom he had offended with the example of his evil deed; and took penance, as they call it, of the congregation, that is, certain discreet injunctions how he should live and order himself in time to come, and tame his flesh, for the avoiding of the said vice; because his confession and repentance, which he seemed to have, should be none hypocrisy, but an earnest thing. For if an open sinner be found among us, we must immediately amend him, or cast him out of the congregation, with defiance and detestation of his sin; as thou seest how quickly Paul cast out the Corinthian that kept his father's wife, and when he was warned would not amend. Or else, if we suffer such to be among us unrebuked, we cannot but at once fall from the constancy of our profession, and laugh and have delectation and consent unto their sin, as it is come to pass throughout all Christendom; which is ten thousand times more abominable, than if we sinned ourselves. For the best man in the world, that hateth sin, might at a time through frailty of the flesh be drawn to sin. But it is altogether devilish, and a sure token that the Spirit of Christ is not in us, nor the profession of our baptism written in the heart, if we laugh at another man's sins, though we ourselves abstain for shame, or fear of hell, or for whatsoever imagination it be, or that we be so blind that we see no other sin in us than our outward deeds. And the penance enjoined frail persons, that could not rule themselves, was under the authority of the curate, and the sad and discreet men of the parish, to release part, or all at a time, if necessity required, or when they saw the person so grown in perfectness that he needed it not. But see whereto it is now come, and after what manner our holy father that is at Rome dispenseth with all together! And see what our bishops' officers do, and where the authority of the curate and of the parish is become! If in ten parishes round there be not one learned and discreet to help the other, then the devil hath a great swing among us, that the bishops' officers, that dwell so far off, must abuse us as they do. And if within a diocese or an whole land we can find no shift, but that the bishop of Rome, that dwelleth at the devil in hell, must thus mock us, what a stroke, think ye, hath Satan among us! And all is because we be hypocrites, and love not the way of truth, for all our pretending the contrary.

What penance was. Ant. ed.

Grievous sin not passed upon. Ant. ed.

Discipline used in the primitive church. Ant. ed.

The description of the parts of the mass. Ant. ed.

And to begin withal, they said *Confiteor*[1], and knowledged themselves to be sinners. And then the priest prayed in general for all estates and degrees, and for increase of grace, and in especial, if need required; unto which prayers the people hearkened, and said, Amen. And then the gospel, and glad tidings of forgiveness of sins, was preached to stir up our faith. And then the sacrament was ministered for the confirmation of the faith of the gospel, and of the testament made between God and us, of forgiveness of sins in Christ's blood for our repentance and faith; as ye see how, after all bargains, there is a sign thereof made, either clapping of hands, or bowing a penny or a groat, or a piece of gold, or giving some earnest; and as I shewed you how, after a truce made, they slew beasts for a confirmation. And then men departed, every man to his business, full certified that their sins were forgiven, and armed with the remembrance of Christ's passion and death for the mortifying of the flesh all the day after. And in all these was neither the sacrament, neither other ceremonies of the mass, image-service unto God; and holy deeds, to make satisfaction for our sins, or to purchase such worldly things as the gospel teacheth us to despise. And now compare this use of the mass to ours; and see whether the mass be not become the most damnable idolatry and image-service that ever was in the world.

The abominable use of the mass. Ant. ed.

We never reconcile ourselves unto our brethren which we have offended; we receive unto our mass the open sinners, the covetous, the extortioners, the adulterer, the backbiter, the common whore, and the whore-keeper, which have no part in Christ by the scripture; yea, such are suffered to say the mass, as the use is now to speak; yea, such are we compelled, with the sword, to take for our pastors and curates of our souls, and not so hardy to rebuke them. Neither do they repent, and confess their sins, and promise amendment, or submit themselves to wholesome injunctions for the avoiding of such sins and taming of their flesh. We say *Confiteor*, and knowledge ourselves to be sinners in Latin[2], but never

[1 I confess. The title of a form of public confession of sins.]

[2 In the Roman breviary, after the priest has recited the *Confiteor* for himself, the choir replies for the people: Confiteor Deo omnipotenti, beatæ Mariæ semper virgini, beato Michaeli archangelo, beato

repent in English. The priest prayeth in Latin, and saith evermore a still mass, as we say: for though he sing and strain his throat to cry loud unto them that be by him, yet as long as no man wotteth what he prayeth, or whether he bless or curse, he is dumb and speechless. And so, in that part, we abide fruitless, and untaught how to pray unto God. And the gospel is sung or said in Latin only; and no preaching of repentance toward the law and faith toward Christ had. And therefore abide we ever faithless, and without studying to amend our livings. And of the ceremonies of the mass we have none other imagination than that they be an holy service unto God; which he receiveth of our hands, and hath great delectation in them, and that we purchase great favour of God with them, as we do of great men here in the world with gifts and presents: insomuch that if the priest said mass without those vestments, or left the other ceremonies undone, we should all quake for fear; and think that there were a sin committed, enough to sink us all, and that the priest for his labour were worthy to be put in the bishop of Rome's purgatory, and there to be burnt to ashes[3].

And of the very sacrament itself we know no other thing than that we come thither to see an unseeable miracle, [which they affirm the angels in heaven have no power to do[4]; *sed solis presbyteris, quibus sic congruit, ut sumant, nec dent ceteris*[5]: how that bread is turned into the body, and wine into the blood, **The abuse of the sacrament. Ant. ed.**

Johanni Baptistæ, sanctis apostolis Petro et Paulo, omnibus sanctis, et tibi, pater (that is, to the officiating priest), quia peccavi nimis cogitatione, verbo, et opere; mea culpa, mea culpa, mea maxima culpa. Ideo precor beatam Mariam semper virginem, beatum Michaelem archangelum, beatum Johannem Baptistam, sanctos apostolos Petrum et Paulum, omnes sanctos, et te, pater, orate pro me ad Dominum Deum nostrum. In feriali officio ad primam.—Ed. Colon. Agripp. 1680, p. 33—4.]

[3 The papal law says, Cum sacerdos ad solemnia missarum accedit, non aliter accedat quam orario utroque humero circumseptus, ita ut de uno eodemque orario cervicem pariter et utrumque humerum premens, signum in suo pectore præparet crucis. Si quis autem aliter egerit, excommunicationi debitæ subjaceat.—Decret. prima pars, Dist. XXIII. c. 9. Ecclesiastica.]

[4 See Vol. I. p. 380, n. 4.]

[5 "But [the power belongs] to the priests only, to whom it is so fitted, that they may take [this power], but not give it to others."]

of Christ, to mock our seeing, smelling, feeling, and tasting; which is a very strong faith, and more a great deal (I think) than the text compelleth a man to[1].] Nevertheless it were somewhat yet, if they had been as loving, kind, careful and diligent to teach the people to repent, and to believe in the blood of Christ for the forgiveness of their sins, unto the glory of the mercy of God, and of his exceeding love to us, and unto the profit of our souls; and, upon that preaching, to have ministered the sacrament as a memorial, remembrance, sign, token, earnest, the seal of an obligation, and clapping of hands together, for the assurance of the promise of God; to quiet, stablish and certify our consciences, and to put us out of all wavering and doubt, that our sins were forgiven us, and God become our father and at one with us, for which cause only Christ ordained it; [as they were zealous and fervent to maintain the opinion of so turning bread and wine into the body and blood of Christ, that it ceaseth to be bread and wine in nature, unto their own glory and profit, without help of scripture, but with subtle arguments of sophistry and with crafty wiles: first, with taking away half the sacrament, lest, if the people should have drunk the blood of Christ, they should have smelled the savour and felt the taste of wine, and so have been too weak to believe that there had been no wine; and secondarily, when they durst not rob the people of all the sacrament, they yet took away common bread, and imagined maunchets which may not be handled, and in sight have no similitude of bread, and in eating very little taste, if there be any at all; and thirdly, whom they could not catch with those crafts, against him they disputed with the sword.] For when they had[2] taken away the signification and very intent of the sacrament, to stablish the ear-confession, their merits, deservings, justifying of works, and like invention, unto their own glory and profit; what had the sacrament been, if they had not made of that opinion an article of the faith[3]? But now, when they have destroyed,

Half of the sacrament kept from the lay people. Ant. ed.

[[1] Those passages in this page and in the remainder of this exposition which are included within brackets are found in D., but not in the earlier P. C. L. edition.]

[[2] In P. C. L. *now they have.*]

[[3] In P. C. L., *what doth the sacrament admonish us, of reconciling us to God?*]

for the nonce, that faith which profited, and have set up with wiles, subtilty, falsehood, guile and with violence, that faith which profiteth not, we have good cause to judge and examine the doctrine of the spirits, whether it be grounded upon God's word or no.

[But I ask, wherefore we believe that Christ's body, and his blood, is there present? Verily, as many heads, as many wits; every man hath his meaning.] We take pains to come thither to see strange holy gestures, whereof, say they to their shame, who knoweth the meaning? [yea, or of the other disguising?] and to hear strange holy voices; whereof, say I also, that no man knoweth the understanding; and to look upon the sacrament; and all to obtain worldly things for that service. Why, may not all men desire worldly things of God? Yes, we ought to ask of God only sufficiency of all worldly things, as we do spiritual things, yet not for bodily service, seeing[4] God is a spirit; but for the goodness and mercy of our Father, and for the truth of his promise and deservings of his Son. And so, when we do men bodily service, we ought to look for our wages of God, lest if he move not the hearts of our masters, we be shrewdly paid; and likewise when we lend or bargain, we ought to desire God for payment, lest through our negligence he forget us, and the appointments be not truly kept. Some there be yet, that ask heaven but for bodily service: which is like abomination.

But who cometh thither with repentance and faith, for to obtain forgiveness of his sins, and with purpose to walk in the life of penance for the taming of the flesh, that he sin no more; and to stablish his heart in that purpose, and to arm his soul against all that move to the contrary; and when he goeth home, is certified in his conscience, through that sign and token, that his sins are forgiven him: as Noah was certified by the sign of the rainbow, that the world should no more be overrun with water; and as Abraham was certified by the sign of circumcision, that God would fulfil to him and his offspring all the mercies that he had promised; and as Abraham, when he asked a sign, to be sure that he should possess the land of Canaan, was certified through the sign that God gave him thereof, and of the four hundred years, that his posterity should be in thraldom in Egypt, and of their de-

The fruitful and profitable doctrine of the sacraments are kept from us. Ant. ed.

Gen. xv.

[4 So P. C. L., but in D. *when* is substituted for *seeing*.]

liverance; and as Gideon was certified, by the sign of his fleece, of the victory that God had promised him; and as many other, that believed in God, were certified by the signs that God gave them, of the promises which God made them? Verily, no man. For our prelates, which lay for themselves, *Compelle intrare*[1], compel not us to enter into any such feast, nor will suffer any such meat to be set before us, for fear of overthrowing the foundation of their false building, whereof springeth so great glory and profit unto them; which foundation, to build their lies upon, they could never have laid, except they had first thrust this doctrine, of our soul's health, clean out of knowledge. And as soon as they had blinded the light, they became leaders in darkness, and made of the mass image-service; so that the strange holy gestures, [and the strange holy voices, and strange holy vestures, with all other strange holy ceremonies,] must be meritorious works, to deserve long life, health, riches, honour, favour, dignity, and abundance of all that we have, forsaking our baptism, and to arm us from bearing of the cross with Christ. And they have made of it a pill, of two contrary operations; so that the same medicine, that preserveth our souls from purgatory, doth purge the body of house, lands, rents, goods and money, [that it is made as bare as Job, and as bald as a coot[2].] And the light that rebuketh them, they call seditious, that it maketh the subjects to rise against their princes: which thing the hypocrites laid some time unto the prophets, as ye may see in the old Testament; and at last they laid it unto Christ's charge, as ye may see in the gospel; and to the charge of the apostles, as ye may see in the Acts. But at all such times the hypocrites themselves stirred up such a sword, to maintain their falsehood, that evermore a great part of the world perished through their own mischievous [incensing and] provoking princes to battle.

[These hypocrites laid to Wicliffe's charge, and do yet, that his doctrine caused insurrection. But they, to quench the truth of his preaching, slew the right king, and set up three false kings a row[3]: by which mischievous sedition they

[1 Compel them to come in. Luke xiv. 23.]

[2 A proverb taken from the appearance of this species of water-fowl, which has a callous white membrane spread over its forehead.]

[3 See Exposition upon Matthew, p. 53. Tyndale charges the

caused half England to be slain up, and brought the realm into such ruin and desolation that M. More could say, in his Utopia, that as Englishmen were wont to eat sheep, even so their sheep now eat up them by whole parishes at once, besides other inconveniences that he then saw. And so the hypocrites say now likewise, that God's word causeth insurrection: but ye shall see shortly that these hypocrites themselves, after their old wont and examples, in quenching the truth that uttereth their juggling, shall cause all realms christian to rise one against another, and some against themselves. Ye shall see them run out, before the year come about, that which they have been in brewing (as I have marked) above this dozen years, &c.]

¶ This much I have said because of them that deceive you, to give you an occasion to judge the spirits.

popish clergy with what he accounted the guilt of deposing Richard II., and of transferring the crown to the house of Lancaster, when the hereditary right had devolved to the house of York.]

NOTES OR GLOSSES

ON

SAINT MATTHEW'S GOSPEL.

A.D. 1525.

[INTRODUCTORY NOTICE.

HAVING arrived at the end of all that is known to be extant of Tyndale's expositions, our promised course leads us to his notes on scripture, of which we can present our readers with no more than those he composed for the margins of his intended first edition of the New Testament in English. It has been already mentioned (Vol. I. p. 3), that the prologue prefixed to that edition was the first address from an English reformer, printed by himself for the edification of our forefathers; and the following notes, originally called glosses, and reprobated under that name by the Romanists (Vol. I. pp. xxiii, xxvi.) are, in like manner, the first approach to a running comment upon the text of scripture ever printed in the English tongue. They were copied by the present editor from that fragment of the first sheets struck off by Tyndale, of which an account was given in Vol. I. pp. 4, 5; and where the fragment terminates, our knowledge of them ceases.]

MARGINAL NOTES

ON THE FIRST TWENTY-ONE CHAPTERS OF ST MATTHEW'S GOSPEL.

CHAPTER I.

Abraham and David are first rehearsed, because that Christ ver. 1.
was chiefly promised unto them.

St Matthew leaveth out certain generations, and describeth ver. 6.
Christ's lineage from Solomon, after the law of Moses. But Lucas describeth it according to nature, from Nathan, Solomon's brother. For the law calleth them a man's children, which his brother begat of his wife left behind him after his death. Deut. xxv.

That is to say, by the working and power of the Holy ver. 18.
Ghost.

That is, he would not put her to open shame, as he well ver. 19.
might have done by the law. Also Matthew rejoiceth of the goodness of Joseph, which, for love's sake, did remit of his right.

Jesus is as much to say as a Saviour; for he only saveth ver. 21.
all men from their sins by his merits, without their deserving.

Christ bringeth God: where Christ is, there is God; and ver. 23.
where Christ is not, there is not God.

Ye shall not suppose that he knew her afterward. But ver. 25.
it is the manner of the scripture so to speak. Gen. viii. "The raven came not again till the water was drunk up, and the earth dry." The scripture meaneth not, he came again afterward: even so here, it followeth not that Joseph knew our lady[1] afterward.

CHAPTER II.

Of Matthew they are called Magi; and in certain countries ver. 1.
in the east philosophers, cunning in natural causes and effects, and also the priests, were so called.

Jewry is the land; Judah is that tribe or kindred that ver. 6.
dwelt therein.

[[1] In the notes to Tyndale's Test. of 1538, of which there is a copy in the Bapt. Coll. Museum, Bristol, *Mary* is substituted for *our lady*.]

ver. 18. Rachael was buried not far from Bethlehem; and the prophet signifieth that as she mourned her son Benjamin, in whose birth she died, so should the mothers of those children mourn. And here may we see how it goeth alway with the right christian men before the world, for the faith's sake which they have in Christ; notwithstanding they are wonderfully maintained and defended alway of God against all power of hell.

CHAPTER III.

ver. 4. Locusts are more[1] than our grasshoppers; and such men used to eat in divers parts of the east.

ver. 9. Put your trust in God's word only, and not in Abraham. Let saints be an ensample unto you, and not your trust and confidence: for then ye make Christ of them.

ver. 15. All righteousness is fulfilled when we forsake all our own righteousness, that God only may be counted he which is righteous, and maketh righteous through faith. This doth John, in that he putteth from him his own righteousness, and would be washed of Christ and made righteous. This also doth Christ, in that he taketh not righteousness and honour on him; but suffereth himself to be baptized and killed: for baptism is none other thing than death.

CHAPTER IV.

CHAPTER V.

ver. 5. The world thinketh to possess the earth, and to defend their own, when they use violence and power; but Christ teacheth that the world must be possessed with meekness only, and without power and violence.

ver. 11. All these deeds here rehearsed, as to nourish peace, to shew mercy, to suffer persecution, and so forth, make not a man happy and blessed; neither deserveth he reward of heaven; but declare and testify that we are happy and blessed, and that we shall have great promotion in heaven; and certify us in our breasts that we are God's sons, and that the Holy Ghost is in us: for all good things are given to us freely of God, for Christ's blood sake and his merits.

ver. 13. When the preachers cease to preach God's word, then

[1 That is, greater.]

must they needs be oppressed, and trod under foot, with man's traditions.

Jot is as much to say as the least letter; for so is the least letter, that the Greeks or Hebrews have, called. ver. 18.

This do they which say that these, Christ's commandments, are not commandments but counsels. ver. 19. First clause.

"Called the least;" that is to say, shall be little set by and despised.

"Called great;" that is to say, shall be much set by and had in reverence.

The goodness of the Pharisees standeth in outward works and appearance; but Christ requireth goodness of the heart. ver. 20.

Racha is the hoarse sound in the throat; and betokeneth all signs of wrath. ver. 22.

To pluck out spiritually is here commanded; that is, when the eyes' lust is put away, and killed in the heart. ver. 29.

All swearing and oaths, which a man of himself doth, are here forbidden. Nevertheless when love, need, thy neighbour's profit, or God's honour requireth it, then is it well done to swear; like as wrath is forbidden, and yet is laudable when it proceedeth of love, to honour God withal. ver. 34.

No man should avenge himself, or seek wreak, no, not by the law. But the ruler, which hath the sword, should do such things of himself; or when the neighbours, of love, warn him and require him. ver. 39.

Publicans gathered rents, toll, custom, and tribute; and were commonly heathen men, thereunto appointed of the Romans. ver. 46.

CHAPTER VI.

Ye shall not think that our deeds deserve anything of God, as a labourer deserveth his hire. For all good things come of the bounteousness, liberality, mercy, promises, and truth of God, by the deserving of Christ's blood only; but it is a manner of speaking, as we say, 'Thy labour, or going was well rewarded,' unto him that hath but fett[2] only the promises of another man. ver. 4.

The eye is single, when a man in all his deeds looketh but on the will of God, and looketh not for laud, honour, or any other reward in this world; neither ascribeth heaven, or a higher room in heaven, unto his deeds, but accepteth heaven ver. 22.

[[2] Brought away, carried off.]

as a thing purchased by the blood of Christ, and worketh freely for love's sake only.

ver. 30. Men heat their furnaces and ovens with such things in those countries.

ver. 34. Trouble[1] is the daily labour. He will it be enough that we labour daily, without farther care.

CHAPTER VII.

ver. 1—4. To judge, or condemn, belongeth to God only. Therefore whosomever judgeth, without God's commandment, taketh God's honour from him; and that is the beam in the eye.

ver. 6. The holy things are the word of God, that sanctifieth all things. Dogs are the persecutors of the word. Swine are they which are drowned in fleshly lusts, and despise the word.

ver. 24. Here Christ requireth faith; for where faith is not, there is not the command fulfilled, Rom. xiii. And all good works after outward appearance, without faith, are sin: contrariwise, where faith is, there must the very good works follow. Christ calleth here *doing*, to do with a pure heart, Acts xv.; and such goodness standeth fast against all winds, that is to say, against all the power of hell; for it is built on the rock, Christ, through faith.

CHAPTER VIII.

ver. 2. Faith knoweth not, yet trusteth in the favour and goodness of God.

ver. 4. Moses calleth the law a witness unto the people (Deut. xxxi.); for the law accuseth us, and is a testimony against our sin. Likewise here, if the priests bare record that Christ had cleansed this leper, and yet believed not, then testified they against themselves.

ver. 5. *Centurion* is a captain of a hundred men; whom I call sometime a centurion, but for the most part a hunder-captain.

ver. 21. Some pretend good works, because they would not follow Christ and believe; but Christ signifieth that such works are dead and lost.

CHAPTER IX.

ver. 1. This city was Capernaum.

[[1] Each day's trouble is sufficient for the self-same day. Tyndale's Version.]

Mourn, that is, to suffer pain. There is pain in many ways: one way, of a man's own choice and election; as is the monks' rules, and as Baal's priests pricked themselves, 3 Kings xviii.: such pain doth all the world, the Pharisees, yea, John's disciples, esteem great; but God despiseth it. Another ways is there pain, and ordained of God, without our election; as shame, rebuke, wrong, death: such to suffer patiently, and with good-will, is the right cross, and pleaseth God well: so Christ's disciples fast not, but are merry at the marriage, while the bridegroom is yet with them; yea, and God had yet ordained no trouble for them. They fain[2] themself no pain; for it pleaseth not God. They must fast after Christ's death, and suffer pain of God's hand and ordinance. So now, whatsoever a man taketh on him by his own election, that is reproved; yea, and where Christ sheweth himself friendly, as a bridegroom, there must needs be a merry heart. ver. 15.

With these words Christ driveth them from him, as them which understood not his learning, as concerning the liberty of his disciples; and saith, "No man mendeth an old garment with new cloth, for the old holdeth not the stitch:" as who saith, "Such spiritual new learning cannot be comprehended with old fleshly hearts." Preach to fleshly people, and they wax worse; as we see, when spiritual liberty is preached, the flesh draweth it unto carnal lust. ver. 16.

The harvest are the people, ready to receive the evangelion; and the labourers are the true preachers. ver. 37.

CHAPTER X.

Beyond the sea, commonly, they have as well brasen money as of gold and silver[3]. ver. 9. Brass in your girdles.

That is, see that ye take nothing of them, insomuch that ye shake off the very dust from your shoes, that they may know how ye sought not your own profit, but their health. ver. 14.

[[2] Fain: desire. So Spenser. F. Q. Cant. IV. St. 47.]

[[3] It was not till the reign of James I. that the English sovereigns issued a copper coinage. As late as 1604 the royal mint issued pence and halfpence in silver. Macpherson's Hist. of Commerce, pp. 242 and 256, under date of 1609. But "beyond the sea," in Ireland for example, copper coin had come into common use in the reign of Edward III., who made a vain effort to restrain the Irish from buying or selling with *black* money, as he styled it.]

ver. 23. Last clause. That is, ye shall not have converted or preached.

ver. 27. That is to say, openly, where every man may hear.

ver. 41. "In the name of a prophet;" that is, in that he pertaineth to God and to Christ.

ver. 42. A cup of cold water. Compare deed to deed, so is one greater than another; but compare them to God, so are they all alike, and one as good as another; even as the spirit moveth a man, and time and occasion giveth.

CHAPTER XI.

ver. 6. Hurt by me. T. V. Offended in me. Auth. Ver. Hurted and offended, throughout all the new Testament, betokeneth to decay and *faule* in the faith. For many, when they saw that Christ was but a carpenter's son, as they supposed, and he himself also a carpenter, and his mother and kin of so low degree, moreover, when they saw him put to so vile a death, fell clean from the faith, and could not believe.

ver. 11. He that is less in the kingdom of heaven. T. V. *Less*, that is Christ[1].

ver. 12. When the consciences perceive the gospel, they thrust in. Nothing can let them.

ver. 20. To *upbraid* is to cast a man in the teeth.

ver. 30. The cross is an easy thing to them that perceive the gospel.

CHAPTER XII.

ver. 7. The understanding of all commandments stands so greatly in love, that the very commandments of God bind not where love and need require.

ver. 25. Shall be desolate. That is, wasted, destroyed, and brought to nought.

ver 31. Sin against the Holy Ghost is despising of the gospel and his working. Where that bideth is no remedy of sin: for it fighteth against faith, which is the forgiveness of sin. If that be put away, faith may enter in, and all sins depart.

ver. 32. Where Matthew saith here, "Neither in the world to come," Mark saith, "He is in danger of eternal damnation."

ver. 34. A viper is after the manner of an adder, viz. a worm most full of poison.

[[1] In his answer to ch. viii. of B. II. of More's Dialogue, [date 1531] Tyndale gives a comment on these words of our Lord to the same purpose, but at greater length. In his new Testament diligently corrected, printed at Antwerp in 1534, this note is changed into the following: "Christ which humbled himself to the cross was less."]

Here may ye see that words and deed declare out- ver. 35—7.
wardly what a man is within, and are witnesses with him or against him, but never make him good or bad; as the fruit declareth what the tree is, but maketh it neither good nor bad.

CHAPTER XIII.

Where the word of God is understood, there it multiplieth, ver. 12.
and maketh the people better. Where it is not understood, there it decreaseth, and maketh the people worse.

The seed is sown in the ground; and the ground is sown ver. 19—23.
with the word of God.

Tares and cockle are weeds that grow among corn. ver. 25.

There is not so simple a thing in the world, or more ver. 32.
despised than the gospel; and yet it saveth and justifieth them that believe thereon. The law and the works doeth it not.

Leaven betokeneth the gospel also; for it changeth a man ver. 33.
into a new creature.

Treasure hid is the gospel, which giveth us grace and ver. 44.
righteousness without our deserving. Therefore we find it, and make joy, and have a merry conscience; a thing that no man can obtain with works.

The *pearl* is also the evangelion. ver. 46.

Old; the law. *New;* the gospel, or evangelion. ver. 52.

CHAPTER XIV.

Tetrarcha is he that hath rule over the fourth part of the ver. 1.
realm. Jewry, with her pertenance, was then divided into four lordships.

The night in the old time was divided into four quarters; ver. 25.
and to every part was given three hours.

CHAPTER XV.

Mark the leaven of the Pharisees. God would that the ver. 5.
son should honour his father and mother with his temporal Whatsoever thing I offer,
goods; and the Pharisees for their temporal lucre interpreted that same doth profit
it, saying, 'God is thy father and thy mother; offer to him.' thee. T. V.
So were the Pharisees' dishes full with robbery and extortion; and the poor fathers and mothers perish for hunger and need.

ver. 9–13. Traditions of men must fail at the last. God's word bideth ever.

CHAPTER XVI.

ver. 3 The *signs* are Christ's wonderful deeds and miracles, which were prophesied of before, that they should be done in Christ's time.

ver. 17–18. *Peter* in the Greek signifieth a stone in English. This confession is the rock. Now is Simon Bar-Jona, or Simon Jonas' son, called Peter, because of his confession. Whosoever then of this wise confesseth Christ is called Peter. Now is this confession common to all that are true Christians. Then is every christian man and woman Peter. Read Bede, Austin, and Hierome of the manner of loosing and binding; and note how Hierome checketh the presumption of the Pharisees in his time, which yet had not so monstrous interpretations as our new gods have feigned. Read Erasmus' Annotations. It was not for nought that Christ bade "beware of the leaven of the Pharisees." Nothing is so sweet that they make not sour with their traditions. The evangelion, that joyful tidings, is now bitterer than the old law. Christ's burden is heavier than the yoke of Moses. Our condition and estate is ten times heavier than was ever the Jews', the Pharisees have so leavened Christ's sweet bread.

ver. 23. It soundeth in Greek, 'Away from me, Satan;' and are the same words which Christ spake unto the devil, when he would have had him to fall down and worship him.

ver. 27. For the deeds testify what a man is inward. The tree shall be praised according to his fruit.

ver. 28. That is, Whosoever believeth on me shall not see death.

CHAPTER XVII.

ver. 21. Strong faith requireth fervent prayer; and prayer requireth fasting to subdue the body, that lusts unquiet not a man's mind.

ver. 26. Though Christ were free, yet gave he tribute for his neighbour's sake. So is a christian man free in all things, as pertaining to his own part; yet payeth he tribute, and submitteth himself to all men for his brother's sake, to serve his brother withal.

CHAPTER XVIII.

Note here, All bind and loose. ver. 18.

CHAPTER XIX.

Laws permit and suffer many things, to avoid a worse inconvenience, which God will judge and punish. ver. 8.

The third chastity must be ghostly understood, *i. e.* voluntary chastity; or else it were all one with the second, which is outward in the flesh. ver. 12. Have made themselves chaste. T. V.

As Christ speaketh, John viii. "My doctrine is not my doctrine," even so saith he here, "I am not good;" for he speaketh of his humanity, wherewith he ever leadeth us to God. ver. 17.

Perfectness is properly the keeping of God's commandments. Therefore it appeareth evidently that this man had not fulfilled God's commandments groundly, as he yet supposed; and that Christ declareth, when he putteth forth unto him the right work of the commandment, and judgeth that none of the rich men can be saved, of whose number this young man was, yet shall all they be safe that keep God's commandments. ver. 21.

CHAPTER XX.

Seven o'clock with us is one with the Jews; and nine is three: twelve is six: three at afternoon is nine; and five is eleven with them, and six is eventide. ver. 1—6.

By this similitude may ye perceive that no similitude serveth throughout; but some one thing contained in the similitude: as this long parable pertaineth but hereunto, that work-holy shall despise weak sinners; which same work-holy shall not there have their reward, as these which come first have here; but shall be reject and put away, because they challenge it of merit, and not of mercy and grace. ver. 8—12.

The cup signifieth the cross and suffering: but the flesh would be glorified yer[1] than crucified; would be exalted and lift up on high, yer than cast down. ver. 22.

Redeem is to deliver out of bondage. ver. 28. For the redemption of many. T. V.

As many as called him son of David believed that he was very Messias, that great prophet promised of God, which ver. 31.

[[1] Ere, before, sooner.]

should come and redeem Israel. For it was promised that Messias should be David's son.

CHAPTER XXI.

ver. 9. Hosanna is as much to say as, O help; or, O give good luck and health.

ver. 25. John taught the very way unto righteousness. For he interpreted the law right; and damned man, and all his deeds and righteousness, and drave men unto Christ to seek true righteousness through mercy obtained by his blood.

ver. 44. All must fall or stumble at Christ; some to their salvation, some to their damnation.

[Title of first edition.]

The Practyse of Prelates.

§ Whether the kinge's grace maye be separated from hys quene, because she was his brother's wyfe.

MARBORCH.

In the yere of oure Lorde, MCCCCC. & XXX.

[Title of edition of 1548.]

The Practyse of Prelates.

Compyled by the faithfull and godly learned man, Wyllyam Tyndale.

Imprinted at London, by Anthony Scoloker and Willyam Seres; dwellynge wythout Temple-barre in the Savoy rentes. Anno 1548. Cum privilegio ad imprimendum solum.

[Title in Day's reprint.]

The practise of papisticall prelates,

made by Wylliam Tyndale,

In the yeare of our Lorde, 1530.

[INTRODUCTORY NOTICE.

The earliest known production of Tyndale, belonging to the class properly styled polemical, was 'The practice of prelates.' It issued from Hans Luft's press at Marburg, in 1530[1]; and the editor has collated a copy of that first edition[2] with the text of an edition published in the reign of Edward VI. by Scoloker and Seres[3], and with that of Day's folio reprint of Tyndale, edited for him by Foxe in the reign of Elizabeth. As the prelates whose conduct Tyndale intended to expose were indisputably those of the church of Rome, it was thought proper to mark this, in an edition issued after the establishment of a protestant prelacy; especially when that prelacy had begun to be assailed by men who might be tempted to cite Tyndale's words as meant to condemn any inequality of ranks, amongst the presbyters of a Christian church. Hence in Day's reprint this treatise is called 'The practise of papistical prelates,' and its running title, at the head of Day's pages, is 'The practise of popishe prelates.'

But, besides this unimportant alteration, there are considerable suppressions in both of the old reprints. For when its author was composing this treatise, it was notorious that Henry VIII. was bent on having his marriage with Catharine of Aragon dissolved as unlawful; and Tyndale, thinking that the king's popish prelates had instilled needless scruples into his breast for treacherous ends, announced in the original title-page, that the question of the lawfulness of putting her away was therein considered; and towards the close of the treatise he contended at some length, that it was neither necessary nor right to deny that Catharine was the king's lawful wife. As the English reformers were eventually well nigh unanimous in holding the contrary opinion, Scoloker and Seres omitted every passage which bore upon this question, to make their edition more acceptable to their protestant customers; and as Day and Foxe must have felt that arguments tending to prove the validity of Catharine's marriage, must also tend to prove that it was not lawful for Henry to marry Anne Boleyn, and consequently made the legitimacy of Elizabeth's birth a disputable point, their attachment to their protestant sovereign naturally led them to continue the like suppressions, though they did not carry their caution to quite the same extent. The Parker Society cannot follow the example of these editors; for whilst it only reproduces the works of such writers as appear to its council to have been faithful expositors of scriptural truths, it does not desire to have them regarded as infallible teachers. Its principle is to issue

[[1] See Biographical notice of Tyndale, pp. xxxix—xli.]
[[2] F. 13, 40 in the Cambridge University Library.]
[[3] In the possession of the Parker Society.]

honest reprints of such works as it selects for republication; leaving it to its readers to compare what is written with "the law and the testimony;" that test which it was the glory of the reformers to have restored to its due authority. In the present instance, suppression could not have consigned to oblivion what may be objectionable; for the 'Practice of Prelates' was reprinted entire but a few years ago, in the Rev. T. Russell's edition of Tyndale's works: and respectable historians would have been unjustly made liable to the suspicion of being either culpably heedless, or dishonest, if a treatise to which they have referred had been republished as correct, after the excision of passages which they have quoted.]

WILLIAM TYNDALE

TO THE

CHRISTIAN READER.

When the old scribes and Pharisees had darkened the scripture with their traditions, and false interpretations, and wicked persuasions of fleshly wisdom; and shut up the kingdom of heaven, which is God's word, that the people could not enter in unto the knowledge of the true way, as Christ complaineth in the gospel (Matt. xxiii.); then they sat in the hearts of men with their false doctrine in the stead of God and his word, and slew the souls of the people to devour their bodies, and to rob them of their worldly substance. But when Christ and John the Baptist had restored the scripture again unto the true understanding, and had uttered their falsehood, and improved their traditions, and confounded their false interpretations with the clear and evident texts, and with power of the Holy Ghost, and had brought all their juggling and hypocrisy to light; then they gat them unto the elders of the people, and persuaded them, saying, 'This man is surely of the devil; and his miracles be of the devil, no doubt. And these good works which he doth in healing the people, yea, and his preaching against our covetousness, are but a cloak to bring him unto his purpose; that, when he hath gotten him disciples enough, he may rise against the emperor and make himself king. And then shall the Romans come, and take our land from us, and carry away our people, and put other nations in our realm: and so shall we lose all that we have, and the most part of us our lives thereto. Take heed, therefore, betimes, while there is remedy, ere he go so far that ye be not able to resist him.'

Matt. xxiii.

An old practice of the Pharisees, newly practised by the pope and his prelates[1].

The elders of the people, which were rich and wealthy, though before they in a manner favoured Christ, or at the

Worldly preferments are lets to true Christianity.

[[1] The marginal notes belonging to the Marburg edition will be marked W. T. The others were probably penned by Foxe for Day's edition.]

least way were indifferent, not greatly caring whether God or the devil reigned, so that they might bide in their authority, feared immediately (as Herod did of the loss of his kingdom, when the wise men asked where the newborn king of the Jews was), and conspired with the scribes and Pharisees against Christ, and took him and brought him unto Pilate, saying, "We have found this fellow perverting the people, and forbidding to pay tribute unto Cæsar, and saying that he is a[2] king, and moving the people from Galilee unto this place." Then Pilate, though he likewise was before indifferent, put[3] now in fear of the loss of his office, through such persuasions, slew innocent Christ. And in very deed, as the scribes and Pharisees were all their lives before blind guides, unto the destruction of their souls; even so were they at their last end blind prophets, unto the destruction of their bodies. For after that they had slain Christ and divers of his apostles, and persecuted those poor wretches that believed on him, God, to avenge the poor innocent blood that bare witness unto his[4] truth, poured his wrath among them, that they themselves rose against the emperor: and the Romans came (according as they blindly prophesied), and slew the most part of them, and carried the rest captive into all nations, and put other nations in the realm. But whose fault was that insurrection against the emperor, and mischief that followed? Christ's and his apostles, whom they falsely accused beforehand? Nay[5], Christ taught that they should give Cæsar that which pertained unto Cæsar, and God that which belonged to God: even that they should give Cæsar their lawful bodily service, and God the heart; and that they should love God's law, and repent of their evil, and come and receive mercy, and let the wrath of God be taken from off them. And the apostles taught that all souls should obey the higher powers, or temporal rulers. But their obstinate malice, that so hardened their hearts that they could not repent, and their railing upon the open and manifest truth, which they could not improve, and resisting the Holy Ghost, and slaying of the preachers of righteousness, brought

The Jews falsely accused Christ.

The cruel Jews, by persecuting Christ and his apostles, procured the vengeance of God to lighten upon themselves.

The apostles taught all obedience.

[2 So Scoloker and Seres, ed. Day omits *a.*]
[3 So Marburg ed. and Day; S. and S. ed. has *but.*]
[4 So both the older edd. Day has *the.*]
[5 So M. ed; S. and S. has *No.*]

the wrath of God upon them, and was cause of their utter destruction.

The practice of our prelates in these days.

Even so our scribes and Pharisees, now that their hypocrisy is disclosed, and their falsehood so brought to light that it can no longer be hid, get them unto the elders of the people, the lords, gentlemen, and temporal officers, and to all that love this world as they do, and unto whosoever is great with the king, and unto the king's grace himself; and after the same ensample, and with the same persuasions, cast them into like fear of losing of their worldly dominions, and roar unto them, saying, 'Ye be negligent, and care nothing at all, but have a good sport that the heretics rail on us. But give them space a while, till they be grown unto a multitude, and then ye shall see them preach as fast against you, and move the people against you, and do their best to thrust you down also, and shall cry havoc, and make all common.' O generation of serpents, how well declare ye that ye be the right sons of the father of all lies! For they, which ye call heretics, preach nothing save that which our Saviour Jesus Christ preached, and his apostles; adding nought thereto, nor plucking aught therefrom, as the scripture commandeth; and teach all men repentance to God and his holy law, and faith unto our Saviour Jesus Christ, and the promises of mercy made in him, and obedience unto all that God commandeth to obey. Neither teach we so much as to resist your most cruel tyranny with bodily violence, save with God's word only; intending nothing but to drive you out of the temple of Christ, the hearts, consciences, and souls of men (wherein with your falsehood ye sit), and to restore again Jesus our Saviour unto his possession and inheritance bought with his blood, whence ye have driven him out with your manifold wiles and subtilty.

The generation of serpents.

A good admonition to all blind guides.

Take heed, therefore, wicked prelates, blind leaders of the blind; indurate and obstinate hypocrites, take heed. For if the Pharisees for their resisting the Holy Ghost, that is to say, persecuting the open and manifest truth, and slaying the preachers thereof, escaped not the wrath and vengeance of God; how shall ye escape, which are far worse than the Pharisees? For though the Pharisees had shut up the scripture, and set up their own professions; yet they kept their own professions, for the most part. But ye will be the chiefest in Christ's flock, and yet will not keep one jot of the right way of his doctrine. Ye have thereto set up wonderful professions, to be more holy thereby than ye think that Christ's doctrine is able to make you, and yet keep as little thereof, except it be with dispensations; insomuch that if a man ask you, what your marvellous fashioned playing coats and your other puppetry mean, and what your disfigured heads and all your apish[1] play mean, ye know not: and yet are they but signs of things which ye have professed. Thirdly, ye will be papists and hold of the pope; and yet, look in the pope's law, and ye keep thereof almost nought at all. But whatsoever soundeth to make for your bellies, and to maintain your honour, whether in the scripture, or in your own traditions, or in the pope's law, that ye compel the lay-people to observe; violently threatening them with your excommunications and curses, that they shall be damned, both body and soul, if they keep them not. And if that help you not, then ye murder them mercilessly with the sword of the temporal powers; whom ye have made so blind that they be ready to slay whom ye command, and will not yet hear his cause examined, nor give him room to answer for himself.

Our prelates seek to be chief and highest.

Swarms of sects set up by the pope and his prelates.

Our prelates profess the pope to be their lord, but yet keep no part of his law.

The pope's clergy are murderers.

And ye elders of the people, fear ye God also. For as the elders of the Jews, which were partakers with the scribes and Pharisees in resisting the Holy Ghost, and in persecuting the open truth, and slaying the witnesses thereof, and in provoking the wrath of God, had their part with them also in the day of wrath and sharp vengeance, which shortly after fell upon them, (as the nature of the sin against the Holy Ghost is, to have her damnation, not only in the world to come, but also in this life, according unto all the ensamples of the bible and authentic stories since the world began;) even likewise ye, if ye will wink in so open and clear light, and let yourselves be led blindfold, and have your part with the hypocrites in like sin and mischief, be sure ye shall have your part with them in like wrath and vengeance, that is like shortly to fall upon them.

A good admonition to all rulers.

And concerning that the hypocrites put you in fear of the rising of your commons against you, I answer: If ye

[[1] M. ed. has *apes*.]

The common persuasion used by hypocrites.

fear your commons, so testify ye against yourselves, that ye are tyrants. For if your consciences accused you not of evil doing, what need ye to fear your commons? What commons were ever so evil, that they rose against their heads for well-doing? Moreover, ye witness against yourselves also that ye have no trust in God: for he hath promised the temporal officers assistance, if they minister their offices truly; and to care for the keeping of them, as much as they care for to keep his laws.

The pope's clergy are liars.

The hypocrites haply bid you take an ensample of the uplandish people of Almany, which they lie that Martin Luther stirred up. For first, what one sentence in all the writing of Martin Luther find they, that teacheth a man to resist his superior? Moreover, if Martin Luther and the preachers had stirred up the common people of Germany, how happened it that Martin Luther and other like preachers had not perished likewise with them; which are yet all alive at this hour[1]? Ye will ask me, Who stirred them up then? I ask you, Who stirred up the commons of the Jews to resist the emperor, after that the scribes and Pharisees, with the elders of the people, had slain Christ and his apostles?

The wrath of God stirreth up the people to destroy the enemies and persecutors of the truth.

Verily, the wrath of God. And even so here, the wrath of God stirred them up; partly to destroy the enemies and persecutors of the truth, and partly to take vengeance on those carnal beasts which abused the gospel of Christ, to make a cloak of it to defend their fleshly liberty, and not to obey it and to save their souls thereby.

God is the defender of kings and princes.

If kings, lords, and great men, therefore, fear the loss of this world; let them fear God also. For in fearing God shall they prolong their days upon the earth; and not with fighting against God. The earth is God's only; and his favour and mercy doth prolong the days of kings in their estate, and not their own power and might.

Wicked kings and rulers, that persecute God's ministers, are the troublers of themselves and their realm, and not the preachers.

And let all men (be they never so great) hearken unto this, and let this be an answer unto them. Wicked king Ahab said unto the prophet Elias, "Art thou he that troublest Israel?" And Elias answered, "It is not I that trouble Israel, but thou and thy father's household, in that ye have forsaken the com-

[[1] So the M. ed. being published in 1530; but in the edition of 1548, it is *which lived long after*. The insurrection alluded to, being that headed by Munzer, occurred in 1525.]

mandments of the Lord and follow idols." Even so the preachers of the truth, which rebuke sin, are not the troublers of realms and commonwealths, but they that do wickedly; and namely high prelates and mighty princes, which walk without the fear of God, and live abominably, corrupting the common people with their ensample. They be they that bring the wrath of God on all realms, and trouble all commonwealths with war, dearth, poverty, pestilence, evil luck, and all misfortune.

And unto all subjects be it said, if they profess the law of God and faith of the Lord Jesus, and will be Christ's disciples; then let them remember that there was never man so great a subject as Christ was; there was never creature that suffered so great unright so patiently and so meekly as he. Therefore, whatsoever they have been in times past, let them now think that it is their parts to be subject in the lowest kind of subjection, and to suffer all things patiently. If the high powers be cruel unto you with natural cruelty; then with softness and patience ye shall either win them, or mitigate their fierceness. If they join them unto the pope, and persecute you for your faith and hope which ye have in the Lord Jesus; then call to mind that ye be chosen to suffer here with Christ, that ye may joy with him in the life to come with joy everlasting, that shall infinitely pass this your short pain here. If they command that God forbiddeth, or forbid that God commandeth, then answer as the apostles did, (Acts v.), "That God must be obeyed more than man." If they compel you to suffer unright; then Christ shall help you to bear, and his Spirit shall comfort you. But only see that neither they put you from God's word; nor ye resist them with bodily violence. But abide patiently awhile, till the hypocrisy of hypocrites be slain with the sword of God's word, and until the word be openly published and witnessed unto the powers of the world, that their blindness may be without excuse: and then will God awake as a fierce lion, against those cruel wolves which devour his lambs; and will play with the hypocrites, and compass them in their own wiles; and send them a dasing in the head, and a swimming in their brains; and destroy them with their own counsel. And then those malicious and wilful blind persecutors, which, refusing mercy when they were called thereto, chose rather to have their part with hypocrites in shedding of innocent

As many as will be the disciples of Christ, must learn of him meekness and obedience to the higher powers.

Ye must suffer with Christ, that ye may joy with him in the life to come.

Acts v.

God will be revenged upon cruel tyrants.

blood, shall be partakers with them also in having their own blood shed again, God giving an occasion that one wicked shall destroy another.

In the treatise following is shewed who are the causers of insurrection.

And as for wickedness, whence it springeth, and who is the cause of all insurrection, and of the fall of princes, and the shortening of their days upon the earth, thou shalt see in the glass following, which I have set before thine eyes, not to resist the hypocrites with violence (which vengeance pertaineth unto God); but that thou mightest see their wicked ways and abominable paths, to withdraw thyself from after[1] them, and to come again to Christ, and walk in his light, and to follow his steps, and to commit the keeping both of thy body and soul also unto him, and unto the Father through him, whose name be glorious for ever. Amen.

[[1] S. and S. edition omits *after;* but it is found in M. and in Day's edition.]

THE PRACTICE OF PRELATES.

Prelates appointed to preach Christ may not leave God's word, and minister temporal offices; but ought to teach the lay-people the right way, and let them alone with all temporal business.

OUR Saviour Jesus Christ answered Pilate, that his kingdom was not of this world. And (Matthew, in the tenth,) he saith, "The disciple is not greater than his master; but it ought to suffice the disciple, that he be as the master is." Wherefore if Christ's kingdom be not of this world, nor any of his disciples may be otherwise than he was; then Christ's vicars, which minister his kingdom here in his bodily absence, and have the oversight of his flock, may be none emperors, kings, dukes, lords, knights, temporal judges, or any temporal officer, or under false names have any such dominion, or minister any such office as requireth violence.

John xviii.

Matt. x.

The ministers of Christ's doctrine may not have any temporal offices.

And, (Matt. vi.) "No man can serve two masters:" where Christ concludeth, saying, "Ye cannot serve God and mammon;" that is, riches, covetousness, ambition, and temporal dignities.

Matt. vi.

And (Matt. xx.) Christ called his disciples unto him, and said: "Ye know that the lords of the heathen people have dominion over them; and they that be great do exercise power over them. Howbeit, it shall not be so among you: but whosoever will be great among you shall be your minister; and he that will be chief shall be your servant: even as the Son of man came not that men should minister unto him, but for to minister and give his life for the redemption of many." Wherefore the officers in Christ's kingdom may have no temporal dominion or jurisdiction, nor execute any temporal authority or law of violence, nor may have any like manner among them: but clean contrary, they must cast themselves down under all, and become servants unto all, suffer of all, and bear the burden of every man's infirmities, and go before them, and fight for them against the world with the sword of God's word, even unto the death, after the example of Christ.

Matt. xx.

The officers in Christ's kingdom may have no temporal dominion.

And (Matt. xviii.), when the disciples asked who should be greatest in the kingdom of heaven, Christ "called a young child unto him, and set him in the midst among them, saying, Except ye turn back, and become as children, ye shall not enter in the

Matt. xviii.

kingdom of heaven." Now young children bear no rule one over another, but all is fellowship among them. And he said moreover: "Whosoever humbleth himself after the ensample of this child, he is greatest in the kingdom of heaven;" that is, to be (as concerning ambition and worldly desire) so childish that thou couldst not heave thyself above thy brother, is the very bearing of rule, and to be great in Christ's kingdom. And, to describe the very fashion of the greatness of his kingdom, he said, "He that receiveth one such child in my name, receiveth me." What is that, to receive a child in Christ's name? Verily, to submit, to meek, and to humble thyself, and to cast thyself under all men; and to consider all men's infirmities and weaknesses; and to help to heal their diseases with the word of truth, and to live purely, that they see no contrary ensample in thee to whatsoever thou teachest them in Christ; that thou put no stumbling-block before them, to make them fall while they be yet young and weak in the faith: but that thou abstain, as Paul teacheth, (1 Thess. v.) *ab omni specie mala*[1], from all that might seem evil, or whereof a man might surmise amiss; and that thou so love them, that whatsoever gift of God in thee is, thou think the same theirs, and their food, and for their sakes given unto thee, as the truth is; and that all their infirmities be thine, and that thou feel them, and that thine heart mourn for them; and that with all thy power thou help to amend them, and cease not to cry to God for them, neither day nor night; and that thou let nothing be found in thee, that any man may rebuke, but whatsoever thou teachest them, that be thou; and that thou be not a wolf in a lamb's skin, as our holy father the pope is, which cometh unto us in a name of hypocrisy, and in the title of cursed Cham, or Ham[2], calling himself *Servus servorum*, the servant of all servants, and is yet found *Tyrannus tyrannorum*, of all tyrants the most

To receive a child in Christ's name, what it is.

1 Thess. v.

The pope is a wolf in a lamb's skin.

[1 From every evil appearance.]

[2 The first letter in the name of this son of Noah having no exact representative in our alphabet, the Latin vulgate puts *ch* for it, writing the name Cham: but *ch*, as pronounced in English, produces a sound more unlike that which belongs to *heth*, than is the sound of our *h*. Hence Tyndale thought it better to write the name Ham; and that improvement in the spelling of this and various other names, which his knowledge of Hebrew enabled him to introduce into the English Old Testament, has been preserved in our authorised version.]

cruel. This is to receive young children in Christ's name; and to receive young children in Christ's name is to bear rule in the kingdom of Christ. Thus ye may see, that Christ's kingdom is altogether spiritual; and the bearing of rule in it is clean contrary unto the bearing of rule temporally. Wherefore none that beareth rule in it may have any temporal jurisdiction, or minister any temporal office that requireth violence to compel withal.

Peter was not greater than the other apostles by any authority given him of Christ.

Why Peter was called chief of the apostles.

They say that Peter was chief of the apostles: verily, as Apelles was called chief of painters for his excellent cunning above other, even so Peter may be called chief of the apostles for his activity and boldness above the other. But that Peter had any authority or rule over his brethren and fellow apostles, is false, and contrary to the scripture. Christ forbade it the last even[3] before his passion, and in divers times before, and taught alway the contrary, as I have rehearsed.

Peter had no authority above the rest of the apostles.

Thou wilt say, 'thou canst not see how there should be any good order in that kingdom, where none were better than other, and where the superior had not a law and authority to compel the inferior with violence.' The world, truly, can see no other way to rule than with violence: for there no man abstaineth from evil, but for fear; because the love of righteousness is not written in their hearts. And therefore the pope's kingdom is of the[4] world: for there one sort are your grace, your holiness, your fatherhood; another, my lord bishop, my lord abbot, my lord prior; another, master doctor, father, bachelor, master parson, master vicar, and at the last cometh in simple sir John[5]. And every man reigneth over other with might; and have every ruler his prison, his jailor, his chains, his torments; even so much as the friars Observants observe that rule, and compel every man other with violence above the cruelness of the heathen tyrants: so that what cometh once in may never out, for fear of telling tales out of school. They rule over the body with violence, and compel it, whether the heart will or not, to observe things of their own making.

The pope's kingdom is of the world.

A rabble of the pope's guard, that wear his badge.

[3 That is, *evening.*] [4 S. and S. ed. *this.*]
[5 See Vol. I. p. 277, n. 3.]

The ministers of the kingdom of God must govern with all love, meekness, and patience.

But in the kingdom of God it is contrary. For the Spirit that bringeth them thither maketh them willing, and giveth them lust unto the law of God; and love compelleth them to work, and love maketh every man's good, and all that he can do, common unto his neighbour's need. And as every man is strong in that kingdom, so love compelleth him to take the weak by the hand, and to help him, and to take him that cannot go upon his shoulders and bear him. And so to do service unto the weaker is to bear rule in that kingdom.

Peter in use of speaking, for his diligence is called (but not in the scripture) the chief of the apostles.

And because Peter did exceed the other apostles in fervent service toward his brethren, therefore is he called, not in the scripture, but in the use of speaking, the chiefest of the apostles; and not that he had any dominion over them. Of which truth thou mayest see also the practice in the Acts of the apostles, after the resurrection. For when Peter had been and preached in the house of Cornelius, an heathen man, the other that were circumcised chode him, because he had been in an uncircumcised man's house, and had eaten with him: for it was forbidden in the law, neither wist they yet that the heathen should be called. And Peter was fain to give accounts unto them (which is no token of superiority), and to shew them how he was warned of the Holy Ghost so to do.

Peter was enforced to render an account to his brethren of his doings. Acts xi.

Acts xv. Peter shewed no part of his authority, but the mighty power of God.

And (Acts xv.) when a council was gathered of the apostles and disciples about the circumcision of the heathen, Peter brought forth, not his commandment and the authority of his vicarship, but the miracle that the Holy Ghost had shewed for the heathen; how at the preaching of the gospel the Holy Ghost had lighted upon them, and purified their hearts through faith; and therefore proved that they ought not to be circumcised.

All the apostles allege the authority of God in Christ, and no authority of their own.

And Paul and Barnabas brought forth the miracles also, that God had shewed by them among the heathen through preaching of faith. And then James brought forth a prophecy of the old Testament for the said part: and therewith the adversaries gave over their hold, and they concluded with one assent, by the authority of the scripture and of the Holy Ghost, that the heathen should not be circumcised; and not by the commandment of Peter, under pain of cursing, excommunication, and interdicting, and like bugs, to make fools and children afraid withal.

Acts viii.

And (Acts viii.) Peter was sent of the other apostles unto

the Samaritans: which is an evident token that he had no jurisdiction over them, (for then they could not have sent him,) but rather (as the truth is,) that the congregation had authority over him, and over all other private persons, to admit them for ministers, and send them forth to preach, whithersoever the Spirit of God moved them, and as they saw occasion.

Peter was sent by the other apostles to preach in Samaria.

And in the epistle unto the Galatians thou seest also how Paul corrected Peter, when he walked not the straight[1] way after the truth of the gospel.

Gal. ii. Paul rebuked Peter to his face.

So now thou seest that in the kingdom of Christ, and in his church or congregation, and in his councils, the ruler is the scripture, approved through the miracles of the Holy Ghost, and men be servants only; and Christ is the head, and we all brethren. And when we call men our heads, that we do not because they be shorn or shaven, or because of their names, parson, vicar, bishop, pope; but only because of the word which they preach. If they err from the word, then may whomsoever God moveth his heart, play Paul, and correct him. If he will not obey the scripture, then have his brethren authority by the scripture to put him down, and to send him out of Christ's church among the heretics, which prefer their false doctrine above the true word of Christ.

Scripture is the chiefest of the apostles. W. T.

We give the ministers reverence, not for themselves, but because of the word that they minister.

How the gospel punisheth trespassers, and how, by the gospel, we ought to go to law with our adversaries.

Though that they of Christ's congregation be all willing; yet, because that the most part is alway weak, and because also that the occasions of the world be ever many and great, insomuch that Christ, which wist all thing before hand, saith, (Matt. xviii.) "Woe be unto the world by reason of occasions of evil:" and saith also, that it cannot be avoided but that occasions shall come, therefore it cannot be chosen but that many shall overfall; when a weak brother hath trespassed, by what law shall he be punished? Verily, by the law of love; whose properties thou readest in the thirteenth of the first to the Corinthians. If the love of God, which is my profession, be written in mine heart, it will not let me hate my weak

Matt. xviii.

Our brethren, when they offend, must be reformed by love, and not by rigour.

[[1] So M. ed., but S. and S. ed. *right*.]

brother when he hath offended me, no more than natural love will let a mother hate her child when it trespasseth against her. My weak brother hath offended me; he is fallen, his weakness hath overthrown him. It is not right by the law of love, that I should now fall upon him, and tread him down in the mire and destroy him utterly: but it is right by the law of love, that I run to him and help him up again.

How we may go to the law with our trespassers. Matt. xviii.

By what process we should go to law with our trespassers, Christ teacheth us, Matth. xviii. Tell him his fault between him and thee with all meekness, remembering thou art a man, and mayest fall also: if he repent and thou love him, ye shall soon agree, and then forgive him. And when thou forgivest thy neighbour, then thou art sure that God forgiveth thee thy trespasses by his holy promise, (Matth. vi.)

Matt. vi.

If he hear thee not, then take a neighbour or two. If he hear them not, then tell the congregation, where thou art: and let the preacher pronounce God's law against him, and let the sad and discreet men rebuke him, and exhort him unto repentance. If he repent, and thou also love him according to thy profession, ye shall soon agree. If he hear not the congregation, then let him be taken as an heathen. If he that is offended be weak also, then let them that be strong go between, and help them. And in like manner, if any sin against the doctrine of Christ and the profession of a christian man, so that he be a drunkard and an whore-keeper, or whatsoever open sin he do, or if he teach false learning; then let such be rebuked openly before the congregation, and by the authority of the scripture. And if they repent not, let them be put out of the congregation as heathen people. If they then be not ashamed, we have no remedy but patiently to abide what God will do; and to pray in the meantime, that God will open their hearts, and give them repentance. Other law than this Christ's gospel knoweth not, nor the officers thereof.

Open and common offenders are to be rebuked openly.

The kingdom of Christ is spiritual.

It is manifest, therefore, that the kingdom of Christ is a spiritual kingdom, which no man can minister well, and a temporal kingdom too, as it is sufficiently proved; because that no man which putteth his hand to the plough, and looketh back, is apt for the kingdom of heaven; as Christ answered (Luke ix.) unto him that would have followed him,

Luke ix.

but would first have taken leave of his household. If a man put his hand to the plough of God's word to preach it, and look also unto worldly business, his plough will surely go awry. And therefore, saith Christ unto another, that would likewise follow him, but desired first to go and bury his father, "Let the dead bury the dead: but come thou and shew, or preach, the kingdom of God." As who should say, He that will preach the kingdom of God (which is Christ's gospel) truly, must have his heart nowhere else. Luke ix.

What officers the apostles ordained in Christ's church; and what their offices were to do.

Wherefore the apostles, following and obeying the rule, doctrine, and commandment of our Saviour Jesus Christ, their master, ordained in his kingdom and congregation two officers; one called, after the Greek word, *bishop*, in English an overseer: which same was called *priest* after the Greek, *elder* in English, because of his age, discretion, and sadness; for he was, as nigh as could be, alway an elderly man: as thou seest both in the new and old Testament also, how the officers of the Jews be called the elders of the people, because (as thou mayest well think) they were ever old men, as nigh as could be. For unto age do men naturally obey, and unto age doth God command to give honour, saying, (Lev. xix.) "Rise up before the hoar head, and reverence the face of the old man." And also experience of things, and coldness, without which it is hard to rule well, is more in age than in youth. And this overseer did put his hands unto the plough of God's word, and fed Christ's flock, and tended them only, without looking unto any other business in the world. Officers first ordained in Christ's church. Bishop. Honour the aged. Lev. xix. In the aged is experience.

Another officer they chose, and called him *deacon* after the Greek, a *minister* in English, to minister the alms of the people unto the poor and needy. For in the congregation of Christ love maketh every man's gift and goods common unto the necessity of his neighbour. Wherefore, the love of God being yet hot in the hearts of men, the rich that had the substance of this world's goods brought of their abundance great plenty unto the sustentation of the poor, and delivered it unto the hands of the deacons. And unto the help of the deacons were widows of sixty years old, holy, virtuous, and destitute of friends, chosen to tend and wait upon the sick, Deacon. In the primitive church they chose deacons to minister to the poor. Widows.

and to wash the saints' feet, that came from one congregation unto another, whether for any business, or for fear of persecution. And those common goods of the church, offered for the succour of the poor, grew in all churches so exceedingly, that in some congregation it was so much, that it was sufficient to maintain an host of men; insomuch that tyrants did oft-times persecute the Christen[1] for those common goods, as thou seest in the life of St Laurence, the deacon of Rome[2].

Common goods. W. T.

The great and fervent charity in the primitive church.

The covetousness of the prelates was the decay of Christendom, and the increasing of the kingdom of Mahomet.

And, moreover, the covetousness of the prelates was the decay of Christendom, and the increasing of the kingdom of Mahomet. For by the first springing of the empire of Mahomet, the emperors, kings, and great lords of Christendom had given their treasure so mightily unto the church, what after great victories, and what at their deaths, that their successors were not able to maintain battle against the Saracens and Turks, (for the world was not yet in such captivity that they could make their subjects swear on books what they were worth, and raise up taxes at their pleasure;) so that a certain writer of stories saith: "The prelates gaped when the laymen would take the war upon them against the Turks; and the laymen looked when the prelates would lay out their money, to make the war withal, and not spend it in worse use, as the most part of them were wont to do; spending the money that was gotten with alms and blood of martyrs upon goodly plate, and great vessels of gold and silver, without care of things to come, despising God, whom they worshipped

The proud clergy, how they spent the treasure of the poor.

[1 *Christen* is frequently used in the earliest editions of Tyndale, and in other old writers, for the plural of Christian, as *men* for plural of *man*. Hence Christendom.]

[2 The church of Rome has dedicated the 10th of August to the memory of Laurence, and the lessons for that day, in the breviary, give a florid account of his merits and martyrdom. It was in the year 258 that a mandate from the emperor Valerian occasioned that persecution under which Sixtus II. bishop of Rome, was put to death; and Platina says that Sixtus bade his attendant deacon Laurence make haste to distribute whatever might be in the church's treasury amongst the poor. Laurence was soon arrested, and the prefect of Rome required him to produce this treasure: upon which he produced the poor whom that treasure had fed, telling the prefect that the poor saints were the treasures of the Christian church. For this, the legend says, the prefect ordered him to be bound upon a red hot iron hurdle, and burnt over a fire. Platina, Vit. Pontificum, and Roman breviary.]

for their belly's sake only, and also man[3]." Moreover, it was the custom even then, saith the author, to ask what the bishoprick was worth[4]; yea, and to leave a worse for a better, or to keep both with a union. And at the same time Isacius, the deputy of the emperor, came to Rome to confirm the pope in his see with the emperor's authority; for the election of the pope was then nothing worth, except it had been confirmed by the emperor: and he found so great treasure in the church of St John Lateran, that for disdain which he had, that they should have such treasure in store, and not to help the emperor in his wars against the Turks, seeing his soldiers lacked wages, he took it away with violence against the will of the prelates, of which he exiled some, and paid his own men of war with one part, and took another part unto himself, and sent the third part unto the emperor: which must needs have been a great treasure in one church[5].

Isacius.

The election was confirmed by the emperor.

Note here the treasure that the bishops of Rome had at this time.

By what means the prelates fell from Christ.

The office of a bishop was a room, at the beginning, that no man coveted; and that no man durst take upon him, save he only which loved Christ better than his own life. For as Christ saith, that no man might be his disciple, except that he were ready to forsake life and all; even so might that officer be sure that it would cost him his life at one time or another, for bearing record unto the truth. But after that the multitude of the Christen were increased, and many great men had received the faith; then both lands and rents, as

The bishop of Rome in the primitive church was a dangerous office.

[3 The 'certain writer of stories' to whom Tyndale refers is Platina, *De vitis pontificum,* who says in his life of Boniface V.: Exspectant sacerdotes ut a secularibus hoc tantum bellum et tam necessarium sumatur. Exspectant item seculares ut presbyteri tuendæ religionis causa [against Mahometan invaders] pecunias in sumptus bellicos polliceantur et sumministrent; nec in pejores usus effundant, quemadmodum facere plerique consuevere, pecunias eleemosynis et sanguine martyrum comparatas, in aurea et argentea vasa et prægrandia quidem pendentes, parum de futuro solliciti, Dei, quem tantum utilitatis gratia colunt, et hominum contemptores.]

[4 Quæritur enim quantum reddat episcopatus; non quot oves pascuæ in eo sint.—Id. Vit. Bonifacii III. Date about 606.]

[5 This last sentence is nearly a translation of what Platina relates, in the beginning of his account of Severinus, pope for but a few months of A. D. 640.—Plat. Vit. Honorii.]

well as other goods, were given unto the maintenance, as well of the clergy, as of the poor: because they gave then no tithes to the priests, nor yet now do, save in certain countries. For it is too much to give alms, offerings, lands, and tithes also. And then the bishops made them substitutes under them to help them, which they called priests, and kept the name of bishop unto themselves[1].

At the first entry of Christ's church, there were no tithes paid to the ministers.

But out of the deacons sprang all the mischief: for through their hands went all things; they ministered unto the clergy, they ministered unto the poor, they were in favour with great and small. And when the bishop's office began to have rest, and to be honourable, then the deacons, through favour and gifts, clamb[2] up thereunto; as lightly[3] he that hath the old abbot's treasure succeedeth with us. And by the means of their practice and acquaintance in the world they were more subtle and worldly wise than the old bishops, and less learned in God's word; as our prelates are, when they come from stewardships in gentlemen's houses, and from surveying of great men's lands, lords' secrets, kings' councils, ambassadorship, from war and ministering all worldly matters, yea, worldly mischief. And yet now they come not thence, but receive all, and bide there still; yea, they have enacted by plain[4] parliament that they must bide in the court still, or

All corruption of the church came first out of the deacons.

Money purchased preferment.

The prelates must bide still in the court. W. T.

[1 Tyndale seems to have held an opinion afterwards maintained by Dr Hammond, and thus noticed by Bingham: "The learned Dr Hammond advances an opinion about this matter" [the original of presbyters], "which is something singular. He asserts (Annot. on Acts xi. 30) that in scripture-times the name of presbyters belonged principally, if not alone, to bishops; and that there is no evidence that any of this second order were then instituted, though soon after, he thinks, before the writing of Ignatius' epistles, there were such instituted in all churches. The authorities he builds upon are Clemens Romanus and Epiphanius, who say that in some churches, at first, there were bishops and deacons without any presbyters." Bing. Orig. Eccles. B. II. ch. xix. § 3, Vol. I. p. 252, ed. 1840.]

[2 Clamb: climbed. The reading of Day's edition is *climed*.]

[3 Easily; and hence, ordinarily.]

[4 The word is spelt *playne* in the black letter editions. Tyndale probably meant to give a version of the old law phrase, Pleno parliamento, used to signify the indisputable authority of a legislative enactment; and had in view an act for 'Abridging spiritual persons from having pluralities of livings.' It was an act which had just passed through parliament, and its 28th clause was to the effect he has stated;

else they may not have plurality of benefices. And then by little and little they enhanced themselves, and turned all to themselves, minishing the poor people's part, and increasing theirs, and joining acquaintance with great men, and with their power clamb up, and entitled them to the choosing and confirming of the pope and all bishops[5], to flatter and purchase favour and defenders; trusting more unto their worldly wisdom than unto the doctrine of Christ, which is the wisdom of God, and unto the defence of man than of God. Then, while they that had the plough by the tail looked back, the plough went awry; faith waxed feeble and fainty; love waxed cold; the scripture waxed dark; Christ was no more seen. He was in the mount with Moses; and therefore the bishops would have a god upon the earth whom they might see, and thereupon they began to dispute who should be greatest.

How the clergy first by riches, and then by flattery, advanced themselves.

When the prelates waxed rich, then they disputed who should be highest.

How the bishop of Rome became greater than other, and called himself pope.

Then, quoth worldly wisdom, Jerusalem must be the greatest, for that was Christ's seat: *Et factum est:* so it came to pass for a season. And in conclusion, where a great city was, and much riches, there was the bishop ever greater than his fellows. Alexandria[6] in Egypt, and Antioch in Greece, were greater than their neighbours. Then, those decaying, Constantinople and Rome waxed great, and strove who should be greater. And Constantinople said, Where the emperor is, there ought to be the greatest seat and chiefest bishop: for the emperor lay most at Constantinople, because it was (I suppose) nigh the midst of the empire; therefore I must be the greatest, said the bishop of Constantinople. Nay, quoth the bishop of Rome, though the emperor lie never so much at Constantinople, yet he is called emperor of Rome, and

Jerusalem was the first seat of our high bishop.

Constantinople. Rome.

How Rome came to be the chiefest city.

for it provided that 'The act should not in any wise extend, nor be prejudicial to any such chaplains as shall be daily or quarterly attending and abiding in the king's or queen's honourable households,' and in like manner for the chaplains of nobles, &c.—21 Hen. VIII. c. 13, § 28.]

[5 He is here giving a sketch of the institution of cardinal presbyters and of their progress to power.—See Bingham, B. II. c. 19, § 18.]

[6 Alexandre in the M. ed. and in Day; but Alexander in the S. S. edition.]

Rome the seat and mother of all wickedness.

Rome is the head of the empire; wherefore of right I must be the father of all whatsoever[1]. And thus, whether they challenged their title by the authority of God or man, or by Peter or pouling[2], it was all one, so they might be greatest.

And great intercession was made unto the emperors of both parties; but in vain a great season: for the emperors stopped their ears at such ambitious requests long time; till at the last there came an emperor called Phocas, which lay long in Italy, and was a very soft man, and a prey for prelates: in whose time Boniface III. was bishop of Rome, a man ambitious and greedy upon honour, and of a very subtle wit, nothing inferior unto Thomas Wolfsee[3], cardinal of York. This Boniface was great with the emperor Phocas, and with his wily persuasions and great intercession together obtained of Phocas to be called the chiefest of all bishops, and that his church should be the chief church[4]: which authority as soon as he had purchased, he sent immediately his commandment, with the emperor's power, unto all the bishops of Almany, commanding that every bishop should call all the priests of his diocese, and charge them that every man should put away his wife, under pain of excommunication; which tyranny, though great resistance was made against it, he yet brought to pass with the emperor's sword and his own subtilty together[5]. For the bishops were rich, and durst not displease the pope, for fear of the emperor.

Phocas.

Pope Boniface the third. W. T.

Phocas the emperor first gave privilege to the bishop of Rome to be the chief bishop.

The chastity of priests, how it came up. W. T.

[1 This word has been printed *waten* in modern editions. In the black letter copies it is *watē*, an abbreviation of *whatsoever*, still employed by lawyers. When a pope is crowned, the cardinal deacon puts the tiara, or *regno*, as it is called, upon his head, and says to him, Accipe tiaram, tribus coronis ornatam; et scias te esse patrem principum et regum, rectorem orbis.]

[2 To poll, or levy a tax, is spelt in the original edition *poule*, and the name of the apostle is also spelt *poul*, though not uniformly. The word pouling may therefore either mean here taxing, or assuming the authority of a Paul, with reference to Peter just mentioned.]

[3 So the two oldest editions; Day, Wolsee.]

[4 So Platina of Boniface III.: Patria Romanus, a Phoca imperatore obtinuit, magna tamen contentione, ut sedes B. Petri Apostoli, quæ caput est omnium ecclesiarum, ita et diceretur et haberetur ab omnibus.]

[5 There seems to be some confusion here of times and persons. Boniface III. died in 606, before he had been pope nine months; when the emperor had no authority in Germany, neither were there any

As soon as Nemroth, that mighty hunter, had caught this prey, that he had compelled all bishops to be under him, and to swear obedience unto him, then he began to be great in the earth; and called himself Papa[6], with this interpretation, Father of fathers. And when the pope had exalted his throne above his fellows, then the unity that ought to be among brethren in Christ's church brake; and division began between us and the Greeks; which Greeks (I suppose) were at that time the one half of Christendom. And when any pope since exhorteth them to unity, they answer, 'That he which will reign over his brethren with violence, breaketh unity, and not they; and that they will not be under his tyranny, whereunto he calleth them under a colour of unity.' And from henceforth, with the help of his bishops, which were sworn to be true liegemen unto him, when beforetime they were admitted to their bishopricks of the emperors and kings, he began to lay a bait to catch the whole empire into his hands also.

Note here the climbing up of the pope.

Division in the church. W. T.

The Greeks will not be under the pope's tyranny.

By what means the pope invaded the empire.

At that same season Mahomet, the author of the sect of the Turks and Saracens, began. And as soon as he had got much people unto him with wiles and feigned miracles, he

Mahomet and the pope began at one time. W. T.

regularly constituted churches in that country. But in 723, pope Gregory II. gave the name of Boniface to the Anglo-Saxon monk, Winfrid, for his good deeds in planting churches in parts of Germany near the Rhine, and desired the Frank ruler, Charles Martel, and all persons in authority to attend to the injunctions of this Boniface, who used the influence thus obtained to elevate the papal authority. Hence some of his dicta were incorporated into the canon law (see Vol. I. p. 328, n. 3), and some of these may have been so quoted as not to distinguish their author from pope Boniface III.—See Hist. des papes, a la Haye, 1733, Tom. I. pp. 518—50. Also Mosheim, Cent. viii. par. 1, cap. I. § 2—4; and Lingard, Antiq. of Anglo-Saxon Ch., pp. 445—53, 2nd edition.]

[6 The word *papa* was in like use among the Greeks as with us. The earliest known instance of its application to a christian minister occurs in Tertullian, De pudicitia, a treatise composed early in the third century. By the middle of that century it was become common to address bishops by this endearing name; but at what period the bishops of Rome began to assume it as exclusively their own, cannot be stated with precision.—Bp. Kaye on Tertullian, ch. IV. p. 241: and Bing. Orig. Eccles. B. II. ch. II. § 7.]

invaded the empire of Rome in those quarters. And look, how busy Mahomet was in those parts, so busy was the pope in these quarters, to invade the empire, (with the help of his sworn bishops, which preached all of none other God than the pope,) while the emperor was occupied afar off in resisting of Mahomet.

Gregory the pope came up by the Frenchmen, and by them he continueth his estate still. W. T.

And within few years after, when the kings of Italy now and then vexed our holy fathers for their covetous ambition, then Gregory III. joined amity with the Frenchmen, and called them to help[1]; by whose power they gat all they have, and also maintain it unto this day. For if any man, since that time hither[2], displeased the pope never so little, he immediately cursed him, and excommunicated him, and proclaimed him no right inheritor, and that it was not lawful to hold of him, and absolved his lords and subjects of their allegiance, and sent his blessing unto the French king and remission of sins to go and conquer his land; the pope and French king alway dividing the spoil between them: the bishops, and all that served God for the belly, preaching the pope's might, how that he had power so to do, and all things to bind and loose at his will; wresting the scriptures to serve for their purpose, corrupting all the laws, both of God and man, to prove his godhead withal.

Pope Zacharias the First. Hildericus.

Then came pope Zacharias the first, in whose time Hildericus[3] was king of France, a man that governed his realm (as it oft chanceth) by a deputy (as parsons[4] preach), one

Pepin.

Pipine, a lord of his own, and his sworn subject. This Pipine sent a holy bishop to pope Zacharias, that he should help to make him king of France, and he would be his defender in Italy (as the manner of scalled horses is, the one to claw the

[1 The French chronologist, president Hainault, confirms Tyndale's statement, under the date of 740, in the following words: "Gregory III. made more advantageous proposals to Charles Martel, when troubled by the king of the Lombards; to wit, that he would cease to recognise the [Greek] emperor's authority, and would proclaim Charles the consul of Rome. Here we have the real epoch of the temporal power of the popes."]

[2 That is, from that time to the date of Tyndale's writing.]

[3 So Marb., but S. and S. ed. Huldericus. In French history he is styled Childeric III., and began to reign in 742.]

[4 So S. and S. ed. By the person, or parson of the parish was meant the rector; the vicar was his deputy.]

other); and Zacharias answered, that he was more worthy to be king, that ruled the realm and took the labours, than an idle shadow that went up and down, and did nought. And so upon that, the lords of France, by the persuasions of the prelates, consented unto Pipine, and thrust down their right king unto whom they were sworn, and made a monk of him; and both the lords, and also Pipine, took dispensations for their oaths of our holy father, and were forsworn[5]. Thus was our holy father, the pope, crept up into the consciences of men with his false interpretation of binding and loosing, good eight hundred years agone[6].

The pope put down the right French king, and set up Pepin.

The king of France was made a monk. W. T.

Then came pope Stephanus the second, out of whose hands Estulphus, king of Lombardy, would fain have scratched somewhat; for he thought that the holy fathers gathered too fast, and had already raked too much unto them. But the new king, Pipine of France, warned of his duty and service promised, and mindful of old friendship, and hoping for part of the prey, came to succour the pope: and when he had subdued the king of Lombardy, he gave unto our holy father, or rather to St Peter, that hungry beggar, great provinces and countries in Lombardy and in Italy, with the isle Corsica, and many great cities, of which some pertained unto the emperor, being then at Constantinople; and yet the emperor had sent before unto king Pipine, that he should not give of his towns unto the pope. But Pipine answered that he came for the same intent, and to enhance our holy father. And our holy father received them[7].

Pope Steven the second.

Estulphus, king of Lombardy.

How the pope was advanced.

And thus the empire was divided into two parts; the pope and the French king parting the one half between them. And as the emperor decayed, the pope grew. And as the

[[5] The history of this transaction is incorporated into the papal law, where Decret. pars. 2da can. xv. q. 6, cap. 3, is as follows. Pontificalis auctoritas a juramento fidelitatis nonnullos absolvit. Alius item Romanus pontifex, Zacharias scilicet, regem Francorum, non tam pro suis iniquitatibus quam pro eo quod tantæ potestati erat inutilis, a regno deposuit, et Pipinum Caroli Magni imperatoris patrem in ejus locum substituit; omnesque Francigenas a juramento fidelitatis absolvit.—Corp. Jur. canonici. Th. Kerver, 1516.]

[[6] The date of this transaction was about 751.]

[[7] Platina has not mentioned Corsica as part of Pepin's gift to Stephen in his life of that pope; but he mentions it as included in that gift, when relating the life of Adrian I.]

By what means Mahomet waxed great. W. T.

pope grew, so the sect of Mahomet grew; for the emperor (half his empire lost) was not able to defend himself against the infidels. And the pope would suffer no help hence to come, for two causes; one, lest the emperor should recover his empire again; and another, because the prelates of the Greeks would not submit themselves unto his godhead, as the prelates of these quarters of the world had done.

Carolus. Magnus.

After Pipine reigned his son the great Charles, whom we call Charlemagne, which knew no other god but the pope, nor any other way to heaven than to do the pope pleasure. For the pope served him for two purposes: one, to dispense with him for whatsoever mischief he did; another, to be established in the empire by his help: for without his favour he wist it would not be; so great a god was our holy father become already in those days.

The pope become a great god on the earth.

This pope Stephen[1] in his latter days fell at variance with Desiderius, king of Lombardy about the archbishop of Ravenna.

Desiderius.

Pope Adrian the first.

After Stephen succeeded Adrian the first; with whom Desiderius, the king of Lombardy, would fain have made peace, but pope Adrian would not. And shortly upon that, the brother of this Charlemagne, which reigned with him in half the dominion of France, died; whose wife, for fear of Charles, fled with her two sons unto Desiderius, king of Lombardy for succour. Desiderius was glad of their coming, trusting by the means of these two children to obtain favour among many of the Frenchmen, and so to be able to resist Charles, if he would meddle, and to bring Italy unto the right emperor again, and would have had that pope Adrian should have anointed them kings in their father's room. But Adrian refused that to do, (for he saw Charles mighty and meet for his purpose,) and was as wily as Desiderius; and thought to keep out the right emperor, and be emperor of Rome himself, though he gave another the name for a season, till a more convenient time came.

The pope purposed to be emperor himself.

Then Desiderius warred upon the pope's jurisdiction; and Adrian sent to Charles: and Charles came with his

[1 By the expression *this* Stephen, Tyndale has marked, though obscurely, that the Stephen of Charlemagne's days is not the same pope as the Stephen whom Pepin assisted. Stephen III. became pope in 768, and was succeeded by Adrian I. in 772.]

army, and drave out Desiderius and his son; which son fled unto the right emperor to Constantinople. And Charles and the pope divided the kingdom of Lombardy between them: and Charles came to Rome; and the pope and he were sworn together, that whosoever should be enemy unto the one, should be enemy also unto the other[2].

Charles and the pope divided the kingdom of Lombardy.

This Adrian gathered a council immediately of an hundred and fifty-three bishops, abbots, and religious persons, and gave unto Charles and his successors the empire of Rome; and ordained that the right and power to choose the pope should be his, and that no bishop should be consecrate till he had obtained of him both consent and the ornaments of a bishop also, (which they now buy of the pope,) under pain of cursing, and to be delivered unto black Satan the devil, and loss of goods. (Dist. lxiii.[3])

The pope gathered a council, and gave unto Charles the empire of Rome.

And Leo the third, which succeeded Adrian, confirmed the same; and crowned Charles emperor of Rome for like service done unto him. And then there was appointment made between the emperors of Constantinople and of Rome, and the places assigned, how far the borders of either empire should reach. And thus of one empire was made twain; and therefore the empire of Constantinople, for lack of help, was shortly after subdued of the Turks.

Leo the third, pope.

Of one whole empire the pope made two.

The said Leo also called Charles "The most christian king[4]," because of his good service; which title the kings of

Most christian king. W. T.

[[2] This was A.D. 774.]

[[3] The heading of Dist. lxiii. is, "Laici nullo modo se debent inserere electioni" [pontificum]; and its first canon begins, Nullus laicorum principum vel potentum semet inserat electioni aut promotioni patriarchæ, metropolitani, aut cujuslibet episcopi. But its ca. XXII. is headed, "Imperator jus habet eligendi pontificem;" and the text of that canon is as follows: Adrianus papa Romam venire Karolum regem ad defendendas res ecclesiæ postulavit... Romam reversus [Karolus] constituit ibi synodum cum Adriano papa in patriarchatu lateranensi, in ecclesia S[ti] Salvatoris; quæ synodus celebrata est cliii. episcopis, religiosis, et abbatibus. Adrianus autem papa cum universa synodo tradiderunt Karolo jus et potestatem eligendi pontificem, et ordinandi apostolicam sedem, dignitatem quoque patriciatus ei concesserat. Insuper archiepiscopos et episcopos per singulas provincias ab eo investituram accipere diffinivit; ut, nisi a rege laudetur et investiatur, episcopus a nemine consecretur; et quicunque contra hoc decretum ageret anathematis vinculo eum innodavit.—Corp. Jur. Canon Decret. par. 1[ma].]

[[4] In the inscription on his tomb, "Magni Caroli Regis Christianissimi Romanorumque Imperatoris." Platin. in Vit. Leon. III.]

France use unto this day, though many of them be never so unchristened: as the last Leo called our king "The defender of the faith;" and as this[1] pope Clemens calleth the duke of Guelder "The eldest son of the holy see of Rome," for no other virtue nor property that any man can know, save that he hath been all his life a pick-quarrel and a cruel and unrighteous bloodshedder, as his father, that sitteth in that holy see, is. So now, above seven hundred years, to be a christian king is to fight for the pope; and most christian, that most fighteth, and slayeth most men for his pleasure.

Defender of the faith. W. T. The eldest son of the holy seat. W. T. Who is a christian king. The life of Charles. W. T.

This Charles was a great conqueror; that is to say, a great tyrant, and overcame many nations with the sword: as the Turk compelleth us unto his faith, so he compelled them with violence unto the faith of Christ, say the stories. But, alas! Christ's faith, whereunto the Holy Ghost only draweth men's hearts through preaching the word of truth, and holy living according thereto, he knew not; but unto the pope he subdued them, and unto this superstitious idolatry which we use clean contrary unto the scripture.

Charles compelled all men to the obedience of the pope.

Practice. W. T.

Moreover, at the request and great desire of his mother, he married the daughter of Desiderius, king of Lombardy; but after one year, unto the great displeasure of his mother, he put her away again; but not without the false subtilty of the pope, thou mayest be sure, neither without his dispensation. For how could Charles have made war for the pope's pleasure with Desiderius her father, and have thrust him out of his kingdom, and banished his son for ever, dividing his kingdom between him and the pope, as long as she had been his wife? And therefore the pope, with his authority of binding and loosing, loosed the bonds of that matrimony (as he hath many other since, and daily doth for like purposes), to the intent that he would with the sword of the French king put the kingdom of Lombardy, that was somewhat too nigh him, out of the way; by the reason of whose kings his fatherhood could not reign alone, nor assign or sell the bishopricks of Italy to whom he lusted, and at his pleasure.

The pope is a dispenser and breaker of the bonds of matrimony.

Charles a filthy whoremonger.

He kept also four concubines, and lay with two of his own daughters thereto. And though he wist how that it was not unknown, yet, his lusts being greater than great Charles, he would not wete, nor yet refrain.

[1 i. e. the pope at the time of Tyndale's writing.]

And beyond all that, the saying is, that in his old age a whore had so bewitched him with a ring and a pearl in it, and I wot not what imagery graven therein, that he went a salt after her as a dog after a bitch, and the dotehead was beside himself, and whole out of his mind: insomuch that when the whore was dead, he could not depart from the dead corpse, but caused it to be embalmed, and to be carried with him whithersoever he went, so that all the world wondered at him; till at the last his lords accombered with carrying her from place to place, and ashamed that so old a man, so great an emperor, and such a most christian king, on whom and whose deeds every man's eyes were set, should dote on a dead whore, took counsel what should be the cause: and it was concluded that it must needs be by enchantment. Then they went unto the coffin, and opened it, and sought and found this ring on her finger; which one of the lords took off, and put it on his own finger. When the ring was off, he commanded to bury her, regarding her no longer. Nevertheless, he cast a fantasy unto this lord, and began to dote as fast on him, so that he might never be out of sight; but where our Charles was, there must that lord also be; and what Charles did, that must he be privy unto: until that this lord, perceiving that it came because of this enchanted ring, for very pain and tediousness took and cast it into a well at Acon[2], in Dutchland. And after that the ring was in the well, the emperor could never depart from the town; but in the said place where the ring was cast, though it were a foul morass, yet he built a goodly monastery in the worship of our lady, and thither brought relics from whence he could get them, and pardons to sanctify the place, and to make it more haunted[3]. And there he lieth, and is a saint, as right is: for he did for Christ's vicar as much as the great Turk for Mahomet; but to save his holiness, that he might be canonized for a saint, they feign in his life, that his abiding there so continually was for the hot-baths' sakes which be there.

Charles hath his whore carried with him.

This was an emperor for the pope's own mouth.

A doting emperor.

The pope made this lecherous emperor a saint.

After Charlemagne Lewis the mild[4] was emperor, which

Lewis the mild.

[[2] Aix la Chapelle.]

[[3] Neither Eginhart, nor Aimon, nor their annotators, nor Gibbon, nor Gaillard have taken any notice of the existence of the above wild legend.]

[[4] Louis le Débonnaire.]

was a very patient man, (another Phocas, and another prey for the pope,) and so meek and soft, that scarcely he could be angry at any thing at all. When our holy fathers had seen his water, and spied what complexion he was, they chose Stephen, the fourth of that name, pope, without his knowledge, and bade him neither good morrow, nor good even, nor once God speed about the matter, against their own grant unto his father for his good service. And his softness was yet somewhat displeased therewith, inasmuch as the election of the pope pertained unto his right. But the pope sent ambassadors, and wrote all the excuses that he could, and came after himself to France to him, and peaced him, and crowned him there emperor, and passed the time a season with him, and they became very familiar together.

Pope Stephen the fourth.

The pope elected and set up without the assent of the emperor.

After that they chose Paschalis pope, of the same manner; which Paschalis sent immediately legates unto the emperor soft Lewis, excusing himself, and saying that it was not his fault, but that the clergy and the common people had drawn him thereto with violence against his will. Then the emperor was content for that once, and bade they should no more do so, but that the old ordinance ought to be kept. The softness of this Lewis did him much care: for he was after prisoned of his own son, with help of pope Gregory the fourth.

Pope Paschal.

The pope, how he abused the emperor.

After this man's days the popes never regarded the emperors, nor did the clergy of Rome sue any more to the emperor, either for the election or confirmation of the pope. Moreover, after this Lewis, there was never emperor in Christendom of any power, or able of his own might to correct any pope; neither was there any king that could correct the outrageous vices of the spiritualty of his own realm after this time. For this Lewis left three sons, among which he divided the realm of France and all Dutchland[1]: which same, for pride and disdain that one should have more than another, fell together (as we say) by the ears, each destroying other's power, so that France was afterward of no might to do any great thing. And then the pope reigned in Italy alone, without care of any emperor: insomuch that Nicholas the first decreed that no secular prince or emperor should have aught to do, or be at the councils of the clergy[2].

The pope setteth not by the emperor.

Alone. W. T.

Pope Nicholas the first.

[1 That is, Germany.]

[2 Approbante Ludovico imperatore instituit [Nicolaus], Ne prin-

And after that Adrian the second was chosen pope; the emperor's deputy being in Rome, and not once spoken to of the matter. And when the emperor's ambassadors disdained, they answered, 'Who can resist the rage of the people?' and prayed them to be content, and to salute him as pope[3]. And Adrian the third decreed that they should not abide or tarry for the emperor's confirmation or authority in choosing the pope[4], and that the pope only should call a general council, and not the emperor; or, if the emperor would presume that to do, the council should be of none effect, though all the prelates of Christendom were there, and though whatsoever they did were but God's word. So mighty was the beast now waxed, when he once began to reign alone. And from this time hitherto[5] perished the power of the emperors and the virtue of the popes, saith Platina, in the life of popes[6]. For since that time, as there was none emperor of might, so was there no pope of any virtue.

Pope Adrian the second.

Pope Adrian the third.

The virtue of the pope and power of the emperor perished together. W. T.

After this Lewis, the empire of France and of all Dutchland was divided between his three sons; which, as I said, fought one with another, and destroyed the strength of the empire of France. And from that time to this, which is above seven hundred years, thou shalt read of few popes that have not led their lives in bloodshedding; insomuch that if thou consider the stories well, thou shalt easily perceive that there hath been slain about their cause far above forty hundred thousand men; beside that there hath been but few princes in Christendom that hath not been busied and cumbered, a great part of his life, about their matter; either in wars begun at their setting on; either in ceasing schisms or division that hath been among the clergy, who should be

The popes have been only bloodshedders above seven hundred years. W. T.

All Christendom hath been troubled with the pope's causes.

ceps ullus secularis aut imperator conciliis clericorum interesse auderet, nisi de fide ageretur: licere tum ac par esse censuit.—Platina. D. V. Pont.]

[3 So Platina, A. D. 867—8.]

[4 Hadrianus III. tanti animi fuit, ut initio pontificatus sui statim ad senatum populumque retulerit ne in creando pontifice imperatoris auctoritas exspectaretur.—Platina relating this gives the date 895; but other chronologists assign the brief popedom of Adrian III. to 884.]

[5 S. and S. ed. *hitherward.*]

[6 Nescio quo fato accidisse dicam, ut una cum industria imperatorum simul etiam pontificum virtus et integritas defecerit.—Plat. D. V. Pont. in vita Formosi. A. D. 891—6.]

pope; or striving of bishops, who should be greatest, as between the bishop of York and Canterbury in England, and between the bishops of England and Wales, whereof all the chronicles be full; or in reforming friars or monks, or in slaying them that uttered their false hypocrisy with God's word.

When the emperor was down, and no man in Christendom of any power to be feared, then every nation fell upon other, and all lands were at variance between themselves. And then, as the Danes came into England, and vexed the Englishmen, and dwelt there in spite of their hearts; even so came strange nations whose names were scarce heard of before in these quarters, (as the Vandals, Huns, and Goths,) and ran throughout all Christendom by hundred thousands together, and subdued the lands and dwelt therein maugre the inhabiters; as thou mayest see in Dutchland, how divers nations are inclosed in the midst of the land, of a strange tongue which no Dutchmen understand; and that rule continued well eight or nine score, or two hundred years. And in all this season, whosoever won the mastery, him the spiritualty received, and him they crowned king, and to him they clave. And whatsoever any tyrant had robbed all his life, that, or the most part thereof, must he deal among them at his death, for fear of purgatory. The spiritualty all that season preached the pope mightily, built abbies for recreation and quietness, shrining them alway for saints which purchased them privileges, or fought for their liberties, or disputed for the pope's power, howsoever they lived, (but after fifty years, when their lives were forgotten;) and if any resisted them, whatsoever mischiefs[1] they went about, him they noted in the chronicles as a cruel tyrant: yea, and whatsoever misfortune chanced any of his posterity after him, that they noted also, as though God had plagued them, because their forefather was disobedient unto holy church; and ever put the stories that uttered their wickedness out of the way; and gathered relics from whence they could get them, and feigned miracles, and gave themselves only unto poetry[2], and shut up the scripture: so that this was the very time of which Christ speaketh, Matt. xxiv.

Vandals. Huns. Goths.

The spiritualty clave to him that gat the victory, how wicked so ever he was.

Building of abbies. Shrining of saints.

This was the time that false prophets did arise in the church. Matt. xxiv.

[1 The two oldest editions have *mischieven.*]

[2 Tyndale uses this word ironically for *fiction.*]

in which false prophets should arise, and shew miracles and wonders, to deceive the very elect, if it had been possible.

Finally, in this busy world, the kings of Lombardy gat a little might, and came up again, and were divers times emperors, though of no great might. And one Beringarius, king of Lombardy, began to meddle with our holy father's business. Wherefore the pope fled unto Otho king of the Saxons, which by that time had gotten might, and brought him into Italy against Beringarium; which Otho overcame Beringarium, and was made emperor for his labour, and thus came the empire first unto Dutchland[3].

Beringarius.

Otho.

And Otho received the empire of one pope John (say they) with this oath: "I Otho do promise and swear unto the lord John, by the Father, the Son, and the Holy Ghost, and by this wood of the cross that maketh living[4], and by these relics of saints, that if I come to Rome, with God's help I will exalt the holy church of Rome, and thee[5] the governor of the same unto my power. Neither shalt thou lose life nor members, or that honour that thou hast, by my will, counsel, consent, or setting awork. Moreover, I will make in Rome no constitution or ordinance, of anything that pertaineth unto thee, or unto the Romans, without thy counsel. And whatsoever of the lands of St Peter cometh unto our hands, I will deliver it thee. And unto whosoever I shall commit the rule of Italy, I will make him swear that he shall help thee to defend the lands of St Peter unto his power."

Pope John the xiith.

The oath of the emperor made to the pope.

Note here the dissimulation of the pope, in calling his possessions St Peter's possessions.

And Gregory the fifth (when they had got at the last that which they long gaped for) made this ordinance of choosing the emperor, to stablish it withal: that six lords of

Pope Gregory the Fifth.

[[3] The events of this paragraph are told in Platina of the popedom of Agapete II., but it is in relating the history of his successor John XII., that he says, Translato tum primum ad Germanos imperio; of which however he confesses that some refer this transaction to the popedom of Leo VIII. Hence Tyndale's expression of uncertainty *they say*, in the next sentence. Agapete II. became pope in 946; Leo, 18 years later.]

[[4] Tyndale is here translating the words, *vivificæ crucis*. This oath is incorporated into the canon law, where it forms ca. 33. of Dist. lxiii. Decret. pars 1ma.]

[[5] *Thee* is wanting in D., but given in the two older editions, and found in the Latin canon.]

Almany, three of the spiritualty, and three of the temporalty, with the king of Bohemia the seventh, to be the odd man and umpire, should choose him for ever, and send him to the pope to receive his oath, and to be crowned[1]. Nevertheless the pope, to keep the emperor afar off, sendeth him his coronation home to him oft-times, much lever than that he should come any nearer, as a meek spirited man that had lever live solitary and alone, than have his holiness seen.

The election of the emperor appertaineth to the lords of Germany.

A proper similitude to describe our holy Father.

And to see how our holy father came up, mark the ensample of an ivy tree: first it springeth out of the earth, and then awhile creepeth along by the ground till it find a great tree. Then it joineth itself beneath alow unto the body of the tree, and creepeth up a little and a little, fair and softly. And at the beginning, while it is yet thin and small, that the burden is not perceived, it seemeth glorious to garnish the tree in the winter, and to bear off the tempests of the weather. But in the mean season it thrusteth roots into the bark of the tree, to hold fast withal; and ceaseth not to climb up, till it be at the top and above all. And then it sendeth his branches along by the branches of the tree, and overgroweth all, and waxeth great, heavy, and thick; and sucketh the moisture so sore out of the tree and his branches, that it choaketh and stifleth them. And then the foul stinking ivy waxeth mighty in the stump of the tree, and becometh a seat and a nest for all unclean birds, and for blind owls, which hawk in the dark, and dare not come at the light.

The ivy tree springeth.

The manner how the pope did spring up to his great authority.

Even so the bishop of Rome, now called pope, at the beginning crope along upon the earth; and every man trod upon him in this world. But as soon as there came a christian emperor, he joined himself unto his feet and kissed them, and crope up a little with begging now this privilege, now that; now this city, now that; to find poor people withal, and the necessary ministers of God's word. And he entitled the emperor with choosing the pope and other bishops; and promoted in the spiritualty, not whom virtue and learning,

The choosing of the pope and all bishops pertained unto the emperor and kings once. W. T.

[1 Plat. D. V. Pont. in Vita. Greg. V. whose popedom extended only from 996 to 999.]

but whom the favour of great men commended; to flatter, to get friends, and defenders withal. And the alms of the congregation which was the food and patrimony of the poor and necessary preachers, that he called St Peter's patrimony, St Peter's rent, St Peter's lands, St Peter's right; to cast a vain fear and a heathenish superstitiousness into the hearts of men, that no man should dare meddle with whatsoever came once into their hands for fear of St Peter, though they ministered it never so evil; and that they which should think it none alms to give them any more (because they had too much already) should yet give St Peter somewhat, (as Nabuchodonesser gave his god Beel) to purchase an advocate and an intercessor of St Peter, and that St Peter should at the first knock let them in. And thus, with flattering and feigning, and vain superstition, under the name of St Peter, he crept up and fastened his roots in the heart of the emperor, and with his sword clamb up above all his fellow-bishops, and brought them under his feet. And as he subdued them with the emperor's sword, even so by subtilty and help of them (after that they were sworn faithful) he clamb above the emperor, and subdued him also, and made him stoop unto his feet and kiss them another while. Yea, pope Cœlestinus crowned the emperor Henry the fifth[2], holding the crown between his feet: and when he had put the crown on, he smote it off with his feet again, saying, that he had might to make emperors and to put them down again[3].

The alms given unto the poor is become St. Peter's patrimony. W. T.

Dan. xiv.

The pope first gat above all the bishops, and then above the emperor.

O Lucifer. W. T.

Note this devilish and abominable pride.

And he made a constitution, that no layman should meddle with their matters, nor be in their councils, or wit what they

A law made by the pope.

[[2] The pope was Cœlestine III., but the emperor was Henry VI., not the fifth. The date 1191.]

[[3] This is related in Hoveden, a chronicler contemporary with Cœlestine III., as follows: Deinde introduxit eos dominus papa in ecclesiam, et unxit eum in imperatorem et uxorem suam in imperatricem. Sedebat autem dominus papa in cathedra pontificali, tenens coronam auream imperialem inter pedes suos; et imperator inclinato capite recepit coronam, et imperatrix similiter, de pedibus domini papæ. Dominus autem papa statim percussit cum pede suo coronam imperatoris, et dejecit eum [eam] in terra, significans quod ipse potestatem ejiciendi eum ab imperio habet, si ille demeruerit: sed cardinales statim corripientes coronam imposuerunt eam capiti imperatoris.—Roger. Hoveden. Annal. Angl. p. 689, in Rerum Anglic. script. post Bed. præcip. Francofurti. MDCI.]

did[1]; and that the pope only should call the council[2], and the emperor should but defend the pope[3]; provided alway that the council should be in one of the pope's towns, and where the pope's power was greater than the emperor's[4]. Then, under a pretence of condemning some heresy, he called a general council, where he made one a patriarch, another cardinal, another legate, another primate, another archbishop, another bishop, another dean, another archdeacon, and so forth, as we now see.

The pope createth his shavelings into dignities.

Qualis pater, talis filius; good natural children. W. T.

And as the pope played with the emperor, so did his branches and his members, the bishops, play in every kingdom, dukedom, and lordship; insomuch that the very heirs of them by whom they came up, hold now their lands of them, and take them for their chief lords. And as the emperor is sworn to the pope, even so every king is sworn to

[1 Dist. xxviii. cap. 17. De presbyteris non est laicis judicandum. De presbyteris vobis qui laici estis nec judicandum est, nec de eorum vita quidpiam investigandum. This sentence is incorporated into the decretal from Nicolaus papa I. ad consulta Bulgarorum, c. 7. Date 866.]

[2 Dist. xvii. cap. 5. Non est concilium sed conventiculum, quod sine sedis apostolicæ auctoritate celebratur. Item Pelagius papa II. Multis denuo apostolicis et canonicis atque ecclesiasticis instruimur regulis, non debere absque sententia Romani pontificis concilia celebrari. The same is affirmed in cap. 1 and 2 of the same Distinctio.]

[3 Uterque ergo est in potestate ecclesiæ, spiritalis scilicet gladius et materialis. Sed is quidem pro ecclesia, ille vero ab ecclesia exercendus: ille sacerdotis, is manu regum et militum, sed ad nutum et patientiam sacerdotis. Oportet autem gladium esse sub gladio, et temporalem auctoritatem spiritali subjici potestati. Boniface VIII. Extrav. comm. Lib. I. Tit. VIII. cap. 1. Corp. juris canonici. Lugduni 1622.]

[4 At the time of Tyndale's writing this it was notorious that the emperor was urging Clement VII. to summon a council, and to let its sessions be held in some German city: this however the pope declined. Il papa, says father Paul, propose per luogo una delle cittá dello stato ecclesiastico; [dicendo] Non poter in alcun modo consentire di celebrarlo in Germania, perche l'Italia non comportarebbe d'esser posposta; e la Spagna e Francia, che nelle cose ecclesiastiche cedono all' Italia per la prerogativa del pontificato, che é proprio di quella, non vorrebbono ceder alla Germania. Quanto al modo di definire le cose in concilio, diceva il pontifice esser cosa chiara che nel concilio non hanno voto, se non i vescovi per dritto del canone, e gli abbati per consuetudine, ed alcuni altri per privilegio pontificio.—Hist. del Concil. Tridentino. Lond. 1619. p. 58.]

the bishops and prelates of his realm: and they are the chiefest in all parliaments; yea, they and their money, and they that be sworn to them, and come up by them, rule altogether.

And thus the pope, the father of all hypocrites, hath with falsehood and guile perverted the order of the world, and turned the roots of the trees upward, and hath put down the kingdom of Christ, and set up the kingdom of the devil, whose vicar he is; and hath put down the ministers of Christ, and hath set up the ministers of Satan, disguised yet in names and garments like unto the angels of light and ministers of righteousness. For Christ's kingdom is not of the world (John xviii.); and the pope's kingdom is all the world. The pope's order compared with Christ's. W. T. John xviii.

And Christ is neither judge nor divider in this world (Luke xii.): but the pope judgeth and divideth all the world, and taketh the empire and all kingdoms, and giveth them to whom he lusteth. Christ and the pope compared together. Luke xii.

Christ saith, "Blessed are the poor in spirit:" so that the first step in the kingdom of Christ is humbleness, or humility; that thou canst find in thine heart to do service unto all men, and to suffer that all men tread thee. Matt. v.

The pope saith, 'Blessed be the proud and high-minded, that can climb and subdue all under them, and maintain their right, and such as will suffer of no man:' so that he which was yesterday taken from the dunghill and promoted this day by his prince, shall to-morrow, for the pope's pleasure, curse him, and excommunicate him, and interdict his realm.

Christ saith, "Blessed be the meek," or soft, that be harmless as doves.

The pope blesseth them that can set all the world together by the ears, and fight, and slay manfully for his sake, that he may come hot from blood-shedding to a bishoprick; as our cardinal did[5], and as St Thomas of Canterbury did, which

[[5] 'The care of providing all that was requisite for the French war of 1513 was confided to Wolsey. He attended the king to his campaign, and became the principal person at his side, being deemed the author of the expedition; and he participated in all the reputation which it gained. He was appointed bishop of the conquered town of Tournay, and in the following year bishop of Lincoln, and also, on the death of one of his patrons, archbishop of York.' Sh. Turner, Hist. Hen. VIII. B. I. ch. 7, Vol. I. p. 179, 2nd ed.]

was made bishop in the field, in complete harness on his horseback, and his spear bloody in his hand[1].

Christ hath neither holes for foxes, nor nests for birds, nor yet whereon to lay his head, nor promised aught in this world unto his disciples, nor took any to his disciple but him that had forsaken all.

The ivy-tree, the pope, hath under his roots throughout all Christendom, in every village, holes for foxes, and nests for unclean birds in all his branches, and promiseth unto his disciples all the promotions of the world.

Christ bringeth a man low, but the pope lifteth up on high.

The nearer unto Christ a man cometh, the lower he must descend, and the poorer he must wax. But the nearer unto the pope ye come, the higher ye must climb, and the more riches ye must gather, whencesoever ye can get them, to pay for your bulls, and to purchase a glorious name, and licence to wear a mitre, and a cross, and a pall, and goodly ornaments.

How the pope receiveth his kingdom of the devil, and how he distributeth it again.

The pope receiveth his riches and kingdoms of the devil. Matt. iv.

Shortly, the kingdoms of the earth and the glory of them, which Christ refused, (Matt. iv.) did the devil proffer unto the pope; and he immediately fell from Christ, and worshipped the devil, and received them. For by falsehead (as he maintaineth them) came he thereto; and by falsehead do all his disciples come thereto. Who of an hundred one is pope, bishop, or any great prelate, but either by necromancy, or simony, or waiting on great men's pleasures, and with corrupting of God's word, and fashioning it after their lusts?

The pope distributeth his father's kingdom. W. T.

And the pope, after he had received the kingdom of the world of the devil, and was become the devil's vicar, took up in like manner all Christendom on high, and brought them from the meekness of Christ unto the high hill of the pride of Lucifer, and shewed them all the kingdoms of the earth, saying: 'Fall down and worship me, and I will give you these.' Unto the spiritualty he saith: 'Fall from Christ, and

[[1] It is not historically correct to say that Becket was made bishop in the field; but the language of his chaplain and biographer, William Fitz-Stephen, might seem to Tyndale to imply that he was so.]

preach me, and take thou that cardinalship, thou that bishoprick, thou that abbotship, and so forth; thou as many benefices as thou wilt, and a dispensation for what thou wilt[2].' And to monks and friars in like manner: 'Take thou that hole, and thou that nest, with what privileges ye will desire, and dispensations of your rules, if ye will preach me.'

And unto the temporalty he saith, first to the emperor: 'If thou wilt fall down and kiss my feet, and swear to hold of me, and to defend me, I give thee the empire.'

And to all kings, in like manner, if they will swear to defend his liberties, and to hold of him, he crowneth them. And even so all temporal lords, from the highest unto the lowest, and all officers, and all manner subjects, if they will enjoy lands, rents, offices, goods, and their very lives, they must run the same way.

The very whores (God's honour unregarded), as long as they despise not him and his ordinances, they shall nest in his rents[3], and among his prelates. And the thieves and murderers shall have dens in his sanctuaries, whatsoever they do against God, so long as they hang on him.

The apostles chose priests to preach Christ only, all other things laid apart, and chose none but learned and virtuous. The pope shaveth whosoever cometh, lever out of the stews than from study: and when they be sworn, he sendeth them unto all great men's houses to preach his godhead, to be stewards, surveyors, receivers, and counsellors of all manner mischief; to corrupt wife, daughter, and maid, and to betray their own master, as oft as it needeth to promote their falsehood withal: for thereto are they sworn together. And when they have done all mischief, there shall no man wot whence it cometh.

The pope's order compared with the order of the apostles. W. T.

The pope's priests. W. T

The apostles chose deacons to minister the alms of the

The pope's widows. W. T.

[2 Clement VII. was neither withheld by the general outcry for a reform of these abuses, nor by shame, from giving to his nephew, Cardinal Ippolito de Medici, authority to take possession of all the vacant benefices in the whole world, secular and regular, dignified and parochial, simple or with cure of souls, and to hold them in commendam for six months, with faculty to dispose of and convert to his own use all the fruits thereof. Concil. Trident. p. 246.]

[3 Tenements, which pay rent immediately to the proprietor of the soil. Certain tenements on the banks of the Thames, called the bishop of Winchester's rents, were then in very ill fame.]

rich unto the poor; and to help the deacons, they chose widows of sixty years old, holy, and destitute of friends, to tend the sick. And the pope instead of such widows maketh whosoever cometh, whether she be young or old, but none save them that be rich and able to pay twenty, thirty, or forty pound for their profession; to whom, for as much more, he will give a dispensation on the morrow to marry again. And instead of such deacons, he maketh both deacons and sub-deacons, which do nothing at all, but are vain names without office; except it be that on some holy day, instead of ministering the goods of the church unto the poor, they sing an epistle or gospel, to beg more from the poor.

The pope's deacons. W. T.

And as his deacons minister the goods of the church unto the poor, even so do his priests preach Christ's gospel unto the flock.

And the alms that was given to the sustentation of the poor, which thou shalt read in stories that it was in some cities above twenty, thirty, and forty, yea, an hundred thousand pound, and all the lands given for the same purpose, they have stolen from them, and have divided it among themselves. And therewith did they at the beginning corrupt the great men of the world, and clamb up to this height, where they now be. And for that have they striven among themselves this eight hundred years: and, to maintain that which they have falsely gotten, hath the pope stirred up a sword of war in all Christendom this eight hundred year, and hath taken peace clean out of the world.

How the pope divideth the poor people's alms. W. T.

When the bishops, priests, and deacons were fallen, and had received of the pope the kingdom that pertained unto the poor people, and had robbed them, and parted their patrimony among themselves, then sprang the orders of monks; whose profession was, to abstain from flesh all their lives[1], to wear vile raiment, to eat but once in the day, and that

Monks. W. T.

[[1] Carnem cuiquam monacho nec sumendi nec gustandi est concessa licentia; non quod creaturam Dei judicemus indignam, sed quod carnis abstinentia utilis et apta monachis æstimetur; servato tamen moderamine pietatis erga ægrotos. Quod si quis monachus violaverit, et contra sanctionem regulæ usumque veterum vesci carnibus præsumpserit; sex mensium spatio retrusioni et pœnitentiæ subjacebit.—Corp. Jur. canon. Decret. pars III. De Consecr. Dist. v. can. 32. Lugduni. 1622.]

but butter, cheese, eggs, fruits, roots, and such things that were not costly, and might everywhere be found. And they wrote books, and wrought divers things, to get their living withal. When the laymen saw that the priests were fallen into such covetousness, and that the monks were so holy, they thought, 'These be meet men to minister our alms unto the poor people: for their profession is so holy that they cannot deceive us as the priests do:' and made the monks tutors[2] and ministers unto the poor; and gave great lands and riches into their hands, to deal it unto the poor. When the monks saw such abundance, they fell after the ensample of the priests; and took dispensations of the pope for their rules and strait profession, which now is as wide as their cowls; and divided all among them, and robbed the poor once more. And out of the abbeys took he the most part of his bishopricks and cathedral churches, and the most part of all the lands he hath, besides that there remain yet so many mighty abbeys, and nunneries thereto.

Monks made ministers to the poor.

Monks rob the poor.

As soon as the monks were fallen, then sprang these begging friars out of hell, the last kind of caterpillars, in a more vile apparel, and a more strait religion; that, if aught of relief were left among the laymen for the poor people, these horse-leeches might suck that also: which drone-bees, as soon as they had learned their craft, and had built them goodly and costly nests, and their limiters had divided all countries among them to beg in, and had prepared livings of a certainty, though with begging; then they also took dispensations of the pope, for to live as largely and as lewdly as the monks.

Begging friars. W. T.

And yet unto the laymen, whom they have thus falsely robbed, and from which they have divided themselves, and made them a several kingdom among themselves, they leave the paying of toll, custom, and tribute (for unto all the charges of the realms will they not pay one mite[3]), and the

The charge of the lay-people.

[2 That is, guardians, defenders of their property.]

[3 In the Corpus Juris canonici, Sexti Decret. Lib. III. Tit. xxiii. præcipit personas ecclesiasticas pro rebus suis vel ecclesiarum nil laicis solvere debere absque licentia apostolicæ sedis, sub quocunque colore mutui, subventionis, doni, vel alio quolibet; ut etiam ipsi laici tallias non exigant, vel recipiant; singulares contra facientes excommunicat; et ab his sententiis solus papa absolvit, præterquam in mortis articulo.]

finding of all the poor, the finding of scholars for the most part, the finding of these foresaid horse-leeches and caterpillars, the begging friars, the repairing of the high-ways and bridges, the building and reparations of their abbeys and cathedral churches, chapels, colleges; for which they send out their pardons daily by heaps, and gather a thousand pounds for every hundred that they bestow truly.

If the lay-people have war, or whatsoever charge it be, they will not bear a mite. If the war be theirs (as the one part almost of all war is to defend them), they will with falsehood make them bear the greatest part; besides that they must leave their wives and children, and go fight for them, and lose their lives. And likewise in all their charges they have a cast to poll the lay-people. The Scots cast down a castle of the bishop of Durham's, on the Scottish bank, called Norham castle; and he gat a pardon from Rome for the building of it again: wherewith I doubt not but he gat for every penny, that he bestowed, three[1].

How the spiritualty bestow their treasure. W. T.

And what do they with their store, that they have in so great plenty everywhere; so that the very begging friars, in short space, to make a cardinal or a pope of their sect, or to do what feat it were for their profit, would not stick to bring above a king's ransom? Verily, make goodly places and parks of pleasure, and gay shrines, and painted posts, and purchase pardons, wherewith they yet still poll and pluck away that little wherewith the poor, which perish for need, and fall into great inconveniences, might be somewhat holpen and relieved; and lay up in store to have alway to pay for the defending of their faith, and for to oppress the truth.

How the pope made him a law, and why.

After that the pope with tyranny was clomb up above his

[[1] Norham Castle, though on the Scottish border, is on the English side of the Tweed; and in a survey of the borders made by Sir Robert Bowes and Sir Ralph Elleker, knts., Dec. 1542, it is reported to be in a very good state, both in reparations and fortifications. But this report was drawn up when Bp Tonstal was in favour at court. Another report drawn up by Sir Robert Bowes but eight years later for the marquess of Dorset, then warden of the Marches, says that "The castle for lack of continual reparation is in much decay," and specifies considerable decays at some length.—Hodgson's Northumberland, Part III. Vol. II. pp. 190 and 197—9.]

brethren, and had made all the spiritualty his subjects, and had made of them and him a several kingdom among themselves, and had separated them from the lay in all things, and had got privileges, that whatsoever they did no man should meddle with them; and after also he had received the kingdoms of the earth of Satan, and was become his vicar to distribute them; and after that the emperor was fallen in like manner at his feet, and had worshipped him as god, to receive his empire of him; and all kings had done likewise to be anointed of him, and to be crowned of him; and after that the world, both great and small, had submitted themselves to receive the beast's badge; then, because that Christ's doctrine was contrary unto all such kingdoms, and therefore had no law therein how to rule it, he went and made him a several law of his own making, which passed in cruelty and tyranny the laws of all heathen princes.

The pope maketh laws.

And in his law he thrust in feigned gifts of old emperors that were out of memory, saying that the emperor Constantinus had given up the empire of Rome unto St Sylvester[2]; which is proved a false lie, for divers causes: one, that St Sylvester, being so holy a man, as he was, would not have received it contrary to his Master's commandments and doctrine; another, that the emperors reigned in Rome many years after, and all bishops sued unto the emperor, and not to the pope, which was but bishop of Rome only, and not called father of fathers: moreover, that no authentic story maketh mention that any emperor gave them their patrimony, but that Pipine, which falsely and with strength invaded the empire, gave it unto him. Then put he in the grant of Phocas; then the gift of Pipine confirmed by the great Charles; then a feigned release of the election of the pope, given up again unto pope Paschal by the emperor Lewis[3]. For they themselves had granted unto Charlemagne and his

The pope hath feigned the gift of Constantine. What subtilty the pope useth to stablish his kingdom. W. T.

[[2] In the papal law, Decreti pars 1ma, Dist. XCVI. can. 13, says, Constantinus imperator coronam et omnem regiam dignitatem in urbe Romana et in Italia et in partibus occidentalibus apostolico concessit. Nam gestis beati Sylvestri (quod beatus papa Gelasius in conventu lxx episcoporum a catholicis legi commemorat, et pro antiquo usu multas hoc imitari dicit ecclesias) ita legitur. And then the pretended deed of gift follows, and constitutes can. 14 of the same Distinctio.]

[[3] His concession is incorporated in the papal law, as can. 30 of Dist. LXIII. Decret. pars 1ma.]

successors for ever the election or denomination of the pope and bishops, to flatter him withal, and to make him a faithful defender, and that in a general council, which (as they say) cannot err. Nevertheless pope Paschal, though he believed the council could not err, yet he thought them somewhat overseen to make so long a grant, and therefore he purchased a release of gentle Lewis, as they pretend. But verily it is more likely that they feigned that grant to excuse their tyranny, after they had taken the election into their hands again with violence, when the emperors were weak, and not able to resist them; as they feigned the gift of Constantine, after they had invaded the empire with subtilty and falsehood. And, last of all, they brought in the oath of Otho, with the order that now is used, to choose the emperor.

How the pope corrupteth the scripture, and why.

The pope corrupteth the scripture, and why.

Moreover, lest these his lies should be spied, and lest haply the emperors following might say, 'Our predecessors had no power to bind us, nor to minish our might;' and lest kings following should say after the same manner, that the sword, and full power to punish evildoers indifferently, is given of God to every king for his time, and therefore that their predecessor could not bind them contrary unto the ordinance of God, but rather that it was unto their damnation to make such grants, and that they did not execute their office; therefore[1] the foul and misshapen monster gat him to the scripture, and corrupted it with false expositions, to prove that such authority was given him of God; and challenged it by the authority of Peter, saying that Peter was the head of Christ's church, and that Christ had made him lord over the apostles, his fellows, in that he bade him feed his sheep and lambs[2], John the last; as who should say that Paul,

Peter (saith the pope) was the head of Christ's church.

John xxi.

[1 Old editions, *and therefore.*]

[2 Igitur ecclesiæ unius et unicæ unum corpus, unum caput, non dua capita, quasi monstrum, Christus videlicet, et Christi vicarius Petrus, Petrique successor, dicente Domino ipsi Petro, Pasce oves meas, inquit et generaliter, non singulariter has vel illas, per quod commisisse sibi intelligitur universas. Sive ergo Græci sive alii se dicant Petro ejusque successoribus non esse commissos, fateantur necesse se de ovibus Christi non esse.—Corp. Jur. canon. Extrav. commun. Lib. I. Tit. VIII. can. 1, Unam sanctam.]

which came long after, was not commanded to feed as especially as Peter, which yet would take none authority over the bodies or over the faiths of them which he fed, but was their servant for Christ's sake, Christ ever the lord and head; and as though the other apostles were not likewise as specially commanded as Peter; and as though we now, and all that hereafter shall love Christ, were not commanded to feed Christ's flock, every man in his measure, as well as Peter. Are not we commanded to love our neighbours as ourselves, as well as Peter? Why then are we not commanded to care for his flock, as well as Peter?

All ministers have as great a charge given them of God as Peter had.

Moreover, if to feed Christ's sheep is to be greatest, (as no doubt to feed Christ's flock is to be great, and most to feed is to be greatest; in which office, though Peter was great, yet Paul was greater;) how cometh it that the pope by that authority challengeth to be greatest, and yet this eight hundred years feedeth not at all; but poisoneth their pasture with the venomous leaven of his traditions, and with wresting the text unto a contrary sense?

Peter preached, but the pope preached not.

Then came he to this text, (Matt. xvi.), "Thou art Peter, and upon this rock I will build my congregation" or church. Lo, saith antichrist, the carnal beast, Peter is the rock whereon the church of Christ is built[3]; and I am his successor, and therefore the head of Christ's church: when Christ meant by the rock the confession that Peter had confessed, saying, "Thou art Christ, the son of the living God," which art come into this world. This faith is the rock whereon Christ's church is built. For who is of Christ's church, but he only that believeth that Christ is God's Son, come into this world to save sinners? This faith is it, against which hell-gates cannot prevail. This faith is it, which saveth the congregation of Christ; and not Peter.

Matt. xvi.

Faith is the rock whereon Christ's church is built. W. T.

[3 Ita Dominus ad omnium apostolorum officium pertinere voluit, ut in beatissimo Petro apostolorum omnium summo principaliter collocaret: ut ab ipso quasi quodam capite dona sua, velut in corpus omne diffunderet, ut exsortem se mysterii intelligeret esse divini, qui ausus fuisset a Petri soliditate recedere. Hunc enim in consortium individuæ unitatis assumptum, id quod ipse erat voluit nominari, dicendo, Tu es Petrus et super hanc Petram ædificabo ecclesiam meam; ut æterni ædificatio templi mirabili munere gratiæ Dei in Petri soliditate consisteret.—Corp. Jur. can. Decr. 1ma pars. Dist. xix. can. 7.]

Then he goeth forth unto that which followeth: "Unto thee I will give the keys of the kingdom of heaven, and whatsoever thou bindest in earth, it shall be bound in heaven," &c. 'Lo, saith he, in that he saith, whatsoever thou bindest in earth, he excepteth nothing; therefore, I may make laws, and bind both king and emperor[1]:' when Christ, as he had no worldly kingdom, even so he spake of no worldly binding, but of binding of sinners. Christ gave his disciples the key of the knowledge of the law of God, to bind all sinners; and the key of the promises, to loose all that repent, and to let them into the mercy that is laid up for us in Christ.

Binding and loosing, how it is to be understood.

The keys. W. T.

Then cometh he unto another text, which Christ rehearseth, Matthew last, saying, "All power is given me in heaven and earth: go ye therefore, and teach all nations, baptizing them in the name of the Father, and the Son, and of the Holy Ghost; teaching them to keep all that I commanded you: and behold, I am with you unto the world's end." Lo, saith the pope, Christ hath all power in heaven and earth without exception, and I am Christ's vicar; wherefore all power is mine, and I am above all kings and emperors in temporal jurisdiction, and they but my servants, to kiss not my feet only, but my .N[2]. also, if I list not to have them stoop so low: when Christ, as I said, because he had no temporal kingdom, even so he meant of no temporal power, but of power to save sinners, which the process of the text declareth, by that he saith, Go ye therefore, and teach and baptize; that is, preach this power unto all nations, and wash off their sins, through faith in the promises made in my blood.

Matt. xxviii.

Behold here antichrist, how he wresteth the scriptures.

Christ's power is to save sinners. W. T.

Then he cometh unto another text, (Heb. vii.) which is, "The priesthood being translated, the law must needs be translated also." Now, saith the pope, 'The priesthood is translated unto me; wherefore it pertaineth unto me to make laws, and to bind every man.' And the epistle meaneth no such thing;

Heb. vii. Of this manner judgeth he with all texts. W. T.

[1 Item Adrianus Papa. Generali decreto censemus et constituimus, ut execrandum anathema sit, et velut prævaricator fidei catholicæ semper apud Deum reus existat, quicunque regum seu episcoporum vel potentum deinceps Romanorum pontificum decretorum censuram in quocunque crediderit vel permiserit violandam.—Decret. 2da. pars, Caus. xxv. qu. 1. can. 11.]

[2 So both in the folio and M. and S. S. ed.]

but proveth evidently that the ceremonies of Moses must cease: for the priests of the old Testament must needs have been of the tribe of Levi, as Aaron was, whose duty for ever was the offering of sacrifices; wherefore, when that priesthood ceased, the sacrifices and ceremonies ceased also. Now that priesthood ceased in Christ, which was a priest of the order of Melchizedec, and not of the order of Aaron; for then he must have been of the tribe of Levi, and that he was not, but of the tribe of Judah, and of the seed of David: wherefore they that are under Christ's priesthood are under no sacrifices or ceremonies. And of this manner juggle they with all the scripture: which falsehood lest the laymen should perceive with reading the process of the text, is all their fear, whatsoever they pretend.

At the suffering of Christ, the offering of sacrifices and ceremonies ceased: for Christ offered himself once for all.

Moreover, that thou mayest perceive the pope's falsehood, mark, Christ said unto Peter, "I will give," and not "I give;" neither said he, 'I will give unto thee only.' Therefore, look in the twentieth chapter of John, where he gave them the keys after his resurrection, and thou shalt see he gave them unto all indifferently, saying, "As my Father sent me, so send I you." Whither sent he them? Unto all the world, and unto all nations. What to do? To preach the law, that the people might repent; and the promises, that they might believe in Christ for the remission of sins; saying, "Receive the Holy Ghost: whosoever's sin ye forgive, they shall be forgiven." By which Holy Ghost he gave them understanding of the scripture, and of all that they should preach: as thou mayest see, Luke last, where he opened their wits to understand the scripture, and said, "That repentance and forgiveness of sins must be preached in his name to all nations," and that they were witnesses to preach it. Whereby thou seest, that to bind and to loose is but to preach and tell the people their faults, and to preach mercy in Christ to all that repent.

Christ gave all his apostles like authority.

John xx.

Luke xxiv.

To bind and loose is to preach. W. T.

And when he saith, "All power is given me," he saith not, Go thou, Peter, and preach: but saith unto all indifferently, Go ye and preach this power given me of my Father to save all that repent; and to damn them that repent not, but follow the lusts of their flesh, with full desire to live beastly, being enemies unto the law of God.

Christ sent out all his apostles, and not Peter alone.

And (Matt. xviii.) Peter asked Christ, how oft he should

Note. W. T. Matt. xviii.

forgive his brother[1], whether seven times? And Christ said, "Seventy times seven times." As who should say, As oft as he repenteth, and asketh forgiveness.

Now, though this was spoken unto Peter only, because Peter only moved the question, yet pertaineth it not unto us all as well as unto Peter? Are not we as much bound to forgive our neighbours that repent and ask forgiveness as Peter? Yes, verily. But because Peter only asked the question, therefore did Christ teach us by Peter. If another had asked, he would have taught us by that other. And in like manner, when Christ asked, "Who say ye that I am?" if any other of the apostles which believed it as well as Peter had said as Peter did, "Thou art Christ, the Son of the living God, which art come into the world of sinners, to save them;" unto him would Christ have answered as he did to Peter, That upon the rock of that his confession he would have built his church; and would have promised him keys, as well as he did Peter. Yea, and in the eighteenth chapter of Matthew Christ saith to all the apostles, yea, and to all congregations where sinners be, That whatsoever they bound should be bound, and whatsoever they loosed should be loosed.

We are bound to forgive our neighbours as well as Peter was.

Christ builded his church upon the confession of Peter, and not upon Peter.

Matt. xviii.

Moreover, every man and woman, that know Christ and his doctrine, have the keys, and power to bind and loose; in an order yet[2], and in their measure, as time, place, and occasion giveth, and privately. May not a wife, if her husband sin against God and her, and take another woman, tell him his fault between him and her secretly, and in good manner humbly, and bind his conscience with the law of God? And if he repent, may she not forgive him, and loose him, as well as the pope? Yea, and better too, as long as the sin is secret; inasmuch as he sinneth specially against her, and not against the pope.

A woman hath power to bind. W. T.

How a woman may bind and loose.

And so may the son do to his father, and a servant to his master, and every man to his neighbour; as thou seest in the said eighteenth chapter of Matthew. Howbeit, to bind and loose in the conscience, by open preaching, pertaineth unto the officers that are appointed thereto. And to bind and loose open sinners, and them that will not repent, till they be complained on unto the congregation, pertaineth unto the congregation.

To bind the conscience, and to reprove open sinners, pertaineth to the congregation.

[1 Marb. brether; S. S. ed. brother; Day, brethren.]

[2 So Marb. and S. S. ed. In day, *yet* is wanting.]

Finally, there were many that preached Christ at Rome, yer[3] Peter came thither, if he came ever thither; as Paul, and many other. Had they not authority to bind and loose? Or else how did they convert the people? Peter also was an apostle, and went from place to place as Paul did; and as Paul ordained bishops in every place to teach the people, so no doubt did Peter. Why then might not those bishops challenge authority by Peter, as well as they of Rome? They say also in their own legends, that Peter had his seat at Antioch first[4]. Did he run to Rome, leaving no man behind him to teach the people at Antioch? God forbid. Why then might not that bishop challenge Peter's authority? They will haply say, sooner than prove it, that Peter died at Rome, and therefore his authority is greatest there. Then by that rule Christ's power is no where so full as at Jerusalem. But what hath Christ's invisible kingdom to do with places? Where Christ's gospel is, there is his power full and all his authority, as well in one place as in another.

Reasons that Peter was not the greatest by authority given him of Christ. W. T.

Peter had first his seat at Antioch.

Christ's power is in the gospel. W. T.

Finally, to get authority whencesoever they can snatch it, they join Paul with Peter in their own laws, *Distinctio* xxii. saying, "By the authority of Peter and Paul:"[5] which is clean against themselves. For they say in their own law, In the presence of the superior the power of the inferior ceaseth, and is none at all[6]. Now if Peter be greater than Paul, then, by

Paul is called to help. W. T.

In the presence of the greater, the power of the lesser doth cease.

[3 Yer: ere.]

[4 Marcellus Papa universis episcopis per Antiochiam constitutis, epist. 1. Ipse enim [Petrus] caput est totius ecclesiæ, cui ait Dominus, Tu es Petrus &c. Ejus enim sedes primitus apud vos fuit, quæ postea, jubente Domino, Romam translata est. Nec ab ejus dispositione vos deviare oportet, ad quam cuncta majora ecclesiastica negotia, divina disponente gratia, jussa sunt referri. Decr. 2da. pars. Caus. XXIV. Qu. i. can. 15.]

[5 In the Corp. Jur. canon. Distinct. XXII. cap. *Sacrosancta*, contains the following sentence: Prima ergo sedes est cœlesti beneficio Romanæ ecclesiæ, quam beatissimi Petrus et Paulus suo martyrio consecrarunt. But the next Distinctio, XXIII, which begins with the decree of pope Nicolas II., De electione summi pontificis, contains, in that decree, more exact language to Tyndale's purpose: Quod si quis contra hoc nostrum decretum synodali sententia promulgatum per seditionem &c. electus fuerit, auctoritate divina et sanctorum apostolorum Petri et Pauli, perpetuo anathemate a liminibus sanctæ Dei ecclesiæ abjiciatur.]

[6 Distinctio XXI. cap. 4. Inferior sedes. Sole clarius exhibuimus, non posse quenquam, qui minoris auctoritatis est, eum qui majoris

that rule, where Peter is present, there Paul is but a subject, and without authority. And where Christ is present bodily and preacheth himself, there the apostles give up their authority, and hold their peace, and sit down at his feet, and become scholars and hearken too. Wherefore, in that they join Paul with Peter, and challenge their superiority as well by the authority of Paul as of Peter, there they make Paul fellow and equal with Peter. And thus it is false that Peter was greater than his fellows. But the blind owls care not what they howl, seeing it is night, and the day-light of God's word shut up, that no man can spy them.

Paul is made equal fellow with Peter.

Moreover, with this term, 'Peter's seat,' they juggle apace (as with infinite other), saying, 'That Peter's seat is the chief seat;' but what Peter's seat is, that they tell you not: for wist ye that, ye should soon perceive that they lie. Peter's seat is no stool, or chair, (for what hath the kingdom of Christ to do with such baggage?) but it is a spiritual thing. Christ saith in the gospel, "The scribes and Pharisees sit on Moses' seat." What was Moses's seat there, a chair, or the temple, or the churches, or synagogue of the land? Nay verily, for Moses came never there. But Moses' seat was Moses' law and doctrine. Even so Peter's seat is Peter's doctrine, the gospel of Christ, which Peter taught. And the same doctrine is Peter's keys: so that Peter's seat, Peter's keys, and Peter's doctrine is all one thing. Now is Peter's doctrine Paul's doctrine, and the doctrine of all the twelve apostles indifferently; for they taught all one thing. Wherefore it followeth, that Peter's keys and Peter's seat be the keys and seat of Paul also, and of all the other twelve apostles, and are nothing save the gospel of Christ. And thus, as Peter's doctrine is no better than Paul's, but one thing; even so Peter's seat is no greater, nor higher, nor holier than the seat of the other twelve. Peter's seat now is Christ's seat, Christ's gospel, on which all the apostles sat, and on which this day sit all they only that preach Christ truly. Wherefore, as antichrist preacheth not Peter's doctrine (which is Christ's gospel), so he sitteth not on Peter's seat, but on the seat of Satan, whose vicar he is, and on the seat of his own laws and ceremonies, and false doctrine, whereunto he compelleth all men with violence of sword.

Matt. xxiii.

Peter's seat, what it is.

Peter's seat, Peter's doctrine, and Peter's keys, are all but one thing.

Peter's seat is Christ's gospel.

The pope sitteth in the devil's seat, whose vicar he is.

potestatis est judiciis suis addicere, aut propriis definitionibus subjugare.]

Then he clamb to purgatory with the ladder of the said text, "Whatsoever thou bindest in earth," &c. "Purgatory," saith he, "is in earth[1]: wherefore I am lord there too." Nevertheless, as he can prove no purgatory, so can he not prove that, if there were any, it should be in the earth. It might well be in the element or sphere of fire under the moon, as well as in the earth. But to bind and loose is, as I have above said, to preach, and to feed, and with Christ's doctrine to purge souls. And they that be dead be not of the flock which Christ bade Peter feed, but they that live only.

Purgatory.

The pope saith that purgatory is in earth.

Then clamb he up, with the same ladder still, over all vows and professions of all religious persons, and over oaths made between man and man, to dispense with them, and over all men's testaments, to alter them. For what thou makest an hospital, that will he shortly make a college of priests, or a place of religion, or what he lusteth. Then all manner monks and friars, and like draff, took dispensations of him, for the ordinances of their old founders. And because, as they thought, they had prayed and distributed for their souls enough to bring them out of purgatory, they thrust them out of their bead-rolls, and took daily more and more.

Vows.

Oaths.

Testaments.

The pope altereth men's wills and testaments at his pleasure.

But ever since they took dispensations of the pope, both for their rules, and to divide all among them, they received in the name, not of the poor, but of purgatory, to quench the raging fire thereof, which is as hot as their bellies can feign it, and fools be out of their wits to believe it; promising a mass daily for forty shillings by the year, of which foundations when they have gotten twenty, they will yet, with an union purchased of the pope, make but one chauntry. For if they should do all that they have promised, from the first founder unto this day, five hundred monks were not enough in many cloisters.

The pope's merchandise.

Union. W. T.

Thinkest thou that men were ever so mad to make the fashions that are now among them; to give the cellarer[2] such a sum, and the prior, and the sub-prior, and the other

[[1] Ordinarius purgatorii locus, qui proprie et communiter nomine purgatorii intelligitur, est sub terra, vicinus inferno.—Tractat. select. De quatuor novissimis. N. 27. P. Dens. op. Lovanii. 1776.]

[[2] Marb. and Day *selerar*. S. and S. ed. *sellerar*. The monk who had charge of the provisions.]

officers so much for their parts as they have yearly; and to exempt the abbot from his brethren, and to send him out of the abbey into such parks and places of pleasure, and give him a thousand, fifteen hundred, two thousand, or three thousand pounds yearly, to sport himself withal? Nay, but when through hypocrisy they had gotten land enough, then they turned unto the pope, and took dispensations both for their rules which were too hard for such abundance, and for the wills of their founders, and served a great sort of founders under one *per Dominum*[1], and divided among few that which was enough for a great multitude.

The great and shameful abuse of abbeys.

Dispensations purchased of the pope.

It was the pope that devised all these fashions, to corrupt the prelates with abundance of worldly pleasures, of which he wist that the worst would be most greedy, and for which he wist also that he should find Judases enough, that would forsake Christ and betray the truth, and be sworn false unto him and his Godhead. He maketh of many chauntries one, of an abbey a cathedral church, and out of the abbeys plucked he the bishopricks. And as bishops pay for their bulls, even so do an infinite number of abbots in Christendom, in all lands some; which abbots be bishops within themselves, and immediately under the pope. And other abbots and priors send after the same ensample daily unto Rome, to purchase licence to wear a mitre[2] and a cross, and gay ornaments, to be as glorious as the best, &c. And where, before God, no man is a priest but he that is appointed to preach Christ's gospel unto the people; and the people ought not to give aught unto the spiritualty, but for the maintenance of the preaching of God's word; the pope taketh six or seven, yea, ten, twenty, and as many benefices as he listeth, and giveth them unto one that preacheth not at all; as he doth all other dignities of the spiritualty. He that will purchase, and pay, and be sworn, shall have what he will.

Chopping and changing used by the pope.

The wicked bestowing of benefices by the pope.

[1 Alluding to the ordinary conclusion of their prayers, viz., Per Dominum, he means that they put all their benefactors into one prayer, to shorten their task.]

[2 In the county of Gloucester alone there were six abbeys, whose abbots had obtained the pope's licence to wear mitres after the manner of bishops.—Anderson's Annals, B. I. § 1.]

How they prove all their general Councils.

When the bishops and abbots and other great prelates had forsaken Christ and his living, and were fallen down before the beast, the vicar of Satan, to receive their kingdom of him; then the pope called together divers councils of such holy apostles, and there concluded and made of every opinion, that seemed profitable, an article of the faith. If thou ask where is the scripture to prove it? they answer, 'We be the church, and cannot err; and therefore,' say they, 'what we conclude, though there be no scripture to prove it, it is as true as the scripture, and of equal authority with the scripture, and must be believed as well as the scripture under pain of damnation.' For, say they, 'Our truth dependeth not of the truth of the scripture;' that is, we be not true in our doing, because the scripture testifieth unto us that we do truly; but contrary, 'The truth of the scripture (say they) dependeth of us:' that is, the scripture is true, because that we admit it, and tell thee that it is true. For how couldst thou know that it were the scripture except we told thee so[3]? And therefore we need no witness of the scripture for that we do: it is enough, that we so say of our own head; for we cannot err. Which reason is like as though young monks, newly professed, should come by the rules of their order and ordinances of their old founders, and would go about to keep them; and the old cankered monks should call them back unto the corrupt and false manner, that now is used, saying: 'Ye err. Do only as we teach you, for your profession is to obey your elders.' 'According unto the rules of our order and ordinances of our founder,' shall they say. 'We can teach you no other,' shall the old monks say, 'nor can lie unto you: ye ought therefore to believe us, and to do as

The church cannot err. W. T.

The pope saith that the scripture is true not of itself, but because he alloweth and approveth it.

A similitude.

[3 Nicolaus papa archiepiscopis, &c. per Gallias constitutis.—Quibus ad hæc asserendum est, quoniam si vetus novumque testamentum recipienda sunt, non quod codici canonum ex toto habeantur annexa, sed quod de his recipiendis Sti Papæ Innocentii prolata videatur esse sententia, restat nimirum, quod decretales epistolæ Rom. pontificum sunt recipiendæ, etiamsi non sint codici canonum compaginatæ, quoniam inter ipsos canones unum B. Leonis capitulum constat esse permistum, quo ita omnia decretalia constituta sedis apostolicæ custodiri mandantur, vel si quis in illa commiserit, noverit sibi veniam denegari.—Decr. 1ma pars. Dist. XIX. c. 1.]

we bid you.' The young monks shall answer, 'We see that ye lie, clean contrary unto all that is written in our rules and ordinances.' The old monks shall say, 'Ye cannot understand them except we expound them unto you, neither yet know that they be your rules, except that ye believe that we cannot lie unto you. For how can ye know that these be your rules and ordinances, but as we your elders tell you so? Now when we tell you that these be your rules and ordinances, how can ye be sure undoubtedly, that it is so, except ye believe undoubtedly that we cannot lie? Wherefore, if ye will be sure that they be your rules and ordinances, then ye must first believe that we cannot lie. Leave such imaginations and disputations therefore, and lay your rules and ordinances out of your hands, and look no more on them; for they make you err: and come and do as we tell you, and captivate your wits, and believe that we cannot lie unto you, and that ye cannot understand your rules and ordinances.' Even so, if thou say it is contrary unto the scripture; they answer, that thou understandest it not, and that thou must captive thy wit, and believe that, though it seem never so contrary, yet it is not contrary: no, if they determine that Christ is not risen again, and though the scripture testify that he is risen again, yet (say they) they be not contrary, if they be wisely understood. Thou must believe, say they, that there is some other meaning in the scripture, and that no man understandeth it. But that we say, whether without scripture, or against it, that must thou believe, that it is true.

This doctrine the papists used in those days.

The common saying and teaching of the papists.

And thus, because that the scripture would not agree with them, they thrust it out of the way first, and shut up the kingdom of heaven, which is Christ's gospel, with false expositions, and with such sophistry, and with false principles of natural wisdom. And the abbots took the scripture from their monks, lest some should ever bark against the abbots' living; and set up such long service and singing, to weary them withal, that they should have no leisure to read in the scripture but with their lips; and made them good cheer to fill their bellies, and to stop their mouths. And the bishops in like manner, to occupy their priests withal, that they should not study the scripture for barking against them, set up long service, wondrous intricate, so that in a dozen years thou couldst scarce learn to turn aright unto it: long matins,

The abbots keep the monks in ignorance, and the bishops the priests. W. T.

long even-songs, long masses, long diriges, with vantage yet to mitigate the tediousness, *quia levis est labor cum lucro;* for 'lucre' (say they) 'maketh the labour light:' ever noselling them in ceremonies, and in their own constitutions, decrees, ordinances, and laws of holy church. Gain joined with pain maketh pain nothing.

And the promises and testament, which the sacrament of Christ's body and blood did preach daily unto the people, that they put out of knowledge; and say now, that it is a sacrifice for the souls of purgatory, that they might the better sell their mass. And in the universities they have ordained that no man shall look on the scripture, until he be noselled in heathen learning eight or nine years, and armed with false principles; with which he is clean shut out of the understanding of the scripture. And at his first coming unto university he is sworn that he shall not defame the university, whatsoever he seeth. And when he taketh first degree, he is sworn that he shall hold none opinion condemned by the church; but what such opinions be, that he shall not know. And then, when they be admitted to study divinity, because the scripture is locked up with such false expositions, and with false principles of natural philosophy, that they cannot enter in, they go about the outside, and dispute all their lives about words and vain opinions, pertaining as much unto the healing of a man's heel, as health of his soul: provided yet alway, lest God give his singular grace unto any person, that none may preach except he be admitted of the bishops. Then came Thomas de Aquino, and he made the pope a god with his sophistry; and the pope made him a saint for his labour, and called him doctor Sanctus[1]: for whose holiness no man may deny whatsoever he saith, save in certain places, where, among so many lies, he said now and then true. The use of universities. W. T. Proviso. W. T. St Thomas de Aquino. W. T.

[[1] The colophon to the work, which will provide us with evidence for what Tyndale has here affirmed, is as follows: Incipit Divi Thomæ Aquinatis opus vigesimum; de regimine principum. And the tenth chapter of its third book is headed, Hic sanctus doctor declarat de dominio hominis secundum gradum et dignitatem: et primo de dominio Papæ qualiter præfertur omni dominio. In this chapter Aquinas presently introduces Matt. xvi. 18, 19; and says of that text, Ubi quatuor ponuntur clausulæ, omnes significativæ dominii Petri suorumque successorum super omnes fideles; et propter quas merito summus pontifex Romanus Christus dici potest, rex, et sacerdos. Si enim, etc.—Th. Aquin. Opusc. f. 231. Lugd. 1562.]

Saints.

And in like manner, whosoever defendeth his traditions, decrees, and privileges, him he made a saint also for his labour, were his living never so contrary unto the scripture; as Thomas of Canterbury[1], with many other like, whose life was like Thomas cardinal's[2], but not Christ's; neither is Thomas cardinal's life anything, save a counterfeiting of St Thomas of Canterbury. Thomas Becket was first seen[3] in merchandise temporal; and then, to learn spiritual merchandise, he gat him to Theobald archbishop of Canterbury; which sent him divers times to Rome about business of holy church. And when Theobald had spied his activity, he shore him deacon[4], lest he should go back; and made him archdeacon of Canterbury, and upon that presented him to the king. And the king made him his chancellor, in which office he passed the pomp and pride of Thomas cardinal, as far as the one's shrine passeth the other's tomb in glory and riches. And after that he was a man of war, and captain over five or six thousand men in full harness, as bright as St George, and his spear in his hand; and encountered whosoever came against him, and overthrew the jolliest rutter[5] that was in all the host of France. And out of the field, hot from blood-shedding, was he made bishop of Canterbury, and did put off his helmet, and put on his mitre; put off his harness, and on with his robes; and laid down his spear, and took his cross, ere his hands were cold; and so came, with a lusty courage of a man of war, to fight another while against his prince for the pope[6]; where his prince's causes were with the law of God, and the pope's clean contrary. And the pomp

Thomas of Canterbury.

Thomas Becket and Thomas Wolsey compared together.

[1 Thomas Becket.]

[2 Thomas Wolsey, the cardinal.] [3 Versed in.]

[4 Made him submit to the clerical tonsure.]

[5 From the old French *ruitre;* which was however imitated from the German *reiter*, a rider, especially a horse-soldier or knight.]

[6 Post reditum regis Angliæ, comitibus omnibus recusantibus, solus cancellarius [Becket] cum sua familia in Gallia remansit. Et postea tria castra munitissima, et quæ inexpugnabilia videbantur, ipsemet lorica indutus et galea cum suis in manu forti cepit. Ipsemet, clericus cum esset, cum valente milite Francorum, Engelramno de Tria, e regione subditis equo calcaribus veniente armato, lancea demissa et equo admisso congressus, ipsum equo dejecit, et dextrarium lucrifecit.—Interim diem suum postremum clausit archiepiscopus Theobaldus. Statuit ergo rex Anglorum cancellarium suum in archiepiscopatum promovere,

of his consecration was after his old worldly fashion. Howbeit yet he is made a saint for his worshipping of the holy seat of St Peter; not that seat of Peter which is Christ's gospel, but another, lied to be Peter's, and is indeed *cathedra pestilentiæ*, a chair of false doctrine. And because he could no skill of our Lord's gospel, he said of matins with our lady. If any man understand the Latin, let him read his life, and compare it unto the scripture; and then he shall see such holiness as were here too long to be rehearsed[7]. And every abbey, and every cathedral church, did shrine them one god or other, and mingled the lives of the very saints with stark lies, to move men to offer: which thing they call devotion.

The pope rewardeth his servants highly when they be dead.

And though in all their doings they oppress the temporalty and their commonwealth, and be grievous unto the rich, and painful to the poor; yet they be so many, and so exercised in wiles, and so subtle, and so knit and sworn together, that they compass the temporalty, and make them bear them, whether they will or will not (as the oak doth the ivy), partly with juggling, and beside that with worldly policy. For every abbot will make him that may do most in the shire, or with the king, the steward of his lands, and give him a fee yearly; and will lend unto some, and feast other, that by such means they do what they will. And little master parson, after the same manner, if he come into an house, and the wife be snout-fair, he will root himself there by one craft or other; either by using such pastime as the good man doth, or in being beneficial by one way or other, or he will lend him, and so bring him into his danger[8] that he cannot thrust him out when he would, but must be compelled to bear him, and to let him be homely[9], whether he will or no.

Policy. W. T.

The practice of little master parson.

intuitu meritorum personæ; confidens quod sibi ad placitum et nutum ut cancellarius fecerat, archiepiscopus obsequeretur.—Sparkes, Hist. Angl. Scriptores varii e Cod. MSS. ed. Lond. 1723.]

[7 In Day, our lady. Such as understand the Latin, read &c. But in the Marburg edition, 'and because he coude no skylle of our Lorde's gospell, he sayde of matēs with our ladye say they. If any mā understond the Latyn, let him reade his life,' &c.]

[8 A state of dependence.] [9 Domesticated.]

An example of practice out of our own chronicles.

King Harold. Robert of Canterbury. W. T.

Take an ensample of their practice out of our own stories. King Harold exiled or banished Robert archbishop of Canterbury[1]: for what cause, the English Polychronicon specifieth not: but if the cause were not somewhat suspect, I think they would not have passed it over with silence. This Robert gat him immediately unto king William the conqueror, then duke of Normandy: and the pope Alexander sent duke William a banner, to go and conquer England[2], and clean remission unto whosoever would follow the banner, and go with king William. Here mark how straight the pope followed Christ's steps and his apostles'! They preached forgiveness of sins to all that repented, through Christ's blood-shedding; the pope preacheth forgiveness of sins to all that will slay their brethren, bought with Christ's blood, to subdue them unto his tyranny. Whatsoever other cause duke William had against king Harold, thou mayest be sure that the pope would not have meddled, if Harold had not troubled his kingdom: neither should duke William have been able to conquer the land at that time, except the spiritualty had wrought on his side. What blood did that conquest cost England, through which almost all the lords of the English blood were slain, and the Normans became rulers, and all the laws were changed into French! But what careth the holy father for shedding of laymen's blood? It were better that ten hundred thousand lay knaves lost their lives, than that holy church should lose one inch of her honour, or St Peter's seat one jot of her right.

Remission of sins to conquer England. W. T.

Note here how well Christ and the pope agree: Christ biddeth save, and the pope biddeth kill.

The pope is a cruel and merciless tyrant.

Anselmus a chaplain of the pope's.

And Anselmus, that was bishop in short time after, never left striving with that mighty prince king William the second, until he had compelled him, maugre his teeth, to deliver up

[1 Robertus, Episcopus Londoniensis, genere Normannorum, (Eadsino) successit; qui expulsus est de Anglia, et sedit annis duobus. Steph. Birchington, Hist. de Archiep. Cantuar. ad ann. 1069.]

[2 Willelmus dux Normannorum, ne justam bellandi causam temeritas deformaret, ad papam Alexandrum nuntios destinavit, ut susceptum negotium auctoritate apostolica firmaretur. Unde papa, consideratis utrinque litigantium causis, vexillum Willelmo in omen regni transmisit.—Matt. Paris, Hist. Angliæ.]

the investiture or election of bishops unto St Peter's vicar, which investiture was of old time the king's duty[3].

And again, when the said king William would have had the tribute, that priests gave yearly unto their bishops for their whores, paid to him; did not Ralph bishop of Chichester forbid God's service (as they call it), and stop up the church doors with thorns, throughout all his diocese, until the king had yielded him up his tribute again[4]? For when the holy father had forbode priests their wives, the bishops permitted them whores of their own, for a yearly tribute; and do still yet in all lands save in England, where they may not have any other save men's wives only.

The pope is well pleased to admit priests to have whores, but not wives.

And again, for the election of Stephen Langton, archbishop of Canterbury, what misery and wretchedness was in the realm a long season! Then was the land interdicted many years: and when that holp not, then Ireland rebelled against king John immediately; and not without the secret workings of our prelates, I dare well say. But finally, when neither the interdicting neither that secret subtilty holp, and when John would in no means consent that St Peter's vicar should reign alone over the spiritualty, and over all that pertained unto them, and that they should sin and do all mischief unpunished, the pope sent remission of sins to the king of France, for to go and conquer his land[5]: whereof king John was so sore afraid, that he yielded up his crown to the pope, and sware to hold the land of him, and that his successors should do so likewise.

Note here the pride and wickedness of the pope.

Remission of sins to conquer. W. T.

And again, in king Richard the second's days, Thomas Arundel, archbishop of Canterbury and chancellor, was exiled with the earl of Derby. The outward pretence of the variance

Thomas Arundel.

[3 That is, the king's due, or right.]

[4 William of Malmesbury confirms part of this statement, though he does not say on what ground the money was to be paid. His words are these: Religiosam contumaciam mandatis Henrici regis exhibuit, volentis per totam Angliam a presbyteris pecuniam exigere. Id aliis vel concedentibus, vel metu silentium tenentibus, in solo Radulfo rigor pontificalis emolliri nequivit, per totam siquidem diœcesin divina vacare officia, januas ecclesiarum spinis obstrui præcepit, monachorum cantum non inhibens, sed tamen laicis aditum arcens. He adds that the king gave way.—De Gest. Pontif. Angl.—Rer. Anglic. Script. Lond. 1596, fol. 146 vers.]

[5 See n. 4, p. 339 Vol. I.]

between the king and his lords was for the deliverance of the town of Brest in Britayne. But our prelates had another secret mystery a brewing. They could not at their own lust slay the poor wretches which at that time were converted unto repentance and to the true faith, to put their trust in Christ's death and blood-shedding for the remission of their sins, by the preaching of John Wicliffe. As soon as the archbishop was out of the realm, the Irishmen began to rebel against king Richard, as before against king John; but not, hardly, without the invisible inspiration of them that rule both in the court and also in the consciences of all men. They be one kingdom, sworn together one to help another, scattered abroad in all realms.

Practice of prelates.

And howbeit that they strive among themselves who shall be greatest, yet against the temporal power they be always at one; though they dissemble it and feign, as though one held against the other, to know their enemy's secrets, to betray them withal. They can inspire privily into the breasts of the people what mischief they list, and no man shall know whence it cometh. Their letters go secretly from one to another throughout all kingdoms. Saint Peter's vicar shall have word in fifteen or sixteen days from the uttermost part of Christendom. The bishops of England at their need can write unto the bishops of Ireland, Scotland, Denmark, Dutchland, France, and Spain, promising them as good a turn another time; putting them in remembrance that they be all one holy church, and that the cause of the tone is the cause of the tother[1]; saying, 'If our juggling break out, yours cannot be long hid.' And the other shall serve their turn, and bring the game unto their hands; and no man shall know how it cometh about.

The pope's clergy are secret and subtle conspirators.

As soon as king Richard was gone to Ireland, to subdue these rebellions, the bishop came in again, and prevented the king, and took up his power against him, and took him prisoner, and put him down and to death most cruelly, and crowned the earl of Derby king. O merciful Christ! What blood hath that coronation cost England! But what care they? Their causes must be avenged. He is not worthy to be king, that will not avenge their quarrels. For do not the kings receive their kingdom of the beast, and swear to wor-

A traitorous practice.

[[1] This antithetical form, *tone* and *tother*, is very common in Sir Thomas More, and other writers of that age.]

ship him, and maintain his throne? And then, when the earl of Derby, which was king Harry the fourth, was crowned, the prelates took his sword, and his son's Harry the fifth after him (as all the king's swords since), and abused them, to shed christian blood at their pleasure. And they coupled their cause unto the king's cause (as now), and made it treason to believe in Christ as the scripture teacheth, and to resist the bishops (as now), and thrust them in the king's prisons (as now), so that it is no new invention that they now do, but even an old practice; though they have done their busy care to hide their science, that their conveyance[2] should not be espied.

The papists are stirrers up of wars and shedders of blood.

And in king Harry the sixth's days, how raged they as fierce lions against good duke Humphry of Glocester, the king's uncle, and protector of the realm in the king's youth and childhood, because that for him they might not slay whom they would, and make what chevisance[3] they lusted! Would not the bishop of Winchester have fallen upon him and oppressed him openly with might and power in the city of London, had not the citizens come to his help?

Duke Humphry.

Papists are cruel.

But at the last they found means to contrive a drift to bring their matters to pass, and made a parliament far from the citizens of London, where was slain the good duke, and only wealth of the realm, and the mighty shield that so long before had kept it from sorrow, which shortly after his death fell thereon by heaps. But the chronicles cannot tell wherefore he died, nor by what means. No marvel, verily: for he had need of other eyes than such as the world seeth withal, that should spy out their privy paths. Nevertheless the chronicles testify, that he was a virtuous man, a godly, and good to the commonwealth. Moreover the proctor of purgatory saith in his dialogue, *Quoth I, and quoth he, and quoth your friend,* how that the foresaid duke of Glocester was a noble man and a great clerk, and so wise that he could spy false miracles, and disclose them, and judge them from the true;[4] which is an hateful science unto our spiritualty, and

A parliament kept at Bury.

The death of Humphry duke of Glocester, protector of the realm of England.

This is Sir Thomas More.

[2 Sleight of hand; fraudulent management.]

[3 Bargain.]

[4 Tyndale calls Sir Thomas More *The proctor of purgatory,* in allusion to his controversial treatise entitled 'The supplication of souls,' which More composed in the form of an address 'To all good christen

The clergy cannot abide them that can judge false miracles. The causes why the duke of Glocester was murdered.

more abhorred amongst them than necromancy or witchcraft; and a thing wherefore a man by their law, I dare well say, is worthy to die, and that secretly, if it be possible. Now to be good to the commonwealth, and to see false miracles, and thirdly to withstand that France, then brought under the foot of the Englishmen, should not be set up again, by whose power the pope holdeth down the emperor and reigneth in his stead, be causes why he might die, though by what means be not known. For to be good to the commonwealth is to be hurtful to the spiritualty, seeing the one is the other's prey, as the lamb is the wolf's. Secondarily, if a man be so clear-eyed that he can spy false miracles, how can jugglers get their living, and be in price, where such a fellow is? Thirdly, to keep down the kingdom of France is to pull St Peter's vicar out of his seat.

Three causes. W. T.

The pope is the whore of Babylon.

Now if the great bawd, the whore of Babylon, were destroyed, then would the brothel and stews of our prelates shortly perish. If Abaddon, that destroyer, king of the grasshoppers which devour all that is green, were destroyed, then were the kingdom of our caterpillars at an end.

By what craft the pope keepeth the emperor down.

Another practice of prelates.

Mark another practice of our most holy prelates. When the empire was translated unto the Germans, though the emperor was fallen down, and had kissed the pope's feet, and was become his sworn servant, yet there was much strife, and open war oft-times, between the popes and the emperors. And the popes have put down many good emperors by help of the bishops, which everywhere secretly persuaded the lords to forsake the emperors, and to take dispensations of the pope for their oaths.

And contrariwise, the emperors have now and then de-

people' from their 'late acquaintance, kindred, spouses, companions, playfellows, and friends—now poor prisoners, the silly souls in purgatory.' But the 'dialogue of Sir Thomas More' is another work, and is kept up by a repetition of Quoth I and quoth he; and in the fourteenth chapter of the first of its four books, More relates, as what he had heard from his father, the well-known tale of duke Humphry's detecting the imposture, of a beggar who pretended to have been miraculously healed of blindness at St Alban's shrine.—Works of Sir T. More, Lond. 1557, p. 134.]

posed divers popes, at the request of the cardinals and other great prelates; by whose help only they were able to do it. For else verily, though all kings christened had sworn to depose one pope out of his seat, if they had not the favour of other prelates thereto, they might haply, by the secret practice of them, be put out of their own seats in the mean time.

Popes have deposed emperors, and likewise emperors have deposed popes.

The pope therefore, to be sure of himself, and out of the fear and danger of the emperor, were he never so mighty, and that the emperor should not see his daily open pastimes, made friendship and amity with the Venetians on the one side of him, and let them come into certain cities of the emperor's in Italy; and with the French king on the other side, and let him also up into certain cities and possessions of the emperor's, and he himself in the midst; and shut out the emperor from coming any more to Rome, and ever sent his coronation home to him. And then he made a law that no man should rebuke the pope for whatsoever he did; saying, that the pope was above all, and judge over all, and none over him; and therefore forbad in his law, *Distinctio*, xl. *Si Papa*, saying, "Though the pope be proved negligent about himself, and also the soul-health of his brethren, and slack in his works, and speechless as concerning any good, and draw with him by his example innumerable people to hell, to be punished with him with divers torments everlastingly; yet see that no mortal man presume once to rebuke his faults here: for he shall judge all men, and no man him[1]." O antichrist! Is he not antichrist, that will not have his life tried by God's word?

No man rebuke the pope. W. T.

If the Venetians catch any of our holy father's towns or possessions, whether by war, or that they have bought it, or that it be laid to mortgage unto them, or that the old pope hath given it with the marriage of some daughter unto the duke of Venice; then the holy father that succeedeth, when he seeth his season, sendeth for it again, saying, 'That it is not lawful for laymen to withhold St Peter's patrimony.' If they allege that they bought it, and so forth, his fatherhood answereth, 'That the old pope had none authority to make any such chevisance with St Peter's inheritance: he could have but the use of it his life long, and after it must needs return unto his successor again.' And upon that he interdict-

Venetians.

The pope may give and take again at his will and pleasure.

[1 See n. 3 to p. 328 of Vol. I.]

eth them, and curseth them as black as coals, down to the pit of hell.

The Venetians care not for the pope's cursing nor blessing.

But the Venetians, knowing more of our holy father's practice, for their nighness, than we which dwell afar off, and wiser than we of cold countries, perceiving also that their colour changeth not with his cursing, and that they sink not, and that their meat digesteth as well as before[1], therefore fear not his interdiction nor excommunication.

Then our holy father raiseth up all the power that he is able to make in Italy against them, and sendeth for the Souchenars[2] to come and help. If he be not yet strong enough, then he sendeth unto the bishops of France, warning them that if his seat decay, theirs cannot long prosper; and therefore that they put their king in remembrance, how that he is called most Christian king, and that they desire him to do somewhat for his title against this disobedient rebellion unto the most holy see of Rome, our mother, holy church.

Frenchmen.

If another time the Frenchmen come to our holy father, as they be ever gaping for Italy, to bring the empire home again to France; then that most holy vicar bringeth his whole power against them, with the power of the Venetians, and with his old friends the Souchenars[3]. If he be not yet strong enough, then he sendeth to the bishops of England to help their god, and to move their king to do somewhat for holy church, putting him in remembrance of whom he holdeth his crown, and of his oath, and how many caps of maintenance have been ever sent unto his forefathers, and what honour it was unto them, and that he may easily get as great honour as they, and haply a more excellent title, if he will take our holy father's part; besides that he shall purchase remission of all his sins.

Englishmen.

The practice of the pope with all kings and princes.

The pope a breaker of peace.

Then must the peace, and all the appointments made between us and France, be broken, and the king must take a dispensation for his oath. For the king of France will attempt nothing in Italy, until he have sent his ambassadors, and have made a perpetual peace with our king, the sacrament

[1 A coarse expression, which Tyndale says he borrowed from Erasmus, is here omitted.]

[2 Souchenars, Marb. ed.; Zwitzers, S. S. ed.; Sochenars, Day. By each of these terms the Swiss are meant. See Vol. I. p. 186. n. 1.]

[3 S. S. ed. has here *Zwitzers*, again.]

of the body of our Saviour broke between them to confirm the appointment. But I suppose that the breaking signifieth that the appointment shall not long endure: for a great deal of flour would not make so many hosts (as they call them), or singing loaves[4], as hath been broken in our days between Christian princes (as they will be called), to confirm promises that have not been kept. Other use of that blessed sacrament will the princes none know: but Christ ordained it to be a perpetual memory that his body was broken for our sins upon the cross, and that all that repent should receive, as oft as they eat of it, forgiveness of their misdeeds through faith. If the kings of the earth, when they break that sacrament between them, do say on this wise, 'The body of our Saviour (which was broken on the cross for the sin of all that repent, and have good hearts, and would fain keep his law) be broke unto my damnation, if I break this oath;' then is it a terrible oath, and they had need to take heed how they make it, and, if it be lawfully made, not to break it at all. But as they care for their oath, which they make in wedlock, so they care for this.

The abuse of the sacrament.

How the sacrament should be broken between kings and princes.

Whatsoever need the pope hath, he will not send to the emperor to come and help him in Italy, for fear lest he would take to himself whatsoever he conquered of the Frenchmen, and wax too strong, and minish our holy father's power, and become our holy father's vicar, as he is St Peter's. Nevertheless, if we Englishmen will hire the emperor to come and fight against France, for the right of the church in these quarters that be next unto us, his fatherhood is content to admit his service.

The pope would not have the emperor too strong.

When our king hath granted to take our holy father's part, then the pretence and cloak outward must be, that the king will challenge his right in France. And, to aid the king in his right, must the commons be milked till they bleed again. Then, to do the king service, the lords sell, or lay their lands to mortgage. Then is clean remission given, to slay French dogs. He that dieth in the quarrel shall never see purgatory, but fly to heaven straight, even with a thought.

Remission of sins, and clean deliverance out of purgatory.

[[4] Loaves; though spelt in the oldest editions loves. The thin loaves, or wafers of meal, intended to be used at mass were called singing loaves, because a psalm was to be sung whilst they were in making].

When the pope hath what he desireth in Italy, then must we make peace with the Frenchmen again immediately, that France be not altogether trodden under the foot; but that it remain alway in a mean state, strong enough to match the emperor and to keep him down, but not too mighty for oppressing the pope. And then our prelates, to bring the peace about, send immediately a friar Forest, or a vicar of Croydon, to preach before the king and his lords; which preacher roareth and crieth unto them, as though he hallooed his hounds, aud maketh exclamations, saying: 'Alas! what will ye do? Spare Christian blood. Will ye slay your own souls? Be not the Frenchmen as well Christians as ye? Moreover, ye slay poor innocents that never offended. Make peace for the passion of Christ. Kill not one another, as though Christ had not died for you; but fight rather against the Turks.'

A friar Forest, or a vicar of Croydon.

Popish practices.

Then come in the ambassadors of France, and money[1] a few prelates, and certain other the king's play-fellows, that be sworn with them to betray both the king and the realm too; and then is peace concluded. But outwardly there is nothing save a truce taken for half an year, till our soldiers be at home again, for fear lest they would not be content. Then cometh the whole host home beggared, both great and small; and the poor, that cannot suddenly get work, fall to stealing, and be hanged at home. This could More tell in his Utopia, before he was the cardinal's sworn secretary, and fallen at his feet to betray the truth for to get promotion[2].

Dissembled truce.

Henry V.

Take an example: the bishops sent king Henry the fifth out to conquer France. The cause was, saith the chronicles, that the king went about to take their temporalities from them;

[1 Money, i. e. bribe.]

[2 In the introductory dialogue to his Utopia, More represents a foreign voyager as describing a conversation at Cardinal Moreton's table, and saying: Laicus quidam...dicebat se mirari, cum tam pauci elaberentur supplicio, quo malo fato fieret uti tam multi tamen ubique grassarentur. Tum ego, Nihil mireris, inquam: nam hæc punitio furum et supra justum est, et non ex usu publico. Est enim ad vindicanda furta nimis atrox, nec tamen ad refrænanda sufficiens. Sæpe vel ab externis bellis vel civilibus mutili redeunt domum, ut nuper apud vos a Cornubiensi prælio, et non ita pridem a Gallico, qui vel reipublicæ impendunt membra vel regi, quos neque pristinas artes exercere debilitas patitur, neque ætas novam discere. Utopia. Lib. I.]

and therefore, to bring the king into another imagination, they monied him, and sent him into France[3].

When they had sent out the king, he conquered more than was their will, and more than they supposed possible for him in so short space, and brought France clean under the foot; so that our prelates had much secret business to set it up again. But what is impossible unto so great gods? King Henry V. conquered more than the prelates thought he should do.

In king Henry's the sixth days, our holy father of Rome made the bishop of Winchester a cardinal; which went shortly after into France, to treat of a truce between England and France. And him met a legate of Rome, and cardinal also: after which meeting Englishmen had ever the worse in France, and their chiefest friend, the duke of Burgaine[4], forsook them[5]. For when cardinals and bishops meet together, they have their secret council by themselves, wherein they conclude neither what is good for England, nor yet for France, but what is best for our holy father's profit, to keep him in his state. Henry VI. The crafty practice of the pope's legate.

When king Henry was of age, there was a marriage between him and the earl of Armainacke's[6] daughter, in Gyan[7]; with the which should have been given many castles and towns in Gyan, and a great sum of money thereto. But that marriage was broken, not without the secret working of our prelates, and dispensation of our holy father, thou

[3 'This year [1513] the king [Henry V.] held his parliament at Leicester, where among other things the foresaid bill put up by the commons of the land, for the temporalities being in the church, was again minded; in fear whereof, lest the king should thereunto give any comfortable audience, as testify some writers, certain bishops and other head men of the church put the king in mind to claim his right in France, and for the exploit thereof they offered unto him great and notable sums. By reason whereof the said bill was again put by, and the king set his mind to the recovery of the same.'—Extract from a copy of Fabian's chronicle in the library of St John's College, Cambridge; having on its fly-leaf the following note in the hand-writing of Baker the antiquarian. "This is the first and uncastrated edition of Fabian, said to be burned by order of cardinal Wolsey.—Bal. cent. VIII. 62."]

[4 Burgundy.]

[5 This had been the subject of Art. xiv. in a list of 21 charges against cardinal Beaufort, bishop of Winchester, presented to Henry VI. by Humphry duke of Glocester, as printed in Foxe's Acts and Mon. B. VI.]

[6 Armagnac.] [7 Guienne.]

mayest be sure; and a marriage was made between him and the king's daughter of Sicily, for which England gave up the whole dukedom of Gyan and earldom of Maine: whereby we lost all Normandy, whereof they were the key[1]; and beside that, the commons gave a fifteen and an half[2], to fetch[3] her in with pomp. And then was the good duke of Glocester traitorously murdered; partly because he could judge false miracles, and partly because of the deliverance of these two countries: for, he being alive, they durst not do it.

The marriage of king Henry VI.

The duke of Glocester traitorously murdered.

And when king Edward had put down king Harry, a marriage was made and concluded between him and the king of Spain, this queen's mother that now is[4]. But ere the ambassadors were come home, our prelates had bewitched king Edward by their apostle, friar Bungay[5], and married him unto

Friar Bungay.

[1 Tyndale seems to have thought that, as Armagnac was an important part of the dutchy of Guienne, the castles &c. given with the count's daughter would have enabled the king of England to secure possession of the whole. It is well known that there was great popular indignation at the setting aside of this match for one with Margaret daughter of Regnier, a French prince who bore the titles of duke of Anjou, and king of Sicily, Naples and Jerusalem, without possessing any corresponding territories.]

[2 A fifteenth was originally a tax to the amount of that portion of the estimated value of every householder's property in moveables. But in the sixth year of Edward III. it was commuted on terms which fixed its amount at no more than £37,930 for all England.—Hollingshed. Vol. I. p. 230. and Blackstone's Comment. pp. 308—9.]

[3 Fol. and S. S. ed. fette.]

[4 The princess here meant must have been Isabella, Queen of Castile, who afterwards married Ferdinand of Aragon, and became mother to Catharine, the first wife of Henry VIII. Sir Thomas More says, that 'after king Edward was in peaceable possession of the realm, he sent over in embassiate the earl of Warwick to entreat and conclude a marriage between king Edward and the king's daughter of Spain. In which thing the earl of Warwick found the parties so toward, that he speedily brought the matter to a very good conclusion.' Hist. Rich. III. Works, Lond. 1557. p. 58. Tyndale seems to have used the word *king* here as rex has been used, to distinguish a queen regnant from a queen consort. The cry of the Hungarian magnates, 'Vivat rex noster, Maria Theresa,' has been admitted into history.]

[5 In the first edition of Fabian's Chronicle, after relating the events of the battle of Barnet, in 1471, he says: "Of the mists and other impediments which fell upon the lord's party, by reason of the incantations by friar Bungay, as the fame went, we list not to write." fol. ccxxiii.]

a widow that was a knight's wife; lest, if Spain and England had been joined together, king Edward should have recovered France again. But what followed after the breaking off the marriage between king Edward and the earl of Warwick? And what came of his children? Yea, and what came on king Henry of Windsor's children also? But what care our prelates, what vengeance or mischief fall on princes, or on their realms, so their kingdom prosper?

Cruel war between king Henry and the earl of Warwick.

In king Henry the seventh's days the cardinal Morton and bishop Fox of Winchester delivered unto the king's grace the confessions of as many lords as his grace lusted. Whosoever was mistrusted, if he shrove himself at the Charter-houses, Sion, Greenwich, at St John's, or wheresoever it was, the confessor was commanded by the authority of the pope to deliver his confession written, and sworn that it was all. And cardinal Morton had a licence of the pope for fourteen to study necromancy, of which he himself was one; and other I have heard named, which at this time I pass over with silence. And how the holy friars observants carried feigned letters, to try who was true, I pass over with silence also. Howbeit, such temptations and feigned proffers were enough to move them that never would have thought amiss: yea, and in confession men will shrive themselves of thoughts, which they never went about in the outward deed.

Confession in the ear was a wicked invention.

Licence of the pope for fourteen to study necromancy.

When any great man is put to death, how his confessor entreateth him, and what penance is enjoined him, concerning what he shall say when he cometh unto the place of execution, I could guess at a practice that might make men's ears glow.

And did not the subtle counsel of the said two prelates feign the siege of Boulogne, to make a pretence to gather in a fifteen, when there was no more war between the king of France and of England than is between a man's head, that hath lust to sleep, and his pillow[6]? which siege yet cost many a man their lives, yea, and some great men thereto,

A subtle practice of prelates.

[[6] Grafton's Chronicle tells how Henry VII. gathered treasure by this threat of war, but ascribes the preparations to an object in which our king was deceived by Maximilian. His account, however, is in unison with Tyndale as to the desire of the French king Charles VIII. to remain at peace with England.]

which knew not of that feigning[1]. The king's grace went over with a ten thousand men to conquer all France, and spent haply an hundred thousand pound, of which he saved the fourth part in the dandyprats[2], and gathered at home five or six hundred, or more. And two other such feigned voyages could I haply rehearse, which I pass over for divers causes, where many an Englishman lost his life. But what care they for men's lives?

He meaneth cardinal Wolsey.

And did not our cardinal with like policy, think ye, (to gather that which he thought would not well be paid, except the commons saw some cause,) bring a great multitude of Scots unto the English pale, either by some bishops of Scotland, or by some great man whom he corrupted with some yearly pension?—against which the poor northern men must go on their own cost, to keep them out. And general procession was commanded at London thrice in the week, and throughout all the land, while the king's receivers gathered the tax of the common people. Which plague, and such like, after the threatening of God, Lev. xxvi. and Deut. xxviii. and xxix., I am sure will fall on all Christendom without cease, until they either defy the name of Christ with the Turks; or, if they will be called Christians, they turn and look on his doctrine.

Lev. xxvi. Deut. xxviii. xxix.

Yea, and what feigned the cardinal at that great loan, to beguile his own priests, to make them swear what they were worth, and the better willing to pay! for the common priests be not so obedient unto their ordinaries that they will pay money, except they know why. Now it is not expedient that every rascal[3] should know the secrets of the very true cause, for many considerations; and therefore another pretence must be made, and another cause alleged: and therefore the priests were charged by their ordinaries to appear before the gentlemen of the country[4], and temporal officers, and swear what every man was worth. Now the priests had lever be slain, and die martyrs, after the ensample of St Thomas of

A practice of the prelates with their poor priests.

[1 Grafton says, 'There was few or none killed, saving only one sir John Savage, knt.,' and ascribes his death to his folly and pride.]

[2 The word is spelt *dandeprats* in Bailey's Dictionary, where the meaning given is a dwarf, or a small coin issued by Henry VII.]

[3 That is, every unimportant personage.]

[4 So Marb. ed. and Day; but in S. and S. it is *of the court.*]

Canterbury, than to swear before a lay judge[5]; for they think it greater sin than to slay their own fathers, and that then the liberties of the church were clean lost, and they no better than the vile lay people. And when they were in that perplexity, that they must either swear, or run into the king's danger, and lose their gods (I would say their goods); then my lord cardinal sent down his gracious power, that they should swear unto their ordinaries only. And then the priests, for joy that they were rid out of the laymen's hands, were so glad and joyous, that they wist not what thanks to give my lord cardinal, and so were obedient to swear, and to lend; or else for all the curses that my lord cardinal hath, and the pope too, they would neither have sworn, or paid a penny.

The practice of our time.

When the king's grace came first to the right of the crown, and unto the governance of the realm, young and unexpert, Thomas Wolfsee, a man of lust and courage and bodily strength, to do and to suffer great things, and to endure in all manner of voluptuousness; expert and exercised in the course of the world, as he which had heard, read, and seen much policy, and had done many things himself, and had been of the secret counsel of weighty matters, as subtle as Sinon that betrayed Troy; utterly appointed to semble and dissemble, to have one thing in the heart and another in the mouth, being thereto as eloquent as subtle, and able to persuade what he lusted to them that were unexpert; so desirous and greedy of honour, that he cared not but for the next and most compendious way thereto, whether godly or ungodly; this wily wolf, I say, and raging sea, and shipwreck of all England, though he shewed himself pleasant and calm at the first (as whores do unto their lovers), came unto the king's grace, and waited upon him, and was no man so obsequious and serviceable, and in all games and sports the first and next at hand; and as a captain to courage other, and a gay finder out of new pastimes, to obtain favour withal[6].

Thomas Wolsey.

The description of cardinal Wolsey.

[5 Because the canon law says, Clericum cujuslibet ordinis absque pontificis sui permissu nullus præsumat ad secularem judicem attrahere, nec laico quemlibet clericum liceat accusare.—Corp. Jur. Can. Decr. 2da. pars, II. qu. 1. can. 3.]

[6 His attached dependent and biographer George Cavendish has

The king's birth calked by the cardinal.

Bishops calk kings' nativities. W. T.

And thereto, as the secret communication went, which by many tokens thou mayest well conjecture and gather to be true, he calked[1] the king's nativity and birth, (which is a common practice among prelates in all lands;) whereby he saw whereunto the king's grace should be inclined all his life, and what should be like to chance him at all times.

King Henry VIII. and cardinal Wolsey in great estimation.

And, as I heard it spoken of divers, he made by craft of necromancy graven imagery to bear upon him; wherewith he bewitched the king's mind, and made the king to dote upon him more than ever he did on any lady or gentlewoman; so that now the king's grace followed him, as he before followed the king. And then, what he said, that was wisdom; what he praised, that was honourable only. Moreover, in the meantime he spied out the natures and dispositions of the king's play-fellows, and of all that were great; and whom he spied meet for his purpose, him he flattered, and him he made faithful with great promises, and to him he sware, and of him he took an oath again, that the one should help the other: for without a secret oath he admitted no man unto any part of his privities.

The manner and practice of cardinal Wolsey.

The king is betrayed. W. T.

And ever as he grew in promotions and dignity, so gathered he unto him of the most subtle-witted, and of them that were drunk in the desire of honour, most like unto himself: and after they were sworn, he promoted them, and with great promises made them in falsehood faithful, and of them ever presented unto the king's grace, and put them into his service, saying, 'This is a man meet for your grace.' And by these spies, if aught were done or spoken in the court against the cardinal, of that he had word within an hour or two;

ascribed Wolsey's influence to the same sinful course. Speaking of Wolsey when he was but dean of Lincoln, and the king's almoner, he says: "He was most earnest and readiest among all the council to advance the king's only will and pleasure, without any respect to the case. The king was young and lusty, disposed all to mirth and pleasure, and to follow his desire and appetite, nothing minding to travail in the busy affairs of this realm. The which the almoner perceiving very well, took upon him therefore to disburden the king of so weighty a charge and troublesome business, putting the king in comfort that he should not need to spare any time of his pleasure for any business that should necessarily happen in the council." Cavendish's Life of Wolsey, 1825. Vol. I. p. 18.]

[1 Calked: calculated.]

and then came the cardinal to court with all his magic, to persuade the contrary. If any in the court had spoken against the cardinal, and the same not great in the king's favour, the cardinal bade him walk a villain[2], and thrust him out of the court headlong. If he were in conceit with the king's grace, then he flattered, and persuaded, and corrupted some with gifts, and sent some ambassadors, and some he made captains at Calais, Hames, Guines, Jersey, and Guernsey, or sent them to Ireland, and into the north; and so occupied them, till the king had forgot them, and other were in their rooms, or till he had sped what he intended.

And in like manner played he with the ladies and gentle- women. Whosoever of them was great, with her was he familiar, and to her gave he gifts: yea, and where St Thomas of Canterbury was wont to come after, Thomas cardinal went oft before, preventing his prince, and perverted the order of that holy man. If any were subtle-witted, and meet for his purpose, her made he sworn to betray the queen likewise, and tell him what she said or did. I know one that departed the court for no other cause, than that she would no longer betray her mistress.

The queen is betrayed. W. T.

Note this devilish practice.

And, after the same example, he furnished the court with chaplains of his own sworn disciples, and children of his own bringing up, to be alway present, and to dispute of vanities, and to water whatsoever the cardinal had planted. If among those cormorants any yet began to be too much in favour with the king, and to be somewhat busy in the court, and to draw any other way than as my lord cardinal had appointed that the plough should go, anon he was sent to Italy or to Spain; or some quarrel was picked against him, and so was thrust out of the court, as Stokesly was.

He promoted the bishop of Lincoln that now is[3], his most faithful friend and old companion, and made him confessor: to whom of whatsoever the king's grace shrove himself, think ye not that he spake so loud that the cardinal heard it? And not unright; for as God's creatures ought to obey God and

The bishop of Lincoln.

[[2] The expression seems to have been equivalent to 'Begone, vile man.' We find in like manner, 'Walk, faytour;' for, 'Begone, impostor.']

[[3] John Longland, principal of Magdalen Hall, Oxford, was made bishop of Lincoln in 1521, and so continued till 1547. He was a fierce persecutor of the protestants.]

serve his honour, so ought the pope's creatures to obey the pope and serve his majesty.

Cardinal Wolsey ruled altogether.

Finally, Thomas Wolfsee became what he would, even porter of heaven, so that no man could enter into promotion but through him.

The cause of all that we have suffered these twenty years.

About the beginning of the king's grace that now is, France was mighty, so that I suppose that it was not mightier this five hundred years. King Lewis[1] of France had won Naples, and had taken Bononia from St Peter's see. Wherefore pope July[2] was wroth, and cast how to bring the Frenchmen down, yet soberly, lest, while he brought him lower, he should give an occasion to lift up the emperor higher. Our first voyage into Spain was to bring the Frenchmen lower: for our meyny[3] were set in the fore-front and borders of Spain, toward Gascoyne, partly to keep those parties, and partly to fear the Gascoynes and to keep them at home, while in the meantime the Spaniards won Naverne[4]. When Naverne was won, our men came to house, as many as died not there; and brought all their money home again, save that they spent there. Howbeit, for all the loss of Naverne, the Frenchmen were yet able enough to match Spain, the Venetians, and the pope, and all the Souchenars[5] that he could make; so that there was yet no remedy but we must set on the Frenchmen also, if they should be brought out of Italy.

King Lewis.

Pope Julius.

This is true story.

Then pope July wrote unto his dear son Thomas Wolfsee, that he would be as good, as loving, and as helping

[1 Louis XII.]

[2 Julius II. pope from 1503 to 1513.]

[3 Meyny: many, a mixed multitude.]

[4 Naverne is Navarre. In March 1511, Henry sent 1000 archers to the aid of Ferdinand, as if to help him in combating the Moors; but they were employed as Tyndale states. In the following November Henry avowed a league with Ferdinand, and sent him a farther reinforcement. Their proposed object was to aid pope Julius to recover Bologna &c. by obliging Louis to draw off his forces from Italy; but the result was the conquest of Navarre by the Spanish monarch.—Sh. Turner's Hen. VIII. B. I. ch. v. and Rymer's Fœdera, Vol. XIII. p. 342.]

[5 In the S. and S. edition they are called Zwitzers, as in the previous mention of the same people.]

to holy church as any Thomas ever was, seeing he was as able. Then the new Thomas, as glorious as the old, took the matter in hand and persuaded the king's grace. And then the king's grace took a dispensation for his oath, made upon the appointment of peace between him and the French king, and promised to help the holy seat, wherein pope Peter never sat. But the emperor Maximilian might in no wise stand still, lest the Frenchmen should money him, and get aid of him, seeing[6] the Almains refuse not money whencesoever it be proffered: then quoth[7] Thomas Wolfsee, 'Oh, and like your grace, what an honour should it be unto your grace if the emperor were your soldier! So great honour never chanced any king christened; it should be spoken of while the world stood; the glory and honour shall hide and darken the cost, that it shall never be seen, though it shall cost half your realm!' *Dixit et factum est*[8]. It was even so. And then a parliament, and then pay: and then upon the French dogs, with clean remission of all his sins that slew one of them; or if he be slain, (for the pardons have no strength to save in this life, but in the life to come only,) then to heaven straight without feeling of the pains of purgatory[9].

The new Thomas. W. T.

Maximilian the emperor was king Henry VIII. his soldier.

Remission of sins. W. T.

Then came our king with all his might, by sea and by land, and the emperor with a strong army, and the Spaniards, and the pope, and the Venetians, all at once against king Lewis of France. As soon as the pope had that he desired in Italy, then peace immediately: and Frenchmen were christian men; and pity, yea, and great sin also, were it to shed their blood; and the French king was 'The most christian king'

Note here the subtilty and craft of the pope.

[6 So M. and S. S. ed. but Day *since*.]

[7 Old editions, *quod*.]

[8 He spake and it was done. "The emperor Maximilian condescended to become one of Henry's soldiers for a hundred crowns a day."—Sharon Turner, B. I. ch. V.]

[9 In the "Articuli bullæ concessæ regi et proficiscentibus cum eo ad bellum contra Ludovicum Francorum regem," 1512, the second clause is as follows: Item qui in castris aut locis dictorum exercituum aliquod opus ad expeditionem hujusmodi necessarium vel opportunum fecerint, aut victualia vel alia necessaria pro opere expeditionis hujusmodi commorantium per se vel alium detulerint, simili modo plenissimam remissionem consequantur:—where the words 'simili modo' must be understood to imply the same thing as was expressed in the words "omnium peccatorum suorum de quibus corde contriti et ore confessi fuerint," in the first clause.—See Rymer, Vol. XIII. p. 343.]

again. And thus was peace concluded, and our Englishmen, or rather sheep, came home against winter, and left their fleeces behind them. Wherefore no small number of them, while they sought them better raiment at home, were hanged for their labour.

How king Henry VIII. with all his army was abused.

Why the king's sister was turned unto France.

When this peace was made, our holy cardinals and bishops (as their old guise is to calk and cast forty, fifty, yea, an hundred years before, what is like to chance unto their kingdom) considered how the emperor that now is[1] was most like to be chosen emperor after his grandfather Maximilian; for Maximilian had already obtained of divers of the electors that it should so be.

The prelates see ever beforehand what is like to follow.

They considered also how mighty he should be: first king of Spain, with all that pertaineth thereto, which was wont to be five, six, or seven kingdoms; then duke of Burgaine, earl of Flanders, of Holland, Zealand, and Brabande, with all that pertain thereto; then emperor; and his brother duke of Austria; and his sister queen of Hungary. Wherefore, thought our prelates, if we take not heed betimes, our kingdom is like to be troubled, and we to be brought under the feet. For this man shall be so mighty, that he shall with power take out of the French king's hands, out of the hands of the Venetians, and from the pope also, whatsoever pertaineth unto the empire, and whatsoever belongeth unto his other kingdoms and dominions thereto; and then will he come to Rome and be crowned there; and so shall he overlook our holy father and see what he doth: and then shall the old heretics rise up again, and say that the pope is antichrist, and stir up again, and bring to light, that we have hid and brought asleep with much cost, pain, and blood-shedding, more than this hundred years long. [They] considered also that his aunt is queen of England, and his wife the king of England's sister[2]; considered the old amity between the house of Burgaine and the old kings of England, so that they could never do aught

Papists are great fore-casters of perils.

[[1] Charles V.]

[[2] Henry's sister Mary had been affianced, and actually married by proxy, Dec. 17, 1508, to Charles, prince of Spain, the boy who was to inherit so many kingdoms. The documents are in Rymer, Tom. XIII. pp. 171—215, 219—31, 236—9.]

in France without their help; and last of all considered the course of merchandise that England hath in those parts, and also the natural hate that Englishmen bear to Frenchmen. Wherefore, if we shall use our old practice, and set the French king against him, then he shall lightly obtain the favour of the king of England, by the means of his aunt and his wife, and aid with men and money: wherefore we must take heed betimes, and break this amity; which thing we may by this our old craft easily bring to pass. Let us take a dispensation, and break this marriage, and turn the king's sister unto the French king: if the French king get a male of her, then we shall lightly make our king protector of France, and so shall England and France be coupled together; and as for the queen of England, we shall trim her well enough, and occupy the king with strange love, and keep her that she shall bear no rule. And as the gods had spoken, so it came to pass. Our fair young daughter was sent to the old pocky king of France[3], the year before our mortal enemy, and a miscreant worse than a Turk, and disobedient unto our holy father, and no more obedient[4] than he was compelled to be against his will.

Practice.

The king's sister sent to France.

The cause of the journey to Calais.

In short space thereafter Thomas Wolfsee, now cardinal, and legate a latere, and greatly desirous to be pope also, thought it exceeding expedient, for his many secret purposes, to bring our king and the king of France that now is[5] together, both to make a perpetual peace and amity between them, and that, while the two kings and their lords dallied together, the great cardinals and bishops of both parties might betray them both, and the emperor and all christian kings thereto.

Traitorous prelates.

Then he made a journey of gentlemen, arrayed altogether in silk, so much as their very shoes and lining of their boots, more like their mothers than men of war; yea, I am sure that many of their mothers would have been ashamed of so nice and wanton array[6]. Howbeit they went not to make war, but

[3 Louis XII. married the princess Mary Oct. 9, 1514, being then very nearly three times her age.]

[4 S. and S. ed. has *yet*.]

[5 Francis I. succeeded Louis XII. in 1515.]

[6 The kings of France and England met near Ardres, in the second

The pomp and apparel of the cardinal and his chaplains passed the twelve apostles.

peace, for ever and a day longer. But to speak of the pompous apparel of my lord himself, and of his chaplains, it passeth the twelve apostles. I dare swear that if Peter and Paul had seen them suddenly, and at a blush, they would have been harder of belief that they or any such should be their successors, than Thomas Didymus was to believe that Christ was risen again from death.

Prelates.

When all was concluded between the king of France and ours, that Thomas Wolfsee had devised, and when the prelates of both parties had cast their penny-worths against all chances, and devised remedies for all mischiefs; then the right reverend father in God, Thomas, cardinal and legate, would go see the young emperor newly chosen to the room, and have a certain secret communication with some of his prelates also; and gat him to Bruges, in Flanders, where he was received with great solemnity, as belongeth unto so mighty a pillar of Christ's church, and was saluted at the entering into the town of a merry fellow, which said, *Salve rex regis tui atque regni sui:* "Hail, both king of thy king, and also of his realm." And though there were never so great strife between the emperor and the French king, yet my lord cardinal juggled him favour of them both; and finally brought the emperor to Calais to the king's grace, where was great triumph, and great love and amity shewed on both parties[1]; insomuch that a certain man marvelling at it asked the old bishop of Dur-

Salutation. W. T.

Cardinal Wolsey was a subtle worker.

week of June, 1520. From the excessive pomp then displayed the place of meeting received the name of 'the field of the cloth of gold.']

[[1] Tyndale has here mingled statements which belong to two different interviews between Wolsey and Charles V. The emperor had come to Dover on the 25th of May, 1520, (where Wolsey had met him,) and had remained with Henry, about to repair to Ardres, till the 31st. On the 10th of July, Henry and the cardinal again met the emperor at Gravelines, from whence Charles returned with the English court to Calais. But it was on July 20th of 1521 that Wolsey, who had gone to Calais to act the impartial umpire between the French and imperial agents commissioned to meet him there, presently proceeded to Bruges, attended by English lords, knights and others, to the number of 460 horse, and was met by the emperor in person, a mile out of the town, who did him 'high honour and reverence.' Grafton's Chron. p. 1048. Sharon Turner says, 'The original letters from Henry, from Charles, and the cardinal, preserved in the British Museum, shew the knavery of this pretended mediation.'—Hist. Hen. VIII. B. I. ch. X. 2nd ed. Vol. I. p. 271.]

ham[2], how it might be that we were so great with the emperor, so shortly upon so strong and everlasting a peace made between us and the Frenchmen, the emperor and the king of France being so mortal enemies? My lord answered, 'That it might be well enough, if he wist all: but there was a certain secret (said he) whereof all men knew not[3].' Yea, verily, they have had secrets this eight hundred years; which though all the laymen have felt them, yet few have spied them, save a few Judases, which for lucre have been confederate with them, to betray their own kings and all other. A certain secret. W. T.

Then were we indifferent and stood still; and the emperor and the French king wrestled together; and Ferdinandus, the emperor's brother, won Milan of the Frenchmen, and the emperor Tournay[4], our great conquest; which yet, after so great cost in building a castle, we delivered up again to the Frenchmen, in earnest and hope of a marriage between the Dolphine and our princess. Milan. Tournay.

How the emperor came through England.

After that the emperor would into Spain, and came through England; where he was received in great honour, and with all that pertaineth to love and amity. The king's grace lent him money, and promised him more; and the emperor should tarry a certain years, and marry our princess: not that the cardinal intended that, thou mayest be sure; for it was not profitable for their kingdom; but his mind was to dally with the emperor, and to keep him without a wife, that (insomuch as he was young and lusty) he might have been noselled and The emperor came through England.

[[2] Thomas Ruthal, lord privy seal, was made bishop of Durham in 1509, and was near the close of his life when these interviews took place.]

[[3] Wolsey had secretly pledged his sovereign to invade France, with permission to pretend to be the faithful ally of its king for eighteen months more. But there was another secret article, by which the emperor and he pledged themselves to coerce and prosecute all and every one in their dominions, who should seem to entertain wrong opinions concerning the catholic faith, or endeavour to disturb the catholic faith or the apostolic see. The articles of this convention are dated Bruges, Aug. 25, 1521, and are quoted by Sharon Turner, B. I. ch. x., from the document in the Brit. Mus. Galba, B. 7. p. 104.]

[[4] Before the end of November, 1521.]

Nurturing of kings. W. T.

entangled with whores (which is their nurturing of kings), and made so effeminate and beastly, that he should never have been able to lift up his heart to any goodness or virtue; that cardinals and bishops might have administered his dominions in the mean time, unto our holy father's profit[1].

Practice. W. T.

The French king sendeth a defiance to king Henry VIII.

The king of France, hearing the favour that was shewed unto the emperor, sent immediately a defiance unto our king[2], not without our cardinals' and bishops' counsel, thou mayest well wit: for Frenchmen are not so foolish to have done it so unadvisedly and so rashly, seeing they had too many in their tops already. Then our king spake many great words, that he would drive the French king out of his realm, or else the French king should drive him out of his. But had he added, as the legate Pandulph taught king John, 'with the pope's licence,' his words had sounded much better: for there can no vow stand in effect, except the holy father confirmed it.

Armies sent into France.

We sent out our soldiers two summers against the Frenchmen, unto whose chief captains the cardinal had appointed how far they should go, and what they should do; and therefore the French king was nothing afraid, but brought all his power against the emperor in other places: and so was the emperor ever betrayed. And thus the cardinal was the emperor's friend openly, and the French king's secretly. For at the meeting with the French king beside Calais, he utterly betrayed the emperor, yet for no love that he had to France, but to

The cardinal was the emperor's friend openly, and the French king's secretly.

[[1] Charles V. landed at Dover May 26, 1522, being met there by cardinal Wolsey, who was attended by a splendid train at the king's especial command. Rymer, p. 767. On the 6th of June the emperor signed a document, preserved in Rymer, p. 769, obliging himself to pay Wolsey a pension of 7000 crowns of gold for his natural life, as an indemnity for what he was likely to lose by a breach with Francis. And on the third of July he signed another obligation pledging himself to secure to Wolsey an annual pension of 2500 ducats from the revenues of a Spanish bishoprick; which obligation is also amongst the documents printed in Rymer, Tom. XIII. p. 770.]

[[2] The contemporary chronicler, Grafton, says, that on the 21st of May Clarencieux king at arms, the English herald, came to the French king's chamber at Lyons; and said to him, 'Sir, I am charged to tell you that the king, my sovereign lord, holdeth you for his mortal enemy from this day forth;' and that Francis replied, 'I looked for this a great while agone: for sith the cardinal was at Bruges, I looked for none other.'—Grafton's Chron. Lond. 1569, p. 105.]

help the pope; yea, and to have been pope haply, and to save their kingdom: which treason though all the world smelled it, yet it brake not out openly to the eye till the siege of Pavie. And the cardinal lent the emperor much money openly; and gave the French king more secretly[3]. He played with both hands to serve their secret that all men know not, as the bishop of Durham said. But whatsoever the Frenchmen did, they had ever the worse, notwithstanding the secret working of our holy prelates on their side. The siege of Pavia.

Finally, unto the siege of Pavie came the French king personally with sixty thousand men of war, of which twelve thousand were horsemen, and with money enough. And the emperor's host was under twenty thousand, of which were but three thousand horsemen, with no money at all[4]: for he trusted unto the pope for aid of men, and unto our cardinal for money. But the pope kept back his men, till that the Frenchmen had given them a field; and our cardinal kept back his money for the same purpose[5]. And thus was the silly emperor betrayed, as all his predecessors have been this eight hundred years. Howbeit there be that say, that the emperor's soldiers so threatened Pace, the king's grace's ambassador, that he was fain to make chevisance with merchants for money, in the king's name, to pay the soldiers withal. Wherefore the cardinal took from him all his promotions, and played tormentors with him, when he came home; because he presumed to do one jot more than was in his commission[6]. Pavia. A false pope, and lewd cardinals. Pace, the king of England's ambassador.

[[3] In January, 1525, the emperor's ambassador in London brought Wolsey to confess, that an agent of the French queen regent had been eight months in London, and in communication with him.—Fiddes's Life of Wolsey, pp. 331—6.]

[[4] The chronicler Grafton makes the French king's army contain only half as many horse as Tyndale has stated; but the accuracy of Tyndale's information respecting the emperor's forces appears remarkable, when tested by the account transmitted to Henry from an English agent in Italy.—See Sharon Turner, pp. 394—5.]

[[5] In a letter now in the British Museum, Galba B. 8. 51, the English ambassador says to Wolsey, writing ten days before the battle, 'As for the king's money, your grace knoweth my commission is *after battle stricken.*']

[[6] Wolsey afterwards persecuted Pace till he became a beggar and a lunatic. S. Turner, B. I. c. XII. Vol. I. p. 355. But Mr. Turner attributes this persecution to a bold remonstrance against Wolsey's conduct, in a letter to the cardinal himself, penned by Pace in 1524.]

But, howsoever it was, the emperor's men, in tarrying for help, had spent out all their victuals. Whereupon Bourbon, the chief captain of the emperor, said unto his under captains: 'Ye see help cometh not, and that our victuals are spent; wherefore there is no remedy but to fight, though we be unequally matched. If we win, we shall find meat enough; if we lose, we shall lose no more than we must lose with hunger, though we fight not.' And so they concluded to set upon the Frenchmen by night. The king of France and his lords, supposing that the moon would sooner have fallen out of the sky than that the emperor's host durst have fought with them, were somewhat negligent, and went the same night a mumming that Bourbon set upon them. The emperor's host therefore with their sudden coming upon them amazed the Frenchmen, and drave them upon heaps together one on another, so that they never could come in array again; and took the king, and divers of his lords, and slew many and won the field. And there came out all the cardinal's privy treason: for in the French king's tent (say men) were letters found[1]; and beside that in the French king's treasure, and in all the host, among the soldiers were English ships found innumerable, which had come sailing a thousand miles by land. But what wonder? Ships be made to sail over the sea, and wings to fly into far countries, and to mount to the top of high hills.

Bourbon.

The emperor setteth upon the French king by night.

These ships were English angels of gold.

When the French king was taken, we sang Te Deum. But for all that singing we made peace with Frenchmen[2]: and the pope, the Venetians, France, and England, were knit together; lest the emperor's army should do any hurt in France. Whereby ye may conjecture of what mind the pope and the cardinal were toward the emperor[3], and with what heart our spiritualty, with their invisible secrets, sang Te

At the taking of the French king Te Deum was sung, and great triumph made in England.

[1 'Searching of the king's treasure, in his coffers there was found among them the league newly concluded between the king of England and the French King under the great seal of England.'—Cavendish's Life of Wolsey, by Singer, p. 80.]

[2 The peace was signed in England, Aug. 30, 1525. Id. p. 457.]

[3 The documents which afford evidence of Wolsey's personal hostility to the emperor at this time, and of that sovereign's knowledge of his abusive language, are cited by Sh. Turner, B. I. ch. XV. Vol. I. pp. 449—55.]

Deum. And from that time hitherto the emperor and our cardinal have been twain.

After that, when the king of France was delivered home again, and his sons left in pledge, many ways were sought to bring home the sons also: but in vain, except the French king would make good that which he had promised the emperor. For the bringing home of those children no man more busied his wits than the cardinal. He would in any wise the emperor should have sent them home; and it had been but for our king's pleasure, for the great kindness that he shewed him in times past. He would have married the king's daughter, our princess, unto the dolphine again, or, as the voice went among many, unto the second brother[4]; and he should have been prince in England, and king in time to come. So that he sought all ways to pluck us from the emperor, and to join us unto France; to make France strong enough to match the emperor, and to keep him down; that the pope might reign a god alone, and do what pleaseth[5] him, without controlling of any overseer. And for the same purpose he left nothing unprovided to bring the mart from Antwerp to Calais[6].

Subtle practices of the cardinal.

The mart should have been at Calais. W. T.

Why the queen must be divorced.

If the cardinal could by such means have made us French, the queen had been queen yet; yea, though she had not been his wife. Neither would he have been more about to separate her, than he hath been to separate other that indeed were not his wives, but hath been rather diligent to couple them to him, to pluck him from his right wife; lest, if she had been (as right is) in his favour, she should have given his grace better counsel for the realm than he hath followed; and lest also the prince's grace should have been moved through her more to have favoured the emperor.

But when there was found no other way, he inspired the king that the queen was not his wife, by the bishop of Lincoln

The bishop of Lincoln. W. T.

[4 At Amiens, Aug. 18, 1527, Wolsey stipulated with Francis that the duke of Orleans should marry her.—Rymer, Tom. XIV. p. 202.]

[5 S. and S. ed. has *pleased.*]

[6 All that follows, of this treatise, except the last three paragraphs, is omitted in S. and S. edition; and the largest part of it is also omitted by Day.]

his confessor, as the saying was[1]; by whom he hath breathed many things into his grace, and by whom he hath heard his confession, and by whom, and like hypocrites, he hath long betrayed him to have married him unto the king's sister of France, as the fame went, by that means at the last to make us French. And then the cardinal's doctors laid their heads together to seek subtle arguments and riddles to prove his divorcement. But all the chancellors of England (say men) which be all lawyers, and other doctors, mumpsimuses[2] of divinity, were called up suddenly to dispute the matter (under a colour to condemn Bilney and Arthur, heard I say), which is their old cast and subtilty, to pretend a contrary thing, and to cast a mist before the eyes of the people, to hide their juggling; that no man should once surmise whereabout they went. And the cardinal's secretaries ministered reasons unto them. And so the matter was discussed with a plain conclusion that he must be divorced. When the queen was warned, she desired learned counsel to defend her quarrel, that she should have no wrong; and it was granted her: and she chose. But, alas! what choice is there among the fox's whelps? All that be shaven be sworn together; and all that be promoted by them must play the Judases with them. They may, to blind the world withal, dispute one against another; but the conclusion shall be the pope's profit, prelates' pleasure, and the lusts of princes, which are their defenders. Finally it is concluded that the queen is not his wife; and the cause why they be not divorced, is peradventure that our prelates are afraid. If they could have brought any

[[1] The contemporary historian, Polydore Vergil, confirms what Catharine declared before Wolsey and Campegio, that Wolsey originated the divorce, because she had censured his dissolute life; and he then adds, "Is [scil. Wolsey] proinde quod cogitarat cum spe magna, id exequi cupiens, cum Joanne Longland, Lincolniensi episcopo, de quæstione futura amicè communicat, quod is esset qui regis confessionem audiret."—Angl. Hist. Lib. 27. p. 1730. Gand. 1557. He proceeds to say, that after this Wolsey first mentioned it to the king, but made little impression upon him, till Longland came to his aid.]

[[2] The allusion is to the well-known tale respecting an ignorant priest, who used to say '*Mumpsimus Domine,*' where his Latin service-book had *sumpsimus*, and being told what he ought to say, replied that he had used the word *mumpsimus* for 30 years, and would not leave his old mumpsimus for a new *sumpsimus*.]

marriage about, to join us unto France, it had been done long since; but because they cannot (for the French king's sister knew too much of Christ to consent unto such wickedness), haply they would it were undone[3]. I doubt not but they bear the king's grace in hand that the pope dare not confirm it for fear of the emperor; but I doubt not, if they feared not the emperor and the lords and commons, it had been done already.

After that my lord cardinal with More, his sworn secretary, and the bishop of London, that still Saturn, the imaginer of all mischief[4], went to France to juggle secretly, and carried with him more than he brought home again. This is of a truth, that he carried great treasure with him. The French galleys lay long in Thames' mouth, and not for nought. The fame went plain, yea, and I know also one that saw in my lord cardinal's court letters sealed with the king's great seal, wherein was contained that the French king should have of us money sufficient for to find twenty thousand men against the emperor in Italy, from the second day of July, in the year of our Lord fifteen hundred twenty-seven, forward[5].

But among all other, as soon as the pope was taken[6], the cardinal wrote unto the emperor that he should make him pope. And when he had got an answer that pleased him not, but according unto his deservings toward the emperor, then he waxed furious mad, and sought all means to displease the

[3 Polydore Vergil, in reference to the circumstance, says: 'Quamvis re vera princeps illa, mulier optima, noluerit quicquam audire de nuptiis, quæ nuptiæ non possent conjungi sine miserabili Catharinæ casu.'—p. 1735. It is well known that Margaret was favourable to the reformation.]

[4 Grafton says, 'The 22d day of July [1527] the cardinal departed out of Calice, and with him was the lord Cutberd Tunstall, bishop of London, Sir Thomas More, &c.'—p. 1151.]

[5 The treaty which the cardinal made with Francis is given in Rymer.]

[6 Day had omitted all the previous part of this chapter; and begins this paragraph as follows; 'But at that time the pope, taking part with the French king, had war with the emperor; and at the last the pope was taken, &c.' The text of Day then proceeds in agreement with that of the first, or Marburg edition, to the close of the next paragraph, with which Day finishes the chapter.]

emperor[1], and imagined this[2] divorcement between the king and the queen, and wrote sharply unto the emperor with menacing letters, that if he would not make him pope, he would make such ruffling between christian princes as was not this hundred year, to make the emperor repent: yea, though it should cost the whole realm of England.

A ruffler. W. T.

The Lord Jesus be our shield! What a fierce wrath of God is this upon us, that a misshapen monster should spring out of a dunghill into such a height that, the dread of God and man laid apart, he should be so malapert, not only to defy utterly the majesty of so mighty an emperor, whose authority both Christ and all his apostles obeyed, and taught all other to obey, threatening damnation to all them that would not; but should also set so little by the whole realm of England, which hath bestowed so great cost and shed so much blood to exalt and maintain such proud, churlish, and unthankful hypocrites, that he should not care to destroy it utterly for the satisfying of his villainous lusts.

The pride and arrogance of cardinal Wolsey.

The emperor sent forth a little book in print, both in Spanish and also in Dutch, in which he answereth unto the cardinal's menacing, and unto many articles that the cardinal layeth against him, and among all other repeateth this threatening of the cardinal. 'Ye will (saith the emperor) to do me displeasure, if I will not make you pope, set such a ruffling among christian princes as was not this hundred year, though it should cost you the whole realm of England.' Whereunto the emperor answereth, saying, 'Ye go about to give your king another wife, which if you do, it may be the next way to cost you the realm of England.' And I believe verily, that the prophecy of this caitiff Caiaphas, the cardinal, through the mischief that he hath wrought for the divorcement of the marriage, shall be fulfilled, and that it will cost the whole realm of England, if it be not seen to betimes. By what means, I will shew you after that I have spoken a word or two of this divorcement.

The emperor writeth against the cardinal. W. T.

[[1] See Sh. Turner, Hist. Hen. VIII. ch. xx. Vol. II. p. 150—1.]
[[2] So M. ed., but D. has *the*.]

Of the divorcement.

If the king's most noble grace will needs have another wife, then let him search the laws of God, whether it be lawful or not; forasmuch as he himself is baptized to keep the laws of God, and hath proposed them and hath sworn them. If the law of God suffer it, then let his grace put forth a little treatise in print, and even in the English tongue, that all men may see it, for his excuse and the defence of his deed, and say, 'Lo, by the authority of God's word do I this.' And then let not his grace be afraid either of the emperor, or of his lords, or of his commons and subjects: for God hath promised to keep them that keep his laws. If we care to keep his laws, he will care for the keeping of us, for the truth of his promises. If it be found unlawful, then let his grace fear God, and cease to shame himself and his blood, his lords, his subjects, and his realm, and specially the blessed name of our Saviour Jesus Christ, and his holy doctrine, and the profession of our faith: for whosoever professeth the faith of Christ, and liveth contrary unto his doctrine, shameth the name of our Saviour Jesus Christ. Moreover whatsoever God coupled, man may not loose, no, though he name himself pope. Wherefore, if this marriage be of God, the pope cannot dispense with it: for God hath given no power against himself; but to preach his ordinances only hath he given power. Therefore if we will see what is right and what is wrong, let us bring it unto the light of God's law, and let us submit our causes unto the judgment thereof, and be content to have our appetites slain thereby, that we lust no farther than God's ordinance giveth us liberty. For verily to desire more than God permitteth, is to tempt God, and to provoke wrath and indignation upon us, unto our destruction, as the children of Israel did under Moses, and perished: whose froward deeds are warning for us (saith Paul, 1 Cor. x.) that we, feared with the terrible ensample of their fall, should abstain from like wickednesses.

The pope hath no authority against God. W. T.

1 Cor. x.

The controversy and strife of the matter, and all the doubt and difficulty, standeth in this, that Moses in the xviiith of Leviticus saith, "Thou shalt not unhele[3] the secrets of thy brother's wife, for they are thy brother's secrets." Which is as

The cause that maketh the doubt, whether a man may marry his brother's wife. W. T.

[[3] Unhele, i. e. uncover.]

Lev. xviii. much to say as, thou shalt not take thy brother's wife. And Deut. xxv. in the xxvth of Deuteronomy he saith, "That if a man die without issue, his brother must marry his wife." Which two texts seem contrary, the one forbidding, the other commanding, a man to take his brother's wife. Wherefore, that we may come unto the true sense and clear meaning of these two texts, and that we may perceive also the ground of the reason that may be made by both parties by the occasion of these texts, and see which reasons do conclude, ye shall understand that the law of Moses is divided into three parts. Part of his laws are ceremonies, that is to say, signs that put men in remembrance either of the benefits of God done already, as the Easter lamb; either signs of the promise and appointment made between God and man, as circumcision; or signs that testify unto the people that the wrath of God is peaced, and their sins forgiven, as all manner sacrifices: which all ceased as soon as Christ had offered up the sacrifice of his body and blood for us; and instead of them come the open preaching of Christ, and our signs which we call sacraments.

The law of ceremonies. W. T.

Another sort are laws of penalty or punishment to avenge sin, if it break out and hurt a man's neighbour, as tooth for tooth, eye for eye, and that the blood-shedder must have his blood shed again, and the breaker of wedlock must be stoned: which laws were given unto the Jews only, and we heathen or Gentiles are not bound unto them, that we should punish every sin after the same manner; but it is enough that every land punish their trespassers as it seemeth best for the commonwealth there, some of one manner and some of another.

The law of penalty. W. T.

Another part pertain unto faith and love; and that a man believe how that there is but one God, and that he is true, good and merciful in all things; and therefore ought to be believed, trusted and loved with all a man's heart, soul, mind and strength; and that a man love his neighbour as himself, for God's sake, which hath created him and made him. And this is the law of nature, and pertaineth unto all nations indifferently, with all that dependeth or followeth thereof. This law was also before Moses; insomuch that though Moses had never written it, yet had the Jews been no less bound thereto by nature and by natural right and equity. For whosoever is of God, the same consenteth unto this law, and unto all that followeth thereof naturally, when he heareth it preached;

The law natural. W. T.

as he consenteth that the fire is hot, when he putteth his finger in it.

Moreover, whosoever hath this law graven in his heart, this same keepeth all laws; and whosoever hath it not written in his heart, the same keepeth no law. For whosoever believeth that there is one God, and loveth him with all his heart, with all his soul, mind and strength, (which is the first of the ten commandments pertaining unto the person of God,) the same will worship nothing of his own imagination without God's word; and then he can make none image to worship it: which is the second commandment pertaining unto the person of God. He cannot also, for very love sake, take the name of God in vain and swear by it unreverently: and so thou hast the third commandment pertaining unto the person of God. Furthermore, he that believeth God and hath his trust only in him, and loveth him as I said, cannot but keep his holy day, not after Moses's fashion, but spiritually: that is, he cannot but observe a time to wait on God's word, to hear it, and learn it, and to knowledge his sins to God, and to desire him of mercy, according to his promises and testament which he hath made with us: and so thou hast the fourth commandment pertaining unto the person of God. Last of all, he that so loveth God cannot disobey father and mother, in which two names are contained all high powers; as grandfather, grandmother, aunt, uncle, king, lord, master, husband, and so forth, persons here in God's stead, by which he made us, and by which he feedeth us, clotheth us, governeth us, teacheth and ruleth us. And thus thou hast the five commandments, which all pertain unto the person of God: for the obedience of father and mother, and of all high powers which rule the world in God's stead, pertaineth unto the person of God, and must be done with love as unto God's self.

All laws spring out of one. W. T.

Furthermore, he that loveth God hath this commandment also, that he love his brother or neighbour, in the fourth chapter of the first epistle of John. For how can a man love the father, and hate the son, whom the father loveth? Even so how canst thou love God the Creator, and hate that creature whom he hath created and made after his own likeness; and so loveth him, that he hath made him lord over all other creatures, and thereto hath given his own Son unto the death for his sake, to shew him kindness, that he might

1 John iv.

see love, and to love again? How also can I love our Saviour Jesus Christ, and hate him whom he hath bought with his blood? Though the son be never so evil, yet if I love his father heartily, I cannot but be sorry that the son is evil, and wish him good in mine heart, and help to the uttermost of my power to make him better, even for his father's sake: until I see him run so far that he go about to slay his father; which thing if he do, then I resist him unto the uttermost of my power. Even so, though my neighbour be never so evil, yet as long as I love God, and Christ our Saviour, with all mine heart, I cannot but love him, and help to better him with all my power; until he run so far, that he beginneth to fight against God, and to destroy the law of God, and the testament that God hath made unto man: then I resist him with all my power, as God hath taught me to resist.

Now if I love my neighbour in God faithfully and unfeignedly, then I cannot find in my heart to slay him: neither to defile his wife: neither to steal his goods: nor to bear false witness against him: neither can mine heart covet his house, wife, man-servant or maid from him, either ox, ass, or whatsoever is his. And thus hast thou other five of the ten commandments, pertaining all unto the person of thy neighbour. This is the law of nature, whose servants Moses and the prophets were, to teach it the Jews; and whose servant Christ our Saviour was, for our sakes, with his apostles, to teach it us. And it is an everlasting law, and pertaineth indifferently to all nations, with all that hangeth thereof; insomuch that though a man be never taught it, yet if it be not found written in his heart, he is the heir of damnation.

Solutions. W. T.

Now they that study to make this divorcement between the king's grace and the queen, will haply say, that the first text is a law depending of the law natural, (for, undoubted, it is no ceremony, nor yet law of penalty,) and therefore pertaineth unto all men indifferently, and ought to be kept of all nations; and that the second is a ceremony, and therefore ceaseth at the coming of Christ. I answer: If it be a ceremony, then it is a sign, and must have a signification. It must signify some benefit of God done already, or some vengeance taken for sin, or some promise, or something that I must do or leave undone at the commandment of God. Now the signification of it they will shew me, when our lady hath a new son.

Ceremonies have significations. W. T.

Moreover, there is no ceremony of Moses, but that I may keep it this day as an indifferent thing; howbeit, not as a thing so necessary unto my soul's health, that I should think that I sinned if I did not. But I may eat the Easter lamb of passover every year, when the time cometh, if I will. And I may circumcise myself for my pleasure, as well as pare my nails, if I list. And I may burn the blood and fat of oxen and calves unto this day without sin, as an indifferent thing; and give this signification thereto, that as the fat consumeth in the fire, even so doth the sin of all men that repent consume in the hot fire of the love of God to us-ward in Christ Jesus the Lord; and so forth. If it be a ceremony, then, how happeneth it that this one ceremony is unlawful among all other? Ceremonies be made of lawful things W. T.

Thereto, inasmuch as Moses in all his laws sought the glory of God and the pureness of his people, as he boasteth of himself, (Deut. iv.), saying, "What nation hath ordinances and laws so righteous as all this law, which I set before you?" how cometh it that Moses was driven into so great a strait, that he would find nought to make a ceremony of, but that which of his own nature is damnable sin, and filthy among the heathen; which heathen made as just laws, out of the law natural graven in their hearts, as Moses did? Might not the heathen of good right say, "See what a filthy nation it is, they marry every one his brother's wife, as hounds?" And so the law shamed the name of God, and honoured it not. If Moses gave his people two contrary commandments, then he was an indiscreet lawgiver, yea, and devilish thereto; for then I cannot but be damned whatsoever I do. If a man say that the first pertaineth unto us heathen, and the last unto the people of Israel, that soundeth not; for when all the other laws contained in the same chapter, and in all his books, pertained unto the same people, how should he, among so many belonging unto them, mingle one for us heathen only, to whom he was no lawgiver; and namely when he wist that one as wise as he should come and teach us, which is our Saviour Jesus Christ? Deut. iv.

If a man will say, the first is a law, and the second a permission, as the permission of divorcements, when a man did hate his wife: nay, verily, it is not a permission, but a flat commandment, and that under pain of great shame and rebuke unto the man, if he did it not, and under the loss of all her husband's possession unto the woman, if she offered not herself. Of which law, also, because thou needest not to dream of a ceremony, a man may shew a good natural reason, profitable unto the commonwealth. For a woman, when she is married, she forsaketh her father's kin, and bringeth her dowry with her, and taketh her name among her husband's kin. Now if her husband die childless, it is not reason that she should be cast out of the kin empty, neither is it right that she should carry her husband's possessions out of his kin away with her, and that a stranger should get a child of her, to possess them. Thou wilt say, that the lands might return unto the next of his kin, and the wife have a portion her life long only. Then should great possessions come into the hands of one man, and so should there many tyrants rise among the people: which to avoid, God ordained that the lands should be scattered ever among as many as might be of the same kin; and for the same cause would suffer no man to buy any lands for ever. For God thinketh it better for his commonwealth, that twenty should spend twenty or forty shillings apiece, than that one should spend twenty or forty pounds, and nineteen never a whit: for then must many poor hang on one rich; which rich for the most part be of corrupt minds, and so sensual that they will look on no man to do him good, except it will be on such as will follow their lusts. And so should the people follow the will of man, and not of God; and be compelled to live wickedly, and to murder, steal, and oppress their brethren, to fill their bellies withal.

Moreover, it was a law in the time of the law natural, four hundred years before Moses, that a man should marry his brother's wife, as thou seest Genesis xxxviii. Also, Moses forbiddeth not a man, when his wife is dead, to marry her sister. If one man may marry two sisters, why may not one woman marry two brethren? Are not two sisters as nigh of kin as two brethren?

Gen. xxxviii.

How the text is to be understood. W. T.

Wherefore I see no remedy, but that a man must understand the text thus: That Moses forbiddeth a man to take his brother's wife as long as his brother liveth; as in the text following, when he forbiddeth a man to take his neighbour's wife, he meaneth while his neighbour liveth; for after his death it is lawful. And therefore John rebuked Herod for taking his brother's wife from him, his brother being yet alive. Or at the uttermost, if they will strive and shew no cause why, it can extend no further than that a man may not take his brother's wife, if he have issue by her; which I suppose an indifferent thing to have her or not, as they can agree: but if his brother die childless, then he ought to have her, and that she is bound to offer herself to the other brother, by the law of Moses; and that it is lawful now, though no commandment.

If it be understood of a man's brother's wife, he being alive, then haply ye will say that it is superfluously added of Moses; for it is included in that which followeth immediately, that a man shall not take his neighbour's wife. Nay, verily: for it is another sin, and a more greater sin for a man to take his brother's wife than his neighbour's wife, that is no kin to him; because that my neighbour's shame is not my shame. For let my neighbour be hanged, and no man casteth that in my teeth. But my brother's shame is my shame, and the shame of my father and mother, and of all my kin. For let whatsoever rebuke bechance my brother, and it is cast in my teeth, and in the teeth of my father and mother, and of all my kin immediately. Wherefore, to be so forgetful of natural honesty, that I should defile my brother's wife unto mine own shame and all my kin, is more grievous and heinous (as they say), and springeth of greater lewdness or malice, than to take my neighbour's wife which is not of my kin. And this doth the xxth chapter of the said Leviticus prove, where Moses saith, If a man lie with his Lev. xx. brother's wife, they shall die immediately, and not tarry the birth: as Judah would have burnt Tamar, his daughter-in- Gen. xxxviii. law, being yet great with child.

They will haply say also, that if it be to be understood of a man's brother's wife, while his brother liveth, then they will understand of the father's and uncle's wives also, while the father and uncle live. Nay, verily, it is far unlike. For my father's wife and mine uncle's wife are my superiors, and persons unto whom I owe obedience by the means of my father and uncle. Now if I should marry them, then I should make them my servants, (for the wife must obey her husband;) and so pervert I the law of nature and natural equity and honesty. Ye will say that when my father and uncle be dead, the obedience is loosed. Verily, it might well stand with the pope's doctrine; for he thrusteth kings down and emperors thereto, and exalteth their sworn subjects into their rooms: he raketh one out of the dunghill on the one day, and out of the most low and vile kind of subjection, and maketh him on the morrow superior unto his own prince, and to all the lords of his realm, in worldly pomp and dignity. But God teacheth his children to humble themselves; and Christ teacheth his disciples to come lower and lower. I suppose, therefore, that a man ought much more to do them service, and obey them, and to give them honour and reverence now after the deaths of their husbands, than before. Moreover, ye see that a man may not marry his daughter-in-law after his son's death, by the story of Judah. And again, ye see that David, after the death of his son Absalom, would not meddle with his own wives, which his son Absalom had before corrupt, but shut them up in perpetual widowhood. Now if the father, after the death of his son, abstain from her that was one flesh with his son, for natural reverence; how much more ought the son, after the death of his father, to abstain from her that was one flesh with his father, to whom also, by the reason of his father, he oweth obedience thereto!

Moreover, if a woman should find a man-child by the streets, and bring him in, and find him up of nought; I would not by my will that she should after marry with him, for perverting of due obedience, which she should haply as unnaturally, even so shrewdly, give unto him again. If she obeyed not, with what face should he correct her? If he corrected her, what would she cast in his teeth, and what wondering would neighbours make? What reverence and service then suppose ye would nature (if we were not so corrupt-minded) teach us to give unto the father's and uncle's wife?

And to go through all the degrees that are forbidden: the mother, grandmother, aunts, father's wife and uncle's wife, are persons to be obeyed as God, with all reverence and service. The daughter and daughter's daughter, and son's daughter, are a man's wife's flesh. The wife's mother and grandmother are persons to be obeyed, besides that the wife is your flesh. Now between a man and his wife's sister, when she is dead, and his brother's wife, when his brother is dead, is there no such cause as between these persons.

And concerning the maid-children, though they be under the obedience of their uncles; yet because, if any be married unto her uncle, she bideth in obedience still, therefore it is not utterly forbidden. And ensamples there be, that maidens have married unto their uncles: which thing yet I could not have drawn into a common use without necessity, or for a commonwealth.

And concerning the sister; she is of egal birth to her brother. It is to be feared, therefore, lest her obedience would be less to her brother than to a stranger. Then note the grief of father and mother, if they agreed not. Moreover, if he were an unkind husband, then had she double sorrow; first, because he is unkind, and also because she hath lost the comfort of a brother. Then the familiar bringing up together. And beside all those and such like, there is yet another, (which I think the chiefest of all,) that the sending out of daughters into another kin, and receiving again out of another kin, is the greatest cause of peace and unity that is in the world. And therefore the heathen people forbad that degree in the laws.

Nevertheless, the marriage of the brother with the sister is not so grievous against the law of nature (thinketh me) as the degrees above rehearsed. And therefore it seemeth me, that it might be dispensed with in certain cases, and for divers considerations. It would be hard to prove that Sarah was not Abraham's sister, whom I think he married because there was none other faithful woman that believed in God. Moreover, the greatest cause to send the daughter out is unity and peace between divers kindreds.

Wherefore, if greater peace and unity might be made with keeping her at home, I durst dispense with it: as, if the king of England had a son by one wife, heir to England, and a daughter by another, heir to Wales; then, because of the great war that was ever wont to be between those two countries, I would not fear to marry them together, for the making of a perpetual unity, and to make both countries one, for to avoid so great effusion of blood. For which cause, I would God that our princess had been married unto the king of Scots. And I doubt not but that had been concluded long ago, if it had been as greatly unto the profit of the pope and his pilpates, (I would say prelates,) as it were to the honour of God. But it is not profitable for them that any kingdom should be strong and mighty, lest, if God should open the eyes of the king, the pope should have too much ado to resist him, and to send in other kings upon him, to conquer his realm.

I did my diligence a long season, to know what reasons our holy prelates should make for their divorcement; but I could not come by them. I searched what might be said for their part, but I could find no lawful cause of myself, by any scripture that I ever read: I communed with divers learned men of the matter, which also could tell me no other way than I have shewed. Then I considered the falsehood of our spiritualty, how that it is but their old practice, and a common custom; yea, and a sport to separate matrimony, for to make division where such marriage made unity and peace. Wherefore I could not but declare my mind, to discharge my conscience withal; which thing I had done long since, if I could have brought it to pass. Howbeit, I had lever now do it at the last, than that any man should cast me in the teeth in time to come, when this old marriage were broken, and a new made, why I had not spoken rather[1]? Neither can the king's grace, or any other christian man, of right be discontent with me. For it is not possible that any person baptized in the heart with repentance of evil, and with faith of forgiveness in the blood of Christ, and stedfast purpose and profession of heart to walk henceforth after the steps of Christ, in the law of God, should once desire or will to do aught openly, with long deliberation, that he would not have compared with the law of God, to see whether it were right or not.

Some man might haply say, that though a great man would be content to have his deeds compared unto the laws of God, he would disdain yet to have so vile a wretch as I am to dispute of them.

I answer, that it is not my fault, but God's, which for the most part even chooseth of the vilest to confound the glorious; which not only clothed his Son with our vile nature, but made him also of the very lowest sort of man, even five hundred

[[1] That is, *earlier*.]

steps beneath the degree of a cardinal, and sent him to rebuke the scribes and the Pharisees which sat on Moses' seat, for their evil doing and false doctrine, beside the law of Moses. And the glorious scribes and the Pharisees, for all their holiness, rebuked not Herod; nor Caiphas and Annas, for all their highness; but vile John the Baptist. By what authority? Verily, by the authority of God's word; which only, whatsoever garment she wear, ought to have all authority among them that have professed it. That word is the chiefest of the apostles, and pope, and Christ's vicar, and head of the church, and the head of the general council. And unto the authority of that ought the children of God to hearken without respect of person; for they that are of God, hear God's word. (John vi.) John vi.
And Christ's sheep hear Christ's voice (John x.), yea, though John x.
he speak by a calf.

Ye will haply say, my reasons be not good. They may be the sooner solved, and shall thereto make the contrary part better, and set it out, and make it appear to all men's sight, and stablish it; and so they shall do good every way.

By what means the divorcement should cost the realm.

Now to that I promised, how that I would shew you by what means this marriage might cost the realm of England, according to Caiphas the cardinal's blind prophecy. This is first as sure as the winter followeth the summer, that our prelates have utterly determined that this marriage that is between the king and the queen must be broken; and so is the princess disinherited, and the king of Scots next to the crown. And we may fortune to find one at home, which, because he is near hand, would look to step in before him; and it may chance thereto that another yet will look to come in, as soon as any of both: peradventure, the third born at home may make friends likewise; yea, and so forth. And then, while ye shed each other's blood, our prelates will sit and laugh, and look upon you out of sanctuary; and when every man hath done his best, they will think to make them a defender, wheresoever shall please them best.

The king's grace, will ye say, shall have another wife, and she shall bear him a prince, and he shall break strife. Who hath promised him a prince? Moreover, if his new marriage be not well proved, and go forth with good authority, so shall we yet follow the princess still; or, if she be sent another way, some other, whom we shall suppose more righteous inheritor: and so the new prince is like to go after king Henry of Windsor's prince, and king Edward's children.

And I will tell you yet another sport. As soon as the cardinal had sent the emperor a defiance, and upon that defiance had arrested the emperor's ships in England, and our ships and men were arrested also in all regions of the emperor; then went the common fame throughout all Dutchland, that the emperor's council, Holland, Braband, and Zealand, had determined, if the war had proceeded, to have set up the king of Denmark that was, to have challenged his right in England. For the Danes challenge England, as we challenge France; and the king of Denmark writeth himself king of England, as our king writeth himself king of England and France. And this is once: the old king of Denmark, with his son, a goodly prince if he had lands, shall never come in Denmark again, of any likelihood[1]. Wherefore, if ye fall together by the ears, may he not by some chance, if God be angry with you, make an appointment with the king of Scots to come in upon you on the one side, and make for his part what friends he can in Dutchland, and send unto the new king of Denmark, and give up his title for ever to get rid of him, so to come in on the other side, and conquer you? And twenty other ways are ye like to come in danger; which I commit unto your own consideration.

The putting down of the cardinal[2].

Cardinal Wolsey a great traitor.

And finally, concerning the cardinal's putting down, I consider many things: first, that I never heard or read that any man, being so great a traitor, was so easily put to death: then the natural disposition and inclination of the man, how that his chief study, yea, and all his felicity and inward joy, hath ever been to exercise that 'angel's wit of his' (as my lord of Lincoln was wont to praise him) in driving of such drifts to

[1 Christiern II., king of Denmark and Norway, and at the beginning of his reign king of Sweden also, had lost all his kingdoms by disgusting his subjects with his cruelty and treachery. He reigned over Denmark from 1513 to 1523; when he was finally expelled, and superseded by his uncle, Frederic duke of Sleswick.]

[2 Day's edition resumes the Marburg text again with the words, *concerning the cardinal's putting down.*]

beguile all men, and to bind the whole world withal. Wherefore I can none otherwise judge by an hundred tokens, evident unto whomsoever hath a natural wit, but that this is also nothing save a cast[3] of his old practice; so that when God had wrapped him in his own wiles, that he wist not which way out, (for the emperor prevailed for all the cardinal's treason, and the French children might not come home,) and he had learned also of his necromancy, this would be a jeopardous year for him, what for the treason that he had wrought against the emperor, and what for the money which he had borrowed of the commons, lest any rising should be against him, then he thought to undo his destiny with his policies, and went and put down himself under a colour (which the process of the tragedy well declareth), and set up in his room, to minister forth, and to fight against God as he had begun, the chiefest of all his secretaries, one nothing inferior unto his master in lying, feigning, and bearing two faces in one hood; a whelp that goeth not out of kind from his sire; the chiefest tasle wherewith the cardinal caught the king's grace, whom he called unto the confirmation of all that he intended to persuade, saying, 'If it like your grace, More is a learned man, and knoweth it, and is also a layman, wherefore he will not say otherwise than it is, for any partiality to us-ward:' which secretary yet must first deserve it with writing against Martin[4], and against 'The Obedience,' and 'Mammon,' and become the proctor of purgatory, to write against 'The supplication of beggars[5].'

Cardinal Wolsey committeth treason against the emperor.

Cardinal Wolsey preferred More to be chancellor.

And then, to blind the world withal, many quarrels were picked: the cardinal might not speak with the king's grace; the broad seal was fetched away; high treason was laid to his charge: first, that he had breathed (heard I say) in the king's face, when he had the French pox: (O hypocrites!) but the very treason that he had wrought was not spoken of at all, nor ought worthy of a traitor done to him at all[6].

Treason laid to the cardinal's charge.

[3 A calculated contrivance.]

[4 Martin Luther.]

[5 A sarcastic attack on the mendicant friars, composed by Simon Fish. It may be seen in Foxe's Acts and Mon.]

[6 The disgusting charge noticed in this paragraph was the subject of Art. 6 in the 44 charges preferred against Wolsey in parliament.—Fiddes' Life of Wolsey, App. of documents, pp. 215—23.]

Then they called a parliament (as though the golden world should come again), wherein the hypocrites, to blear men's eyes withal, made a reformation of mortuaries, and probates of testaments; the root yet left behind, whence all that they have for a time weeded out will spring again by little and little as before, if they, as their hope is, may stop this light of God's word that is now abroad. They made also a reformation of pluralities of benefices, ordaining that henceforth no man may come by plurality of benefices with virtue and cunning, but with serving for them in the court[1]. Which what other thing is it save plain simony? O blind buzzards and shameless hypocrites! what care they to do, whether against God or their own laws, to flatter great men withal and to blind them! But hark here: the tithes were ordained, at the beginning, to find the preachers and the poor people, which now go a begging; so that the church-wardens ought to take the benefices into their hands in the name of the parishens, and to deliver the preachers of God's word their dwelling and present a sufficient living, and divide the rest among the poor people. And the king is bound to maintain that order, and not to resist them, except he will be an open tyrant. Now I appeal to the consciences of the king's grace and of his lords. What answer will they give, when they come before Christ in the last judgment, for their robbing of so many souls in so many parishes of God's word, with holding every man so many chaplains in their houses with pluralities of benefices, and for the robbing of so many poor and needy of their due and daily food; whose need, for lack of succour, crieth to God continually for vengeance against them, which we see daily, by a thousand misfortunes, fall on them and on their wives and children? Let them read Exodus and Deuteronomy, and see what they find there. Yea, and what shall so many chaplains do? First

Mortuaries, probate of testaments.

Pluralities of benefices.

Tithes.

The church-wardens have been accustomed to gather the tithes, and to give the parson his reasonable stipend, and to give the rest to the poor.

Princes have here much to answer.

[1 Cunning is here used for learning. Tyndale alludes to the statute 21 Henry VIII. c. 13, which had just been enacted, to abridge 'Spiritual persons from having pluralities of livings;' but its seeming stringency was rendered nugatory by the proviso in § 28, which said, 'Provided alway that this act shall not in any way extend, ne be prejudicial to any such chaplains as shall be daily or quarterly attending and abiding in the king's or queen's most honorable housholds'—'and so for chaplains of nobles, &c.']

slay their souls, and then defile their wives, their daughters, and their maidens, and last of all betray them.

When this reformation, the colour and cloak of their hypocrisy, was made, then the spiritualty came ducking before the king's grace, and forgave him the money which they had lent their pope to bring in the temporalty; and to make them after their example to do likewise, as loving subjects, and no less kind unto their prince than the spiritualty[2]. Whereupon the temporalty forgave their part also, in hope of that they obtained not: for as soon as the loan was forgiven, the parliament broke up; because our prelates, and their confederate friends, had found that they sought, and caught the fish for which they laid the bait of all those faces of reformations; and for which the cardinal, to bring the world into a fool's paradise, was compelled even with his own good will to resign his chancellorship, and that to whom he listed himself. And as for the bishoprick of Durham, to say the very truth, he could not of good congruity but reward his old chaplain, and one of the chief of all his secretaries withal, still Saturn, that so seldom speaketh, but walketh up and down all day musing and imagining mischief, a ducking hypocrite, made to dissemble[3]: which, for what service done in Christ's gospel came he to the bishoprick of London; or what such service did he therein? He burnt the new Testament, calling it *Doctrinam peregrinam*, 'strange learning[4].' Yea, verily, look how strange his living, in whose blood that testament was made, was from the living of the pope; even so strange is that doctrine from the pope's law, in which only, and in the practice thereof, is Tunstal learned. Which also, for what cause left he the bishoprick of London? Even for the same cause he took it, after that he had long served for it, covetousness and ambition. Neither is it possible naturally, that there should be any good bishop, so long

The loan first forgiven by the clergy.

The loan forgiven by the temporalty.

The bishoprick of Durham.

Tonstal bishop of Durham burnt the new Testament.

[2 A coarse expression is here omitted.]

[3 Wolsey held the bishoprick of Durham in commendam with the archbishoprick of York from 1523 to 1529, when he resigned Durham in favour of Tonstal, but took possession of the see of Winchester. He also held the rich abbey of St Alban's in commendam; and the bishoprics of Bath, Worcester, and Hereford in farm, because the incumbents were foreigners.—Cavendish's Wolsey, Vol. I. p. 32. Singer's ed. Also Lord Herbert's Hen. VIII. p. 57.]

[4 See Life of Tyndale, p. xxxviii.]

A bishoprick is a superfluous honour, and a lewd liberty.

as the bishopricks be nothing save worldly pomp and honour, superfluous abundance of all manner riches, and liberty to do what a man listeth unpunished; things which only the evil desire, and all good men abhor.

The cardinal clearly discharged.

And as soon as the parliament was ended, the cardinal had his charter, and gat him home; and all bishops gat them every fox to his hole; leaving yet their attornies behind them, to come again themselves as soon as the constellation is somewhat overrun, whereof they be afraid.

What the cause of all this mischief is.

Whence cometh all this mischief? Verily it is the hand of God to avenge the wantonness of great men, which will walk without the fear of God, following the steps of the high prelates, contrary unto their profession; and to avenge also the wrongs, the blasphemies, and subtle persecuting of his word.

Defender of the faith. W. T.

For when Martin Luther had uttered the abominations of the pope and his clergy with God's word, and divers books were come into England, our cardinal thought to find a remedy against that well enough, and sent to Rome for this vain title, 'Defender of the faith;' which the vicar of Croydon preached that the king's grace would not lose for all London, and twenty miles round about it. Neither is it marvel: for it had cost more than London and forty miles about it is able to make (I think) at this hour; beside the effusion of innocent blood that was offered unto the idol, and daily is offered thereto. When this glorious name was come from our holy father, the cardinal brought it unto the king's grace at Greenwich. And though the king had it already, and had read it, yet against the morning were all the lords and gentlemen that could in so short space be gathered together, sent for, to come and receive it in with honour. And in the morning after the cardinal gat him, through the back side, into the friars Observants. And part of the gentles went round about, and welcomed him from Rome, as representing the pope's person; part met him half way, part at the court gate, and last of all the king's grace himself met him in the hall, and brought him up into a great chamber, where was a seat prepared on high for the king's grace and the cardinal, while the bull was read; insomuch that not the wise only, but

The title of the defender of the faith came from Rome.

The popish and vain-glorious manner of cardinal Wolsey.

men of mean understanding, laughed the vain pomp to scorn, not far unlike to the receiving of the cardinal's hat: which when a ruffian had brought unto him to Westminster under his cloak, he clothed the messenger in rich array, and sent him back to Dover again; and appointed the bishop of Canterbury to meet him, and then another company of lords and gentles, I wot not how oft, ere it came to Westminster; where it was set on a cupboard, and tapers about, so that the greatest duke in the land must make courtesy thereto, yea, and to his empty seat, he being away.

The cardinal's hat. W. T.

The falsest and vainest cardinal that ever was.

And shortly, for lack of authority of God's word, Martin must be condemned by the authority of the king. And the king's grace, to claw the pope again, must make a book; in which, to prove all that they would have stablished, for lack of scripture, yea, and contrary to the open scripture, is made this mighty reason: Such prelates are the church; and the church cannot err; and therefore, all that they do is right; and we ought to believe them without any scripture[1], yea, and though the scripture be contrary. Wherefore God (offended with such blasphemy, to make his enemies feel that they would not see in the open scripture, nor in the practice of their livings and doings, clean contrary unto the scripture and unto the living of Christ and his apostles, this eight hundred years,) hath poured this wrath upon us, and hath snared the wise of the world with the subtilty of their own wits. For either the pope and cardinals, with other prelates, that made this first marriage, or they that would break it, err; to speak no more grievously[2].

The church erreth, if the pope and bishops be the church. W. T.

[1 Such is the gist of the king's arguments, where the royal printer, Pynson, has placed in the margin, *Lutherus prostratus;* and further on (sign. m.) where the king says, 'Si nihil omnino recipiat [Lutherus] quod non tam aperte legat in evangelio ut tergiversandi non sit locus, quomodo credit (si modo credit, qui nihil fere credit,) perpetuam Mariæ virginitatem? De qua adeo nihil invenit in scripturis, ut Helvidius non aliunde quam ex scripturarum verbis corripuerit ansam decernendi contrarium. Nec aliud opponitur illi quam totius ecclesiæ fides,' etc: the margin has, 'Efficax ratio adversus Lutherum, quod recipi oporteat etiam quæ nusquam sunt scripta.' And, 'Hic locus fortiter premit Lutherum, ut veneretur ecclesiæ traditiones non scriptas.'—From 'Henrici Octavi Opera,' a quarto volume in the library of St John's College, Cambridge.]

[2 The last sentence is omitted in Day's ed.]

Martin Luther submitted himself to king Henry VIII.

Moreover, when Martin Luther had submitted himself in an epistle, let his grace consider what answer he gave again. Where is the glory of that great praise become, that his grace gave the cardinal for his goodly acts and benefits, which all the commonwealth of the whole realm should feel[1]? And let his grace remember, how he inveigheth against Martin's wedlock, and fear lest God, to avenge wilful blindness, tangle his grace with matrimony (beside the destruction of the realm that is like to follow) much more dishonourable than his grace thinketh Martin shameful. His grace promised to keep his wedlock, as well as Martin did his chastity: and his grace's vow hath authority of God, and Martin's not, but is damned by the word of God as he did vow, and as the hypocrites do yet teach to vow.

More is proved a liar.

And More, among his other blasphemies in his dialogue, saith, that none of us dare abide by our faith unto the death. But shortly thereafter God, to prove More that he hath ever been a false liar, gave strength unto his servant, Sir Thomas Hitton, to confess, and that unto the death, the faith of his holy Son Jesus; which Thomas the bishops of Canterbury and Rochester, after they had dieted and tormented him secretly, murdered at Maidstone most cruelly[2].

Sir Thomas Hitton.

I beseech the king's most noble grace, therefore, to consider all the ways by which the cardinal and our holy bishops have led him, since he was first king; and to see whereunto all the pride, pomp, and vain boast of the cardinal is come, and how God hath resisted him and our prelates in all their wiles. We, having nothing to do at all, have meddled yet in all matters, and have spent for our prelates' causes more than all Christendom, even unto the utter beggaring of ourselves, and have gotten nothing but rebuke and shame and hate among all nations, and a mock, and a scorn thereto, of them whom we have most holpen.

A dance in Paris.

For the Frenchmen (as the saying is) of late days made a play, or a disguising, at Paris, in which the emperor danced

[1 Day omits the remainder of this paragraph.]

[2 This sufferer is here called Sir Thomas, after the usual manner of styling priests in Tyndale's time; but Foxe only calls Hitton 'an honest poor man and religious.' The Archbishop of Canterbury was Warham; and the bishop of Rochester was Fisher. The date of Hitton's marytrdom is said by Foxe to have been Feb. 20, 1529.]

with the pope and the French king, and wearied them; the king of England sitting on a high bench, and looking on. And when it was asked, why he danced not, it was answered, that he sat there but to pay the minstrels their wages only. As who should say, we paid for all men's dancing. We monied the emperor openly, and gave the Frenchmen double and treble secretly, and to the pope also. Yea, and though Ferdinandus[3] had money sent him openly, to blind the world withal, yet the saying is throughout all Dutchland, that we sent money to the king of Pole, and to the Turk also; and that by help of our money Ferdinandus was driven out of Hungary. Which thing, though it were not true, yet it will breed us a scab at the last, and get us, with our meddling, more hate than we shall be able to bear, if a chance come, unless that we wax wiser betime.

Here Tyndale prayeth for the ceasing of persecution.

And I beseech his grace also to have mercy of his own soul, and not to suffer Christ and his holy testament to be persecuted under his name any longer; that the sword of the wrath of God may be put up again, which for that cause, no doubt, is most chiefly drawn.

And I beseech his grace to have compassion on his poor subjects, which have ever been unto his grace both obedient, loving, and kind; that the realm utterly perish not, with the wicked counsel of our pestilent prelates. For if his grace, which is but a man, should die, the lords and commons not knowing who hath most right to enjoy the crown, the realm could not but stand in great danger.

Tyndale prayeth the understanding of such as of right should succeed to the crown.

And I exhort the lords temporal of the realm, that they come and fall before the king's grace, and humbly desire his majesty to suffer it to be tried, who of right ought to succeed; and if he or she fail, who next, yea, and who third. And let it be proclaimed openly: and let all the lords temporal be sworn thereto, and all the knights, and squires, and gentlemen, and the commons, above eighteen years old, that there be no strife for the succession. For if they try it by the sword, I promise them, I see none other likelihood but that, as the cardinal hath prophesied, it will cost the realm of England.

And all that be sworn unto the cardinal, I warn them yet

[[3] Ferdinand king of Hungary, who eventually succeeded his brother Charles V. as emperor of Germany.]

once again to break their oaths, as I did in 'The Obedience.' And all my lord cardinal's privy secretaries and spies, by whom he worketh, yet I warn them to beware betime. My lord cardinal, though he have the name of all, yet he wrought not all of his own brain: but of all wily and exercised in mischief he called unto him the most expert, and of their council and practice gathered that most seemed to serve his wicked purpose. Let them remember Emson and Dudley, and such like in all chronicles[1].

Tyndale warneth all the cardinal's secretaries to repent, and turn to God.

And all that be confederate with the cardinal and with the bishops upon any secret appointment, be they never so great, I rede[2] them to break their bonds, and to follow right by the plain and open way, and to be content, and not too ambitious: for it is now evil climbing; the boughs be brittle. And let them look well on the practice of bishops, how they have served all other men in times past, and into what troubles they have brought them that were quiet. Many a man, both great and small, have they brought to death in England, even in my days, (beside in times past,) whose blood God will seek once. Let them learn at the last, that it is but the cast of the bishops to receive the sacrament with one man secretly upon one purpose, and with another man as secretly upon the contrary, to deceive all parties. For of perjury they make as much conscience as a dog of a bone; for they have power to dispense with all things, think they.

A general exhortation to all kinds of people.

Popish bishops make no account of perjury.

At the beginning of the war between the French king and the emperor the prognostication said, year by year, that there should be great labour for peace: but it shall not come to pass; for there is *Bicorporeum*, or *Corpus neutrum*[3], that cometh between and letteth it; that is to say, a body that is neither-nother[4], or holdeth on neither part: and that body is the spiritualty, which hold but of themselves only. For when any ambassadors go between, to entreat of peace, the bishops are ever the chief; which, though they make a goodly oration for the peace openly, to deceive the laymen, yet secretly, by the bishops of the same country, they cast a bone in the way: and there can be no peace, until the peace be for their profit, let it cost in the mean season what blood it will.

The spiritualty are neither of the one side nor of the other for there is no truth in them, more than shall serve their turn.

[1 So Marb. ed. but this last sentence is wanting in the later eds.]
[2 Advise.] [3 Of the nature of two bodies, or a neutral body.]
[4 That is, neither the one nor the other.]

And as for them which for lucre, as Judas, betray the truth, and write against their consciences; and which for honour, as Balaam, enforce to curse the people of God; I would fain (if their hearts were not too hard) that they did repent. And as fain I would, that our prelates did repent, if it were possible for them to prefer God's honour before their own[5]. And let them remember what wrong they have done to the queen, and what fruit they have lost her, that never could come unto the right birth, for sorrow which she suffered through their false means; than which what greater treason could they work unto the realm of England?

And unto all subjects I say, that they repent. For the cause of evil rulers is the sin of the subjects, testifieth the scripture. And the cause of false preachers is, that the people have no love unto the truth, saith Paul in the second chapter of the second epistle to the Thessalonians. We be all sinners, an hundred times greater than all that we suffer. Let us therefore each forgive other, remembering, the greater sinners the more welcome, if we repent; according to the similitude of the riotous son (Luke xv.) For Christ died for sinners, and is their Saviour, and his blood their treasure, to pay for their sins. He is that fatted calf which is slain to make them good cheer withal, if they will repent, and come to their father again; and his merits is that goodly raiment, to cover the naked deformities of our sins.

An admonition to all subjects.

2 Thess. ii.

Luke xv.

These[6] be sufficient at this time, although I could say more, and though other have deserved that I more said: yea, and I could more deeply have entered into the practice of our cardinal, but I spare for divers considerations; and namely for his sake, which never spared me, nor any faithful friend of his own, nor any that told him truth; nor spareth to persecute the blood of Christ, in as clear light as ever was, and under as subtle colour of hypocrisy as ever was any persecution since the creation of the world. Neither have I said for hate of any person or persons, (God I take to record,) but of their wickedness only, and to call them to repentance, knowledging that I am a sinner also, and that a grievous. Howbeit, it is a devilish thing, and a merciless, to defend wickedness against

Here Tyndale shewed himself to be void of malice to any private person.

[5 The remainder of the paragraph is omitted in Day's ed.]

[6 S. and S. edition does not resume Tyndale's text, till it comes to the words, 'These be sufficient.']

the open truth, and not to have power to repent. And therefore, I doubt not, if men will not be warned hereby, but that God will utter more practice by whom he will, and not cease until he have broken the bond of wily hypocrites which persecute so subtilly.

God is merciful to the ignorant; but he pleaseth the malicious and wilful offender.

And[1], finally, if the persecution of the king's grace, and of other temporal persons conspiring with the spiritualty, be of ignorance, I doubt not but that their eyes shall be opened shortly, and they shall see and repent, and God shall shew them mercy. But and if it be of a set malice against the truth, and of a grounded hate against the law of God by the reason of a full consent they have to sin, and to walk in their old ways of ignorance, whereunto (being now past all repentance) they have utterly yielded themselves, to follow with full lust, without bridle or snaffle, which is the sin against the Holy Ghost; then ye shall see, even shortly, that God shall turn the point of the sword, wherewith they now shed Christ's blood, homeward to shed their own again, after all the examples of the bible.

The Obedience of a Christian Man, written three years before this book.

And let them remember that I, well toward three years agone[2], to prevent all occasions and all carnal beasts that seek fleshly liberty, sent forth 'The true Obedience of a Christian Man,' which yet they condemned, but after they had condemned the new Testament, as right was, whence 'The Obedience' had his authority. Now then, if when the light is come abroad, in which their wickedness cannot be hid, they find no such obedience in the people unto their old tyranny, whose fault is it? This is a sure conclusion: none obedience, that is not of love, can long endure; and in your deeds can no man see any cause of love: and the knowledge of Christ, for whose sake only a man would love you, though ye were never so evil, ye persecute. Now then, if any disobedience rise, are ye not the cause of it yourselves[3]?

Say not but that ye be warned!

[1 S. and S. ed. omits all this paragraph except the first two words, which it connects with, 'And let them remember,' &c.]

[2 S. and S. ed. omits this clause.]

[3 So the two old editions; but Day has, *ye are the cause of it yourselves.*]